# Women and Exercise:
# Physiology and Sports Medicine

# Women and Exercise:
# Physiology and Sports Medicine

**MONA M. SHANGOLD, M.D.**

Assistant Professor of Obstetrics and Gynecology
Georgetown University School of Medicine
Director, Sports Gynecology Center
Georgetown University Hospital
Washington, D.C.

**GABE MIRKIN, M.D.**

Associate Clinical Professor of Pediatrics
Georgetown University School of Medicine
Washington, D.C.

**CONTEMPORARY EXERCISE AND SPORTS MEDICINE SERIES**
**ALLAN J. RYAN, M.D., Editor-in-Chief**

 F. A. Davis Company • Philadelphia

Printed in the United States of America

Last digit indicates print number: 10 9 8 7 6 5 4 3 2

NOTE: As new scientific information becomes available through basic and clinical research, recommended treatments and drug therapies undergo changes. The author(s) and publisher have done everything possible to make this book accurate, up-to-date, and in accord with accepted standards at the time of publication. However, the reader is advised always to check product information (package inserts) for changes and new information regarding dose and contraindications before administering any drug. Caution is especially urged when using new or infrequently ordered drugs.

**LIBRARY OF CONGRESS**
**Library of Congress Cataloging-in-Publication Data**

Women and sports: physiology and sports medicine / [edited by] Mona M. Shangold, Gabe Mirkin.
    p. cm.
    Includes bibliographies and index.
    ISBN 0-8036-7816-9
    1. Women athletes—Physiology. 2. Exercise for women—Physiological aspects. 3. Sports for women—Physiological aspects. 4. Sports medicine. I. Shangold, Mona M. II. Mirkin, Gabe.
    [DNLM: 1. Physical Fitness. 2. Sports. 3. Sports Medicine. 4. Women. QT 260 W8715]
RC1218.W65W65 1988
617′.1027′088042—dc19
DNLM/DLC
for Library of Congress

87-33038
CIP

# Dedication

To Kenneth,
Our greatest treasure
and
Our greatest joy

# Preface

We have prepared this book to assist physicians and other health care professionals in caring for women who exercise. Included are chapters covering the many fields necessary to provide comprehensive care to women who range from novice exercisers to elite athletes and who may require information about training, health maintenance, treatment of disease or injury, and rehabilitation. Chapters have been written by leading authorities in each of these fields to supply the necessary depth of scientific background and clinical experience. In each case, relevant basic science is explained, and pertinent literature is reviewed and interpreted. When sufficient data are present, most authors have outlined and justified their personal recommendations, based on these data. Because clinical medicine often requires action even when sufficient data are lacking or inconclusive, many contributors have outlined their advice for these situations, based on their own expertise and clinical experience. We believe readers will find these recommendations invaluable.

Contributors to this volume include both basic scientists and practicing physicians. We purposely have encouraged some basic scientists and clinicians to cover the same topics from their different perspectives. We feel that this approach adds greatly to the value of this book.

Although elementary textbooks must oversimplify in order to teach students, this book is aimed at scientists and educators, who appreciate that research may, at times, lead to conflicting conclusions and different recommendations based upon these conclusions. We are confident that the sophisticated reader will find the controversy generated by these different perspectives refreshing, stimulating, and representative of the state of the art in this field.

No other book to date has covered so many relevant topics dealing with exercise and sports medicine for women in the depth that is provided in this volume. We hope this volume meets the needs of generalists caring for women athletes and specialists wanting information outside of their own specialty. Above all, we hope it will enable exercising women to receive the best care possible.

Mona Shangold, M.D.
Gabe Mirkin, M.D.

# Acknowledgments

We are very grateful to Bernard Gutin, Ph.D., for his comprehensive and sagacious review of material included in this text and for sharing his expertise and time with us. We also are very grateful to Sylvia Fields, Ed.D., and to Linda Weinerman for their help and patience in preparing this volume.

# Foreword

Here is an authoritative, referenced scientific book on sports medicine for women. Just 20 years ago, most women were discouraged from exercising, and those women who wanted to exercise and to compete had fewer and inferior facilities than men for fitness and competition. That all changed with the Education Amendments Act of 1972, which mandated that schools supply equal facilities for boys and girls in organized sports. Now women climb dangerous mountains, run ultramarathons, ride in long-distance bicycle races, and play in such "masculine" sports as rugby and ice hockey. Virtually all sports and athletic endeavors are open to women.

Female athletes ask questions that can't possibly be answered by sports medicine books for men. How does menstruation affect athletic performance? How do contraceptives taken by women affect performance? How does exercise affect fertility? How does exercise affect girls at puberty and women at menopause? Are women susceptible to injuries that are different from those suffered by men? Should women train differently from the way men do? Do women have different nutritional requirements?

All these questions and more are answered in this book by experts who are authorities in their respective fields on the basis of their own scientific research, publications, and lectures. This book is for sportswomen and those who teach, train, treat, and communicate with female athletes.

Allan J. Ryan, M.D.

# Contributors

Oded Bar-Or, M.D.
  *Professor of Pediatrics*
  *McMaster University*
  *Director, Children's Exercise and Nutrition Centre*
  *Chedoke-McMaster Hospitals*
  *Hamilton, Ontario, Canada*

Kelly D. Brownell, Ph.D.
  *Professor, Department of Psychiatry*
  *University of Pennsylvania School of Medicine*
  *Philadelphia, Pennsylvania*

David H. Clarke, Ph.D.
  *Professor and Chairman*
  *Department of Physical Education*
  *University of Maryland*
  *College Park, Maryland*

Pamela S. Douglas, M.D.
  *Assistant Professor of Medicine*
  *Hospital of the University of Pennsylvania*
  *Philadelphia, Pennsylvania*

Thomas D. Fahey, Ed.D.
  *Professor of Physical Education*
  *California State University*
  *Chico, California*

Christine E. Haycock, M.D.
  *Associate Professor of Surgery*
  *UMDNJ, New Jersey Medical School*
  *Newark, New Jersey*

Letha Y. Hunter-Griffin, M.D., Ph.D.
  *Clinical Instructor*
  *Emory University College of Medicine*
  *Staff, Peachtree Orthopaedic Clinic*
  *Atlanta, Georgia*

Frank I. Katch, Ed.D.
*Professor and Chairman*
*Department of Exercise Science*
*University of Massachusetts*
*Amherst, Massachusetts*

Victor L. Katch, Ed.D.
*Professor, Department of Kinesiology*
*Associate Professor, Department of Pediatric Cardiology*
*University of Michigan*
*Ann Arbor, Michigan*

Jack L. Katz, M.D.
*Professor of Clinical Psychiatry*
*Cornell University Medical College*
*New York, New York*
*Director, Division of Acute Treatment Services*
*New York Hospital-Cornell Medical Center, Westchester Division*
*White Plains, New York*

Frederik K. Lotgering, M.D., Ph.D.
*Assistant Professor, Department of Obstetrics and Gynecology*
*Erasmus University Medical School*
*The Netherlands*

Robert M. Malina, Ph.D.
*Professor of Anthropology*
*University of Texas*
*Austin, Texas*

Gabe Mirkin, M.D.
*Associate Clinical Professor of Pediatrics*
*Georgetown University School of Medicine*
*Washington, D.C.*

Morris Notelovitz, M.D., Ph.D.
*Founder/President*
*Midlife Centers of America*
*The Climacteric Clinic*
*Gainesville, Florida*

Mary L. O'Toole, Ph.D.
*Director, HealthPlex Center for Human Performance Research*
*Baptist Memorial Hospital*
*Assistant Professor, Department of Orthopaedic Surgery*
*University of Tennessee*
*Memphis, Tennessee*

Cindy J. Rubin, M.S.
*Research Assistant*
*Department of Psychiatry*
*University of Pennsylvania*
*Philadelphia, Pennsylvania*

Mona M. Shangold, M.D.
*Assistant Professor of Obstetrics and Gynecology*
*Georgetown University School of Medicine*
*Director, Sports Gynecology Center*
*Georgetown University Hospital*
*Washington, D.C.*

Arthur J. Siegel, M.D.
*Medical Director*
*Hahnemann Hospital*
*Brighton, Massachusetts*

Everett L. Smith, Ph.D.
*Director, Biogerontology Laboratory*
*Department of Preventive Medicine*
*University of Wisconsin*
*Madison, Wisconsin*

Jordan W. Smoller, A.B.
*Research Assistant*
*Department of Psychiatry*
*University of Pennsylvania*
*Philadelphia, Pennsylvania*

# Contents

# PART I

# Basic Concepts of Exercise Physiology

# CHAPTER 1

# Fitness: Definition and Development

MARY L. O'TOOLE, Ph.D.
PAMELA S. DOUGLAS, M.D.

The term "physical fitness" connotes a state of optimal physical well-being. However, a universally accepted definition of physical fitness is difficult to find. Cureton, a pioneer in the fitness movement, defined it as "the ability to handle the body well and the capacity to work hard over a long period of time without diminished efficiency."[1] Others have used physical fitness to describe a quality of life rather than a precise set of conditions. For example, in monographs published by the President's Council on Physical Fitness[2,3] to offer guidance to those interested in improving their physical fitness, a physically fit individual is described as one able to perform vigorous work without undue fatigue and still have enough energy left for enjoying hobbies and recreational activities as well as for meeting emergencies. Exercise physiology texts[4-8] have similar descriptive rather than quantitative definitions of physical fitness. For example, Lamb[6] defines it as "the capacity to meet successfully the present and potential physical challenges of life." So, despite all the interest generated by physical fitness, a need remains for a clear definition of fitness to allow accurate assessment of an individual's level of fitness.

The most successful definitions used to quantify "fitness" have been based on its measurable components. Muscular strength and endurance, body composition, flexibility, and cardiovascular-respiratory capacity are generally agreed upon as the major components of physical fitness.[9] Therefore, for purposes of this text, an operational measure of fitness based on combined capabilities in these four components will be assumed to quantify an individual's level of physical fitness.

A further problem in evaluating fitness is the wide variation in individual need for physical work capacity. For example, a healthy adult who wishes to pursue active recreation needs to achieve and maintain a certain degree of physical fitness, while a competitive ultra-endurance athlete needs to maintain a greater capacity for physical work. Therefore, the adequacy of one's physical fitness cannot be judged simply by the attainment of some magic number. Normative values for these parameters of muscular strength and endurance, body composition, flexibility, and cardiovascular-respiratory capacity have been developed based on age, sex, and habitual activity level.[10,11] An interested individual can compare her own values to the appropriate (based on desired activity level) normative values to assess the adequacy of her "fitness level."

## COMPONENTS OF FITNESS

**Muscular strength and endurance.** Muscular strength refers to the force or tension that can be generated by a muscle or muscle group during one maximal effort.[5,6,9] Muscular endurance is the ability to perform many repetitions at submaximal loads.[5,6,12] For example, it takes a certain amount of strength to lift and swing a tennis racquet, but it takes muscular endurance to repeat that swing hundreds of times during the course of a 2-hour match. An individual may have a great deal of strength but little endurance, or may have extraordinary strength in one muscle group but not in others. Although women usually have a smaller muscle fiber area and, therefore, lower absolute strength levels than men, the trainability of their muscles for strength and endurance performance is similar to that of men. The topics of muscular strength and endurance are covered in detail in Chapters 4 and 5.

**Body composition.** Body composition makes an important contribution to an individual's level of physical fitness. Performance, particularly in activities that require one to carry one's body weight over distance, will be facilitated by a large proportion of active tissue (muscle) in relation to a small proportion of inactive tissue (fat).[13] In general, women have a greater percentage of fat then do men, whether trained or untrained. Therefore, when performing in a distance running event women tend to be at a disadvantage compared with their male counterparts. The role of exercise in reaching and maintaining a desirable weight and percentage of body fat is discussed at length in Chapters 2 and 3.

**Flexibility.** Flexibility is the degree to which body segments can move or be moved around a joint.[5,6] The flexibility, or range of motion around a particular joint, is determined by the configuration of bony structures and the length and elasticity of ligaments, tendons, and muscles surrounding the joint.[5,6] Although there are no research data to support the concept that flexibility aids in coordinated movements, it certainly makes sense that by allowing free movement without unnecessary restriction, the body's efficiency and grace would be increased and the potential for injury reduced.[14]

**Cardiovascular-respiratory capacity.** The cardiovascular-respiratory component of fitness reflects the integrity of the heart and lungs as well as the ability of the muscle cells to use oxygen as fuel. It therefore reflects the degree to which an individual can increase metabolism above resting levels.[4-6,8,9] Incremental tests up to maximal oxygen uptake ($\dot{V}_{O_2max}$) are used to measure this component and to define the limits of physical work capacity. This measurement is considered to be the best single measure of an individual's overall functional capacity.[15] This and other measures of fitness will be discussed below.

## BENEFITS OF FITNESS

Regular physical activity, resulting in fitness, has benefits to disease-free individuals as well as implications for the medical care of individuals with certain diseases.[4,16-25] There is general agreement that exercise performed by healthy individuals has both physical and psychologic benefits, including improved physical performance and enhanced quality of life. In contrast, although exercise clearly does not change the course of most diseases, there are certain medical implications that are important.

## For Healthy Individuals

**Physical benefits.** In reviewing the physiologic aspects of exercise in women, Drinkwater[16] cites numerous studies that support the hypothesis that women of all ages benefit from programs of physical conditioning. The observed changes in the women are similar to those in men and include increases in maximal aerobic capacity, maximal minute ventilation, $O_2$ pulse, and increases in submaximal work performance.[17] With training, one can perform the same amount of work with lower heart and respiratory rates and with a lower systolic blood pressure. Some studies show that beneficial effects occur after 4 weeks of training.[16] Getchell and Moore[24] report that middle-aged women and men responded to an exercise training program in a similar fashion; they increased aerobic capacity by 21 percent and decreased heart rate by 6 percent during submaximal work tests given before and following training.

There have also been suggestions that exercise may affect longevity or that a "reversal of aging" may occur. A number of epidemiologic studies have attempted to examine the long-term effects of exercise upon longevity. Although no study has yet demonstrated a negative effect, in general such studies may have limited applicability because of the many methodologic problems inherent in choosing subject populations for this type of study. Of primary importance, from the viewpoint of this text, is the fact that few have examined female populations. Other limitations include inclusion of ex-athletes who may have had intense exercise training for short periods of time; classification of activity level based on workplace activity; and the interaction of a number of covariables such as obesity, smoking, environment, other life habits, and importantly, concomitant medical diseases.

Exercise training, however, has been well documented to modify or retard aspects of the aging process.[18,19] Exercise training slows the normal age-related declines in peak performance and maximal aerobic capacity, and it retards the loss of muscle and bone mass

and the increase in body fat. The exercising older woman has an aerobic capacity and body composition similar to those of much younger, sedentary women.[20,21] It has been suggested that the rate of decline in many physiologic parameters may be reduced by approximately 50 percent in physically fit as compared with sedentary women.

**Psychologic benefits.** Although subjective parameters are extraordinarily difficult to measure and a small number of participants may note a negative effect of exercise, it is generally thought that fitness leads to an improved quality of life. In several studies, the majority of participants in an exercise program noted enhancement of mood, self-confidence, and feelings of satisfaction, achievement, and self-sufficiency.[22-25] Interestingly, in one study, those with the greatest improvement in endurance also had more marked improvement on psychologic testing.[22] In general, women who exercise regularly are more likely to be more comfortable with day-to-day physical exertion and to have reduced anxiety and improved body image.[23-25]

## Medical Implications

Women with medical illnesses may have a lower level of fitness than their counterparts in a comparable but healthy, sedentary population. Although this may be due to limitations imposed by either the primary or an associated illness, it may also be related to the adoption of a less active lifestyle. In the latter case, increased fitness through participation in regular exercise programs encourages the patient to increase her level of activity in daily life and in recreation, thus yielding at least a subjective improvement in health.

Fitness or exercise training may have salutary effects upon specific medical disease in three ways: (1) as primary prevention (e.g., in modifying factors known to increase the risk of acquiring heart disease); (2) as secondary prevention or modification of the natural history of a disorder (e.g., decreases in both systolic and diastolic resting blood pressures); and (3) for rehabilitation or palliation of a specific disorder. The last is more closely related to task-specific exercise and is beyond our consideration of the benefits of overall fitness.

## Cardiovascular Disease

**Coronary artery disease.** Although coronary artery disease is more common in men, it is a leading cause of death in women as well. Studies examining the effects of fitness upon the risk of developing coronary artery disease find either a reduced or, less often, an unchanged risk associated with higher levels of physical activity.[26-32] Unfortunately, methodologic problems similar to those inherent in studies of longevity also limit the usefulness of these studies.

The amount of activity necessary to reduce cardiovascular risk is similarly unclear. It appears that no amount of exercise will lower the incidence of cardiovascular disease in those at especially high risk. However, in women at "usual" risk, it is likely that moderate amounts of exercise are protective, with benefit accruing to those expending 200 to 500 kcal per day or 2000 kcal per week pursuing vigorous activity.[33-35] Although most studies have examined the effects of aerobic exercise, recent studies have shown that cardiovascular endurance may be increased by resistive exercise as well.[36]

The mechanisms by which exercise may improve cardiovascular health are unclear. Certainly, training enhances cardiac efficiency, allowing a given workload to be achieved at a lower heart rate and blood pressure level. This is equally true in the healthy individual and in a patient with known coronary disease. Table 1-1 groups these and other physiologic changes occurring in the cardiovascular system with exercise according to the method by which they might prevent coronary heart disease, additionally noting the likelihood of each adaptation of being an important factor in prevention.[37] The beneficial effects of exercise are likely multifactorial, and the mechanisms are still unclear.

Exercise may also affect cardiovascular disease by altering risk factors for its development. In healthy women, fitness, as determined by exercise duration on treadmill testing, has been associated with lower body weight, a lower percentage of body fat, lower incidence of cigarette smoking, lower systolic and diastolic blood pressures, lower total cholesterol with a higher high-density lipoprotein (HDL) subfraction, and lower triglycerides.[38] Gibbons and colleagues,[38] using multiple regression analysis, demonstrated independent associations between fitness level and lipid profiles, blood pressure, and smoking, suggesting that risk factors for coronary heart disease may be modified by fitness level. Other studies have partly confirmed these results, finding more favorable lipid profiles in active women;[39] however, an exercise-related increase in HDL cholesterol has been demonstrated only in men, not in women.[40]

The benefits of exercise in the modification of pre-existing coronary disease are much less clear. At least one well-controlled study in men with heart disease showed a modest decrease in deaths due to myocardial infarction, with a trend toward a reduction in deaths from all causes in individuals pursuing exercise programs.[41] Although cardiac patients are generally encouraged to avoid resistive exercise because of the resultant unfavorable cardiac-loading conditions, some successfully used forms of exercise (e.g., rowing, bicycling) have significant resistive as well as aerobic components. No study has demonstrated a harmful effect of carefully performed exercise in selected cardiac patients.

**Hypertension.** Appropriately tailored exercise programs have been shown to result in 5 to 10 mm decreases in both systolic and diastolic resting blood pressures.[42-44] Although the mechanisms of these changes are unknown, exercise may be a useful adjunct to more conventional therapy. Care must be taken in the exercise prescription, however, because the normal increases in systolic and diastolic blood pressure levels with exercise are enhanced in patients with hypertension. Further, exercise blood pressure has been correlated with left ventricular mass, an independent risk factor for cardiovascular mortality.[45] Thus, it is important for the hypertensive individual to pursue dynamic or aerobic types of exercise that have less marked increases in blood pressure than those requiring resistive activity.

Associated with hypertensive disease are cerebrovascular accidents. Exercise has been shown to enhance fibrinolysis and may therefore reduce the incidence of or morbidity from stroke.[46]

## Obesity

The benefits of exercise with regard to obesity are discussed in detail in Chapter 3. Obe-

**Table 1–1.** BIOLOGIC MECHANISMS BY WHICH EXERCISE MAY
CONTRIBUTE TO THE PRIMARY OR SECONDARY PREVENTION OF
CORONARY HEART DISEASE*

**Maintain or increase myocardial oxygen supply.**
　Delay progression of coronary atherosclerosis (possible).
　　Improve lipoprotein profile (increase HDL-C/LDL-C ratio) (probable).
　　Improve carbohydrate metabolism (increase insulin sensitivity) (probable).
　　Decrease platelet aggregation and increase fibrinolysis (probable).
　　Decrease adiposity (usually).
　Increase coronary collateral vascularization (unlikely).
　Increase coronary blood flow (myocardial perfusion) or distribution (unlikely).
**Decrease myocardial work and oxygen demand.**
　Decrease heart rate at rest and submaximal exercise (usually).
　Decrease systolic and mean systemic arterial pressure during submaximal exercise (usually) and at
　　rest (possible).
　Decrease cardiac output during submaximal exercise (probable).
　Decrease circulating plasma catecholamine levels (decrease sympathetic tone) at rest (probable) and
　　at submaximal exercise (usually).
**Increase myocardial function.**
　Increase stroke volume at rest and in submaximal and maximal exercise (likely).
　Increase ejection fraction at rest and in exercise (possible).
　Increase intrinsic myocardial contractility (unlikely).
　Increase myocardial function resulting from decreased "afterload" (probable).
　Increase myocardial hypertrophy (probable); but this may not reduce CHD risk.
**Increase electrical stability of myocardium.**
　Decrease regional ischemia at rest or at submaximal exercise (possible).
　Decrease catecholamines in myocardium at rest and at submaximal exercise (probable).
　Increase ventricular fibrillation threshold due to reduction in cyclic AMP (possible).

*Expression of likelihood that effect will occur for an individual participating in endurance-type training program for 16 wk or longer at 65–80% of functional capacity for 25 min or longer per session (300 kcal) for 3 or more sessions per week ranges from unlikely, possible, likely, probable, to usually.
Abbreviations: HDL-C = high-density lipoprotein cholesterol; LDL-C = low-density lipoprotein cholesterol; CHD = coronary heart disease; AMP = adenosine monophosphate.
(From Haskell,[37] p. 65, with permission.)

sity is probably an independent risk factor for cardiovascular disease in both sexes; its reduction would therefore be expected to contribute to cardiac health.[47] Exercise clearly increases caloric expenditure through the effort necessary to maintain activity, favorably alters metabolic rate and heat production, and is useful in preserving muscle mass during dieting. In addition to the subjective enhancement of perceived health, the toning effects of exercise may have a positive effect on self-image and may therefore encourage the dieter to adhere to both exercise and dietary programs.

## Osteoporosis

With aging, the mineral content of bone decreases much more rapidly in women than in men, such that, after menopause, up to 8 percent of bone mass may be lost per decade.

Although this has been regarded as an inevitable effect of aging and hormonal changes, it is clearly accelerated by inactivity or disuse. Further, most studies of athletes engaged in weight-bearing exercise (e.g., not swimmers) have shown up to a 40 percent increase in bone mass over more sedentary control subjects.[48–49] Controlled trials, with or without calcium supplementation, have demonstrated that exercise may retard or even reverse the normal loss of bone mineral content.[50–52] Thus, stresses imposed by exercise may be beneficial in preventing osteoporosis. However, exercise is more effective when estrogen and calcium supplements are also given.

### Selected Other Diseases

Exercise training has been found to be of benefit in a variety of other chronic diseases.

In general, it improves cardiovascular function, muscle strength, endurance, flexibility, adjustment to disease, activity level, and overall well-being. Additional benefits may be specific to the underlying disease. For example, in patients with chronic obstructive airways disease, exercise is useful for ventilatory muscle training, increased tolerance of dyspnea, and reduction in associated anxiety.[53] In those with end-stage renal disease and in diabetes mellitus, exercise may lower blood pressure and otherwise modify cardiovascular risk.[54] Additionally, in patients with diabetes, a regularly followed exercise regimen may decrease insulin requirements and improve glucose tolerance. In patients with depression, exercise seems to improve mood or at least provide a physical vigor important in counteracting affective illness.[55]

## FITNESS EVALUATION

### Flexibility

Flexibility can be measured directly or assessed indirectly during movement tasks.[5] Direct measurement of resting or static range of motion around a specific joint can be obtained with a goniometer. Dynamic flexibility or movement around a particular joint during an activity can be measured by digitizing of video, high-speed film analysis, or electrogoniometers. For a complete assessment of movement during activity, range of motion must be measured simultaneously in several planes. A less precise assessment of flexibility can be obtained using field tests such as the sit-and-reach test of Wells and Dillon[56] or the trunk flexion/extension tests of Cureton.[1]

As with the other components of fitness, each individual's need for flexibility may differ. However, the prevailing clinical opinion is that normal ranges of motion for specific joints are necessary for pain-free movement. These normal values can be found in texts on athletic training[57] or physical therapy.[58] The degree and type of any additional flexibility varies with the activity an individual wants to participate in.[57]

### Functional Capacity

Maximal oxygen uptake is the best single measure of the overall functional capacity of an individual. Since human metabolism depends on oxygen utilization, an indirect estimate of energy metabolism can be made by measuring the amount of oxygen required to perform a given task. Because this is equal to the amount inhaled minus the amount exhaled, oxygen uptake can be used to estimate the maximum level of metabolism (work) of which an individual is capable.

Maximal oxygen uptake ($\dot{V}_{O_2max}$) can be calculated from actual measurement of expired oxygen and carbon dioxide during any work task of sufficient intensity and duration to require maximal use of aerobic energy systems.[4,6,9] The most commonly used exercise tests make use of a treadmill, cycle ergometer, rowing ergometer, or any other device that can be calibrated to allow the quantification of the work being done. The volume and concentration of respiratory gases is measured either breath by breath or averaged for a certain time period (e.g., 15 seconds), using some kind of volume-metering device such as a Tissot spirometer or volume transducer, along with oxygen and carbon dioxide analyzers. Commercial metabolic carts with these components are available.

Most often the test is incremental, with the workload increased at the beginning of each stage.[4,6,9] During an incremental test, oxygen uptake will increase in a linear relationship with the increasing workload. The test protocol ideally should reflect the exercise capabilities of the subject population being tested. Healthy individuals can usually begin with a workload that requires an oxygen uptake of approximately 24 $mL \cdot kg^{-1} \cdot min^{-1}$. Work increments should require 3 to 7 $mL \cdot kg^{-1} \cdot min^{-1}$ increases in oxygen uptake. Endurance athletes, because of expected higher maximal capacities, can be started at workloads greater than 30 $mL \cdot kg^{-1} \cdot min^{-1}$ with increments of 3 to 7 $mL \cdot kg^{-1} \cdot min^{-1}$. Elderly women or those with known or suspected limitations should begin much lower and increase workloads more gradually. Duration of the early stages should be at least 2 minutes to ensure gradual physiologic adjustments. The later stages can be 1 minute in duration. When the maximum capacity for aerobic energy transfer has been reached, a further increase in workload will not be accompanied by an increase in oxygen uptake.[6]

Because the direct measurement of maximal oxygen uptake depends on subject mo-

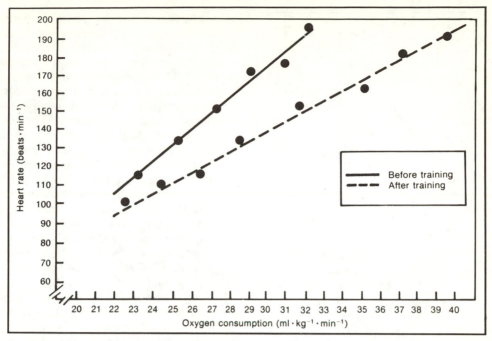

**Figure 1–1.** HR–$\dot{V}_{O_2}$ *line for a 20-year-old woman before and after a 10-week aerobic conditioning program.* (From McArdle, Katch, and Katch,[9] *with permission.)*

tivation and the use of rather elaborate laboratory equipment, various submaximal laboratory tests and field tests have been devised to estimate maximal aerobic capacity. Many of the submaximal predictive tests are based on a linear relationship between heart rate and oxygen uptake.[4,6,9] The slope of this line is unique to each individual and depends on state of training but not on gender (Fig. 1–1). A widely used predictive test is the Åstrand-Rhyming Nomogram.[4] This nomogram allows the prediction of $\dot{V}_{O_2max}$ from the heart rate attained during one 6-minute work bout on a cycle ergometer, but can also be used with a step-test protocol. Alternately, if oxygen uptake and heart rate are measured at two submaximal exercise intensities, the line representing the relationship between heart rate and oxygen uptake can then be extrapolated to the age-predicted maximal heart rate (220 − age) and $\dot{V}_{O_2max}$ estimated (Fig. 1–2). McArdle and associates[9] have also developed a set of norms for the estimation of $\dot{V}_{O_2max}$ from measurement of recovery heart rate following a bench-stepping protocol. Since one of the more practical uses of $\dot{V}_{O_2max}$ test data is for monitoring an individual's progress in fitness programs over a period of time, it is unimportant which protocol is used as long as the same one is used in follow-up tests.

Several tests of distance covered in a given time period (walking, running, or a combination of the two) have also been used to predict aerobic capacity. The most widely known is the 12-minute walk/run test first suggested by Cooper in *Aerobics.*[59] Cooper[60] reported a correlation (based on tests of 47 male military personnel) of 0.90 between distance covered and maximal oxygen uptake actually measured in the laboratory. However, Maksud and colleagues,[61] repeating this correlation for women, reported a correlation of only 0.70 between actually measured oxygen uptake and distance covered, in a group of 26 female athletes. Katch and co-workers[62] noted a similarly low correlation (r = 0.67) between these two measurements in 36 untrained female subjects. Because factors such as body weight, body fatness, and movement efficiency contribute to distance covered, these tests have error ranges of from 10 to 20 percent of actual maximal oxygen uptake.[9] They can be used only as a rough estimate of aerobic capacity.

**Terminology.** Oxygen uptake measurements or estimations used to quantify activity or exercise can be reported in several dif-

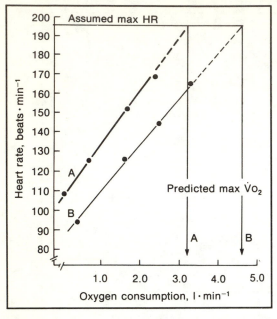

***Figure 1-2.*** *Application of the linear relationship between submaximal heart rate and oxygen consumption to predict* $\dot{V}_{O2max}$. *(From McArdle, Katch, and Katch,*[9] *with permission.)*

ferent ways. It can be reported simply as liters of oxygen used per minute. Because 1 liter of oxygen is roughly equivalent to 5 kcal,[9] the approximate energy cost for any particular activity level can be calculated. One disadvantage of using liters per minute is the discrepancy between energy costs for individuals of varying weights.[9] For example, a 200-lb man will consume more oxygen during activity (or even sitting at rest) than will a 100-lb woman. For this reason, oxygen uptake is more often reported as milliliters of oxygen consumed per kilogram of body weight per minute ($mL \cdot kg^{-1} \cdot min^{-1}$). This allows the energy cost of various tasks to be compared among individuals without the bias of body weight. It is in these terms that $\dot{V}_{O2max}$ is most often reported for athletes. Although a high $\dot{V}_{O2max}$ may be taken as a "badge of honor" by endurance athletes, it actually has poor predictive ability for sports performance.[4] Nonetheless, a high $\dot{V}_{O2max}$ is indicative of a large aerobic capacity. The highest $\dot{V}_{O2max}$ reported in the literature for men is 14 $mL \cdot kg^{-1} \cdot min^{-1}$ higher than that

**Table 1-2.** ENERGY REQUIREMENTS IN METS FOR HORIZONTAL AND UPHILL JOGGING/RUNNING*

**a. Outdoors on Solid Surface**

| % Grade | mph<br>m/min | 5<br>134 | 6<br>161 | 7<br>188 | 7.5<br>201 | 8<br>215 | 9<br>241 | 10<br>268 |
|---|---|---|---|---|---|---|---|---|
| 0 | | 8.6 | 10.2 | 11.7 | 12.5 | 13.3 | 14.8 | 16.3 |
| 2.5 | | 10.3 | 12.3 | 14.1 | 15.1 | 16.1 | 17.9 | 19.7 |
| 5.0 | | 12.0 | 14.3 | 16.5 | 17.7 | 18.8 | 21.0 | 23.2 |
| 7.5 | | 13.8 | 16.4 | 18.9 | 20.2 | 21.6 | 24.1 | 26.6 |
| 10.0 | | 15.5 | 18.5 | 21.4 | 22.8 | 24.3 | 27.2 | |
| 12.5 | | 17.2 | 20.6 | 23.8 | 25.4 | 27.1 | | |

**b. On the Treadmill**

| % Grade | mph<br>m/min | 5<br>134 | 6<br>161 | 7<br>188 | 7.5<br>201 | 8<br>215 | 9<br>241 | 10<br>268 |
|---|---|---|---|---|---|---|---|---|
| 0 | | 8.6 | 10.2 | 11.7 | 12.5 | 13.3 | 14.8 | 16.3 |
| 2.5 | | 9.5 | 11.2 | 12.9 | 13.8 | 14.7 | 16.3 | 18.0 |
| 5.0 | | 10.3 | 12.3 | 14.1 | 15.1 | 16.1 | 17.9 | 19.7 |
| 7.5 | | 11.2 | 13.3 | 15.3 | 16.4 | 17.4 | 19.4 | 21.4 |
| 10.0 | | 12.0 | 14.3 | 16.5 | 17.7 | 18.8 | 21.0 | 23.2 |
| 12.5 | | 12.9 | 15.4 | 17.7 | 19.0 | 20.2 | 22.5 | 24.9 |
| 15.0 | | 13.8 | 16.4 | 18.9 | 20.3 | 21.6 | 24.1 | 26.6 |

* Differences in energy expenditures are accounted for by the effects of wind resistance.
(From American College of Sports Medicine,[65] with permission.)

**Table 1–3.** ENERGY EXPENDITURE IN METS DURING BICYCLE ERGOMETRY

| Body Weight | | Exercise Rate (kg/min and watts) | | | | | | | |
|---|---|---|---|---|---|---|---|---|---|
| *kg* | *lb* | *300*<br>*50* | *450*<br>*75* | *600*<br>*100* | *750*<br>*125* | *900*<br>*150* | *1050*<br>*175* | *1200*<br>*200* | *(kg/min)*<br>*(watts)* |
| 50 | 110 | 5.1 | 6.9 | 8.6 | 10.3 | 12.0 | 13.7 | 15.4 | |
| 60 | 132 | 4.3 | 5.7 | 7.1 | 8.6 | 10.0 | 11.4 | 12.9 | |
| 70 | 154 | 3.7 | 4.9 | 6.1 | 7.3 | 8.6 | 9.8 | 11.0 | |
| 80 | 176 | 3.2 | 4.3 | 5.4 | 6.4 | 7.5 | 8.6 | 9.6 | |
| 90 | 198 | 2.9 | 3.8 | 4.8 | 5.7 | 6.7 | 7.6 | 8.6 | |
| 100 | 220 | 2.6 | 3.4 | 4.3 | 5.1 | 6.0 | 6.9 | 7.7 | |

*Note:* $\dot{V}_{O_2}$ for zero-load pedaling is approximately 550 mL/min for 70–80 kg subjects.
(From American College of Sports Medicine,[65] with permission.)

reported for women.[63,64] (This apparent sex discrepancy will be discussed later.)

With the advent of large-scale exercise testing and prescription at hospitals, universities, and health clubs, energy expenditure has been classified in METS. One MET is the equivalent of a resting oxygen consumption taken in a sitting position. For an average man, that is approximately 250 mL per min, and for an average woman, 200 mL per min.[9] METS can also be expressed in terms of oxygen consumption per unit of body weight, in which case 1 MET is equivalent to 3.5 mL per kg per min ($mL \cdot kg^{-1} \cdot min^{-1}$). One MET is also equal to 1 kcal per kg per hr ($kcal \cdot kg^{-1} \cdot hr^{-1}$).[65] The MET cost of a particular exercise can be calculated by dividing the metabolic rate $\dot{V}_{O_{2max}}$ during exercise by the rest-

ing metabolic rate. The American College of Sports Medicine (ACSM) has constructed tables listing the energy cost in METS for walking, jogging, and running during a range of speeds and grades of the treadmill (Tables 1–2 and 1–3).[65] Similar tables have been constructed for MET levels during bicycle ergometry and bench-stepping (Tables 1–4 and 1–5).[65] These tables are equally applicable to men and women.

**Anaerobic threshold.** Traditionally, the term "anaerobic threshold" has been used to describe the level of exercise at which aerobic metabolism becomes insufficient to meet the required energy demands. This is assumed to be the point at which the resultant increase in anaerobic glycolysis causes lactate to accumulate in the muscles and blood.[6]

**Table 1–4.** APPROXIMATE ENERGY REQUIREMENTS IN METS FOR HORIZONTAL AND GRADE WALKING

| % Grade | *mph*<br>*m/min* | *1.7*<br>*45.6* | *2.0*<br>*53.7* | *2.5*<br>*67.0* | *3.0*<br>*80.5* | *3.4*<br>*91.2* | *3.75*<br>*100.5* |
|---|---|---|---|---|---|---|---|
| 0 | | 2.3 | 2.5 | 2.9 | 3.3 | 3.6 | 3.9 |
| 2.5 | | 2.9 | 3.2 | 3.8 | 4.3 | 4.8 | 5.2 |
| 5.0 | | 3.5 | 3.9 | 4.6 | 5.4 | 5.9 | 6.5 |
| 7.5 | | 4.1 | 4.6 | 5.5 | 6.4 | 7.1 | 7.8 |
| 10.0 | | 4.6 | 5.3 | 6.3 | 7.4 | 8.3 | 9.1 |
| 12.5 | | 5.2 | 6.0 | 7.2 | 8.5 | 9.5 | 10.4 |
| 15.0 | | 5.8 | 6.6 | 8.1 | 9.5 | 10.6 | 11.7 |
| 17.5 | | 6.4 | 7.3 | 8.9 | 10.5 | 11.8 | 12.9 |
| 20.0 | | 7.0 | 8.0 | 9.8 | 11.6 | 13.0 | 14.2 |
| 22.5 | | 7.6 | 8.7 | 10.6 | 12.6 | 14.2 | 15.5 |
| 25.0 | | 8.2 | 9.4 | 11.5 | 13.6 | 15.3 | 16.8 |

(From American College of Sports Medicine,[65] with permission.)

**Table 1–5.** ENERGY EXPENDITURE IN METS DURING STEPPING AT DIFFERENT RATES ON STEPS OF DIFFERENT HEIGHTS

| Step Height | | Steps/min | | | |
|---|---|---|---|---|---|
| cm | in | 12 | 18 | 24 | 30 |
| 0 | 0 | 1.2 | 1.8 | 2.4 | 3.0 |
| 4 | 1.6 | 1.5 | 2.3 | 3.1 | 3.8 |
| 8 | 3.2 | 1.9 | 2.8 | 3.7 | 4.6 |
| 12 | 4.7 | 2.2 | 3.3 | 4.4 | 5.5 |
| 16 | 6.3 | 2.5 | 3.8 | 5.0 | 6.3 |
| 20 | 7.9 | 2.8 | 4.3 | 5.7 | 7.1 |
| 24 | 9.4 | 3.2 | 4.8 | 6.3 | 7.9 |
| 28 | 11.0 | 3.5 | 5.2 | 7.0 | 8.7 |
| 32 | 12.6 | 3.8 | 5.7 | 7.7 | 9.6 |
| 36 | 14.2 | 4.1 | 6.2 | 8.3 | 10.4 |
| 40 | 15.8 | 4.5 | 6.7 | 9.0 | 11.2 |

(From American College of Sports Medicine,[65] with permission.)

appearance and rise of blood lactate).[6] The need to dispose of excess carbon dioxide produced from the buffering of excess hydrogen ions (from the lactic acid) drives the peripheral chemoreceptors that stimulate increased ventilation. Ventilation breaking points can be found during gas exchange measurements, whereas lactate breaking points can be found through frequent analysis of a small amount of blood usually taken by a fingerstick. Most experiments with highly trained athletes use the 4 mM value rather than the more reproducible 2 mM value, since athletes can exercise for several hours with lactate values greater than 2 mM but less than 4 mM. As with the ventilation breaking point, there is no universally accepted explanation for the lactate breaking point. Among the explanations offered are increased production of lactate, decreased clearance of lactate, a combination of these two, and increased recruitment of fast twitch (glycolytic) motor units.

Because this explanation is no doubt an oversimplification of the physiologic changes occurring, many investigators now avoid the term "anaerobic threshold" and prefer either "lactate breaking point" or "ventilation breaking point" to describe this alteration in metabolism.[66]

During light and moderate exercise, minute ventilation increases in a linear manner with increasing exercise intensity (oxygen uptake). However, at some point during the increasing exercise, the ventilation increases out of proportion to the increase in oxygen consumption. This point has been designated as the "ventilation breaking point." In an untrained individual, this point generally falls between 40 and 60 percent of $\dot{V}_{O_2max}$ and is associated with a more rapid rise in blood lactate to a concentration of 2 millimoles (mM) per liter (20 mg/dL blood). A second upswing in both ventilation and blood lactate can be seen at between 65 and 90 percent $\dot{V}_{O_2max}$ and a lactate concentration of 4 millimoles per liter (36 mg/dL).[67] In highly trained athletes, these "ventilation breaking points" occur at higher percentages of $\dot{V}_{O_2max}$.

The mechanism of the ventilation breaking point has not been satisfactorily explained but is usually associated with accumulation of lactic acid in the blood (hence,

## FITNESS DEVELOPMENT AND MAINTENANCE

### Fitness Development

#### Flexibility

Flexibility can best be improved through the use of sustained static stretches.[5,6,12] The muscles and connective tissue to be stretched should be slowly elongated to the point at which the exerciser feels a mild tension.[5,12] Usually, this position is then held for between 10 and 30 seconds.[12] During this time period, the exerciser should feel a gradual release of this feeling of tension as the stretch or myotatic reflex is overcome. As the tension is released, the exerciser should slowly move a fraction further, again to the point of tension and continue to hold for approximately 30 seconds.[12] Stretching following an exercise session, when the muscle and connective tissues are warm, has been found to be the best time for improving flexibility.[6]

#### Cardiovascular Fitness

The ACSM has developed guidelines for developing and maintaining fitness in healthy adults.[65,68] In recommending the quantity and quality of exercise, the ACSM cites five components that are applicable to the development of exercise programs for adults regardless of age, sex, or initial level of fitness: (1) type of activity, (2) intensity, (3) duration, (4) frequency, and (5) progression.

**Type of activity.** The exercise program shold include activities that use large muscle groups in a continuous, rhythmic manner. Activities such as walking, hiking, jogging/running, swimming, bicycling, rowing, cross-country skiing, skating, dancing, and rope skipping are ideal. Because control of exercise intensity within rather precise limits is often desirable at the beginning of an exercise program, these activities are useful since they are easily quantifiable. Various endurance game activities such as field hockey, soccer, and lacrosse may also be suitable but should not be used in the exercise prescription until participants are able to exercise at a minimum level of 5 METS.[65] If intensity, duration, and frequency are similar, the training result appears to be independent of

the mode of aerobic activity. Therefore, a similar training effect on functional capacity can be expected, regardless of the endurance activity used.

**Intensity.** The conditioning intensity of the aerobic portion of the exercise session is best expressed as a percentage of the individual's maximal or functional capacity. Effective training intensities are from 50 to 85 percent of $\dot{V}_{O2max}$ or 60 to 90 percent of the maximum heart rate achieved during a graded exercise test.[65,68,69] These intensities can be translated into MET levels. The intensity of training sessions can be monitored through the use of target heart rates (Fig. 1–3) or through MET levels. The energy cost in METS of various activities can be found in the ACSM *Guidelines for Exercise Testing and Exercise Prescription* (Tables 1–2 through 1–5).[65]

**Duration.** Each training session should last between 15 and 60 minutes with an

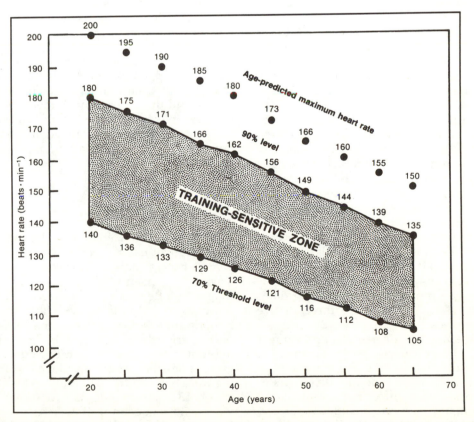

**Figure 1–3.** *Maximal heart rates and training-sensitive zones for use in aerobic training programs for people of different ages. (From McArdle, Katch, and Katch.[9] with permission.)*

aerobic component of at least 15 minutes. Typically, an exercise session should include a 5- to 10-minute warm-up, 15 to 60 minutes of aerobic exercise at the appropriate training level, and a cool-down of 5 to 10 minutes.[65,68,69] The function of the warm-up is gradually to increase the metabolic rate from the 1 MET level to the MET level required for conditioning. In planning the aerobic portion of the workout, one must consider that duration and intensity are inversely related. That is, the lower the exercise intensity, the longer the workout needs to be. Although significant cardiovascular improvements can be made with very intense (more than 90 percent $\dot{V}_{O2max}$) exercise done for short periods of time (5 to 10 minutes), high-intensity, short-duration sessions are not appropriate for individuals starting a fitness program.[65] Because of potential hazards (including an unnecessary risk of injury) for untrained individuals embarking on a high-intensity program, low to moderate intensity for longer durations is recommended for those beginning a fitness program. Although the recommended duration of the aerobic or conditioning part of the workout is 15 to 60 minutes, an adequate training response can be elicited by maintaining the prescribed exercise intensity for a period of approximately 15 minutes.[65] With the warm-up and cool-down, a reasonable amount of total workout time for a person beginning an exercise program would be 30 minutes. The cool-down phase should include exercise of diminishing intensity to return the physiologic systems of the body to their resting states.

**Frequency.** The frequency of exercise sessions is somewhat dependent on the intensity and duration of the exercise. For example, exercise programs for individuals with very low functional capacities (less than 5 METS) may start out with several short (5-minute) sessions per day. For most individuals, exercise programs for improving one's fitness level should be done three to five times per week.[65]

**Progression.** The degree of improvement in $\dot{V}_{O2max}$ (the best measure of functional capacity) is directly related to the intensity, duration, and frequency of the training. Research has documented improvements in $\dot{V}_{O2max}$ ranging between 5 and 25 percent, with the largest changes usually seen in the individuals who have the lowest initial fit-

ness levels.[70] Both men and women respond to aerobic training with similar increments in maximal oxygen uptake.[68] An individual starting a fitness program can expect a significant improvement in functional capacity to occur during the first 6 to 8 weeks.[4,6,9] The length of time necessary to reach one's true $\dot{V}_{O2max}$ depends on initial fitness level and intensity of training. As conditioning takes place, exercise intensity will need adjustment in order to keep the participant exercising in the training range. During the initial phases of a program, this is best done by changing the MET level to correspond to the desired exercise heart rate. Since with conditioning the heart rate will drop for any given submaximal workload, intensity adjustments will result in more actual work being done during each exercise session.[65] Follow-up graded exercise tests should be done during the first year of the program to help in the intensity adjustment and in motivating the participant. The goals of the participant need to be taken into account to determine when the exercise program can be changed from one with a goal of increasing fitness level to one with the goal of maintaining the newly acquired level. Sample exercise programs for sedentary, active, and competing women are shown in Appendix 1–1. It must be stressed that no program should be undertaken lightly and that, for many women, the ideal program may be a highly individualized "exercise prescription" developed in conjunction with a physician and exercise physiologist.

## Fitness Maintenance

**Activity level.** Exercise must be continued on a regular basis in order to maintain a given fitness level. Hickson and colleagues[25,71,72] have shown that duration and frequency of exercise may be reduced by as much as two thirds without affecting the training-induced $\dot{V}_{O2max}$, but that intensity plays a critical role in maintaining the training-induced changes. When the duration of exercise sessions following 10 weeks of training were reduced from 40 minutes per day to 26 or 13 minutes per day for the next 5 weeks, no reduction in the exercise-induced $\dot{V}_{O2max}$ was seen.[71] Similarly, when sessions were reduced from 6 days per week to 4 or 2 days per week, there again was no reduction in $\dot{V}_{O2max}$.[72] However, data suggest that in order to maintain training-induced gains, an individual must continue to exercise at an intensity of at least 70 percent of the training intensity.[25] Therefore, after achieving a desired level of fitness, an individual can theoretically be expected to maintain this level by exercising at least twice a week at 70 percent or more of her training intensity for a minimum of 13 minutes per session. Caution is advised, however, in the interpretation of these data, since the subjects from whom these conclusions were reached were highly conditioned men and women and the results may not be applicable to individuals training at lower intensities. It should also be kept in mind that body composition is one of the components of "physical fitness." Thus, if the participant is using the exercise program to maintain caloric balance and to keep body fat at a reasonable level, a maintenance program of 4 to 5 days per week would be a better choice.

When an individual stops training, a significant detraining effect occurs within 2 weeks, as measured by a decrease in physical work capacity.[9] A 50 percent reduction of the newly acquired gain in fitness has been shown to occur by 4 to 12 weeks after cessation of training, while a return to pretraining fitness level can be expected after cessation of training for between 4 weeks and 8 months.[68] Although much of this research has used men, the deconditioning pattern and time-course are expected to be similar in women.[70]

**Role of recreational sports.** Recreational sports that require an energy expenditure of sufficient intensity and duration to fall within ACSM guidelines for developing and maintaining fitness can be used for training.[65,68] Many recreational activities, however, are intermittent in nature and their energy expenditure difficult to quantify. Although there are tables listing average energy expenditures,[9,68] the amount of energy expended often depends on the skill level of the participants. For example, it is difficult to imagine that the energy expended by a professional tennis player such as Martina Navratilova is in any way similar to that expended by some weekend players. Recreational activities, then, are best used to supplement a planned program for the development and maintenance of physical fitness.

## FACTORS AFFECTING FITNESS DEVELOPMENT AND MAINTENANCE

**Age.** Increased age alone is not a contraindication to participation in a fitness program. Regular training will result in positive physiologic adaptations, regardless of age.[6,68] Some studies have shown that older individuals may require longer to adjust to physical training programs and may not make as large an absolute improvement in fitness level as a younger person.[68] However, comparison of improvements is often difficult because younger individuals tend to train at higher intensities than do older individuals. As an individual ages, there will be some drop in $\dot{V}_{O2max}$ regardless of training, since there is an age-related drop in maximal heart rate, which reduces maximal cardiac output.[4] An age-related decrease in $\dot{V}_{O2max}$ does not imply that an older individual cannot or should not participate in activities requiring a great deal of fitness. For example, each year there are several contestants and finishers over age 60 in the Hawaiian Ironman Triathlon, a contest that takes 9 to 17 hours to complete.

**Gender.** Although most of the research supporting the quantity and quality of exercise necessary to develop and maintain fitness has used male subjects, it seems equally applicable to women, since the training response appears to be identical for men and women.[68] Before puberty, there is no difference in maximal aerobic power between boys and girls.[4] After that, however, there is a difference between men and women in the potential to develop maximal aerobic capacity. There seem to be at least three basic physiologic differences between men and women that affect the capacity for aerobic power.[16] Women usually have a higher percentage of body fat, a smaller oxygen-carrying capacity, and a smaller muscle fiber area than do men. When the effects of body weight and percentage of body fat are corrected mathematically, the differences in $\dot{V}_{O2max}$ are lessened. Studies have averaged these differences to be approximately 50, 20, and 9 percent when $\dot{V}_{O2max}$ is expressed as liters per minute, milliliters per kilogram per minute, and milliliters per kilogram fat-free mass, respectively. The remaining difference (approximately 9 percent) is either still a difference in conditioning or more probably a sex-linked difference in the ability to transport and utilize oxygen. Since women usually have a lower hemoglobin concentration than men (normal range equals 12 to 16 g/dL for women; 14 to 18 g/dL for men) and a smaller blood volume, they have a smaller maximal oxygen-carrying capacity than men. In addition, endurance-trained women have approximately 85 percent of the muscle fiber areas of endurance-trained men. Although the fiber area is different, the muscle composition is much the same for male and female endurance athletes.[16]

**Underlying disease.** For any woman with known or suspected medical illness, embarking upon a fitness program should be preceded by consultation with a physician with special training in the patient's disease and, when indicated, by continued close medical supervision. Although it is rare when an individual should be excluded from exercise, many patients will need special considerations in the design and implementation of appropriate exercise training. Any aspect of an exercise program may be changed to adapt to the individual's needs, as long as the core features of intensity, duration, and frequency are preserved. Although reductions in intensity are most common, exercise modality may be altered (e.g., using non–weight-bearing or low-impact activities for the patient with arthritis, extreme obesity, or musculoskeletal abnormalities). Regardless of initial fitness level or absolute level of achievement, the positive effects of enhanced well-being, muscular strength, and activity tolerance may be expected. Monitoring methods may also need to be adapted to the individual situation (e.g., use of respiratory rate rather than heart rate for exercise intensity in the patient with a pacemaker). Detailed discussion of exercise prescription is beyond the scope of this chapter.

**Sudden death.** Sudden death during exercise has been well publicized, yet is extremely rare and most unlikely in an otherwise healthy individual without known cardiac disease.[73–75] Although sudden death may occur more often during activity than during rest, most occurences are related to usual daily activities and not to exercise programs.

The causes of sudden death during exercise have been examined in male athletes.[76] In the young, nearly 65 percent have some form of hypertrophic cardiomyopathy, 14 percent have congenital coronary artery anomalies, 10 percent have coronary heart disease, and 7 percent ruptured aorta or Marfan's syndrome. In contrast, of those over 35 years dying suddenly, more than 80 percent have coronary heart disease. Other associated diseases include hypertrophic cardiomyopathy, mitral valve prolapse, and acquired valvular disease. For this reason, women with known or suspected cardiovascular disease and previously sedentary individuals over 50 years of age should seek the advice of an internist or cardiologist before pursuing a vigorous exercise program. While most cardiovascular illnesses do not preclude the achievement of fitness, the exercise program should be individually tailored to meet the needs and limitations of the participant. Further, there are a small number of illnesses in which any form of vigorous activity should be strictly limited.

**Injury.** Most of the injuries resulting from participation in fitness programs are musculoskeletal injuries. Although occasionally there are traumatic injuries, such as fractures and torn ligaments, more frequently the injuries are the result of chronic microtrauma or overuse. These injuries include muscle strains, tendinitis, synovitis, bursitis, and stress fractures. In most cases, these injuries are not serious enough to prevent training but often require alterations in training patterns. Overuse injuries have been attributed mainly to errors in training, such as progressing too fast and not allowing enough time for recovery and adaptation.[77]

**Practical considerations.** Practical considerations are often critical to whether or not an individual participates in a fitness program. The most important of these considerations for most people is time. Everyone has certain constraints on her time, whether they be job-related or home-related. An individual wishing to participate in an exercise program to improve fitness must make a time commitment. A minimum of at least 1 hour three times per week is necessary. This could comprise a bare minimum of 30-minute exercise sessions plus time to change clothes, travel, and so forth. Cost is another factor to be considered. Most exercise test evaluations with an exercise prescription cost between

$100 to $400. Following this initial financial outlay, each individual can spend as little as the cost of a good pair of shoes and comfortable exercise clothing, or much more. Costs for the use of facilities can be from less than $100 per year for a YMCA/YWCA- or local university-based program to $500 or $600 per year for a health club membership. Individuals can join exercise classes, such as one in aerobic dance, or they may choose to carry out their prescription on their own. Equipment for walking or jogging programs is minimal, but that for a bicycling program is more.

## TRAINING FOR COMPETITION

Training for competition differs from training for fitness in that its main objective is improvement of performance rather than improvement of health. Training for competition should begin using the same ACSM guidelines for intensity, frequency, and duration. A period of approximately 8 weeks is necessary to lay the groundwork for a more intense training program.[6] Physiologic adaptations occurring in ligaments and muscles during that time make them less susceptible to overuse injuries, which otherwise might occur as a result of high-intensity training. Once the fitness base is laid, the competitive athlete must overload her system further to continue improving. The overload should be progressive and individualized to the specific goals of the athlete. At this point, training should be as specific to the competition as possible. That is, the exerciser needs to train the specific muscles to be involved in the desired performance in a manner specific to the competition.

Because most competition involves an element of speed, the exerciser may benefit from interval as well as continuous training.[6] Interval training is a means of accomplishing a great deal of work in a short period of time by interspersing work intervals with rest intervals. The work intervals may be of any desired length from just a few seconds to several minutes. The length of the work interval is determined by the specific demands of the competition and by the energy system the athlete wishes to train. Intervals of less than 4 seconds can be used to develop strength and power for activities such as a high jump, shot put, golf swing, or tennis stroke. Intervals of up to 10 seconds are used to develop sustained power for activities such as sprints, fast breaks, and so on. The length of these intervals force the body to use immediate, short-term energy systems. Intervals of up to 1½ minutes are used to develop the intermediate, glycolytic energy systems for activities such as 200- to 400-meter dashes or 100-meter swims. Intervals lasting longer than 1½ minutes tax the aerobic as well as the glycolytic systems. Training intervals should include all the energy systems expected to be taxed during competition. Recovery times or rest between intervals should be of a length that allows recovery of that particular energy system before the next work bout.

**Cross training.** Recently, the term "cross training" has been used to describe training in one exercise mode and deriving benefits in a different exercise mode. For example, triathletes often attribute improved running performance to concurrent bicycling training. Research, however, does not provide much support for a cross-training effect.

Although there is some evidence that the functional capacity of the cardiovascular system improves with different exercise modes, peripheral adaptation occurs only in the muscles involved in training.[7,8] Thus, while oxygen delivery may be enhanced through cross training, oxygen extraction is not. Therefore, cross training is not likely to improve competitive performance.

## SUMMARY

In conclusion, physical fitness for women is very similar to physical fitness for men. That is, a certain level of fitness is necessary for general well-being and protection against some disease states. A greater degree of fitness is beneficial for certain recreational and competitive sport activities. Cardiovascular fitness can be developed according to the guidelines of the American College of Sports Medicine. Rate and degree of improvement for women can be expected to be similar to that expected for men and is dependent on intensity, duration, and frequency of exercise sessions.

### References

1. Cureton TK: Physical Fitness Appraisal and Guidance. CV Mosby, St Louis, 1947.
2. President's Council on Physical Fitness: Adult Physical Fitness—A Program for Men and Women. US Government Printing Office, 1979.

3. President's Council on Physical Fitness: The Fitness Challenge . . . in the Later Years. US Government Printing Office, 1977.

4. Åstrand PO, and Rodahl K: Textbook of Work Physiology. Physiological Bases of Exercise, ed 3. McGraw-Hill, New York, 1986.

5. deVries HA: Physiology of Exercise for Physical Education and Athletics, ed 4. Wm. C. Brown, Dubuque, IA, 1986.

6. Lamb DR: Physiology of Exercise. Responses and Adaptations, ed 2. MacMillan, New York, 1984.

7. Mathews DK: Measurement in Physical Education, ed 2. WB Saunders, Philadelphia, 1963.

8. Mathews DK, and Fox EL: The Physiological Basis of Physical Education and Athletics, ed 2. WB Saunders, Philadelphia, 1976.

9. McArdle WD, Katch FI, and Katch VL: Exercise Physiology. Energy, Nutrition, and Human Performance. Lea and Febiger, Philadelphia, 1986.

10. Berg A, and Keul J: Physiological and metabolic responses of female athletes during laboratory and field exercise. Med Sport 14:77, 1981.

11. Drinkwater BL, Horvath SM, and Wells CL: Aerobic power of females, ages 10 to 68. J Gerontol 30(4):385, 1975.

12. Gutin, B: A model of physical fitness and dynamic health. Journal of Health, Physical Education, and Recreation 51:48, 1980.

13. Gutin B, Trinidad A, Norton C, et al: Morphological and physiological factors related to endurance performance of 11- to 12-year-old girls. Res Q 49:44, 1978.

14. Anderson B: Stretching. Shelter Publications, Bolinas, CA, 1980.

15. Palgi Y, Gutin B, Young J, et al: Physiologic and anthropometric factors underlying endurance performance in children. Int J Sports Med 5:67, 1984.

16. Drinkwater BL: Women and exercise: physiological aspects. Exerc Sport Sci Rev 12:21, 1984.

17. Flint MM, Drinkwater, BL, and Horvath SM: Effects of training on women's response to submaximal exercise. Med Sci Sports 6(2):89, 1974.

18. Pollock ML, Miller HS, Jr, and Ribisl PM: Effect of fitness on aging. The Physician and Sportsmedicine 6:45, 1978.

19. Shepard RJ, and Kavanagh, T: The effects of training on the aging process. The Physician and Sportsmedicine 6:33, 1978.

20. Vaccaro P, Dummer GM, and Clarke DH: Physiologic characteristics of female master swimmers. The Physician and Sportsmedicine 9(12):75, 1981.

21. Adams GM, and deVries HA: Physiological effects of an exercise training regimen upon women aged 52 to 79. J Gerontol 28:50, 1973.

22. Prosser G, Carson P, Phillips R, et al: Morale in coronary patients following an exercise programme. J Psychosom Res 25(6):587, 1981.

23. Franklin B, Buskirk E, Hodgson J, et al: Effects of physical conditioning on cardiorespiratory function, body composition and serum lipids in relatively normal weight and obese middle-aged women. Int J Obes 3:97, 1979.

24. Getchell LH, and Moore JC: Physical training: comparative responses of middle-aged adults. Arch Phys Med Rehabil 56:250, 1974.

25. Hickson R, Foster C, Pollock ML, et al: Reduced training intensities and loss of aerobic power, endur-ance, and cardiac growth. J Appl Physiol 58:492, 1985.

26. Morris JN, Heady JA, Raffle PAB, et al: Coronary heart-disease and physical activity. Lancet 2:1053, 1111, 1953.

27. Paffenbarger RS, Wing AL, and Hyde RT: Physical activity as an index of heart attack in college alumni. Am J Epidemiol 108:161, 1978.

28. Morris JN, Pollard R, Everitt MG, et al: Vigorous exercise in leisure time: protection against coronary heart disease. Lancet 2:1207, 1980.

29. Costas R, Garcia-Palmieri MR, Nazario, E, et al: Relation of lipids, weight and physical activity to incidence of coronary heart disease: The Puerto Rico Heart Study. Am J Cardiol 42:653, 1978.

30. Salonen JT, Puska P, and Tuomilehto J: Physical activity and risk of myocardial infarction, cerebral stroke and death: A longitudinal study in Eastern Finland. Am J Epidemiol 115:526, 1982.

31. Chapman JM, and Massey FJ: The interrelationship of serum cholesterol, hypertension, body weight and risk of coronary disease. J Chron Dis 17:933, 1964.

32. Paul O: Physical activity and coronary heart disease, Part II. Am J Cardiol 23:303, 1969.

33. Skinner JS, Benson H, McDonough JR, et al: Social status, physical activity and coronary proneness. J Chron Dis 19:773, 1966.

34. Rose G: Physical activity and coronary heart disease. Proc Roy Soc Med 62:1183, 1969.

35. Paffenbarger RS Jr, Brand RJ, Sholtz RI, et al: Energy expenditure, cigarette smoking, and blood pressure level as related to death from specific diseases. Am J Epidemiol 108:12, 1978.

36. Stewart KJ, and Kelemen MH: Circuit weight training: A new approach to cardiac rehabilitation. Pract Cardiol 12(10):41, 1986.

37. Haskell WL: Cardiovascular benefits and risks of exercise: The scientific evidence. In Strauss RH: Sports Medicine. WB Saunders, Philadelphia, 1984, pp 57–76.

38. Gibbons LW, Blair SN, Cooper KH, et al: Association between coronary heart disease risk factors and physical fitness in healthy adult women. Circulation 67(5):977, 1983.

39. Haskell WL, Taylor HL, Wood PD, et al: Strenuous physical activity, treadmill exercise test performance and plasma high-density lipoprotein cholesterol. Circulation 62(Suppl IV):53, 1980.

40. Busby J, Notelovitz M, Putney K, et al: Exercise high density lipoprotein cholesterol and cardiorespiratory function in climacteric women. South Med J 78:769, 1985.

41. Shaw LW: Effects of a prescribed supervised exercise program on mortality and cardiovascular morbidity in patients after a myocardial infarction. The national exercise and heart disease project. Am J Cardiol 48:39, 1981.

42. Tipton CM, Matthes RD, Bedford TB, et al: Exercise, hypertension, and animal models. In Lowenthal DT, Bharadwaja K, and Oaks WW (eds): Therapeutics Through Exercise. Grune and Stratton, New York, 1979, pp 115–132.

43. Choquette G, and Ferguson RJ: Blood pressure reduction in "borderline" hypertensives following physical training. Can Med Assoc J 108:699, 1973.

44. Hagberg IM, Goldring D, Ehsani AA, et al: Effect of exercise training on the blood pressure and hemo-

dynamic features of hypertensive adolescents. Am J Cardiol 52:763, 1983.

45. Douglas PS, O'Toole ML, Hiller WDB, et al: Left ventricular structure and function by echocardiography in ultraendurance athletes. Am J Cardiol 58:805, 1986.

46. Williams RS, Logue EE, Lewis JL, et al: Physical conditioning augments the fibrinolytic response to venous occlusion in healthy adults. N Engl J Med 302:987, 1980.

47. Hubert HB, Feinleib M, McNamara PM, et al: Obesity as an independent risk factor for cardiovascular disease: A 26-year follow-up of participants in the Framingham heart study. Circulation 67(5):968, 1983.

48. Aloia JF, Cohn SH, Babu T, et al: Skeletal mass and body composition in marathon runners. Metabolism 27(12):1793, 1978.

49. Lane NE, Bloch DA, Jones HH, et al: Long-distance running, bone density, and osteoarthritis. J Am Med Assoc 255(9):1147, 1986.

50. Krolner B, Toft B, Nielsen SP, et al: Physical exercise as prophylaxis against involutional vertebral bone loss: a controlled trial. Clin Sci 64:541, 1983.

51. Smith EL, Reddan W, and Smith PE: Physical activity and calcium modalities for bone mineral increase in aged women. Med Sci Sports Exerc 13(1):60, 1981.

52. Aloia JF, Cohn SH, Ostuni JA, et al: Prevention of involutional bone loss by exercise. Ann Intern Med 89:356, 1978.

53. Unger KM, Moser KM, and Hansen P: Selection of an exercise program for patients with chronic obstructive pulmonary disease. Heart Lung 9(1):68, 1980.

54. Richter EA, Ruderman NB, and Schneider SH: Diabetes and exercise. Am J Med 70:201, 1981.

55. Brown RS, Ramirez DE, and Taub JM: The prescription of exercise for depression. The Physician and Sportsmedicine 6:35, 1978.

56. Wells KF, and Dillon EK: Sit and reach, a test of back and leg flexibility. Res Q 23:115, 1952.

57. Klafs CE, and Arnheim DD: Modern Principles of Athletic Training. CV Mosby, St Louis, 1973.

58. Rothstein JM: Measurement in Physical Therapy. Churchill Livingstone, New York, p 105, 1985.

59. Cooper KH: Aerobics. Bantam Books, New York, 1968.

60. Cooper K: Correlation between field and treadmill testing as a means for assessing maximal oxygen intake. JAMA 203:201, 1968.

61. Maksud MG, Cannistra C, and Dublinski D: Energy expenditure and $\dot{V}_{O_{2max}}$ of female athletes during treadmill exercise. Res Q 47:692, 1976.

62. Katch FI, McArdle WD, Czula R, et al: Maximal oxygen intake, endurance running performance, and body composition in college women. Res Q 44:301, 1973.

63. Bergh U, Thorstensson A, Sjodin B, et al: Maximal oxygen uptake and muscle fiber types in trained and untrained humans. Med Sci Sports 10(3):151, 1978.

64. O'Toole ML, Hiller WDB, Crosby LO, et al: The ultraendurance triathlete: a physiological profile. Med Sci Sports Exerc 19(1):45, 1987.

65. American College of Sports Medicine: Guidelines for Graded Exercise Testing and Exercise Prescription, ed 3. Lea and Febiger, Philadelphia, 1986.

66. Gutin B: Prescribing an exercise program. In Winick M (ed): Nutrition and Exercise. John Wiley and Sons, New York, 1986, pp 30–50.

67. Skinner JS, and McLellan TH: The transition from aerobic to anaerobic metabolism. Res Q Exerc Sport 51:234, 1980.

68. American College of Sports Medicine: Position statement on the recommended quantity and quality of exercise for developing and maintaining fitness in healthy adults. Med Sci Sports 10(3):vii, 1978.

69. Wilmore JH: Individual exercise prescription. Am J Cardiol 33:757, 1974.

70. Pollock ML: The quantification of endurance training programs. Exerc Sports Sci Rev 1:155, 1973.

71. Hickson RC, Kanakis C Jr, Davis JR, et al: Reduced training duration effects on aerobic power, endurance, and cardiac growth. J Appl Physiol 53:225, 1982.

72. Hickson R, and Rosenkoetter MA: Reduced training frequencies and maintenance of aerobic power. Med Sci Sports Exerc 13:13, 1981.

73. Gibbons LW, Cooper KH, Meyer B, et al: The acute cardiac risk of strenuous exercise. JAMA 244:1799, 1980.

74. Thompson P, Stern M, Williams P, et al: Death during jogging or running: A study of 18 cases. JAMA 242:1265, 1979.

75. Thompson P, Funk E, Carleton R, et al: Incidence of death during jogging in Rhode Island from 1975 through 1980. JAMA 247:2535, 1982.

76. Maron BJ, Epstein SE, and Roberts WC: Causes of sudden death in competitive athletes. J Am Coll Cardiol 7:204, 1986.

77. Clancy WG: Runners' injuries. Am J Sports Med 8(2):137, 1980.

78. Clausen JP: Effect of physical training on cardiovascular adjustments to exercise in man. Physiol Rev 57(4):779, 1977.

# Appendix 1-1

## Sample Training Programs

The following are sample training schedules for women starting a fitness program. They are, however, only examples of types of activities that would be appropriate for women in these categories and should not be undertaken without proper medical and fitness evaluation. Also included are general guidelines to be followed by an athlete training for competition. Since a competitive athlete must train specifically for the requirements of her sport, a program appropriate for one athlete may be of little benefit to someone in another sport.

### Sample 8-Week Program for a Sedentary 30-Year-Old Woman

**Weeks 1-4** (Initial Stage—The energy cost of the exercise in this stage should be approximately 200 kcal per session. Exercise sessions should be 3 times per week or every other day.)

*Warm-up:* 5 min walking (heart rate [HR] = 110 beats per minute [bpm]); 5 min stretching (areas to stretch: Achilles tendon, hamstrings, lower back, and shoulders).
*Aerobic phase:* 15 min vigorous walking, jogging, stationary cycling, or any combination of these (HR = 135–145 bpm). After the 2nd week, the time for this phase should be gradually increased (by 1 min every other day) to 20 min.
*Cool-down:* 5 min walking (HR = 100–110 bpm); 5 min stretching (same as in warm-up).

**Weeks 4-8** (Improvement Stage—The energy cost of exercise in this stage should be approximately 300 kcal per session. Exercise sessions should be 3 to 5 times per week.)

*Warm-up:* 5 min walking (HR = 115 bpm); 5 min stretching, as previously.
*Aerobic phase:* 20 min initially; gradually increase to 25 min, as above. Aerobic activities can include walking, jogging, cycling, or any other continuous, rhythmic exercise. (HR = 140–150 bpm.)
*Cool-down:* 5 min walking (HR = 100–110 bpm); 5 min stretching, as previously.

**Week 8 and afterward** (Maintenance Stage—The energy cost should still be approximately 300 kcal per session.)

*Warm-up:* Same as above.
*Aerobic phase:* Intensity and duration of sessions should be the same as in Improvement Stage. Exercise should be done at least 3 times per week. Recreational sport activities of approximately the same intensity may be substituted 1 day per week.
*Cool-down:* Same as above.

### Sample 8-Week Program for Sedentary 60-Year-Old-Woman

**Weeks 1-4** (Initial Stage—200 kcal per session; 3 times per week.)

*Warm-up:* 5 min walking (HR = 100 bpm); 5 min stretching (areas to stretch: Achilles tendon, hamstrings, lower back, and shoulders).

*Aerobic phase:* 12–15 min vigorous walking or stationary cycling (HR = 110–120 bpm).
*Cool-down:* 5 min walking (HR = 95–105 bpm); 5 min stretching, as previously.

**Weeks 4–8** (Improvement Stage—300 kcal per session, 3–5 times per week.)

*Warm-up:* 5 min walking (HR = 110 bpm); 5 min stretching, as previously.
*Aerobic phase:* 15 min initially; gradually increase to 25 min of walking, jogging, stationary cycling or any combination of these (HR = 120–130 bpm)
*Cool-down:* 5 min walking (HR = 100–105 bpm); 5 min stretching, as previously.

**Week 8 and afterward** (Maintenance Stage—The energy cost per session should remain at 300 kcal. Exercise should be done at least 3 times per week.) Exercise program can remain the same as in the Improvement Stage with recreational sport activities substituted once a week if desired.

## Sample 8-Week Program for a Moderately Active 45-Year-Old Woman

**Weeks 1–2** (Initial Stage—Energy cost approximately 300 kcal per session. The purpose of this stage in a moderately active woman is to allow adaptation [particularly musculoskeletal] to occur in response to specific aerobic activity, such as jogging.)

*Warm-up:* 5 min walking or slow jogging (HR = 120–125); 5 min stretching (Achilles tendon, hamstrings, lower back, shoulders).
*Aerobic phase:* 25 minutes of vigorous walking, jogging, stationary cycling, rowing, or any other continuous, rhythmic activity of choice. (HR = 135–140)
*Cool-down:* 5 min slow jogging and/or walking (HR = 110 bpm); 5 min of stretching, as previously.

**Weeks 3–8** (Improvement Stage—300–500 kcal per session.)

*Warm-up:* 10 min (same as previously).
*Aerobic phase:* 25 min initially; gradually increase to 45 min per session. Any activity that will keep the heart rate 140–145 bpm for this length of time may be used.
*Cool-down:* 10 min (same as previously).

**Week 8 and afterward** (Maintenance Stage—Exercise sessions should be similar to those in the Improvement Stage and should be done at least 3 times per week with an energy cost of 500 kcal per session.)

## Guidelines for the Competitive Athlete

**1.** Training should be in 3 stages, comparable to those shown earlier but on a higher level—laying a base, increasing intensity, and fine tuning.
**2.** When adding sport-specific activities, training should be under conditions as similar to competitive conditions as possible.
**3.** Set reasonable goals in a reasonable time frame.
**4.** Keep a training diary to discover your own personal pattern of optimal training and to discover practices that lead to injury for you.
**5.** Use an overload/adaptation/progression system. That is, allow enough time for adaptation to occur after a hard workout, by following the hard workout with several easy or moderate ones. For example, after a race, some running coaches suggest waiting one day for each mile that was run, before beginning the next hard workout.
**6.** Balance the high energy output of training with a high caloric intake.

**Sample Program for a USTS Distance Triathlete**
(0.9-mile swim, 25-mile bike, 6.2-mile run)

**Weeks 1–4**   (Initial Stage—Goals are gradually to increase weekly mileage to 3 miles of swimming, 45 miles of bicycling, and 20 miles of running.)

Each workout should follow the format given previously (that is, warm-up, aerobic phase, and cool-down). The warm-up and cool-down phases should include gradual transition from rest to swimming, cycling, or running, as well as stretching of the muscles specific to that activity.

Each activity should be done 3 times per week, or 9 total workouts for the week. Since there are a variety of muscle groups being used, each with their own stresses, the triathlete can safely exercise every day. In order to complete the 9 workouts, single workouts can be done on 5 days and double workouts on 2 other days. Workouts in the same sport should not be done on 2 consecutive days.

Training mileages per workout should be up to 1500 meters swimming, 25 miles cycling, and 6 miles running. No interval training should be done. All training mileages should be accomplished aerobically; that is, at the end of the workout, the triathlete should feel that she could repeat the workout immediately.

**Weeks 4–12** (Improvement Stage—The time to increase the intensity of the workouts.)

Mileages should be increased to 5 miles of swimming, 75 miles of bicycling, and 25 miles of running per week.

During this stage, the emphasis should be on increasing the mileages so that some workouts are done slower than race pace at distances longer than race distances. Other workouts should be done using interval training. One interval training workout per week per sport is sufficient, and interval training should probably not be done on consecutive days. Time trials at race distances can be added during this phase.

Each activity should be done 4 or 5 times per week for a total of no more than 15 workouts per week. Hard workouts should be followed by easy workouts in each activity so that hard workouts are not done on two consecutive days. Occasionally, a swim workout should be immediately followed by a bike workout and a bike workout immediately followed by a run.

## Weeks 12 through the competitive season

The emphasis during this time should be on race performance. The total amount of training should be cut down, particularly on weeks when the triathlete is competing. The emphasis in workouts should be on quality rather than quantity. Short intervals concentrating on speed rather than endurance should be done once a week for each activity. Other days can either be at race pace for distances shorter than the race, or slower for longer distances. One day a week can be complete rest or a very easy workout.

# CHAPTER 2

# Optimal Health and Body Composition

FRANK I. KATCH, Ed.D.
VICTOR L. KATCH, Ed.D.

Maintenance of a relatively high degree of physiologic fitness can play an important role in human well-being. Physical fitness courses such as aerobic conditioning, circuit training, "slimnastics," body movement, figure control, aerobic dance, and body conditioning are flourishing in the public schools, universities, health clubs, and YMCA/YWCAs in this country and abroad. The corporate setting is also gaining the full benefits from a properly integrated approach to fitness, health, or wellness. Although opportunities for participation in vigorous physical activities have long been available to men, the involvement of women in such fitness-oriented programs is relatively new. Even 10 years ago, exercise programs for women were generally relegated to the figure salon or health spa where a woman would be passively exercised by machines and patronized by fancy and shiny gadgetry, but this is no longer the case. Opportunities to engage in vigorous exercise for women and men are now commonplace and not the exception. Women run fast marathons, they perform exquisitely in triathlons, and they train with all the vigor and zeal of their male counterparts in cycling, body building, mountain climbing, swimming, tennis, and just about every sport and recreational activity. **Research shows clearly that the training process in terms of physiologic adaptations is essentially the same for both sexes.** Because few physiologic processes or acute and chronic adaptations to exercise are peculiar just to women, in this chapter we have attempted to present current research information about the topics of optimal health and body composition in a more general way. In the section on body composition, we highlight several subtopics that do pertain uniquely to females.

## OPTIMAL HEALTH

Many exercise enthusiasts believe that exercise prolongs life. Research evidence is equivocal, however, concerning the association between longevity and regular exercise participation, as are data that show conclusively that exercise facilitates quality of life, delays the onset of aging, or serves as a possible prophylactic agent in degenerative diseases.

This section reviews pertinent data on the relationship between exercise participation and prospective health benefits. Discussions include exercise training and longevity and exercise and coronary heart disease (CHD) risk in adults and in children.

**Exercise training and longevity.** Because older fit individuals have many of the functional characteristics of younger people, it can be argued that improved physical fitness may help retard the aging process and maintain health in later life. In one of the first studies to test this hypothesis, Hill in 1927[1] showed that former Harvard oarsmen exceeded their predicted longevity by 5.1 years per man. Earlier studies showed similar but more modest results.[2] These studies, how-

ever, were plagued with methodologic problems that included inadequate record keeping, small sample size, improper statistical procedures for estimating expected longevity, and an inability to account for other important factors such as socioeconomic background, body type, cigarette smoking, and family history.

Thirty years later, other researchers attempted to overcome these limitations by studying the longevity of former college athletes.[3] Because collegiate athletes usually have a longer involvement in habitual physical activity prior to entering college than nonathletes, and because they may remain more physically active after college,[4] such factors would seem to provide insight concerning exercise and longevity.

Figure 2–1 shows that essentially no difference existed in the longevity of the ex-athletes compared with their nonathletic cohort. Such findings illustrate that participation in athletics as a young adult does not necessarily ensure increased longevity, at least in men. Longitudinal data on women are not available. It will be interesting to track the longevity of today's female athletes to see if they follow the same trend as for male athletes. Within the next three decades or so, we should know whether or not female athletes will have a longer life expectancy than their male counterparts, just as women generally now have a longer life expectancy than men.

An important question to be answered is whether *regular* physical activity *throughout life* promotes health and longevity. A recent long-term follow-up study of 16,936 Har-

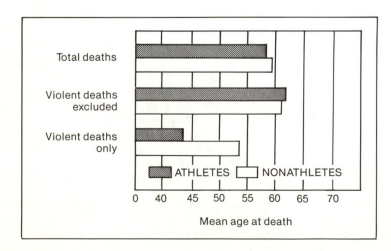

*Figure 2–1.* Age at death of athletes and nonathletes. None of the differences between the groups is statistically significant. (From Montoye,[3] with permission.)

**Table 2–1.** RELATIVE AND ATTRIBUTABLE RISKS* OF DEATH (FROM ALL CAUSES) AMONG 16,936 HARVARD ALUMNI, 1962 TO 1978, ACCORDING TO SELECTED ADVERSE CHARACTERISTICS

| Alumnus Characteristic | Prevalence (Man-Years, %) | Relative Risk of Death† | P Value | Clinical Attributable Risk (%) | Community Attributable Risk (%) |
|---|---|---|---|---|---|
| Sedentary lifestyle‡ | 62.0 | 1.31 (1.15–1.49) | 0.0001 | 23.6 | 16.1 |
| Hypertension§ | 9.4 | 1.73 (1.48–2.01) | <0.0001 | 42.1 | 6.4 |
| Cigarette smoking¶ | 38.2 | 1.76 (1.56–1.99) | <0.0001 | 43.2 | 22.5 |
| Low net weight gain‖ | 35.1 | 1.33 (1.17–1.51) | 0.0001 | 24.6 | 10.3 |
| Early parental death** | 33.3 | 1.15 (1.02–1.30) | 0.0248 | 13.1 | 4.8 |

*Adjusted for differences in age and each of the other characteristics listed.
†Figures in parentheses are 95% confidence intervals.
‡Energy expenditure of <2000 kcal per week in walking, climbing stairs, and playing sports.
§Physician-diagnosed.
¶Any amount.
‖Net gain in body-mass index of <3 units since college—i.e., not more than 7 kg (15 lb).
**One or both parents dead before the age of 65.
(From Paffenbarger,[5] with permission.)

vard alumni, aged 35 to 74 years, studied physical activity and other lifestyle characteristics in relation to rates of mortality from all causes and to influences on length of life.[5] Data on mortality were analyzed for men who entered Harvard in the period 1916 to 1950. A total of 1413 alumni died during 12 to 16 years of follow-up. The underlying causes of death were cardiovascular disease (45 percent), cancer (32 percent), trauma (10 percent), and natural causes (13 percent). Table 2–1 shows age-adjusted rates of death from all causes during the 16-year follow-up period in relation to physical activity, as well as relative risks of death. Such data reveal several important findings.

First and foremost was that risk of death could be reduced by up to 16 percent if the individuals were physically active (defined as expending 2000 kcal per week). Extirpation of hypertension could cut the community death rate another 6 percent, and total abstinence from cigarette smoking would cut the death rate by an additional 23 percent. There was a clear and consistent trend toward a lower death rate with increased physical activity.

Based on this 1986 epidemiologic study, it would seem prudent for individuals to increase their amount of physical activity. While this may seem like a simple prescription, the fact remains that the average American is really quite sedentary.

Figure 2–2 shows data on the percent of adults who participate in fitness/recreational activities. The ages range from 19 to 64 years, grouped in five age categories. On the abscissa are the number of days of participation per year. These data include men and women from the most recent American study based on a random sample of over 15,000 people who participated in walking, jogging, running, cycling, swimming, and weight lifting.[6] These data reveal that with increasing age, there is a progressive and predictable decline in participation in fitness activities. Also, the percent of the population who participate in fitness activities is really quite small, especially in the older age groups. Other findings showed that age accounted for 4.5 percent of the variance in fitness participation, whereas gender accounted for less than 1 percent of the variance. After adjusting for age and education, women were only one-half day per year less active than men. However, participation in fitness-type activities by both men and women must be considered minimal at best.

The reasons why people become less active as they become older are complex and require further study. It is unknown, for example, if regular participation in physical activity during earlier years ensures greater than normal participation as one ages? If this turns out to be the case, then the nation's youth should be encouraged to participate to

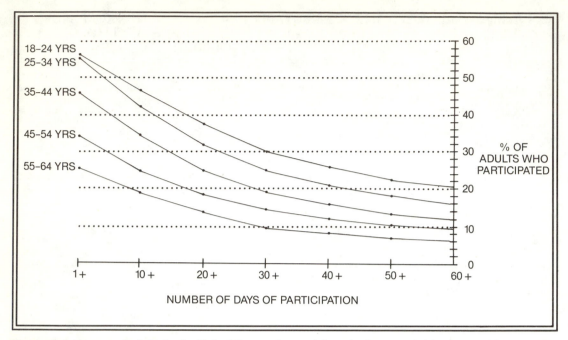

**Figure 2-2.** *Percent of adults in the United States who participate in fitness activities, grouped by age. (From Brooks,[6] by permission of author, Professor Christine Brooks, Sports Marketing, Dept. of Sports Management and Communication, University of Michigan, Ann Arbor, MI.)*

a much greater extent in fitness-type activities, especially at the elementary school grade levels. Newer approaches are certainly needed to help alleviate the trend toward sedentary living observed in adulthood. A way must be found to increase exercise compliance. This will take a coordinated effort between physical education specialists and the medical professions (particularly physicians in all of the various specialties and subspecialties, not just those who profess an interest in "sports medicine").

**Exercise and coronary heart disease (CHD) risk in adults.** Coronary heart disease has reached epidemic proportions throughout the United States and most technologically advanced societies. Beginning at age 30 for men and age 40 for women, CHD is the single greatest cause of death. For example, about twice as many people die from CHD as from cancer. As depicted in Figure 2–3, the chances of dying from CHD increase progressively and dramatically after age 35 in men and age 45 in women. Between the ages of 55 and 65, about 13 of every 100 men and 6 of every 100 women will die from CHD.

Regardless of the specific mechanism of coronary disease, significant information is now available on its natural history and dynamics. Various personal characteristics, physiologic alterations, and environmental factors are frequently implicated as risk factors. These include (1) age and gender, (2) elevated blood lipids, (3) hypertension, (4) cigarette smoking, (5) physical inactivity, (6) diet, (7) diabetes mellitus, (8) heredity, (9) personality and behavior, (10) high uric acid levels, (11) pulmonary function abnormalities, (12) race, and (13) ECG abnormalities at rest and during exercise. Stress has also been implicated as a risk factor, but the association between this factor and coronary disease has not been firmly established.

It is difficult to determine quantitatively the importance of a single CHD risk factor in comparison to any other, because many of the factors are interrelated. For example, blood lipid abnormalities, diabetes, heredity, and obesity often go hand-in-hand. One research study, for example, reported that men living in Ireland consumed more saturated fat than their blood brothers who lived in the United States, yet the former had a much

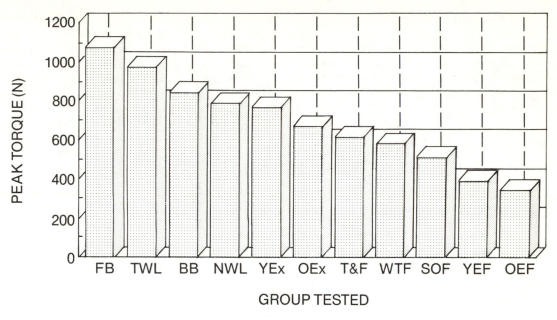

**Figure 2–3.** *Comparison of female track and field athletes with other male and female groups. The designation for the symbols is as follows: FB = male varsity collegiate football players; TWL = trained male weight lifters; BB = male varsity collegiate baseball players; NWL = non–weight-trained males: YEx = young male corporate executives; OEx = older male corporate executives; T&F = female collegiate track and field athletes; WTF = weight-trained females; SOF = female varsity collegiate soccer players; YEF = young female executives; OEF = older female executives. Peak torque scores were obtained at resistance (dial) setting 10 during chest press exercise on a Total Power exercise device (Hydra-Fitness Industries, Belton, TX). (Data courtesy of the Muscle Strength Laboratory, Exercise Science Department, University of Massachusetts, Amherst, MA, 1987, with permission.)*

lower incidence of CHD.[7] Protection was attributed to higher physical activity levels for those living in Ireland. Similar results of a high saturated fat intake, high physical activity, and low incidence of CHD have been reported for Masai tribesman of East Africa and farm laborers in Georgia.[8,9]

Lack of agreement in results do indeed cloud the issues, but a major point is that several factors are closely related to CHD. In each case, the degree of causality is unknown, and it still remains to be shown that risk factor modification offers effective protection from developing CHD. One could assume that elimination or reduction of one or more CHD risk factors would decrease the probability of risk for CHD. This line of reasoning has prompted the American Medical Association, for example, to recommend guidelines and prescriptions for consuming an optimal dietary intake of saturated fat and cholesterol, as well as a recommendation to increase physical activity and maintain body weight at a desirable level.

It is also known that the distribution of cholesterol among the various types of lipoproteins is a more powerful predictor of heart disease than the total quantity of plasma lipids. An elevated high-density lipoprotein (HDL) level is linked to a lower CHD risk, whereas an elevated low-density lipoprotein (LDL) and very low–density lipoprotein (VLDL) levels represent an increased CHD risk. LDL is targeted for peripheral tissue, and HDL may reflect the removal aspect of lipid dynamics by promoting the movement of cholesterol from peripheral tissue (including arterial walls) for transport to the liver and excretion through bile synthesis.[10] HDL may retard cholesterol build-up by directly blocking LDL uptake.

Cigarette smoking and obesity also appear to be potent predictors of CHD risk. While mild obesity per se does not predict CHD, its correlation to hypertension, diabetes mellitus, hyperlipoproteinemia, and smoking is undeniable.[11] Weight loss and accompanying fat reduction generally reduce cholesterol and triglyceride levels and can have a normalizing effect on blood pressure and adult-onset diabetes.

Physical **inactivity** may also be important as a CHD risk factor. Although the data on physical inactivity and increased risk for CHD generally fall short of critical proof, there is no evidence that the prudent application of exercise is "harmful" in terms of health. Regular exercise may mitigate against CHD in a variety of ways. In addition to the mechanisms listed in Table 2–1, other effects of exercise may include the following:

1. *More desirable body composition.* For the obese and borderline obese (see next section), regular aerobic exercise reduces body weight and body fat. Increases in lean body weight also accompany fat loss. When dietary restriction is combined with exercise, more of the lost weight is fat because exercise appears to conserve the body's lean tissues. Such favorable changes can improve cardiovascular functioning, most likely because of a decrease in body fat and an increase in muscle mass.

2. *More favorable neural-hormonal balance.* Exercise can positively affect hormone balance. Because of the complex interactions between endocrine secretions and the nervous system, the research literature is sparse with respect to multiple hormone secretions and changes consequent to physical training. Most of the research is limited to studies on a single hormone response; thus, a global picture of hormone balance resulting from exercise training is not available. What is known is that regular exercise affects the pancreatic hormones and results in increased insulin sensitivity and smaller increases in glucose levels mediated via glucagon. Such effects have implications for individuals that are insulin insensitive.

3. *Favorable outlet for release of psychologic "stressor."* This area of inquiry is fraught with methodologic considerations, mostly because anecdotal evidence and case studies provide little hard data. Nevertheless, this is a fertile field for developing psychobiologic models and correlation to physiologic correlates of behavior.

**Exercise and coronary heart disease risk in children.** CHD risk factors develop during early childhood.[12] The disease matures slowly, generally becoming recognizable during adulthood. However, multiple risk factors for CHD have now been documented in young children.[13-15]

Table 2–2 presents the prevalence of risk factors for active and apparently healthy boys and girls ages 7 to 12 years. Obesity and a family history of heart disease were the two most frequently occurring risk factors. A large percentage of children showed abnormal serum lipid profiles. For the group, 65 percent had at least one or two risk factors, and 31 percent had three or more risk factors! Whether risk factor identification in children is linked to premature heart disease remains unclear. Equally important is the question of whether "risk intervention" in children improves the long-term health outlook in adulthood. A recent study considered this question.[16] Sixty-seven obese adolescents who exhibited initially high levels of coronary risk (89 percent of the subjects had four or more CHD risk factors) were enrolled in a 20-week intervention program. Subjects were randomly placed in either control (C); diet and behavior modification therapy (DB); or exercise, diet, and behavior modification (EDB) groups.

The pre- and post-treatment means are shown in Table 2–3 for eight CHD risk variables for each group. These data are striking for several reasons. First, elevated blood pressure and other risk variables in obese ad-

**Table 2–2.** PREVALENCE OF CHD RISK FACTORS IN ACTIVE CHILDREN, 7–12 YEARS OF AGE

| Risk Factor | Prevalence | | | | Percent in Total Sample |
| --- | --- | --- | --- | --- | --- |
| | *Male* | *Female* | Total | N | |
| Obesity (>20% body fat) | 10 | 4 | 14 | 47 | 30 |
| Low work capacity (<31 mL·kg$^{-1}$·min$^{-1}$) | 3 | 1 | 4 | 34 | 12 |
| Elevated blood lipids | | | | | |
|   Cholesterol (>200 mg%) | 1 | 3 | 4 | 38 | 10 |
|   Triglycerides (>100 mg%) | 4 | 3 | 7 | 38 | 18 |
| Lipoprotein classification | | | | | |
|   Type II | 1 | 1 | 2 | 38 | 5 |
|   Type IV | 4 | 3 | 7 | 38 | 18 |
| Family history of CHD | 7 | 5 | 12 | 47 | 26 |

(From Gilliam,[15] with permission.)

olescents were reduced with the diet and exercise intervention. Second, the exercise training effect, independent of the amount of change in body fat or body weight, was important in reducing the magnitude and number of risk factors.

Small differences in the change in fat and body weight were found between DB and EDB subjects, and large differences occurred in the *change* in multiple risk prevalence. Before entering the program, all but one of the EDB subjects had three or fewer risk factors, and two had only one risk factor. In contrast, for the DB and C subjects, only two and three subjects dropped below four risk factors post-treatment, respectively. This suggests that the exercise training effect caused the greatest change in multiple and specific CHD risk prevalence.

## BODY COMPOSITION

### Evaluation of Body Composition

A variety of techniques are available for quantitative assessment of body composition. Within the last 20 years, newer methodologies have become available, and the popular height-weight tables are no longer required to determine the extent of "overweight" or obesity. In fact, the height-weight tables serve little useful purpose other than categorization and description of populations in terms of height and weight. Height and weight (or their dubious ratios that include the body mass index) correlate poorly with more objective measures of body composition such as percent body fat, absolute fat weight, or skeletal (bone) mass. Body weight does correlate highly with lean body weight, but the relationship is spurious because the body weight is involved in the calculation of lean body weight.

The purpose of this section is to provide information about the following topics: (1) composition of the human body, (2) essential and storage fat, (3) exercise, leanness, and menstrual irregularity, (4) valid measurement of body composition, and (5) body composition and strength performance.

**Composition of the human body.** The three major structural components of the human body include muscle, fat, and bone. Because there are marked sex differences in body composition, an objective basis for evaluation and comparison is to employ the concept proposed by Behnke[17,18] of the *reference man and reference woman*. Table 2–4 presents data on the gross body composition for a reference man and woman in terms of muscle, fat, and bone. This theoretical model is based on the average physical dimensions obtained from detailed measurements of thousands of individuals who were subjects in large-scale anthropometric surveys.[19–21]

The reference man is taller by 4 inches, heavier by 29 lb; his skeleton weighs more (23 versus 15 lb); and he has a larger muscle mass (69 versus 45 lb) and lower total fat content (23.1 versus 33.8 lb) than the refer-

# Table 2-3. PRETREATMENT AND POST-TREATMENT MEANS FOR A GROUP OF OBESE ADOLESCENTS UNDERGOING A WEIGHT REDUCTION PROGRAM

| | Control (n = 14) | | EDB (n = 11) | | DB (n = 11) | |
|---|---|---|---|---|---|---|
| | Pre | Post | Pre | Post | Pre | Post |
| TAG (mg/dL) | 117.79 ± 59.13 | 122.21 ± 50.75 | 135.82 ± 54.71 | 91.64 ± 60.91 | 117.27 ± 46.24 | 99.91 ± 57.59 |
| HDL:C (mg/dL) | 29.5 ± 6.1 | 32.0 ± 5.7 | 35.3 ± 7.6 | 43.4 ± 7.5*† | 34.5 ± 9.0 | 38.4 ± 9.8 |
| Chol (mg/dL) | 176.93 ± 39.95 | 167.14 ± 33.50 | 170.55 ± 33.73 | 149.27 ± 30.40 | 181.18 ± 40.88 | 171.91 ± 37.77 |
| SBP-Z (sd) | 1.12 ± 1.04 | 1.41 ± 1.15 | 1.27 ± 0.46 | −0.07 ± 0.66*‡ | 1.61 ± 1.28 | 0.53 ± 1.23 |
| DBP-Z (sd) | 0.44 ± 1.17 | 0.76 ± 1.44 | 0.59 ± 0.97 | −0.50 ± 0.82*† | 1.34 ± 1.59 | 0.51 ± 1.32* |
| BW (kg) | 68.73 ± 17.02 | 71.92 ± 18.07 | 67.89 ± 9.32 | 66.26 ± 9.81 | 77.15 ± 21.86 | 76.76 ± 21.74 |
| % Fat | 39.80 ± 6.67 | 40.54 ± 7.42 | 38.28 ± 3.95 | 35.26 ± 5.32 | 43.95 ± 7.58 | 40.47 ± 6.30 |
| $\dot{V}_{O_2max}$ (mL·kg$^{-1}$·min$^{-1}$) | 30.56 ± 6.86 | 29.67 ± 6.49 | 32.69 ± 5.18 | 33.42 ± 9.25 | 28.51 ± 5.41 | 28.65 ± 9.16 |

*Post-treatment significantly different from pretreatment ($p < 0.05$).
†EDB post-treatment significantly different from Control and DB post-treatment ($p < 0.05$).
‡EDB post-treatment significantly different from Control post-treatment ($p < 0.05$).
(From Becque F, and Katch V: Unpublished data. Section of Pediatric Cardiology and Department of Kinesiology, University of Michigan, Ann Arbor, MI, 1987, with permission.)

**Table 2–4.** GROSS BODY COMPOSITION OF A
REFERENCE MAN AND WOMAN FOR MUSCLE,
FAT, AND BONE

| Reference Man | Variable | Reference Woman |
|---|---|---|
| 20–24 | Age, yr | 20–24 |
| 68.5 | Height, in | 64.5 |
| 154 | Weight, lb | 125 |
| 69 (44.8%) | Muscle, lb | 45 (36.0%) |
| 23.1 (15.0%) | Total fat, lb | 33.8 (27.0%) |
| 4.6 (3.0%) | Essential fat, lb | 15.0 (12.0%) |
| 18.5 (12.0%) | Storage fat, lb | 18.8 (15.0%) |
| 23.0 (14.9%) | Bone, lb | 15.0 (12.0%) |
| 136 | Lean body weight, lb | — |
| — | Minimal weight, lb | 107 |

Adapted from McArdle WD, Katch FI, and Katch VL: Exercise Physiology, ed
2. Lea and Febiger, Philadelphia, 1986.

ence female. Such sex differences exist even
when the amount of fat, muscle, and bone
are expressed as a percentage of body
weight. It is not known how much of this difference in body fat is biologic or how much
is behavioral, owing perhaps to the more
sedentary lifestyle of the average female.
More than likely, however, hormonal differences between the sexes play an important
role. The concept of a reference standard
does not mean that men and women should
strive to achieve the body composition of the
reference models, nor that the reference man
and woman are in fact "average." The models serve as a useful frame of reference for
statistical comparisons and interpretation
with the data from other studies, as well as
for contrast of the data of individuals.

**Essential and storage fat.** The total
amount of body fat exists in two depots or
storage sites. The first depot, termed *essential
fat*, is stored in the marrow of bones as well
as in the heart, lungs, liver, spleen, kidneys,
intestines, muscles, and lipid-rich tissues of
the central nervous system. This fat is required for normal physiologic functioning. In
the female, essential fat also includes *sex-
specific* or *sex-characteristic fat*. It is not at all
clear whether this fat depot is expendable or
serves as reserve storage.

The other major fat depot, the *storage fat*,
accumulates in adipose tissue. This nutritional reserve includes the fatty tissues that
protect the various internal organs from
trauma, as well as the larger subcutaneous
fat volume deposited beneath the skin sur-

face. Although the proportional distribution
of storage fat in men and women is similar
(12 percent in men and 15 percent in
women), the total quantity of essential fat in
women plus the sex-specific fat is four times
higher than in men. The additional essential
fat may be biologically important for childbearing and other hormone-related functions.

Table 2–5 illustrates a proposed theoretical
model of body tissue distribution for the ref-

**Table 2–5.** THEORETICAL
DISTRIBUTION OF BODY FAT
FOR A REFERENCE FEMALE*

| Fat | |
|---|---|
| a. Sex-specific fat (reserve) | 5–9% |
| Location: breast, genitals, lower body, subcutaneous, intramuscular, other | |
| b. Essential fat | 4–7% |
| Location: bone marrow, spinal cord, liver, heart, spleen, kidneys, other | |
| c. Storage fat (expendable) | 15% |
| Location: mainly subcutaneous, intra-organ | |
| Bone | 14% |
| Muscle | 37% |
| Remainder | 25% |

*Weight 125 lb, height 64.5 in, and body fat 23.6% of
body weight; values for the various components differ
slightly from those in Table 2–4.
Adapted from Katch,[22] with permission.

erence female. Note that there is a subclassification of the essential body fat stores that includes sex-specific fat. As part of the 5 to 9 percent sex-specific reserve fat, the breasts contribute approximately 4.4 percent of the total weight of body fat, or no more than 12.5 percent to the quantity of sex-specific fat.[22] We interpret this to mean there must be other substantial sex-specific depots in the female such as in the pelvic and thigh regions that contribute importantly to female body fat stores.

*Minimal weight.* In contrast to the lower limit of body weight in men that includes about 3 percent essential fat in adipose tissue, the lower limit of body weight for the reference woman includes 12 percent essential fat in adipose tissue. This theoretical limit for *minimal weight* in the reference woman is equivalent to 107 pounds. In general, the leanest women in the population do not have body fat levels below about 10 to 12 percent of body weight.[17,22] This probably represents the lower limit of fatness for most women in "good health." In carefully conducted studies based on body density or total body potassium, values of body fat lower than 8 to 10 percent fat are very uncommon, even in highly trained endurance athletes and body builders.[23,24] The concept of minimal weight in the female that incorporates about 12 percent essential fat is equivalent to lean body weight in males that includes 3 percent essential fat. Minimal weight can be estimated from bone diameters. If body weight is lower than the computed minimal weight, then the woman would be classified as "underweight," and should not reduce body weight further without medical supervision. The following equation is used to calculate minimal weight:

Minimal weight
$$= (D/33.5)^2 \times ht,dm \times 0.111$$

where D is the sum of eight bone diameters; ht,dm is height in decimeters; and 33.5 and 0.111 are constants.[17,25] The data in Table 2–6 illustrate the computation of minimal weight for a thin-appearing woman who weighed 38.7 kg (85.3 lb) and was 65.6 inches tall (166.7 cm, or 16.67 dm). The bone diameters were taken according to established procedures.[17,25] The example shows that this woman was clearly underweight,

because her body weight of 85.3 lb (38.7 kg) was about 8 percent below her recommended minimal weight.

**Leanness, exercise, and menstrual irregularity.** It is believed that female athletes with a relatively "low" body fat content increase their chances of a delayed onset of menstruation, an irregular menstrual cycle, or amenorrhea. In support of this position are studies of ballet dancers who are quite lean and report a greater incidence of menstrual irregularities and a higher mean age at menarche compared with age-matched, nondancer counterparts.[26,27] It is estimated that from one third to one half of female athletes have some menstrual irregularity.[28-31] The speculation is that in some way the body "senses" when energy reserves are inadequate to sustain a pregnancy, and thus ceases ovulation to prevent conception. Often cited is the maintenance of at least 17 percent body fat as the "critical level" for the onset of menstruation, and 22 percent body fat as the level required to maintain a normal cycle. It is argued by some that hormonal and metabolic disturbances are triggered that affect the menses if body fat goes below these levels of fat.[32]

**Table 2–6.** PROCEDURE FOR COMPUTING A WOMAN'S MINIMAL WEIGHT

| Diameter | Measurement (cm) |
|---|---|
| Biacromial | 34.4 |
| Chest | 23.8 |
| Bi-iliac | 22.7 |
| Bitrochanteric | 29.8 |
| Knees* | 16.1 |
| Ankles* | 11.5 |
| Elbows* | 11.1 |
| Wrists* | 10.0 |
|  | 159.4 |

*Sum of right and left sides.

Step 1. Compute D, the sum of the 8 diameters. Note that the last 4 measurements represent the sum of the right and left sides.

Step 2. Substitute in the equation for minimal weight.
Minimal weight = $(D/33.5)^2 \times h_{dm} \times 0.111$
= $(159.4/33.5)^2 \times 16.67 \times 0.111$
= 41.9 kg

Although the lean-to-fat ratio does appear to be important for normal menstrual function (owing perhaps to the role of peripheral fat in the conversion of androgens to estrogens), other factors must also be considered. There are many active women with less than 17 percent body fat who have normal menstrual cycles and who maintain a high level of physiologic and performance capacity.[33–35] On the other hand, there are amenorrheic athletes with average levels of body fat (21 to 28 percent body fat assessed by densitometry). In addition, when the menstrual cycle returns to normal, it is not always associated with an increase in body weight or body fat. As would be expected, many outstanding female distance runners, gymnasts, and body builders have normal menses during intensive training and competition, and compete successfully at a body fat level below 17 percent.

In a study from one of our laboratories,[36] 30 female athletes and 30 nonathletes, all with less than 20 percent body fat, were compared for menstrual cycle regularity, irregularity, and amenorrhea. Four of the athletes and three of the nonathletes, whose body fat ranged from 11 to 15 percent, had regular cycles, whereas seven athletes and two nonathletes had irregular cycles or were amenorrheic. For the total sample, 14 athletes and 21 nonathletes had regular cycles, respectively. These data illustrate that the hypothesis of a "critical fat level" based on an estimate of body fat derived from regression equations that use height and weight is simply invalid.[32]

The complex interplay of physical, nutritional, psychologic, and environmental factors on menstrual function must be considered. Research shows that for active women, an intense bout of exercise triggers the release of an array of hormones, some of which have antireproductive properties.[37] It has been shown that regular bouts of heavy exercise exert a cumulative effect sufficient to alter normal menstrual function. It is noteworthy that when young amenorrheic ballet dancers received injuries that prevented them from exercising, normal menstruation resumed even though body weight remained unchanged.[26] Exercise-associated disturbances in menstrual function can probably be reversed with changes in lifestyle without serious consequences.[28,37]

If a critical fat level does exist, it may be specific for each woman, but could change throughout life. Based on current data, approximately 13 percent body fat can be regarded as an upper-bound estimate of some yet to be determined minimal level of fatness associated with the regularity of menstrual function.[36] The effects and risks of sustained amenorrhea on the reproductive system have still to be determined. Failure to menstruate or cessation of the normal cycle should be evaluated by a gynecologist or reproductive endocrinologist, because it may reflect a significant medical condition such as pituitary or thyroid gland malfunction or premature menopause. Additional studies are needed to define the lower limits of body fatness compatible with regularity of menstrual status and to determine if a low level of body fat per se acts to modify hormonal regulation of ovulatory patterns. What is clear is that height-weight–based regression equations to predict body fatness should not be employed to provide answers to such questions.[32] The relationship of exercise and menstruation is extensively discussed in Chapter 10.

**Valid measurement of body composition.** Two general procedures are used to evaluate body composition: (1) direct (chemical analysis of the animal carcass and human cadaver), and (2) indirect (hydrostatic weighing, fat folds, girths, bone diameters, isotope dilution, neutron activation, potassium-40 counting, arm roentgenograms, total body electrical conductivity, and ultrasound). Although the direct methods provide the theoretical validity for the indirect procedures,[38–46] it is the indirect, noninvasive techniques that permit estimation of the fat and nonfat components of humans. For purposes of clinical evaluation or fitness assessment, what method is "best" for evaluation of body composition?

The answer is not very simple, although many practitioners prefer expediency to validity. By this we mean that if a measurement is simple to take and the end result provides a direct answer (i.e., a value for percent body fat or lean body weight gleaned from a computer printout and the latest high-tech "body fat machine"), then such a procedure will probably be used as the method of choice. This is usually the case when large numbers of patients are to be measured, when fitness and sports medicine specialists want an easy way to target the degree of obesity or overweight, or when school teachers require that their students "know" their body composition because of state-mandated physical fitness tests. But, as with most things that are "simple and easy," there must be a trade-off with accuracy and validity. The real inequity, however, is that the person being evaluated gets short-changed in terms of technically correct information. Consider the fat-fold technique. There is no question that subcutaneous fat thickness measured with a given caliper at some site does in fact give an indication of the thickness of the underlying fat width plus a double layer of skin at that site. If fat thickness turns out to be 22 mm, for example, does this mean that 22 mm thickness will be obtained when another measurement is taken 5 minutes later, or the next day, or even the next week or month (assuming constant state of hydration, caloric intake, and expenditure)? Under the best of laboratory conditions, when such measurements are performed by a so-called expert, the degree of unreliability in repeated measurements can easily approach 50 to 100 percent! For a large fat thickness in more obese individuals, intravariation in repeated testing could mean a ±5 to 10 mm difference in repeated testing. Even this degree of inaccuracy for trained technicians means that the resultant percent body fat, calculated from a regression equation that used the particular fat-fold score, could be in error by ±100 percent or more! This level of inaccuracy does not include the "error" inherent in the regression equation. Even the "best" equations based on gender and age have standard errors of estimate in the range of about 3 to 5 percent.

If we now translate information obtained from the laboratory to the "field" (i.e., doctor's office, school, fitness center), we are left with the inescapable conclusion that in the hands of a technician less trained than laboratory personnel, the inaccuracy in taking measurements can be 100 percent or more of the criterion values. The situation is compounded when the fat-fold information is used to assess *changes* as a result of some intervention program. It is all too common to observe that body fat calculated from fat-fold regression equations actually *increases* as a result of weight loss, rather than decreasing as should occur when subcutaneous fat stores are reduced. The culprit, of course, is not the particular fat-fold caliper that is used but the individual who takes the measurements. Unless the tester is truly an expert in such measurement taking, fat folds are rather useless for quantitative assessment of changes in body composition.

If an individual is tested only once and is given a score for body fat and lean body weight, then no one will know how "incorrect" the values really are. That is why control groups are crucial for assessing the extent of variability in the measurement process, as well as having someone with real expertise perform the fat-fold assessments (preferably without knowledge of the make-up of the experimental and control groups). As a minimum, the tester should have measured 100 people on two different days, with five repeated measurements at each fat-fold site, before the reliability of test scores can be assessed. If the resulting reliability is consistently above r = 0.9, with no significant variance between repeated measures or test days, then there is probably sufficient accuracy to expect less than about 2 to 5 percent inaccuracy in fat-fold assessment. If this level of proficiency cannot be achieved, our recommendation is to *not* use the fat-fold technique for assessment of body composition, at least not for predicting body fat with regression equations. Prediction equations developed by a particular researcher (that may be highly valid for the sample measured) may be almost useless to predict accurately the body fat for an individual when another person measures the fat folds. As an alternative, we have argued for the use of girth measurements to assess body composition, because these measurements are easier to reproduce, and because the standard errors of estimate for the resulting regression equations give the same or higher validity than do fat-fold regressions.[47,48]

If one uses the girth equations and constants presented elsewhere for young and older men and women,[48-50] the error in predicting an individual's body fat is generally ±2.5 to 4.0 percent. These relatively low prediction errors make the girth equations particularly useful to those without access to laboratory facilities, especially because the measurements are easy to take and a tape measure is inexpensive. A variety of other surface anthropometric procedures can be used to evaluate body composition, without the inherent limitations imposed by the fat-fold technique.[51-59] Of course, a better alternative to surface anthropometry would be to rely on a more precise indirect procedure such as densitometry with correction for residual air volume.[60-62]

**Body composition and strength performance.** A recent article reviewed more than 100 studies concerning the relationship between various measures of body composition and different modes of muscular strength training.[63] A current experiment provides further information about the role of body composition in relation to maximal muscular performance. Twenty female track and field athletes at the University of Massachusetts, Amherst, were tested for various measures of strength with isokinetic, isotonic, and hydraulic concentric methods. The age range was 18 to 23 years, mean height was 165.8 cm (SD = 6.31), and mean weight was 59.4 kg (SD = 4.48). To assess isokinetic strength, subjects performed a conventional bench press at 5 degrees per second. The best of three sets of three was used as the criterion strength score. For isotonic strength, subjects lifted 70 kg as fast as they could during a bench press; the criterion score was the highest velocity of movement during three sets of four repetitions. Subjects were also tested during maximal effort in a seated bench press-lat pull concentric exercise with hydraulic resistance equipment at a slow speed of movement (resistance setting 10; Total Power Machine, Hydra-Fitness Industries, Belton, TX).

Table 2-7 presents the correlations among the various expressions of maximal strength and height, weight, and body fat determined from a generalized fat-fold regression equation.[64] Height was unrelated to strength (r ≤ 0.17), but body weight and body fat correlated moderately with maximal force production (r = 0.41-0.67). The magnitude of the correlations, however, accounted for less than 50 percent of the common variance between body size and body fat and the various expressions of strength.

Figure 2-3 displays the results for the track and field athletes in relation to other groups of females and various groups of males. All of the female groups scored more poorly than the male groups for concentric, maximal force production during chest press exercise at a relatively slow speed of movement on a hydraulic resistance device. It is hoped that future studies will try to separate the influence of the purely body composition factors (body morphology and limb size and volume) related to maximal force production from factors related to the mechanical characteristics of maximal force production. Of particular interest will be the influence of different regimens of "strength" training in relation to changes in overall body composition, as well as changes in limb and trunk composition of the musculature involved in training. It will also be necessary to study the relationship between endurance performance and body composition of women, as well as various indices of neuromuscular performance (speed, static and dynamic balance, agility, resisted and unresisted reaction and movement time, coincidence timing, eye

**Table 2-7.** CORRELATIONS AMONG HEIGHT, WEIGHT, BODY FAT, AND VARIOUS MEASURES OF MUSCULAR STRENGTH IN FEMALE TRACK AND FIELD ATHLETES (N = 20)

|  | Body Weight (kg) | Body Fat | Isokinetic Strength | Isotonic Strength | Hydraulic Strength |
|---|---|---|---|---|---|
| Height (cm) | 0.44 | 0.19 | 0.03 | 0.04 | 0.17 |
| Body weight (kg) | — | 0.60 | 0.61 | 0.41 | 0.69 |
| Body fat (%) |  | — | 0.67 | 0.55 | 0.57 |
| Isokinetic strength |  |  | — | 0.59 | 0.83 |
| Isotonic strength |  |  |  | — | 0.75 |

Means and SDs are as follows: body fat (21.0 ± 2.38); isokinetic squat "speed" strength, degrees/sec (86.7 ± 9.1); isotonic squat strength, kg (126.9 ± 29.63); hydraulic chest press strength, newtons (614.3 ± 91.6).
(Data courtesy of the Muscle Strength Laboratory, Department of Exercise Science, University of Massachusetts, Amherst, MA, 1987.)

and hand coordination) in relation to valid measures of body morphology and composition, as well as different expressions of muscular force. Currently, such data on females are unavailable.

### Effects of Diet and Exercise on Body Composition During Weight Loss

Historically, the major focus of weight-reducing programs has been weight loss without real concern for its composition. The composition of the lost weight (fat, protein, and water) is highly variable and can be affected by body composition, level of caloric restriction, initial fatness level, amount and type of exercise, and techniques used to assess changes. Generally, weight loss by only caloric restriction includes a large proportion of lean body mass (LBM), with the proportion lost increasing relative to the severity of the caloric deficit. Losses in LBM can range from 15 percent of body weight for mild caloric restriction[65] to as high as 70 percent during semistarvation.[66,67] Exercise alone or in combination with caloric restriction appears to minimize LBM losses. Studies reporting

"gains" in LBM during periods of weight loss are not available. Chapter 3 discusses exercise and weight loss in greater detail.

Reports of the interactive effects of caloric restriction plus exercise on the composition of weight loss have included relatively low-intensity, aerobic-type programs (walking, jogging, running, bicycling, and swimming). While low-intensity aerobic exercise produces a substantial caloric expenditure, there are no data that show the effects on muscle growth and hypertrophy from "light aerobics." Thus, it is not surprising that there is little conservation of the LBM during weight reduction by aerobic exercise. Resistance exercise training that promotes an increase in LBM has been used in only one study as a stimulus during diet-induced weight loss.[68] The experimental results are shown in Figures 2–4 and 2–5.

Figure 2–4 shows the body composition changes for 40 moderately obese females enrolled in either a *control* (C; N = 12); an *exercise only* (EO; N = 12, heavy resistance, free weight exercises 3 days/week, and aerobic exercise 2 days/week); a *diet only* (DO; N = 10, reduced caloric intake of approxi-

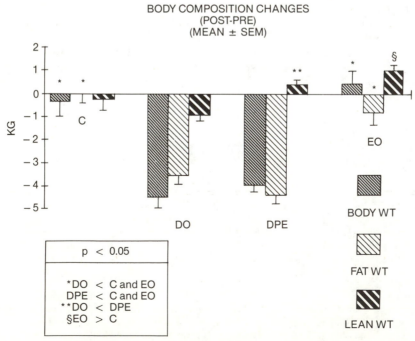

*Figure 2–4.* Changes in body composition consequent to diet and weight training. See text for complete explanation. (From Ballor D, and Katch V: Unpublished data. Behnke Laboratory for Body Composition Research, Department of Kinesiology, University of Michigan, Ann Arbor, MI, 1987, with permission.)

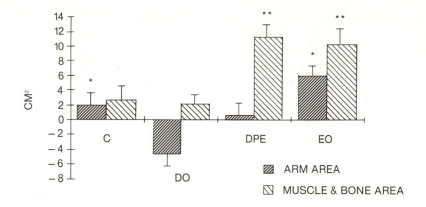

**Figure 2-5.** *Changes in total arm and muscle-plus-bone area, determined by roentgenogram in female subjects undergoing weight loss. (From Ballor D, and Katch V: Unpublished data. Behnke Laboratory for Body Composition Research, Department of Kinesiology, University of Michigan, Ann Arbor, MI, 1986, with permission.)*

mately 1200 kcal/day); or a *diet-plus-exercise* group (DPE; N = 12, same weight training as the EO group, and same caloric restriction as the DO group).

The DO and DPE groups lost substantial amounts of body weight in the 8 weeks, compared with the C and EO groups. Similarly, the DO and DPE groups lost significant amounts of body fat. The most important aspect of the study, however, was the gain in LBM for the DPE and the EO groups, and the loss of LBM for the DO group. Apparently, it *is* possible to gain LBM during weight reduction by performing heavy resistance exercise. This is in contrast to what occurs with only aerobic exercise.

Figure 2–5 shows the changes in arm and muscle-plus-bone area computed from individual roentgenographic measurements of the right arm for these four groups. It is noteworthy that the DPE and EO groups significantly increased their muscle component. Such evidence of local muscular hypertrophy

despite weight loss (DPE group) is truly remarkable. These results argue strongly for the inclusion of resistance-type muscular training in programs to enhance fitness for purposes of LBM conservation during weight loss.

## SUMMARY

The volume of research in the area of optimal health and its corelationships has increased tremendously during the past 15 years, yet most of the research relates to men. We certainly have come a long way, as the saying goes, but unfortunately, the important clinical trials and basic studies that relate health to disease risk, optimal exercise for maintaining health, and the role of body composition in health and performance have not really focused on women. If the position we have taken is correct—that is, that the training process in terms of physiologic adaptations is essentially the same regardless of gender—then the overall pattern of results found for men probably can be applied to women. But if the crux of our thesis is incorrect, then it will certainly take several decades of concentrated research effort to tease out the answers. What we do know for certain is that the acute and chronic response pattern of women to exercise and training is much more favorable than commonly believed. It is hard to imagine that only 10 years ago, women were discouraged from participation in vigorous, endurance-type activities such as a marathon, a triathlon, "pumping iron" with resistance exercise, or body building competition.

To promote continuing research as well as effective practical applications of research findings, medical professionals must join in harmony with those who can provide leadership in marrying the "medical" domain with the exercise science specialists who are also keenly interested in bridging the gap. The ivory towers of the university (as well as the medical school) will always exist, but the modern-day clinician can go a long way in unlocking previously restricted territories. A cross-disciplinary approach that combines medicine and the biologic sciences, exercise physiology, basic and applied nutrition, exercise biochemistry, epidemiology, biomechanics, neural control, sensorimotor functioning, human ergonomics and engineering, and a host of other subdisciplines seems to us to be the wave of the future. An integrated approach will help to refine the relationships in women between longevity and exercise prescription and various markers for health (i.e., blood profiles, maximal and submaximal physiologic parameters), as well as to define optimal standards for body composition in relation to health and physical performance. Many more studies of a cross-disciplinary nature are sorely needed.

## References

1. Hill AV: Cricket and its relation to the duration of life. Lancet 2:949, 1927.
2. Andersen WG: Further studies on the longevity of Yale athletes. Med Times 44:75, 1916.
3. Montoye HJ, et al: The Longevity and Morbidity of College Athletes. Phi Epsilon Kappa, Indianapolis, 1957.
4. Montoye HJ: Physical Activity and Health: An Epidemiologic Study of an Entire Community. Prentice-Hall, Englewood Cliffs, NJ, 1975.
5. Paffenbarger RS, Hyde RT, et al: Physical activity, all-cause mortality, and longevity of college alumni. N Engl J Med 314(10):605, 1986.
6. Brooks C: Promoting Physical Activity in the United States. Part II. Fitness Activity. Unpublished Working Document #2. Department of Sports Management and Communication, University of Michigan, Ann Arbor, MI, 1986.
7. Truison MF, et al: Comparisons of siblings in Boston and Ireland. J Am Diet Assoc 45:225, 1964.
8. Mann GV, et al: Physical fitness and immunity to heart disease in Masai. Lancet 2:1308, 1965.
9. McDonough JR, et al: Coronary heart disease among Negroes and Whites in Evans County, Georgia. J Chron Dis 18:443, 1965.
10. Toll A, and Small DM: Current concepts: plasma high density lipoproteins. N Engl J Med 229:1232, 1978.
11. Hubert HA, et al: Obesity as an independent risk factor for cardiovascular disease. A 26-year follow-up of participants in the Framingham heart study. Circulation 67:968, 1983.
12. Newman WP, Freedman DS, Voors AW, et al: Relation of serum lipoprotein levels and systolic blood pressure to early atherosclerosis: The Bogalusa Heart Study. N Engl J Med 314:138, 1986.
13. Wilmore JH, and McNamara JJ: Prevalence of coronary heart disease risk factors in boys, 8 to 12 years of age. J Pediatr 84:527, 1974.
14. Lauer RM, Connor WE, Leaverton PE, et al: Coronary heart disease risk factors in school children: the Muscatine study. J Pediatr 87:1187, 1975.
15. Gilliam TB, Katch V, Thorland W, et al: Prevalence of coronary heart disease risk factors in active children, 7 to 12 years of age. Med Sci Sports 9:21, 1977.
16. Becque MD, Katch VL, Rocchini AP, et al: Exercise plus diet intervention reduces coronary risk incidence of obese adolescents. J Pediatr, in press, 1988.
17. Behnke AR: New concepts in height-weight relationships. In Wilson N (ed): Obesity. FA Davis, Philadelphia, 1969.
18. Behnke AR, and Wilmore JH: Evaluation and Regulation of Body Build and Composition. Prentice-Hall, Englewood Cliffs, NJ, 1974.
19. Hertzberg HTE, et al: Anthropometry of Turkey, Greece, and Italy. AGARDograph 73. Elmsford. New York, Pergamon Press, 1963.
20. Clauser CE, et al: Anthropometry of Air Force women AMRL-TR-70-5. Wright Patterson Air Force Base, Ohio, 1972.
21. Behnke AR, et al: Quantification of body weight and configuration from anthropometric measurements. Hum Biol 31:213, 1959.
22. Katch VL, et al: Contribution of breast volume and weight to body fat distribution in females. Am J Physical Anthropol 53:93, 1980.
23. Boyden T: Prolactin responses, menstrual cycles and body composition of women runners. J Clin Endocrinol Metab 54:712, 1982.
24. Freedson PS, et al: Physique, body composition, and psychological characteristics of competitive female body builders. Phys Sportsmed 11(5):85, 1983.
25. Katch FI, and Katch VL: The body composition profile: techniques of measurement and applications. Clin Sports Med 3:31, 1984.
26. Calabrese LH, et al: Menstrual abnormalities, nutritional patterns, and body composition in female classical ballet dancers. Phys Sportsmed 11(2):86, 1983.

27. Frisch RE, et al: Delayed menarche and amenorrhea in ballet dancers. N Engl J Med 303:17, 1980.
28. Shangold MM: Sports and menstrual fucntion. Phys Sportsmed 8(8):66, 1980.
29. Shangold MM: Do women's sports lead to menstrual problems? Contemp Obstet Gynecol 17:52, 1981.
30. Bonen A, et al: Profiles of selected hormones during menstrual cycles of teenage athletes. J Appl Physiol 50:545, 1981.
31. Dale ED, et al: Menstrual dysfunction in distance runners. Obstet Gynecol 54:47, 1979.
32. Grisch RE, and McArthur JW: Mentrual cycles: fatness as a determination of minimum weight for height necessary for their maintenance or onset. Science 185:449, 1974.
33. Martin BJ: Is athletic amenorrhea specific to runners? Am J Obstet Gynecol 143:859, 1982.
34. Carlberg KA, et al: Body composition of oligo/amenorrheic athletes. Med Sci Sports Exerc 15:215, 1983.
35. Wakat DK, et al: Reproductive system function in women cross-country runners. Med Sci Sports Exerc 14:263, 1982.
36. Katch FI, and Spiak DL: Validity of the Mellits and Cheek method for body-fat estimation in relation to menstrual cycle status in athletes and non-athletes below 22 percent fat. Ann Hum Biol 11:389, 1984.
37. Bullen BA, et al: Endurance training effects on plasma hormonal responsiveness and sex hormone excretion. J Appl Physiol 56:1453, 1984.
38. Rathbun EW, and Pace N: Studies on body composition. I. Determination of body fat by means of the body specific gravity. J Biol Chem 158:667, 1945.
39. Body Composition in Animals and Man. National Academy of Sciences, Publication 1598, Washington, DC, 1968.
40. Siri WE: Gross composition of the body. In Lawrence JH and Tobias CA (eds): Advances in Biological and Medical Physics, Vol IV. Academic Press, New York, 1956.
41. Brozek J (ed): Body Composition. Parts 1 and 2. Ann NY Acad Sci 110:1, 1963.
42. Brozek J (ed): Human Body Composition, Approaches and Application. Pergamon Press, Oxford, 1965.
43. Brozek J, et al: Densitometric analysis of body composition: revision of some quantitative assumptions. Ann NY Acad Sci 110:113, 1963.
44. Brozek J, and Henschel A: Techniques for Measuring Body Composition. National Academy of Sciences—National Research Council, Washington, DC, 1961.
45. Kodama AA: In vivo and in vitro determinations of body fat and body water in the hamster. J Appl Physiol 31:218, 1971.
46. Morales MF, et al: Studies on body composition: II. Theoretical considerations regarding the major body tissue compartments with suggestions for application to man. J Biol Chem 158:677, 1945.
47. Katch FI, and Katch VL: Measurement and prediction errors in body composition assessment and the search for the perfect prediction. Res Q Exerc Sport 51:249, 1980.
48. Katch FI, and McArdle WD: Nutrition, Weight Control, and Exercise, ed 3. Lea and Febiger, Philadelphia, 1987.
49. Katch FI, and McArdle WD: Prediction of body density from simple anthropometric measurements in college-age men and women. Hum Biol 45:445, 1973.
50. Katch FI, and McArdle WD: Validity of body composition prediction equations for college men and women. Am J Clin Nutr 28:105, 1975.
51. Katch FI: The assessment of lean body tissues by radiography and by bioelectrical impedance. In Roche AF (ed): Body-Composition Assessments in Youth and Adults. Report of the Sixth Ross Conference on Medical Research. Ross Laboratories, Columbus, OH, 1985.
52. Behnke AR, et al: Routine anthropometry and arm radiography in assessment of nutritional status: its potential. JPEN 2:532, 1978.
53. Lukaski HC, et al: A comparison of methods of assessment of body composition involving neutron activation analysis of total body nitrogen. Metabolism 30:777, 1981.
54. Forbes GB, and Hersh JB: Age and sex trends in lean body mass calculated from $K^{40}$ measurements: with a note on the theoretical basis for the procedure. Ann NY Acad Sci 110:255, 1963.
55. Tokunaga K: A novel technique for the determination of body fat by computed tomography. Int J Obes 7:437, 1983.
56. Myhre LG, and Kessler WV: Body density and potassium 40 measurements of body composition as related to age. J Appl Physiol 21:1251, 1966.
57. Kushner RF, et al: Comparison of total body water (TBW) determination by bioelectrical impedance analysis (BIA), anthropometry, and $D_2O$ dilution. Am J Clin Nutr 39:658, 1984.
58. Katch FI, and Behnke AR: Arm x-ray assessment of body fat in men and women. Med Sci Sport Exerc 16:316, 1984.
59. Katch FI: Reliability and individual differences in ultrasound assessment of subcutaneous fat: effects of body position. Hum Biol 55:789, 1983.
60. Behnke AR, et al: The specific gravity of healthy men. JAMA 118:495, 1942.
61. Katch FI, et al: Estimation of body volume by underwater weighing: description of a simple method. J Appl Physiol 23:811, 1967.
62. Katch FI: Practice curves and errors of measurement in estimating underwater weight by hydrostatic weighing. Med Sci Sports 1:212, 1969.
63. Katch FI, and Drumm S: The effects of different modes of strength training on body composition and anthropometry. Clin Sports Med 5:413, 1986.
64. Jackson AS, et al: Generalized equations for predicting body density of women. Med Sci Sports 12:175, 1980.
65. Young CM, Scanlan HS, et al: Effect on body composition and other parameters in obese men of carbohydrate level of reduction diet. Am J Clin Nutr 24:290, 1971.
66. Ball MF, Canary JJ, and Kyle LH: Comparative effects of caloric restriction and total starvation on body composition in obesity. Ann Int Med 67(1):60, 1967.
67. Buskirk ER, Thompson RH, et al: Energy balance of obese patients during weight reduction: influence of diet restriction and exercise. Ann NY Acad Sci 110:918, 1963.
68. Ballor D: Weight Loss and Lean Body Weight Maintenance. PhD dissertation. Department of Kinesiology, University of Michigan, Ann Arbor, MI, 1986.

# CHAPTER 3

# Exercise and Regulation of Body Weight

KELLY D. BROWNELL, Ph.D.
CINDY J. RUBIN, M.S.
JORDAN W. SMOLLER, A.B.

Exercise is becoming increasingly popular. When asked why they exercise, many people list weight control as a primary reason. There is a clear belief that exercise aids in weight maintenance in persons at normal weight and in weight loss in overweight individuals. The booming business in fitness equipment, jogging shoes, fashionable exercise clothes, and exercise clubs is testimony to the strength of this belief.

The concern for thinness in industrialized countries is especially pronounced in women.[1] The eating disorders of anorexia nervosa and bulimia, both of which involve preoccupation with weight, are seen almost exclusively in women. Obesity occurs more equally in men and women, yet women more frequently attend clinical programs, buy diet books, and enter figure salons to lose weight.

Society tolerates less excess weight in women than in men. Many women internalize this as an unrelenting, self-induced pressure to be thin. The result is that a large proportion of American women go on diets. A Gallup poll in November 1985 found that 90 percent of Americans think they weigh too much, that 31 percent of women ages 19 to 39 diet *at least once a month*, and that 16 percent of women consider themselves "perpetual dieters." There are countless variations among these women in the combination of diet and exercise programs they follow. It is important, therefore, to understand the physiologic and psychologic effects of such programs and to isolate an approach that is safe and effective. Exercise physiology and sports medicine are central to such an enterprise.

In this chapter, we discuss the prevalence, severity, and refractory nature of weight problems. The effects of exercise on food intake, metabolism, and the regulation of body weight are outlined, with specific focus on the effects of exercise on females. We then discuss the results of programs in which various combinations of diet and exercise approaches have been used. We end by describing the role exercise can play in weight regulation and by outlining an approach to exercise that accounts for metabolic factors, psychologic issues, and the challenge of long-term adherence.

## NATURE AND SEVERITY OF WEIGHT DISORDERS

At this point it may be helpful to distinguish between "overweight" and "obesity." "Overweight" refers to excess weight using height-weight tables as the standard. These tables present weights at which people are considered most healthy, i.e., the weight at which large numbers of people of the same sex and frame size live longest. "Obesity" refers to excess body fat. This can be estimated by using skin-fold calipers, by weighing the person underwater (hydrostatic weighing), or with other more sophisticated laboratory techniques. For the most part, increasing degrees of overweight reflect increasing degrees of obesity, so height-weight tables can provide some indication of an individual's fatness. There are exceptions, however. A football player will appear overweight but may not be obese. Some thin people in poor physical condition are not overweight but may have excess body fat if their ratio of fat to lean tissue is high.

There is considerable debate about the point at which a person becomes overweight or obese. Since the actual measurement of body fat is not practical in many settings, most health professionals must rely on the height-weight tables. The conservative approach is for the cut-off for overweight to occur at 20 percent above ideal weight. This is the weight at which risks for health problems are thought to increase. The field is moving toward the specification of health risks, ability to lose weight, and other factors based on the combination of behavioral (e.g., dietary history) and metabolic (e.g., distribution of body fat, basal metabolic rate) variables, but for now the height-weight tables remain the standard.

By far the most common disorder of weight is obesity. Estimates of prevalence vary depending on the criteria used to define obesity, but at least 25 percent of adult Americans are more than 20 percent overweight.[2] This degree of overweight is associated with an increased risk of cardiovascular disease and perhaps certain cancers.[3] As important as the health risks are, most people who struggle with their weight are more concerned with the psychologic and social disadvantages of being overweight.[4] Weight loss programs have been notoriously ineffective. Therefore, obesity is a disorder with sufficient prevalence, severity, and resistance to treatment to be considered a significant public health issue.

At the opposite end of the continuum lies anorexia nervosa.[5] This involves pathologic dieting, weight loss, and physical activity, to the point at which body weight drops low enough to be life-threatening. It occurs primarily in adolescence and the early 20s and, with few exceptions, is confined to females. It is not the "flip side" of obesity. Anorexics have characteristic family backgrounds and psychologic patterns that are not common among the obese. Further, few anorexics are formerly obese persons in whom dieting has "gone too far."

Bulimia is the newest addition to the list of eating disorders.[5,6] It involves fluctuation between extreme dietary restriction and binge eating. In some cases, the binges are followed by some type of purging (vomiting or laxatives). As with anorexia, it is most common in young females. Among the contributing factors are cultural pressures to be thin; role conflicts in women who are expected to be competent mothers, wives, and professionals; and dieting itself.[6-8]

In each of these disorders of weight and eating, complex interactions exist among food intake, physical activity, metabolism, psychology, and culture. The remainder of this chapter is designed to help the reader understand these interactions by isolating them and discussing the role they play in the lives and health of modern women.

## WEIGHT AND HEALTH

People feel that they should exercise to improve their physical and emotional well-being. Although many people feel the health benefits are secondary to weight control and appearance, the fact that so many people are exercising makes it important to consider the implications for health.

Physical activity can produce several medical benefits. These include changes in plasma insulin, blood lipid levels, total cholesterol, blood pressure, and coronary efficiency. These same factors are influenced by changes in body weight.

### Cardiovascular Disease

Many studies have examined the relationship of body weight to cardiovascular disease (CVD).[3,9–11] Although a consistent relationship has been noted between obesity and CVD risk factors, the relationship of obesity to the incidence of CVD is less certain, as is the influence of less severe degrees of overweight. Possible explanations for the divergent results found in epidemiologic studies of obesity are differences in populations, length of surveillance, varying sample sizes, and perhaps most importantly, heterogeneity in risk among persons at the same weight.

Some studies have found that obesity is not a risk factor for CVD independent of its effect on the established risk factors of cholesterol, blood pressure, and diabetes. However, the Framingham Study[10] found greater risk of CVD with increasing degrees of overweight using a large sample cohort and a particularly long follow-up. This notion of obesity as an independent risk factor has been strengthened by the report of an NIH Consensus Conference on the Health Implications of Obesity.[3]

A recent and exciting development in the field may help explain some of the confusion about weight and health. Researchers have now begun to study distribution of body fat in the hope of finding an association between risk and *where* fat is distributed on the body.[12] Several studies from Sweden[13,14] have shown that there is a significant correlation

between the ratio of waist-to-hip circumference and the incidence of myocardial infarction, angina pectoris, stroke, and death. A high ratio of waist-to-hip circumference (abdominal or upper body obesity) was associated with an increased risk of ischemic heart disease in both men and women. Females who have this typically masculine distribution of body fat, a high waist-to-hip circumference ratio, have a greater risk for CVD than women with fat distributed below the waist. The simple measure of waist-to-hip circumference is a stronger predictor than other indices of obesity such as body mass index or skin-fold thicknesses.

It is unclear why these patterns of fat distribution are associated with a greater risk for CVD. One explanation is that sex hormones determine the distribution of adipose tissue and also influence the risk of CVD. If true, this theory could explain why fewer women than men suffer from CVD. However, no hormonal differences have been demonstrated between those who store fat primarily in the abdomen and those who store it primarily in the hip and thigh. Another possibility is that differences in receptors in adipose tissue above and below the waist determine whether fat can be mobilized from the cells to create metabolic damage.[15] We must await studies that evaluate the effects of weight reduction (and the associated decreases in waist-to-hip ratios) on CVD to know whether weight loss achieves the reduction in risk that is assumed to occur.

Much is known about the positive effects of physical activity on blood lipid levels and total cholesterol, both of which are closely related to risk for CVD. Wood and colleagues[16] found that male and female long-distance runners had significantly lower total cholesterol concentrations and lower triglyceride levels than an age- and sex-matched, randomly selected control group. The runners also had higher levels of high-density lipoprotein (HDL) cholesterol and lower levels of low-density lipoprotein (LDL) cholesterol than the control group. Recent studies have shown that there is a consistent relationship between high levels of HDL cholesterol and reduced risk of CVD.

Brownell and associates[17] found significant changes in the HDL cholesterol levels of men, but not women, who were participating in a 16-week weight reduction program. Although these individuals were not engaged in vigorous activity, they were still able to alter their cholesterol levels.

Diet, exercise, and body weight each influence lipids and lipoproteins. For example, both a low-calorie and a low-fat diet will lower total cholesterol, low-density cholesterol, and high-density cholesterol.[18,19] Substituting monounsaturated fats for saturated ones will lower low-density cholesterol and raise or not change high-density cholesterol.[20]

Few studies have specifically looked at the effects of physical training, changes in weight, and health risk in women. Hanson and co-workers[21] conducted a study in which sedentary women were put on a long-term physical training program. The results indicated significant improvements in oxygen utilization, carbon dioxide production, respiratory exchange ratio, and exercise heart rates. This suggests that regular exercise can result in positive health benefits for both women and men. Drinkwater[22] also suggests that women get much the same physiologic benefit from exercise as men.

### Metabolic Disease

A strong correlation exists between excessive body weight and risk for metabolic aberrations such as glucose intolerance, hyperinsulinemia, and hypertriglyceridemia.[2,3,9–12] Although the exact mechanism for these metabolic complications is not fully understood, it is known that physical activity and weight loss can lead to improved glucose tolerance and decreased plasma insulin and triglyceride levels.

Bjorntorp and colleagues[23] found that obese individuals who participated in a 6-week physical training program had significantly lowered plasma insulin levels. Several theories have been proposed to explain the decrease in insulin levels: changes in amino acid concentrations,[24] alterations in the antagonistic hormones to insulin,[23] or changes in the sensitivity of the beta cell.[25] None of these theories have been proved.

Kissebah and associates[26] found a significant relationship between body fat distribution and the prevalence of metabolic complications. Women with upper body obesity—a higher waist-to-hip ratio—were found to have higher plasma glucose, insulin, and tri-

glyceride levels than those with lower body obesity, or a lower waist-to-hip ratio. It was concluded that in women, the sites of fat depots are an important prognostic marker for glucose intolerance, hyperinsulinemia, and hypertriglyceridemia.

To summarize this discussion, body weight and physical activity, which are related to one another, are both related to many health indices. Exercise, which is used by many women to control their weight, may also influence other risk factors. The changes are likely to be positive, but studies showing negative effects may also exist,[17,27] so this is an area in need of more research. In obese persons, health risk is high and activity levels are typically low. Exercise, therefore, is a natural approach to include in a treatment program, but direct evidence of reduced cardiovascular disease in formerly obese persons has not been documented.

## EFFECTS OF EXERCISE

### Energy Expenditure

The expenditure of energy results from four mechanisms of heat generation (thermogenesis): (1) resting metabolic rate—the energy of basic cellular and body maintenance; (2) diet-induced thermogenesis—the thermic effect of food ingestion; (3) exercise-induced heat production; and (4) thermogenesis in response to changes in environmental conditions.[2,28,29]

For individuals between the ages of 23 and 50 years, average daily energy expenditure is 2700 kcal for men and 2100 kcal for women.[30] As much as 60 to 75 percent of this is attributable to resting metabolic rate (RMR), while exercise-induced thermogenesis accounts directly for only 750 kcal per day.[31] In very active individuals, however, the contribution of thermogenesis during exercise to total energy expenditure may be increased severalfold.[32] Evidence for sex differences in exercise-induced energy expenditure is conflicting. Even when expressed per unit body weight, the energy cost of exercise may be smaller for women.[22]

**Metabolic rate.** Although the terms may generally be used interchangeably, a distinction should be made between resting metabolic rate (RMR) and basal metabolic rate (BMR). The RMR is measured when an individual is at rest in a thermoneutral environment at least 8 to 12 hours after the last meal or any significant physical activity. BMR is measured in the morning upon awakening after 12 to 18 hours of rest.[30]

The notion that exercise increases metabolic rate beyond the duration of the activity is not new. A sustained effect of exercise on metabolic rate was first identified in several studies conducted in the 1920s and 1930s. The effect appeared to be quite dramatic in these early reports: after a bout of strenuous exercise, metabolic rate remained elevated by 10 percent or more for up to 48 hours.[33] Subsequent studies have generally substantiated the postexercise metabolic effect, although reports of the magnitude of this effect have varied widely. This variability reflects differences in the experimental tasks and metabolic measurements that make it difficult to determine the optimal conditions for producing the postexercise effect.

In a review of studies in this area, Thompson and co-workers[33] estimated that light exercise produces a postexercise elevation in metabolic rate equivalent to 40 to 50 kcal, whereas studies of strenuous exercise suggest an expenditure of 450 kcal following such activity. For a given individual, actual expenditures may depend on body composition, weight, and fitness level.

The metabolic effect of exercise may be of particular importance to individuals who are dieting. Caloric restriction is known to decrease RMR in both obese and lean persons. The decline begins within 24 to 48 hours of caloric restriction and may exceed 20 percent in only 2 weeks.[2,28,33-34] Besides diminishing overall metabolic rate, dieting produces a significant decrease in the energy cost of performing particular tasks.[34] This suppression of energy expenditure may be responsible for the plateau in weight loss that is commonly observed among dieters. As the body becomes more energy-efficient, a level of caloric intake that had produced weight loss previously may result in weight maintenance or even gain.

Citing the increase in RMR that accompanies physical activity, some researchers have argued that exercise may counter the decline in RMR that follows caloric restriction and weight loss.[33,34] Evidence for this hypothesis is sparse, but a number of studies have produced intriguing results. Donahoe and colleagues[35] evaluated the effect of exercise on 10 obese women participating in a behavioral weight loss program. Consistent with earlier reports, when they were simply restricting caloric intake, their RMR fell at twice the rate of weight loss. When exercise was combined with the diet, however, RMR per unit body weight increased to its original predieting baseline level.

Another recent report suggests that women stand to gain the most from exercise during calorie restriction. Lennon and associates[36] put men and women on a diet and divided them among three conditions of physical activity: no exercise, 30 minutes of daily self-directed aerobic activity, or prescribed exercise training performed every other day. Overall, the prescribed exercise program produced the greatest enhancement of RMR, but the effect was significant only among the women. The authors concluded that "the incorporation of exercise, even moderate daily activity, may be of greater importance for females than males to prevent the decline in RMR during caloric restriction for weight loss."

The relationship between exercise and RMR may reverse if caloric restriction is severe. In a preliminary report, Phinney[37] evaluated the metabolic effects of a very-low-calorie diet (720 kcal) on two groups of obese women. The first group maintained their sedentary lifestyle, while the second group received vigorous aerobic training. Surprisingly, the trained women experienced a *fall* in resting energy expenditure that was three times as great as the fall among the sedentary dieters. Exercise under conditions of severe caloric restriction, then, may trigger a compensatory decrease in RMR designed to conserve endangered energy reserves.

It is tempting to accept the notion that exercise enhances metabolic rate to a sufficient degree to help individuals control their weight, and that this increase can partially or completely offset the decline in resting energy expenditure that accompanies dieting. We hope this is the case, because exercise is a natural activity to recommend for weight control and one that brings other positive changes (e.g., improvement in coronary risk factors, enhanced well-being). However, the results of the study by Phinney,[37] which were obtained in carefully controlled metabolic conditions, did not support this notion.

It is possible that the additional energy drain imposed by exercise would stimulate a body to defend a "set point"[38] to protect energy stores by lowering metabolic rate. It is important for future research to identify the conditions and characteristics of the individual which influence the metabolic effects of exercise. Female-male differences might be important in this regard.

**Diet-induced thermogenesis.** Diet-induced thermogenesis (also called the thermic effect of food) refers to the increase in metabolic rate that follows the ingestion of food; it usually involves 7 to 10 percent of the caloric intake.[2,28] Several researchers have found that the thermic response to food increases when exercise follows the meal, although it is unclear whether this effect is over and above the increase in RMR that is normally associated with exercise.[33]

Unfortunately, however, there is evidence that the obese, who would benefit most from this effect, have a lower resting and exercise-induced thermic response to food, and that dieting further diminishes the response.[33,39] For example, Segal and Gutin[40] found that, for lean women, the thermic effect of food was more than two and one half times as great with exercise as at rest; there were no differences among obese women. A follow-up study of men[41] yielded similar results, although these researchers noted that "blunted thermogenesis" is probably not a major cause of obesity since the energy differences involved are generally small.

It should also be noted that the exact relationship between exercise and diet-induced thermogenesis is still controversial. In fact, several studies report a diminished response to food among exercise-trained individuals. Trembley and colleagues,[42] for example, compared the metabolic functioning of elite long-distance runners with that of untrained subjects. No differences were found in RMR, but the thermic response to a meal was lower in the trained subjects. These investigators suggest that, among individuals who regularly engage in endurance activities, diminished thermogenesis is an adaptive mechanism for energy conservation.

Some authors have based exercise prescriptions for obese persons on this notion that activity may enhance the thermic effect of food.[43] The idea is to schedule exercise in proximity to meals so that the dieter incurs the energy cost of the exercise along with the increased thermic cost of the meal.

For several reasons, we feel this is premature and could potentially be counterproductive. First, the practice of prescribing meals and exercise close together is based primarily on work with animals, in which the brown fat organ can be an important vehicle for the dissipation of heat. The transfer of these findings to humans is speculative at best. Second, the studies that do exist on obese humans suggest that they respond differently from lean persons and specifically do not show the desired synergistic thermogenic responses.[40-41] Third, even if the effect were to be documented, it may be of no practical significance. Fourth, and perhaps most important, prescribing exercise at specific times leaves the individual less flexible for scheduling, and this may be an obstacle to adherence. In sum, we feel that there is not sufficient evidence to justify exercise prescriptions based on the timing of meals.

## Body Composition

**Lean body mass and body fat.** The effect of exercise on metabolic rate is related at least partially to the changes in body composition that accompany exercise. Body fat (BF) is less metabolically active than lean body mass (LBM), and since the average woman has about 10 to 15 percent more BF than the average man, her RMR is lower. When RMR is expressed per unit LBM, however, this sex difference disappears.[30]

Exercise increases LBM (by increasing muscle mass) while reducing BF.[33,34,44,45] Since muscle is denser than the fat that is lost in both obese and normal-weight individuals, sometimes fat loss occurs without significant weight change. The fat losses produced solely by exercise rarely exceed 5 percent.[34] Indeed, the average loss of BF was only 1.6 percent in a review of 55 exercise programs of up to 2 years' duration.[44] Obese individuals may encounter further difficulty in maintaining a loss of BF. Franklin and co-workers[46] measured changes in body composition in obese and normal-weight individuals after 12 weeks of physical training. By 18 months' follow-up, the obese subjects had regained all the weight and BF they had lost during the program.

Body composition changes usually require

sustained physical activity. The American College of Sports Medicine[47] has concluded that significant BF loss requires a program of exercising at least 20 minutes per day, 3 days per week, with sufficient intensity and duration to burn 300 kcal per session. A variety of aerobic activities appear to be equally effective in changing body composition. One study compared changes in body composition achieved by walking, running, and cycling, and found similar, significant reductions in body weight and body fat for all three programs.[48] Anaerobic activities (e.g., weight training) increase LBM but have less effect on BF levels than do aerobic activities.[33]

The effect of regular physical activity on BF is strikingly demonstrated by trained athletes. Compared with average young men and women (whose percentages of BF are about 15 percent and 25 percent, respectively), athletes are often much leaner. Table 3–1, taken from the review by Wilmore[44] indicates that athletes in endurance activities (e.g., long-distance running) have particularly low levels of BF. As with sedentary individuals, however, a female athlete has more BF than her male counterpart.[44]

Physical training also can counter the increase in BF that accompanies aging. Older female athletes may have significantly less BF than sedentary females of the same age.[22] For example, female distance runners in their 30s average about 15 percent BF, while a sedentary 30-year-old woman averages 27 percent. Female tennis players (20 percent BF) and mountaineers (19 percent BF) in the same age range also have levels closer to the average for an active 20-year-old (20 percent) than for a woman of their own age.[22]

Although exercise alone produces a modest loss of BF, much greater losses can be accomplished when exercise is accompanied by caloric restriction.[32,49] Conversely, a significant reduction in physical activity—such as the interruption of training or a shift to a sedentary lifestyle—results in an increase in BF, even if caloric intake is significantly reduced.[50] In fact, such a reduction in habitual activity is accompanied by a disproportionate increase in BF.

As much as 35 percent of the weight lost by caloric restriction alone may be LBM, particularly when intake is severely restricted.[51] Exercise may prevent the loss of LBM that accompanies caloric restriction. Thus far, evidence for this phenomenon comes mainly from animal studies. (See Chapter 2 for additional data.) Among calorically restricted animals, 35 to 45 percent of total weight loss is lean tissue; when exercise accompanies restriction, there is a sparing of LBM and substantially greater loss of body fat.[44] Evidence for a similar effect in humans is sparse, but what does exist is supportive.[52]

**Fat cells.** When exercise is undertaken to remedy obesity, the results may depend on the nature of the excess fat. Obesity may be the result of an excessive number of fat cells (hyperplastic obesity), excessively large cells (hypertrophic obesity), or a combination of the two. Once formed, fat cells are permanent, and loss of BF is due exclusively to the shrinkage of enlarged cells.

Bjorntorp[49] has reported a series of studies that support the conclusion that fat cell number sets an upper limit for BF loss with exercise. In a study of men who had suffered a myocardial infarction, BF levels varied widely after an exercise training program although fat cell size was fairly uniform: the differences were attributable to differences in fat cell number. Among obese persons, exercise induces BF loss only to the extent that enlarged fat cells can shrink to normal size. As a consequence, moderately obese individuals with enlarged cells may lose up to 40 lb with physical training, while the same training produces little or no weight loss among severely obese individuals with hyperplastic disease.[49]

Is there any role for exercise in the management of hyperplastic obesity? The answer may be that an ounce of prevention is worth many pounds of fat. While exercise cannot eradicate fat cells, it may slow their proliferation. Animal studies consistently demonstrate that in young, growing animals physical training slows the rate of increase in body weight, total fat, and fat cell number. When these animals reach maturity, they have lower body weights, body fat, and fat cell numbers than untrained animals.[44]

## Appetite and Hunger

Exercise may increase hunger in some cases and decrease it in others. Athletes are thought to compensate for their high level of

**Table 3–1.** WEIGHT (KG) AND PERCENT BODY FAT OF MALE AND FEMALE ATHLETES*

| | Males | | Females | |
|---|---|---|---|---|
| | *Weight* | *% Fat* | *Weight* | *% Fat* |
| Baseball | 83–88 | 12–14 | — | — |
| Basketball | 84–109 | 7–11 | 63–64 | 21–27 |
| Canoeing | 80 | 12 | | |
| Football | | | | |
|   Defensive backs | 77–85 | 10–12 | — | — |
|   Offensive backs | 80–91 | 9–12 | — | — |
|   Linebackers | 87–102 | 13–14 | — | — |
|   Offensive linemen | 99–113 | 16–19 | — | — |
|   Defensive linemen | 98–117 | 18–19 | — | — |
|   Quarterbacks, kickers | 90 | 14 | | |
| Gymnastics | 69 | 5 | 52–60 | 10–24 |
| Ice hockey | 77–87 | 13–15 | — | — |
| Jockeys | 50 | 14 | — | — |
| Orienteering | 72 | 16 | 58 | 19 |
| Pentathlon | — | — | 65 | 11 |
| Racquetball | 80 | 8 | | |
| Skiing | | | | |
|   Alpine | 70–76 | 7–10 | 59 | 21 |
|   Cross-country | 67–73 | 8–13 | 56–59 | 16–22 |
| Soccer | 76 | 10 | — | — |
| Speed skating | 77 | 11 | — | — |
| Swimming | 78–79 | 5–9 | 57–67 | 15–26 |
| Tennis | 77 | 15–16 | 56 | 20 |
| Track and field | | | | |
|   Runners | | | | |
|     Distance | 63–72 | 8–18 | 53–57 | 15–19 |
|     Middle distance | 72 | 12 | — | — |
|     Sprint | 74 | 17 | — | — |
|   Discus | 105–111 | 16 | 71 | 25 |
|   Jumpers, hurdlers | — | — | 59 | 21 |
|   Shot put | 113–126 | 17–20 | 78 | 28 |
| Volleyball | — | — | 60–64 | 21–25 |
| Weight lifting | | | | |
|   Power | 92 | 16 | — | — |
|   Olympic | 88 | 12 | — | — |
|   Body builders | 83–88 | 8 | — | — |
| Wrestling | 66–82 | 4–14 | — | — |

* Data adapted from a review of studies on body composition in athletes by Wilmore.[44] In cases in which more than one study were available, the minimum and maximum values for weight and body fat are presented. The studies reviewed by Wilmore varied widely in techniques for measuring body fat, so these numbers are to provide a general range for various groups of athletes but do not necessarily reflect the weights or fat levels at which performance is maximized.

activity with increased food consumption, so that the balance of energy in and out remains stable. For overweight persons, it would be desirable if exercise decreased appetite. This may be the case, although much extrapolation from animal studies is necessary to accept this concept.

**Animal studies.** Mayer and associates[53] found that various levels of activity had different effects on appetite. A linear relationship was found between activity level and caloric intake in obese rats for the moderate-to-heavy activity range, so that body weight remained stable. At the lowest levels of activity, however, caloric intake declined and weight dropped. These results were used for years to suggest that low-level activity in overweight persons would be beneficial because of both increased output and decreased intake.

Oscai[54] found that the intensity of the work rather than the duration exerts the greatest effect on appetite suppression. He concluded that high-intensity, short-term exercise suppresses the appetite while low-intensity, long-term exercise does not. Katch and colleagues[55] also demonstrated this effect. Both researchers, however, concluded that exercised growing animals have depressed food consumption and rate of body weight gain compared with the nonexercised control animals. The results of their studies appear to conflict with those of Mayer and co-workers,[53] but the resolution may lie in differences between lean and obese laboratory animals. These researchers found that appetite suppression was more pronounced in obese than in lean animals.

Some researchers have also noted differences in appetite suppression between male and female laboratory animals. Mayer and associates[53] were the first to find that exercise stimulates the appetite of female animals. Similarly, Oscai and colleagues[56] found that exercised female rats consumed more calories than the sedentary female rats. These differences were not found in male rats. In general, animal studies demonstrate that activity decreases caloric intake in males but not in females. The physiologic mechanism responsible for this sex difference remains unclear.

**Human studies.** Mayer and co-workers[57] supported their original findings with animals[53] when they measured the caloric intake and activity levels of 213 men in various occupations in West Bengal. Workers in sedentary occupations consumed more calories than individuals who were engaged in light-to-moderate activity. Not surprisingly, the sedentary men also weighed more.

More recent studies have also supported Mayer's nonlinear relationship between caloric intake and exercise level.[58–61] Dempsey[58] studied obese and nonobese young men who exercised vigorously for 18 weeks. The obese subjects were able to significantly decrease their body weight and total body fat and to increase their lean body mass. Although daily caloric intake remained unchanged during the 18 weeks as compared

with the 3-week pretraining period, there was a substantial increase in energy expenditure, which resulted in a daily caloric deficit. The fact that calorie intake did not increase in response to this deficit may result from the appetite-depressing effect of exercise or from voluntary restriction of food intake.

Epstein and co-workers[60] found that lunchtime food intake could be decreased in obese school children by scheduling recess before rather than after lunch. The children voluntarily decreased food intake following prelunch programmed exercise. There was an inverse relationship between prelunch exercise and lunchtime caloric intake.

Several studies specifically examined the effect of exercise on appetite in women. Katch and associates[62] found that college women participating in "moderate" or "strenuous" daily activity for 4 months consumed fewer calories. Johnson and colleagues[63] also studied college women and found similar results after a 10-week period of exercising for 30 minutes, five times a week. These results contradict the previously described results for female rats. The fact that both of the human studies were conducted on college-age women, who are generally very concerned with their body weight, may have influenced the results. Studies are needed to examine the factors responsible for decreased food consumption in exercising women and to confirm the lack of sex differences in humans, despite such differences in animals.

## Psychologic Changes

People who engage in some form of regular physical activity sometimes feel better about themselves. Exercise appears to play an important role in the improvement of both physical and mental health.[64] Whether this is due to physiologic or psychologic factors is unclear. Nevertheless, physical activity can result in improved mood-states,[65] decreased depression,[66] and improved self-esteem.[67,68] This may have important implications for the regulation of body weight, which itself is influenced by psychologic factors that stimulate or suppress eating.

Vigorous physical activity may be relevant for the control of stress and tension. Raglin and Morgan[69] conducted several studies on individuals who were characterized as having moderate as well as elevated anxiety. The exercise was thought to have an effect that was more persistent than that achieved with interventions such as tranquilizers designed to "quiet" the individual.

Several theories have been proposed to explain the possible mechanisms for these psychologic benefits. Dimsdale and Moss[70] suggest that exercise changes levels of norepinephrine and catecholamines. Appenzeller and colleagues[71] suggest that the release of beta-endorphins during exercise create the "opiate-like" effect. It has further been suggested that these biochemical effects of exercise may create a "positive addiction."[72]

These psychologic changes with exercise may combine with the metabolic effects to explain why physical activity is so important in the control of body weight. In persons attempting to lose weight or to keep their weight low (e.g., models and some athletes), exercise may help relieve the stress that can provoke unwanted eating. The improved self-concept from exercise may generalize to other aspects of functioning, so the individual may have extra resolve to control dietary practices. These issues deserve more attention in research and should be studied with an eye to possible interactions between psychologic and metabolic changes.

## THE CHALLENGE OF ADHERENCE

Poor adherence has long been considered a problem in exercise programs. One of the early studies reporting adherence rates was by Taylor, Buskirk, and Remington.[73] Men at high risk for coronary artery disease were monitored during a regular exercise program. Nearly 50 percent of the men dropped out within the first 6 months. This rate of 50 percent has been reported in other studies with different populations.[33,34,64] These high rates are surprising, especially in groups in which there is a special health incentive to comply.

Less is known about adherence rates in women. Gwinup[74] reported the results of a walking program for obese women. Only 32 percent of the women remained in the program for 1 year. Little is known about adherence rates for women of normal weight. The rates probably vary depending on many factors, including age, previous exercise history, reason for initiating an exercise program, the type and intensity of the exercise itself, and

so forth. This is a rich area for study. We encourage researchers to include men and women in their samples, to address the important issue of sex differences.

Some work has appeared recently on predicting and improving adherence patterns. Oldridge and colleagues[75] examined adherence in 733 men prescribed an exercise program after myocardial infarction. Nearly 47 percent of the men dropped out; the two significant predictors of drop-out were smoking and employment in a blue collar job. Martin and Dubbert[64] reviewed the literature in this area and found that predictors of poor exercise adherence tend to be low self-motivation, smoking, inactive leisure-time pursuits, type A behavior pattern, high body weight, lack of social support, strenuous exercise, and inconvenient time or location of exercise.

Studies on improving adherence are relatively recent and have tested primarily behavioral strategies.[64] A systematic series of studies on the topic was published by Martin and associates.[76] They examined adherence in 12-week programs of aerobic jogging and brisk walking. They found that adherence could be increased greatly with stimulus control (reminders), reinforcement from others, self-control techniques, and cognitive approaches such as goal-setting. These studies are the most intensive and well-controlled to date, so it appears there is promise to a combination of these approaches. Further testing is needed to evaluate their long-term effectiveness.

## EXERCISE AND WEIGHT LOSS

Exercise is nearly always prescribed in weight loss programs. For many years it was done almost as a reflex. Professionals thought exercise was important, but the prospect of doing sit-ups and calisthenics held little appeal for the overweight individuals, and the professionals held little hope of compliance. Consequently, typical admonitions consisted of little more than "exercise more."

Several changes occurred in subsequent years to change this picture. In one development, studies began to show that exercise is a correlate of long-term success at weight reduction.[77] People who exercise are more likely to maintain their weight loss after a program ends. The association between exercise and weight loss is not as strong as would be helpful (i.e., many people who do not exercise lose weight and some who exercise do not). However, the association is encouraging, considering that only exercise and social support tend to correlate with success despite hundreds of attempts in the literature to predict weight loss with questionnaires, scales, demographic factors, and so forth.

This finding led some researchers to manipulate exercise as an independent variable in weight loss studies. Gwinup[74] did not manipulate exercise as a variable, but he added a regular program of walking to a diet program for obese women. Many of the participants (68 percent) dropped out, but those who remained lost significant amounts of fat. Dahlkoetter and co-workers[78] found that obese subjects randomly assigned to an exercise program combined with dietary modification lost more weight than subjects who restricted diet but did not receive an exercise program. Several other studies confirm the finding that adding exercise facilitates weight loss.[32,64,77]

In summary, individuals who exercise tend to lose more weight and keep it off more effectively than do sedentary individuals. In programs in which exercise has been manipulated experimentally, groups that exercise lose more weight than groups that do not. Adherence, however, is a barrier, and developing an exercise program that is enjoyable and beneficial and that promotes long-term adherence is difficult. The following section describes what is known about this complex subject.

## RECOMMENDATIONS

We have now covered basic and applied issues related to exercise and body weight in women. This information has been assembled from many fields including exercise physiology, nutrition, metabolism, and psychology. It is time to integrate the information and to provide specific recommendations for exercise programs.

### Exercise: Alone or Combined With Diet?

Many people exercise, at least in part, to control their weight. For individuals who are at their ideal weight, exercise can be a useful

and healthy way either to control weight or to afford the luxury of more calories in the diet. For people who are mildly overweight, in the range of 10 to 20 percent overweight, exercise alone can sometimes be sufficient to control weight. For heavier people, a combination of diet and exercise is necessary.

Metabolic requirements vary greatly from person to person. Some women can maintain normal weight on 2400 calories per day, while others can consume no more than 800 calories. If a 2400-calorie individual expends more than 300 calories per day via exercise and the associated metabolic changes, she could then eat 2700 calories per day and maintain constant weight. Using the 800-calorie example, a woman who adds 300 calories to her expenditure through exercise could afford to eat no more than 1100 calories without gaining weight. Therefore, she must still restrict her calories. This makes nutrition important because it becomes more difficult to consume adequate nutrients as caloric intake drops.

As mentioned earlier, exercise and diet combined are more effective than either used alone for people who are overweight. This may occur for both physiologic and psychologic reasons. The challenge is to combine changes in diet, exercise, attitude, and social support into a comprehensive lifestyle program that focuses on long-term adherence.

We have worked to develop such a program and have collected the material in a manual.[79] It is entitled the LEARN Program: LEARN is an acronym for the five components (Lifestyle, Exercise, Attitudes, Relationships, and Nutrition). The manual is for use by individuals and professionals. Information about obtaining the manual can be obtained by writing to Dr. Brownell, Department of Psychiatry, University of Pennsylvania, 133 South 36th Street, Philadelphia, PA 19104. Some aspects of this program related to exercise are presented below.

### Attitude and Personality Factors

**Exercise threshold.** One pervasive attitude held by both the public and many health professionals is that a "threshold" exists for exercise. Such a threshold implies that exercise must occur in a specific amount to be beneficial. Thresholds do exist if one wishes to show measurable improvements in cardiovascular function or to develop exceptional ability at a sport. However, most people do not exercise for these reasons, but remain active to control their weight, look better, feel better, or have fun. Suggesting that a threshold exists conveys the message that activity must be quite vigorous, must remain vigorous for some time (15 to 20 minutes), and must be done regularly. These are laudable goals but are not attainable, at least in the short term, for many or most people. Thresholds may hinder more than help.

We take a strong stand on this issue. We explain to people in our programs that *any* exercise is better than no exercise and that they should not aspire to arbitrary levels until they are in good condition. If such a threshold exists, it is to put an *upper* limit on exercise to cease the activity when it becomes unpleasant.

Our position on the threshold concept will seem unusual and counterintuitive to many professionals who work in the sports medicine area. Such professionals typically are very active themselves and work with individuals who are also active. For someone at a high level of training, a threshold may provide an inspiration and may be helpful for psychologic reasons. For the majority of individuals, however, the threshold may not be helpful. This argues for tailoring this attitudinal aspect of exercise to the needs and level of conditioning of the individual.

**Solo versus social personalities.** In our work we have identified several personality types that respond differently to various forms of activity. Before describing this further, we must add that we base our ideas on clinical and practical experience. We are not aware of research that supports or refutes this notion.

There appear to be differences among individuals in whether they prefer to exercise alone or with others. The "solo" type individual does not desire the company of others and might select activities such as riding a stationary bicycle or walking or jogging alone. A "social" exerciser may prefer an aerobics class, tennis, a team sport, or jogging with a partner.

Most individuals gravitate toward an activity that matches their personality, even if they do not articulate the solo-social distinction. Problems can arise when programs prescribe the same activity for all individuals.

Our hope is that this and other personality issues will receive more attention in research studies and that we can perfect the notion of matching exercises to individuals.

## Obstacles to Exercise

Several obstacles can impede the transition from the desire to exercise to exercise itself. One obstacle and predictor of poor adherence is the absence of a history of being physically active. Persons who have been regular exercisers at some time in the past, particularly those who have enjoyed some success at a sport or activity, can usually begin exercising again with little difficulty, assuming motivation is high. Others may not have been active because of some physical limitation, lack of coordination, social upbringing, or negative attitudes about exercise. Such a person requires special consideration in choosing a type of activity that is enjoyable and at a level that is achievable.

There are special and sometimes formidable obstacles for overweight people to overcome in order to exercise regularly. For people who have been overweight since childhood, early memories of exercise may be negative because they were picked last for teams, were teased about their abilities, and were self-conscious about their bodies, unable to buy appealing clothes, and so forth. It is not surprising that the negative associations emerge when such a person is encouraged to exercise as an adult. Not only does the excess weight add a physical burden, but persistent negative body image may discourage a person from exercising with others, and the lack of self-confidence may prevent a person from starting an exercise program.

## Selecting an Activity

For a person who wishes to become more active, many activities exist. Several factors may be relevant in choosing from such a wide selection.

**Purpose of exercising.** An exercise can be chosen according to the reasons a person is exercising. If a person is of normal weight but wants a more athletic or muscular build, weight-training or strength-building activities will be helpful. If endurance and cardiovascular training are the focus, aerobic activities are the choice. If total energy expenditure and weight control are the issue, sustained movement activities are in order. A combination of all these activities is desirable, but not all people have the time, energy, or resources to follow an ideal program.

**Maximizing enjoyment.** Since adherence is a major problem with exercise, enjoyment is an important issue. When professionals encourage people to exercise, they often assume their own experience is applicable to others, and there may be a tendency to push others to do what the professional does. This type and level of activity may not be pleasing for the individual, who will not continue the exercise program.

Some people sustain enjoyment by undertaking more than one activity. A person might jog, ride a stationary cycle, and play racquetball, in some sort of rotating fashion. Social support from others can also be helpful in making an activity more enjoyable. Running with a friend while having a lively conversation has a different character than running alone.

### Maintenance of Exercise Habits

With exercise, it is easy to make the conviction to change and to take the first few steps, but it is difficult for many people to follow through over the long term. The maintenance of exercise habits is an important issue.

Some of the issues discussed previously (selecting an activity, maximizing enjoyment) must be considered for improving the maintenance of exercise habits. Another key aspect is *relapse prevention.*[80,81] This refers to a system of behavioral and cognitive strategies for preventing return of old habits.

Individuals making any change in lifestyle inevitably make mistakes. These can be considered "lapses," which are defined as temporary setbacks that may or may not be followed by further mistakes. If the initial lapse weakens restraint, relapse will follow and this negative cycle can end in complete collapse. Preventive strategies are available and are detailed in the manual described earlier[79] and in an excellent book by Marlatt and Gordon.[80]

### SUMMARY

Considering the preoccupation with dieting and thinness in our culture, the interactions among nutrition, exercise, and the regulation of body weight are important for many reasons. Body weight, diet, and exercise are all related to health status and are related to one another in complex ways.

Exercise increases caloric expenditure via the direct use of energy and indirectly through possible increases in resting metabolic rate and the thermic effect of food. It is not clear, however, that exercise will offset the decline in metabolic rate that accompanies dieting. Also, scheduling exercise near meal times in an attempt to increase the thermic effect of food has not been proven effective in humans and may interfere with compliance. Exercise can help preserve lean body mass during weight reduction.

For nonathletic and overweight persons, compliance is a major problem. We have described specific methods that can help enhance compliance and have attempted to develop a comprehensive picture of exercise in women by combining what is known about both physiology and psychology.

### References

1. Brownell KD, and Foreyt JP (eds): Handbook of Eating Disorders: Physiology, Psychology, and Treatment of Obesity, Anorexia, and Bulimia. Basic Books, New York, 1986.
2. Bray GA: The Obese Patient. WB Saunders, Philadelphia, 1976.
3. National Institutes of Health Consensus Conference on Obesity: Consensus conference statement. Ann Int Med 103:1073, 1985.
4. Wadden TA, and Stunkard, AJ: Social and psychological consequences of obesity. Ann Int Med 103:1062, 1985.
5. Garner DM, and Garfinkel PE (eds): Handbook of Psychotherapy for Anorexia Nervosa and Bulimia. Guilford Press, New York, 1985.
6. Fairburn CG, Cooper Z, and Cooper PJ: The clinical features and maintenance of bulimia nervosa. In Brownell KD, and Foreyt JP (eds): Handbook of Eating Disorders: Physiology, Psychology, and Treatment of Obesity, Anorexia, and Bulimia. Basic Books, New York, 1986, p 389.
7. Striegel-Moore RH, Silberstein LR, and Rodin J: Toward an understanding of risk factors for bulimia. Am Psychol 41:246, 1986.
8. Polivy J, and Herman CP: Dieting and binging: A causal analysis. Am Psychol 40:193, 1985.
9. Keys A: Seven Countries: A Multivariate Analysis of Death and Coronary Heart Disease. Harvard University Press, Cambridge, 1980.
10. Hubert HB, Feinleib M, McNamara PM, et al: Obesity as an independent risk factor for cardiovascular disease: a 26-year follow-up of participants in the Framingham Heart Study. Circulation 67:968, 1983.
11. Simopoulos AP, and Van Itallie TB: Body weight, health and longevity. Ann Int Med 100:285, 1984.

12. Bjorntorp P: Fat cells and obesity. In Brownell KD, and Foreyt JP (eds): Handbook of Eating Disorders: Physiology, Psychology, and Treatment of Obesity, Anorexia, and Bulimia. Basic Books, New York, 1986, p 88.

13. Larsson B, Svardsudd D, Welin L, et al: Abdominal adipose tissue distribution, obesity, and risk of cardiovascular disease and death: 13 year follow up of participants in the study of men born in 1913. Br Med J 288:1401, 1984.

14. Lapidus L, Bengtsson C, Larsson B, et al: Distribution of adipose tissue and risk of cardiovascular disease and death: a 12 year follow-up of participants in the population study of women in Gothenburg, Sweden. Br Med J 289:1257, 1984.

15. Leibel RL, and Hirsch J: A radioisotopic method for the measurement of lipolysis in small samples of human adipose tissue. Am J Physiol 248:E140–E147, 1985.

16. Wood PD, Haskell WL, Stern MP, et al: Plasma lipoprotein distributions in male and female runners. Ann NY Acad Sci 2:748, 1979.

17. Brownell KD, and Stunkard AJ: Differential changes in plasma high-density lipoprotein cholesterol levels in obese men and women during weight reduction. Arch Intern Med 141:1142, 1981.

18. Thompson PD, Cullinane E, Eshelman R, et al: Lipoprotein changes when a reported diet is tested in distance runners. Am J Clin Nutr 39:368, 1984.

19. Thompson PD, Cullinane EM, Eshelman R, et al: The effects of caloric restriction or exercise cessation on the serum lipid and lipoprotein concentrations of endurance athletes. Metabolism 33(10):943, 1984.

20. Grundy SM: Comparison of monounsaturated fatty acids and carbohydrates for lowering plasma cholesterol. N Engl J Med 314(12):745, 1986.

21. Hanson BF, and Nedde WH: Long-term physical training effect in sedentary females. J Appl Physiol 37:112, 1978.

22. Drinkwater BL: Physiological characteristics of female athletes. In Welsh RP and Shephard RJ (eds): Current Therapy in Sports Medicine. Decker, Toronto, 1985.

23. Bjorntorp P, Holm G, Jacobsson B, et al: Physical training in human hyperplastic obesity. IV. Effect on the hormonal status. Metabolism 26:319, 1977.

24. Holm G, Sullivan L, Jagenburg R, et al: Effects of physical training and lean body mass on plasma amino acids in man. J Appl Physiol 45:177, 1978.

25. Bjorntorp P, deJounge K, Sjostrom L, et al: The effect of physical training on insulin production in obesity. Metabolism 19:631, 1970.

26. Kissebah AH, Vydelingum N, Murray R, et al: Relation of body fat distribution to metabolic complications of obesity. J Clin Endocrin Metab 54:254, 1982.

27. Thompson PD, Jeffery RW, and Wing RR: Unexpected decrease in plasma high density lipoprotein cholesterol with weight loss. Am J Clin Nutr 32:2016, 1979.

28. Garrow JS: Energy Balance and Obesity in Man. Elsevier/North Holland, Amsterdam, 1978.

29. Garrow JS: Physiological aspects of obesity. In Brownell KD, and Foreyt JP (eds): Handbook of Eating Disorders: Physiology, Psychology, and Treatment of Obesity, Anorexia, and Bulimia. Basic Books, New York, 1986, pp 45–62.

30. Katch FI, and McArdle WD: Nutrition, Weight Control, and Exercise, ed 2. Lea and Febiger, Philadelphia, 1983.

31. Woo R, Garrow JS, and Pi-Sunyer FX: Effect of exercise on spontaneous calorie intake in obesity. Am J Clin Nutr 36:470, 1982.

32. Stern JS, and Lowney P: Obesity: The role of physical activity. In Brownell KD, and Foreyt JP (eds): Handbook of Eating Disorders: Physiology, Psychology, and Treatment of Obesity, Anorexia, and Bulimia. Basic Books, New York, 1986, p 145.

33. Thompson JK, Jarvie GJ, Lahey BB, et al: Exercise and obesity: Etiology, physiology, and intervention. Psychol Bull 91:55–79, 1982.

34. Brownell KD, and Stunkard, AJ: Physical activity in the development and control of obesity. In Stunkard AJ (ed): Obesity. WB Saunders, Philadelphia, p 300.

35. Donahoe CP Jr, Lin DH, Kirschenbaum DS, et al: Metabolic consequences of dieting and exercise in the treatment of obesity. J Consult Clin Psychol 52:827, 1984.

36. Lennon D, Nagle F, Stratman F, et al: Diet and exercise training effects on resting metabolic rate. Int J Obes 9:39, 1985.

37. Phinney SD: The metabolic interaction between very-low-calorie diets and exercise. In Blackburn GL, and Bray GA (eds): Management of Obesity by Severe Caloric Restriction. PSG Publishing Co, Littleton, MA, 1985.

38. Keesey RE: A set-point theory of obesity. In Brownell KD, and Foreyt JP (eds): Handbook of Eating Disorders: Physiology, Psychology, and Treatment of Obesity, Anorexia, and Bulimia. Basic Books, New York, 1986, p 63.

39. Kaplan ML, and Leveille GA: Calorigenic responses in obese and nonobese women. Am J Clin Nutr 29:1108, 1976.

40. Segal KR, and Gutin, B: Thermic effects of food and exercise in lean and obese women. Metabolism 32:581, 1983.

41. Segal KR, Presta E, and Gutin, B: Thermic effect of food during graded exercise in normal weight and obese men. Am J Clin Nutr 40:995, 1984.

42. Trembley A, Cole J, and LeBlanc J: Diminished dietary thermogenesis in exercise-trained human subjects. Eur J Appl Physiol 52:1, 1983.

43. Miller PM: The Hilton Head Metabolism Diet. Warner Books, New York, 1983.

44. Wilmore JH: Body composition in sport and exercise: Directions for future research. Med Sci Sports Exerc 15:21, 1983.

45. Pollock ML, Cureton TK, and Greninger L: The effects of frequency of training on working capacity, cardiovascular function, and body composition of adult men. Med Sci Sports Exerc 1:70, 1969.

46. Franklin BA, MacKeen PC, and Buskirk ER: Body composition effects of a 12-week physical conditioning program for normal and obese middle-aged women, and status at 18-month follow-up. Int J Obes 2:394, 1978.

47. American College of Sports Medicine: The recommended quantity and quality of exercise for developing and maintaining fitness in healthy adults. Med Sci Sports Exerc 10:vii, 1978.

48. Pollock ML, Dimmick J, Miller HS, et al: Effect of mode of training on cardiovascular function and body composition of adult men. Med Sci Sports Exerc 7:139, 1975.

49. Bjorntorp P: Physical training in the treatment of obesity. Int J Obes 2:149, 1978.
50. Parizkova J: Body Fat and Physical Fitness. Martinus Nifhoff, The Hague, Netherlands, 1977.
51. Wadden TA, Stunkard AJ, and Brownell KD: Very-low-calorie diets: Their safety, efficacy, and future. Ann Int Med 99:675, 1983.
52. Trembley A, Despres JP, and Bouchard C: The effects of exercise training on energy balance and adipose tissue morphology and metabolism. Sports Med 2:223, 1985.
53. Mayer J, Marshall NB, Vitale JJ, et al: Exercise, food intake and body weight in normal rats and genetically obese adult mice. Am J Physiol 177:544, 1954.
54. Oscai LB: The role of exercise in weight control. In Wilmore JH (ed): Exercise and Sports Sciences Reviews (Vol. 1). Academic Press, New York, 1973, p 103.
55. Katch NL, Martin R, and Martin J: Effects of exercise intensity on food consumption in the male rat. Am J Clin Nutr 32:1401, 1979.
56. Oscai LB, Mole PA, and Holloszy JO: Effects of exercise on cardiac weight and mitochondria in male and female rats. Am J Physiol 220:1944, 1971.
57. Mayer JE, Roy P, and Mitra KP: Relation between caloric intake, body weight, and physical work: Studies in an industrial male population in West Bengal. Am J Clin Nutr 4:169, 1956.
58. Dempsey, JA: Anthropometrical observations on obese and nonobese young men undergoing a program of vigorous physical exercise. Res Q 35:275, 1964.
59. Epstein LH, Masek BJ, and Marshall WR: A nutritionally based school program for control of eating in obese children. Behav Ther 9:766, 1978.
60. Epstein LH, Masek BJ, and Marshall WR: Pre-lunch exercise and lunch time caloric intake. Behav Ther 1:15, 1978.
61. Epstein LH, Wing RR, and Thompson JK: The relationship between exercise intensity, caloric intake, and weight. Addictive Behav 3:185, 1978.
62. Katch FI, Michael ED, and Jones EM: Effects of physical training on the body composition and diet of females. Res Q 40:99, 1969.
63. Johnson RE, Mastropaolo JA, and Wharton MA: Exercise, dietary intake, and body composition. J Am Dietet Assoc 61:399, 1972.
64. Martin JE, and Dubbert PM: Exercise applications and promotion in behavioral medicine: current status and future directions. J Consult Clin Psychol 50:1004, 1982.
65. Morgan WP: Anxiety reduction following acute physical activity. Psych Ann 9:141, 1979.
66. Greist JH, Klein MH, Eischens JF, et al: Running as treatment for depression. Comp Psychiatr 20:41, 1979.
67. Collingwood TR, and Willett L: The effects of physical training upon self-concept and body attitudes. J Clin Psychol 27:411, 1971.
68. Folkins CH, and Sime WE: Physical fitness training and mental health. Am Psychol 36:373, 1981.
69. Raglin JS, and Morgan WP: Influence of vigorous exercise on mood state. Behav Ther 8:179, 1985.
70. Dimsdale JE, and Moss J: Plasma catecholamines in stress and exercise. JAMA 243:340, 1980.
71. Appenzeller O, Standefer J, Appenzeller J, et al: Neurology of endurance training: V endorphins. Neurology 30:418, 1980.
72. Glasser W: Positive Addiction. Harper and Row, New York, 1976.
73. Taylor HL, Buskirk ER, and Remington RD: Exercise in controlled trials of the prevention of coronary heart disease. Fed Proc 32:1623, 1973.
74. Gwinup G: Effect of exercise alone on the weight of obese women. Arch Int Med 135:676, 1975.
75. Oldridge NB, Donner AP, Buck CW, et al: Predictors of dropout from cardiac exercise rehabilitation: Ontario Exercise-Heart Collaborative Study. Am J Cardiol 51:70, 1983.
76. Martin JE, Dubbert PM, Katell AD, et al: Behavioral control of exercise: Studies 1–6. J Consult Clin Psychol 52:795, 1984.
77. Brownell KD: Behavioral, psychological, and environmental predictors of obesity and success at weight reduction. Int J Obes 8:543, 1984.
78. Dahlkoetter J, Callahan EJ, and Linton J: Obesity and the unbalanced energy equation: Exercise vs. eating habit change. J Consult Clin Psychol 47:898, 1979.
79. Brownell KD: The LEARN Program For Weight Control. University of Pennsylvania, Philadelphia, 1987.
80. Marlatt GA, and Gordon J: Relapse Prevention. Guilford Press, New York, 1985.
81. Brownell KD, Marlatt GA, Lichtenstein E, et al: Understanding and preventing relapse. Am Psychol 41:765, 1986.

# CHAPTER 4

# Training for Strength

## DAVID H. CLARKE

With proper training, women can become very strong. However, even with the same strength-training program, their muscles will not enlarge as much as those of men. The data-based studies regarding the adaptations resulting from strength training have come predominantly from research conducted on male subjects, but, aside from questions raised concerning muscle hypertrophy, it seems tenable to conclude that principles that apply to men also apply to women.

## DEFINITION OF STRENGTH

The first concept that needs to be defined is that of strength. A dictionary definition is unacceptable, as the terms "tough," "powerful," and "muscular" do very little to describe what is actually a functional concept. Attempts at obtaining a true measure of muscle force show that maximum tension varies from 1.5 to 2.5 $kg \cdot cm^{-2}$ in vertebrate nonhuman muscles and perhaps slightly higher in the normal human.[1] Thus, if one assumes a value of 3 $kg \cdot cm^{-2}$ and that large muscles of the thigh may have 100 $cm^2$ of cross section, the resulting internal force that could be developed would be 300 kg. Obviously, the amount of useful torque that can be marshaled during normal activities must be expressed somewhat differently, since it is not feasible to determine true internal tensions. Thus, it is customary to employ the concept of the maximal voluntary contraction (MVC), which implies that the effort is not submaximal, nor is it created by some external stimulus, such as a tetanic shock. Yet one does not know whether the contraction resulted in

55

any movement, whether it caused any muscle shortening or lengthening, and, if movement did occur, whether it was at a fixed speed or whether the tension on the muscle was constant or variable.

Mastering the terminology helps one not only to understand the literature on strength training but also to comprehend the difficulty faced by investigators in quantifying the results of various training regimens. There are few absolute standards available for the assessment of strength, so a wide variety of procedures has been employed. Thus, there has been great difficulty in making clear comparisons among various studies. In the present context, *isotonic strength* (or dynamic strength) of a muscle is defined as the maximum force that can be exerted by that muscle during contraction as it moves through its full range of motion. This can be further delineated into concentric (i.e., shortening) and eccentric (i.e., lengthening) forms. *Isometric strength* (or static strength) is a single MVC performed by a muscle group in a static position, in which no shortening or lengthening of the muscle occurs; *isokinetic strength* resembles the isotonic contraction, since the joint moves through a range of motion, but the speed of movement is held constant. This latter system requires specialized equipment to control for a variety of movement speeds.

## ISOTONIC TRAINING

The usual method of training has been to follow a routine of isotonic exercises. A system described by DeLorme and Watkins[2] during the period immediately following World War II became known as progressive resistance exercise (PRE) and was based on a set of 10 repetitions maximum (10 RM), which is the heaviest weight that can be lifted and lowered 10 times in succession. The manner in which these exercises were to be employed was first to perform a set of 10 repetitions of one half of the weight of the 10 RM, then to perform a second set of 10 repetitions at three fourths of the weight of the 10 RM, and finally to perform as many repetitions as possible at the weight of the 10 RM. When an appropriate number of additional repetitions of the 10 RM could be performed, more weight was added and the process continued at this new 10-RM weight.

It is generally thought that keeping the total number of repetitions for the three sets somewhere in the range of 30 to 35 enhances the development of muscular strength. Using a program with reduced resistance and increased repetitions is thought to emphasize muscular endurance. Houtz, Parrish, and Hellebrandt[3] applied the PRE principle to female subjects, exercising the quadriceps and forearm muscles, and found that strength more than doubled in 4 weeks. Thus, it seems probable that the principles of strength development can be successfully applied to women as well as men.

Interest in refining the procedures for PRE for effective strength gains has been the subject of fairly intense investigation in the subsequent years. Berger[4] has provided considerable insight into the strength development process using various combinations of repetitions, sets (number of repeated sequences the exercise is performed during a given session), and number of training sessions per week. The criterion measure of muscular strength was the 1 RM, defined as the maximum amount of weight that could be successfully moved through a complete range of motion for 1 repetition. In one study,[4] Berger trained six groups for 12 weeks employing the bench press exercise. The groups used resistances of 2, 4, 6, 8, 10, and 12 RM as their training modalities and performed only one set of repetitions per training session. At the end of this time it was found that those training at four, six, and eight repetitions gained significantly greater amounts of strength than any of the other groups, suggesting that an optimum target for training would be to perform between three and nine repetitions. Using one, two, and three sets of repetitions and employing 2, 6, and 10 RM as the weights and numbers of repetitions in each set, he found that no advantage was gained by exercising with heavier loads for 2 RM than with lighter loads at 10 RM.[5] All combinations resulted in significant strength increases, but strength gains were maximal when the number of repetitions per set was 6 RM for three sets. To determine whether increasing the number of sets beyond three would lead to greater gains in strength, Berger[6] compared the strength achieved by performing 2 RM for six sets, 6 RM for three sets, and 10 RM for three sets. He found that all three groups gained significantly and similarly in strength. This suggests that there is a point beyond which gains in muscular strength should not be anticipated.

Berger and Hardage[7] studied an alternate, somewhat unique modification of the 10-RM training technique. One group performed 10 repetitions for one set, but each repetition was adjusted so that it required maximum effort, that is, a 1 RM. Subsequent repetitions were performed by gradually reducing the load, so that at the 10th repetition the subjects were still exerting maximum tension. When compared with the regular 10-RM group, it was found that both groups improved significantly in the 1-RM bench press after 8 weeks of training. However, the 1-RM group improved significantly more than the regular 10-RM group, indicating the relative importance of intensity of effort in training. It should be noted that almost all studies have shown the importance of attaining maximal tension of the muscles during the course of the exercise.

To compare the strength achieved by performing many repetitions using light weight with that gained by performing few repetitions using heavy weight, Anderson and Kearney[8] trained 43 male subjects using three sets of 6 to 8 RM for one group, 30 to 40 RM for a second group, and 100 to 150 RM for a third group, all subjects employing the bench press three times per week for 9 weeks. Strength was assessed with the 1-RM bench press, administered before and after the training. Gains in strength were achieved by all three groups, but only the high-resistance, low-repetition (6- to 8-RM) group was significantly stronger than the other two groups, which did not differ from each other. Thus, it appears that strength gains are greatest when resistance is high. Since few repetitions can be done using high resistance, a smaller time expenditure is required for this training.

It has generally been found that men have greater absolute amounts of strength than women under most conditions.[9–12] Even untrained men who have not been specifically weight training[13] exhibit greater upper and lower body strength than female athletes trained in such sports as basketball and volleyball but not weight training. The ratios comparing the strength of women to that of men are on the order of 0.46 to 0.73 when compared on maximal strength of elbow flexion, shoulder flexion, back extension, and handgrip.[14] Even though this is the case, the established principles of strength training are applicable to both men and women.

## ISOMETRIC TRAINING

The systematic use of isometric training principles can probably be traced to the 1953 report of Hettinger and Muller,[15] who found an average strength increase of 5 percent per week when the muscle tension was held for 6 seconds at two thirds of maximum strength. Even when the tension was increased to 100 percent, or when the length of time was increased, very little additional improvement was noted. Isometric exercises are normally performed by establishing a given joint angle and exerting isometric tension at that point in the range of motion (e.g., pushing against a stationary wall). As with isotonic exercises, more than one set may be performed and the length of time for which the tension is exerted may vary. However, the amount of the strength gain suggested by Muller[16] has not been confirmed in subsequent experimentation. It seems more likely that the amount of strength gain would depend on the relative state of training of a given muscle group. Thus, the closer one is to a theoretical maximum, the more likely the gains are to be small.[17]

Isometric exercise does increase muscular strength. Josenhans[18] employed isometric exercises for the grip and the flexor and extensor muscles of the finger, the elbow, and the knee and found a 40 percent increase in muscular force at the end of the training period. When 5-second maximal isometric contractions of the quadriceps muscles were employed it was found that strength increases vary between 80 and 400 percent.[19] Morehouse[20] separated some trained subjects into high- and low-strength groups and employed either 1, 3, 5, or 10 maximum isometric contractions each session. Subjects increased significantly in strength after 5 weeks, with similar improvements found regardless of level of initial strength. Apparently, most individuals can anticipate increases in strength regardless of how strong they are at the outset, unless they are already in an advanced state of muscular training.

These principles were applied to postpubescent young men who were trained in wrist flexion employing the Hettinger and Muller strategy[15] of two-thirds maximum tension for one 6-second period each day. This was compared with a technique in which 80 percent of maximum strength was employed in five 6-second periods.[21] Both groups of subjects improved significantly after 4 weeks of training, although no significant difference resulted between the two groups. This suggests that a single 6-second bout of isometric exercise on a daily basis is about as effective for developing muscular strength as bouts practiced more frequently and at higher tensions. Furthermore, high school boys and girls training for one contraction per day at 25, 50, 75, and 100 percent of maximum isometric elbow flexion strength were compared after training.[22] With the exception of the 25 percent resistance group, all groups became stronger. Thus, the age of subjects seems to be of little consequence for achieving strength-training results.

Increasing the number of isometric contractions appears to increase the strength gain over a greater range of motion.[23] One group of subjects held three maximum isometric contractions at an elbow joint angle of 170 degrees' flexion, each for 6 seconds, in a program that was of 6 weeks' duration. Another group performed 20 6-second maximum contractions at the same joint angle. Maximum strength was assessed before and after the experiment at angles of both 90 and 170 degrees. All tests used isometric maximum contractions. The subjects who performed more contractions gained strength significantly at both joint angles, while those who performed fewer contractions became stronger only at the angle of 170 degrees, the training angle. Thus, the longer duration of work seems to be more beneficial for strength development, but the difference is small, compared with the amount of effort required.

Whereas most investigations have employed either male subjects or a combination of male and female subjects, Hansen[24,25] used female subjects, employing sustained and repeated isometric contractions. The gains in isometric strength in this study ranged from approximately 4 percent to 11 percent over a 5-week training program.

A more recent development has been the incorporation of functional isometrics into an isotonic strength training program. In a given range of motion, it is common to locate a given point at which the muscle is most inefficient. Weight lifters refer to this as the "sticking point" of exercise. It represents the point at which the force available is equal to the resistance of the weight. To determine whether the incorporation of maximum isometric contractions at this point would permit the development of strength beyond that provided by the isotonic exercise alone, subjects[26] in a control group trained on the bench press exercise using an isotonic training procedure employing 6 to 8 RM, while the experimental group added to this routine an isometric program consisting of six maximal voluntary contractions at a predetermined "sticking point" in the bench press. Analysis of the 1-RM bench press before and after the training program revealed significant improvements for both groups. However, the experimental group was significantly stronger than the control group, providing evidence that isometric training enhances the standard isotonic training routine in the achievement of maximum strength.

## ISOTONIC VERSUS ISOMETRIC TRAINING

It has been difficult to compare the improvements in strength resulting from isotonic and isometric training methods, because the intensities of training in the two methods cannot be equated. The ideal method of comparison would employ two exercise regimens, both of equal workloads. However, this has been difficult to accomplish because isometric exercises involve no movement and, thus, are difficult to quantify in physical terms.

Despite the problems inherent in comparing isotonic and isometric training effects, Rasch and Morehouse,[27] in one of the earlier studies, compared these two methods by having one group (isotonic) perform a 5-RM procedure involving three sets of arm presses and curls, taking a total of 15 seconds to perform, and having the other group (isometric) employ a 15-second exercise period contracting the muscles isometrically at two-thirds maximum. Following 6 weeks of training, substantial increases were found for the isotonic exercise group in elbow flexion and arm elevation and for the isometric exercise group in arm elevation alone. No significant gain was made in elbow flexion for the isometric training group. Thus, subjects employing isotonic exercise gained a greater amount of strength than did those subjects employing isometric exercises. It was suggested by the investigators that some of the strength development may have come from the acquisition of skill, since subjects tended to do better when performing familiar procedures. This may help explain sudden early increases in strength; they may be attributable more to neuromuscular coordination than to true muscle hypertrophy.

Isometric and isotonic training procedures were applied to subjects engaging in exercise over a 12-week training period, exercising three times per week and employing the larger muscles of the back.[28] The isometric group trained with a back pull machine, contracting the muscles for 6 seconds maximally, three sets per exercise session, and the isotonic group employed back hyperextension exercises based on an 8- to 12-RM regimen. Both groups improved significantly in muscular strength, but the isometric group gained significantly more when an isometric test was employed, and the isotonic group performed better when a test of isotonic strength, such as the 1-RM procedure, was used. This finding suggests that training is specific, a concept that has received additional support from some studies. However, this is in contrast to the work of many other investigators who reported similar gains in strength from these two different training methods. For example, Berger[29] trained subjects for 12 weeks both isometrically and isotonically and used the criterion of the 1-RM test. The final strength of the isometrically trained group was not significantly different from seven of the nine groups that trained isotonically. Coleman[30] employed the elbow flexor muscle in a program of 12 weeks' duration, using an isometric regimen consisting of two 10-second contractions and an isotonic training program consisting of a 5-RM regimen. In this instance, there was an attempt to equate the load, duration, and range of motion of the exercise. No significant difference was found between the two methods, although both produced significant strength gains.

Salter[31] investigated the effect on muscular strength of maximum isometric and isotonic contractions, performed at different repetition rates. The isometric group gradually increased force to maximum over approximately 4 seconds. The isotonic group lifted a load equivalent to 75 percent of maximum as far as possible, also over a duration of 4 seconds. The exercise involved supination of the left hand and involved 12 male and 8 female subjects. All training procedures resulted in a significant improvement in strength. However, no significant differences were found between the different procedures. Chui[32] noted similar findings. Two groups trained with rapid and slow isotonic contractions and were compared with a group employing isometric contractions. The slow isotonic contractions required a cadence of 4 seconds for movement and recovery, and the isometric contractions were held for 6 seconds. All groups employed a weight equal to a 10-RM resistance. No advantage was found for either procedure over the other, although each group gained significantly in muscular strength. When isometric contractions were lengthened to 30 seconds,[33] the development of strength was found to be less than by isotonic methods by some 14 percent, even though both isotonic and isometric methods caused increases in muscular strength. Thus, it would seem desirable to employ isotonic procedures whenever possible. Gains in strength with isometric exercise tend to be less consistent than those with isotonic exercise, when many training techniques and strength tests are employed.

## ECCENTRIC TRAINING

As pointed out earlier, isotonic movement can be divided into a concentric (shortening) and an eccentric (lengthening) phase. It is generally concluded that in isotonic training the greatest force is exerted concentrically, and this usually means that the muscle is shortening and the load is being lifted against gravity. Thus, loads are adjusted so that the greatest tension is provided during this phase. The eccentric phase is ordinarily employed to complete the movement so that the muscle returns to its original length. The weight is simply lowered slowly with gravity assistance. It is generally accepted that the amount of weight that can be lowered maximally is about 20 percent greater than that which can be lifted against gravity. Logically, one would expect the added force that can be resisted with an eccentric contraction to be a greater stimulus to strength gain. However, scientific studies have failed to show any advantage of eccentric over concentric training.

Bonde Peterson[34] studied isometric, isotonic, and eccentric contractions in female and male subjects for a period lasting from 20 to 36 days. Training for each subject consisted of one of the following protocols: 1 maximum isometric contraction daily, 10 maximum isometric contractions daily, or 10 eccentric contractions daily. It was found that performance of 1 maximum isometric contraction daily had no effect on the isometric strength of the subjects; performance of 10 isometric contractions daily caused no change in the strength of the female subjects but led to a significant increase (13 percent) for the male subjects. Subjects who trained with the 10 daily eccentric contractions failed to demonstrate any significant increase in strength. This lack of significant strength gain may have been due to training every day rather than every other day. It is possible that insufficient time was allowed between training sessions to recover completely from the previous training session.

Singh and Karpovich[35] designed a study to determine the effect of eccentric training on a muscle group as well as on its antagonist (the opposing muscle complex). In this instance, the forearm extensors were given 20 maximum eccentric contractions four times per week for 8 weeks, and the extensors as well as the forearm flexors were tested for maximum strength before and after training. Concentric and isometric strength of the exercised muscles increased approximately 40 percent, but the eccentric strength increased only 23 percent. When the antagonistic muscles were examined, it was found that they also increased in strength, ranging from 17 to 31 percent. This suggests that during maximum contractions in eccentric movement, the antagonistic muscles are also contracted. The investigators verified that this occurs, by palpation and by examination of the electromyographic activity emanating from the antagonistic muscle. This finding illustrates the fact that it is very difficult to isolate muscle activity in the human body.

More recently, Johnson and co-workers[36] trained subjects with eccentric movements on one arm and leg and concentric movements on the opposite arm and leg, three times weekly for a period of 6 weeks. The specific exercises included the arm curl, arm press, knee flexion, and knee extension. Each exercise lasted for 3 seconds. The concentric movement was performed against a resistance of 80 percent of the subject's 1-RM strength, and the eccentric movement was against 120 percent of 1 RM. Both exercise programs resulted in significant gains in strength in all subjects, but neither training procedure produced gains that were significantly different from the other. Interestingly, the subjects felt that the eccentric training movements were easier to perform than the concentric movements. Normally, one might expect this perception of the subjects to lead to greater compliance and acceptability of eccentric training. However, present equipment and common training habits do not permit isolation of eccentric contractions. Moreover, since a muscle can resist greater force in an eccentric contraction than in a concentric contraction, considerably greater tension is required in the eccentric movement in order to promote strength gains. Thus, in a regular isotonic exercise encompassing both concentric and eccentric contractions, the eccentric phase contributes relatively little to strength development, since the amount of force is undoubtedly well below the training stimulus during that phase of the exercise.

## ISOKINETIC EXERCISE

The newest form of exercise used for training is isokinetic exercise. It is often referred to as "accommodating resistance exercise," because, as explained earlier, it has the unique feature of adjusting to the ability of the muscles throughout the range of motion, so that weak spots are eliminated and the muscles remain under constant tension throughout the movement. Actually, few activities produce and maintain isokinetic tension, the arm strokes in swimming and oar strokes in rowing being the major exceptions. Properly designed equipment offers exercise at any one of a range of fixed speeds; the subject determines the resistance by the applied force. Thus, it is possible to exercise maximally throughout a full range of motion using any one of several speeds. In isokinetic exercise, increased force does not produce increased acceleration, but simply increased resistance.

One of the earlier studies[37] compared isokinetic training with isotonic and isometric training over an 8-week period. The isokinetic group increased in total muscular ability by 35 percent, the isotonic group increased 28 percent, and the isometric group increased approximately 9 percent. Employing quadriceps and hamstring muscle exercises on 12 male and 48 female subjects, Moffroid and associates[38] studied groups that exercised isometrically, isotonically, and isokinetically for a 4-week period. Significant increases in isometric strength occurred for all groups, with one exception: when the isotonic group was tested at 90 degrees rather than 45 degrees, no significant improvement was noted. None of the groups improved significantly in the quadriceps muscles when tested for isokinetic work, but all were significantly better when the hamstring muscles were tested.

Lesmes and colleagues[39] trained male subjects isokinetically on knee extensors and flexors four times per week for 7 weeks, at maximal intensity and at a constant velocity of 180 degrees per second. One leg was trained at 6-second work bouts and the other leg at 30-second work bouts, the ratio of work to rest providing a method of keeping workloads equal. Isokinetic testing was accomplished at various intervals between 60 and 300 degrees per second. Increased peak torque occurred at both 6 and 30 seconds at all intensities except those between approximately 180 and 300 degrees per second.

Thus, isokinetic exercises are effective in increasing muscular strength, but probably not more so than isotonic training. The ability of isokinetic movements to create maximum tension throughout the range of motion is clearly desirable, but methods of measuring strength may not illustrate this advantage. Perhaps future studies using more refined methods to measure gains in strength may show increased gains in strength with isokinetic training compared with isotonic and isometric training. However, the specificity of training and the bias inherent in that situation make it difficult to compare results.

## HYPERTROPHY OF SKELETAL MUSCLE

Based on the evidence presented so far, heavy resistance exercise unquestionably results in increases in muscular strength for men. While some of the experimentation has included women, the extent of strength development and muscle hypertrophy for women has not been studied as extensively. One of the most striking occurrences for men engaged in weight training over an extended period of time is the obvious evidence of hypertrophy, as shown by changes in muscle size accompanying increases in strength. The extent of these changes depends on a number of factors surrounding the strengthening regimen. However, for men, high blood levels of androgens account for the increased muscle size.

One of the reasons for the reluctance of women to engage in serious weight training in the past has been a fear that they would develop the same hypertrophy that men do and would look "masculine." Wilmore[10] examined strength and body composition of 47 women and 26 men before and after a 10-week intensive weight-training program. Men were found to be stronger than women in most measures of strength, but women were stronger in leg strength per unit of lean body weight. Both groups made similar relative gains in strength, but the degree of muscular hypertrophy for women was considerably less than that noted for men. The conclusion seems warranted that increases in strength for women are not accompanied by the same degree of changes in muscle size as for men. Low blood concentrations of testosterone in women apparently limit the development of large muscles. Anabolic steroid administration during training will promote muscle hypertrophy in women. However, the adverse metabolic effects of anabolic steroid use outweigh their potential desirability for enhancing muscle size.

One of the major issues examined over the years has been to clarify the nature of hypertrophy itself. It is clear that size increases with strength development, and examining the structural changes that take place within the muscle has been of interest to exercise physiologists and biologists. The term "hypertrophy" denotes an increase in the size or bulk of the muscle fibers, rather than an increase in the number of muscle fibers (called hyperplasia). The question of whether the latter actually occurs as a result of systematic weight training has been the subject of a number of investigations. Early studies concentrated on laboratory animals as subjects. Goldspink[40] trained mice by means of an exercise requiring the pulling of a weight to retrieve food. He reported a 30 percent increase in cross-sectional area of the average fiber. He also reported a threefold or fourfold increase in the number of myofibrils per fiber. In working with guinea pigs, Helander[41] found an increase of some 15 percent in actomyosin as a result of training. The studies suggest that both hypertrophy and hyperplasia take place.

One of the earliest studies to report the formation of new muscle fibers (hyperplasia) was published by van Linge,[42] who surgically implanted the plantaris muscle of female rats into the calcaneus. He cut the nerve of the other plantar flexors so that the plantaris muscle would provide plantar flexion. The formation of new muscle fibers was observed at the end of a prolonged heavy training period. Several studies have performed muscle tenotomy (severing the muscle tendon at its insertion) to observe the effect of training on the muscle that must take over the function of the cut muscle. A very rapid hypertrophy takes place after this procedure, and fiber splitting and branching have been reported, as well as increases in strength and fiber diameter.

If a muscle is examined repeatedly for several months after removal of its synergists, hyperplasia is noted.[43] Gonyea[44] subjected 20 cats to a conditioning program involving lifting of weights with the right forelimb against increasing resistance to receive a food reward. The program lasted for 34 weeks, and the flexor carpi radialis muscle was examined to determine any increase in fiber number as a result of low-resistance and high-resistance training. The control group experienced no difference in the number of fibers in either the left or right limb, and no difference in the number of fibers was found in those that lifted a "light-resistance" weight. There was a significant increase in fiber number (20.5 percent) for those lifting the heavy load. This was attributed to muscle fiber splitting.

Male albino rats were trained by Ho and co-workers,[45] in a progressive training program against high resistance for 8 weeks. There was a significant increase in the number of fibers per unit of cross-sectional area in the weight-lifting animals. The authors suggested that the fiber splitting appeared to be due to some sort of "pinching-off" of a small segment from the parent fiber or to an invagination of the sarcolemma deep into the muscle fiber in a plane parallel to the sarco-meres. Under certain conditions, fiber splitting seems to occur, but hypertrophy still remains the major mechanism for the size increase that results from intense weight training. In addition to the structural changes evident from hypertrophy and hyperplasia are a number of enzymatic changes that occur in skeletal muscle. Many of these enzymatic changes are important for the attainment of muscle endurance, and many occur during weight training. The biochemical changes that take place for the weight-lifting individual are those that are involved primarily in anaerobic metabolism.

## SUMMARY

The unmistakable conclusion that can be drawn is that training for strength is a goal that can be pursued by both men and women. There seems to be an optimal regimen of exercises to be followed, consisting of six to nine repetitions maximum undertaken for three sets at least three times a week. Most individuals will be working with a system that is at the very least an isotonic one. However, because some of the equipment currently available is specifically designed to maximize the tension throughout the full range of motion, many people now use isokinetic machines. It seems reasonably clear that both isotonic and isokinetic exercises can be used successfully for developing muscle strength. Less effective are isometric exercises and eccentric contractions. Gains are greater for untrained than for trained individuals. Most athletes, male or female, find increases in strength to come more slowly near the peak of training.

Training with heavy-resistance exercise can be safely employed by women without fear of developing markedly hypertrophied muscles. The external size of the muscle is not the only determinant of its strength. Many of the changes associated with hypertrophy are cellular and thus are not associated with noticeable enlargement. With training, men develop greater muscle hypertrophy than women, because they have much higher levels of androgenic hormones. Women can become very strong through weight training and still not develop markedly enlarged muscles. The average woman should find a number of advantages in being physically strong as she carries out normal activities and engages in other fitness exercise.

The principles outlined, not the type of equipment available, should form the basis for exercise selection. Selecting appropriate exercises and establishing an acceptable routine are more important to strength development than the use of certain commercial fitness machines. Training with free weights can accomplish the same gains in strength as training with machines. However, free weights are more likely to cause injury, since the weights are unsupported and require somewhat greater skill to use. The individual should choose the appropriate exercises and engage in a systematic and progressive program. Early gains are due to an increase in motor coordination. Those gains that occur after several months of training are due to greater muscle strength. Expecting great gains in strength after a few weeks of training is unrealistic, since the acquisition of strength is a slow and progessive process. Such unrealistic expectations about improvement are a common cause of attrition among novices. Qualified instruction may be beneficial to many seeking gains in muscular strength.

# References

1. Ralston HJ, Polissar MJ, Inman VT, et al: Dynamic features of human isolated voluntary muscle in isometric and free contractions. J Appl Physiol 1:526, 1949.
2. DeLorme TL, and Watkins AL: Technics of progressive resistance exercise. Arch Phys Med 29:263, 1948.
3. Houtz SJ, Parrish AM, and Hellebrandt FA: The influence of heavy resistance exercise on strength. Physiother Rev 26:299, 1946.
4. Berger RA: Optimum repetitions for the development of strength. Res Q 33:334, 1962.
5. Berger RA: Effect of varied weight training programs on strength. Res Q 33:168, 1962.
6. Berger RA: Comparative effects of three weight training programs. Res Q 34:396, 1963.
7. Berger RA, and Hardage B: Effect of maximum loads for each of ten repetitions on strength improvement. Res Q 38:715, 1967.
8. Anderson T, and Kearney JT: Effects of three resistance training programs on muscular strength and absolute and relative endurance. Res Q Exerc Sport 53:1, 1982.
9. Montoye HJ, and Lamphiear DE: Grip and arm strength in males and females. Res Q 48:109, 1977.
10. Wilmore JH: Alterations in strength, body composition and anthropometric measurements consequent to a 10-week weight training program. Med Sci Sports 6:133, 1974.
11. Heyward V, and McCreary L: Analysis of the static strength and relative endurance of women athletes. Res Q 48:703, 1977.
12. Clarke DH: Sex differences in strength and fatigability. Res Q Exerc Sport 57:144, 1986.
13. Morrow JR, and Hosler WW: Strength comparisons in untrained men and women athletes, age 10 to 69. Med Sci Sports 13:194, 1981.
14. Yates JW, Kamon E, Rodgers SH, et al: Static lifting strength and maximal isometric voluntary contractions of back, arm and shoulder muscles. Ergonomics 23:37, 1980.
15. Hettinger TL, and Muller EA: Muskelleistung und muskeltraining. Arbeitsphysiol 15:111, 1953.
16. Muller EA: Physiology of muscle training. Rev Can Biol 21:303, 1962.
17. Muller EA, and Rohmert W: Die geschwindigkeit der muskelkraft zunahme bei isometrischen training. Int Z Angew Physiol 19:403, 1963.
18. Josenhans WKT: An evaluation of some methods of improving muscle strength. Rev Can Biol 21:315, 1962.
19. Rose DL, Radzyminski SF, and Beatty RR: Effect of brief maximal exercise on the strength of the quadriceps femoris. Arch Phys Med Rehabil 38:157, 1957.
20. Morehouse CA: Development and maintenance of isometric strength of subjects with diverse initial strengths. Res Q 38:449, 1967.
21. Rarick GL, and Larsen GL: Observations on frequency and intensity of isometric muscular effort in developing static muscular strength. Res Q 29:333, 1958.
22. Cotten D: Relationship of the duration of sustained voluntary isometric contraction to changes in endurance and strength. Res Q 38:366, 1967.
23. Meyers CR: Effects of two isometric routines on strength, size, and endurance in exercised and nonexercised arms. Res Q 38:430, 1967.
24. Hansen JW: The training effect of repeated isometric muscle contractions. Int Z Angew Physiol 18:474, 1961.
25. Hansen JW: The effect of sustained isometric muscle contraction on various muscle functions. Int Z Angew Physiol 19:430, 1963.
26. Jackson A, Jackson T, Hnatek J, et al: Strength development: using functional isometrics in an isotonic strength training program. Res Q Exerc Sport 56:234, 1985.
27. Rasch PJ, and Morehouse LE: Effect of static and dynamic exercises on muscular strength and hypertrophy. J Appl Physiol 11:29, 1957.
28. Berger RA: Comparison of static and dynamic strength increases. Res Q 33:329, 1962.
29. Berger RA: Comparison between static training and various dynamic training programs. Res Q 34:131, 1963.
30. Coleman AE: Effect of unilateral isometric and isotonic contractions on the strength of the contralateral limb. Res Q 40:490, 1969.
31. Salter N: The effect on muscle strength of maximum isometric and isotonic contractions at different repetition rates. J Physiol 130:109, 1955.
32. Chui EF: Effects of isometric and dynamic weight-training exercises upon strength and speed of movement. Res Q 35:246, 1964.
33. Lawrence MS, Meyer HR, and Matthews NL: Comparative increase in muscle strength in the quadri-

ceps femoris by isometric and isotonic exercise and effects on the contralateral muscle. J Am Phys Ther Assoc 42:15, 1962.

34. Bonde Petersen F: Muscle training by static, concentric and eccentric contractions. Acta Physiol Scand 48:406, 1960.

35. Singh M, and Karpovich PV: Effect of eccentric training of agonists on antagonistic muscles. J Appl Physiol 23:742, 1967.

36. Johnson BL, Adamczyk JW, Tennøe KO, et al: A comparison of concentric and eccentric muscle training. Med Sci Sports 8:35, 1976.

37. Thistle HG, Hislop HJ, Moffroid M, et al: Isokinetic contraction: a new concept of resistive exercise. Arch Phys Med Rehabil 48:279, 1966.

38. Moffroid M, Whipple R, Hofkosh J, et al: A study of isokinetic exercise. Phys Ther 49:735, 1969.

39. Lesmes GR, Costill DL, Coyle EF, et al: Muscle strength and power changes during maximal isokinetic training. Med Sci Sports 10:266, 1978.

40. Goldspink G: The combined effects of exercise and reduced food intake on skeletal muscle fibers. J Cell Comp Physiol 63:209, 1964.

41. Helander EAS: Influence of exercise and restricted activity on the protein composition of skeletal muscle. Biochem J 78:478, 1961.

42. van Linge B: The response of muscle to strenuous exercise. J Bone Joint Surg 44-B:711, 1962.

43. Reitsma W: Some structural changes in skeletal muscles of the rat after intensive training. Acta Morphol Neerl Scand 7:229, 1970.

44. Gonyea WJ: Role of exercise in inducing increases in skeletal muscle fiber number. J Appl Physiol 48:421, 1980.

45. Ho KW, Roy RR, Tweedle CD, et al: Skeletal muscle fiber splitting with weight-lifting exercise in rats. Am J Anat 157:433, 1980.

# CHAPTER 5

# Endurance Training

THOMAS D. FAHEY

Until recently, systematic studies of female endurance athletes were limited. This is understandable because, prior to the passage of Title IX of the Civil Rights Act (legislation that mandated equal opportunity for sports participation in the schools), the number of women competing in endurance sports was small.[1]

In 1971, the American College of Sports Medicine, perhaps the premier organization for the study of sports medicine in the world, published the *Encyclopedia of Sport Sciences and Medicine*.[2] Although this monumental work consisted of over 1700 pages, fewer than 10 pages were devoted to women and sports medicine. Until 1958, the longest event in women's track and field in meets hosted by the Amateur Athletic Union of the United States was 440 yards. In 1965, top female runners were threatened with banishment from international competition if they ran in a race longer than 1.5 miles. In 1984, the first Olympic marathon for women was held in Los Angeles. Now, it is common for women to compete in endurance events such as ultramarathons, triathlons, and long-distance swimming and cycling.

## FACTORS THAT DETERMINE SUCCESS IN ENDURANCE EVENTS

The factors that help to determine success or failure in endurance performance include maximal oxygen consumption ($\dot{V}_{O_2max}$), mitochondrial density, performance efficiency, and body composition.[3] Although sex differences exist in endurance performance, the relative changes that occur with training and the basic underlying mechanisms that determine performance are the same in men and women.

## Maximal Oxygen Consumption

$\dot{V}_{O_2max}$ is considered to be the best measure of cardiovascular capacity and is referred to by many sports medicine experts as the single most important criterion of physical fitness. It is defined as the point at which $O_2$ consumption fails to rise despite an increased exercise intensity or power output. In response to increased exercise intensity, both trained and untrained individuals respond with an increase in $\dot{V}_{O_2max}$. The greater ability of trained people to sustain a high exercise intensity or power output is largely due to a greater $\dot{V}_{O_2max}$.

$\dot{V}_{O_2max}$ is equal to the product of maximum cardiac output and maximum arteriovenous oxygen difference (Eq. 5–1):

**(Eq. 5–1)**

$$\dot{V}_{O_2max} = \dot{Q}_{max} (a\text{-}v)O_{2max}$$

where $\dot{V}_{O_2max}$ is the maximal rate of $O_2$ consumption (in $L \cdot min^{-1}$), $\dot{Q}_{max}$ is the maximum cardiac output in ($L \cdot min^{-1}$), and $(a\text{-}v)O_{2max}$ is the maximum arterial-venous $O_2$ difference (in liter $O_2 \cdot$ liter blood$^{-1}$). In other words, $\dot{V}_{O_2max}$ is a function of the maximum rate of oxygen transport and oxygen utilization.

During the transition from rest to maximal exercise, there is a linear increase in $(a\text{-}v)O_2$. Arterial oxygen partial pressure ($P_aO_2$) is well maintained in most athletes during exercise, so the increase is attributable to the decrease in venous oxygen partial pressure ($P_vO_2$). The body has only a limited capacity to increase oxygen extraction through endurance training because the venous blood draining the active muscles of both trained and untrained people during maximal exercise contains relatively little oxygen.

To be successful in competition, athletes in sports that require great endurance must have a large cardiac output capacity. Maximum cardiac output is the product of maximum heart rate (HR) and maximum stroke volume (SV) (Eq. 5–2).

**(Eq. 5–2)**

$$\dot{Q}_{max} = (HR_{max})(SV_{max})$$

Maximum heart rate is largely determined by heredity and age and is not appreciably affected by training. Because $HR_{max}$ and $(a\text{-}v)O_{2max}$ are relatively stable, changes in $\dot{V}_{O_2max}$ with training are mostly due to changes in stroke volume.

Stroke volume is affected by hemodynamic and myocardial factors and is closely linked to venous return of blood to the heart. The ability of the heart to contract with increased force as its chambers are stretched (a phenomenon known as preload) is described by the Frank-Starling principle.[4] A large number of factors affect preload, including total blood volume, body position, intrathoracic pressure, atrial contribution to ventricular filling, pumping action of skeletal muscle (muscle pump), venous tone, and intrapericardial pressure.[4] These hemodynamic factors can have both acute and chronic effects on stroke volume, oxygen transport capacity, and the perception of fatigue. As examples, during endurance exercise a decrease in blood volume due to dehydration or a decrease in venous tone will result in a compensatory increase in heart rate and an increased level of perceived exertion. Likewise, the increase in blood volume resulting from endurance training causes an increase in stroke volume.

Stroke volume is also affected by myocardial contractility. The contractile force of the myocardium changes in response to circulating catecholamines, the force-frequency relationship of the muscle, sympathetic nerve impulses, intrinsic depression, loss of myocardium, pharmacologic depressants, inotropic agents such as digitalis, anoxia, hypercapnia, and acidosis.[4] Endurance training increases myocardial contractility by increasing $Ca^{++}$-myosin ATPase activity.[5,6] The combination of increased preload and contractility is responsible for the increase in stroke volume that occurs with endurance training. Both of these factors are limited by ventricular volume, which is affected by genetic and environmental factors during growth and development and can be modified to some extent through endurance training.[7,8]

The oxygen consumption capacity of a muscle varies according to fiber type.[9] The ability of the mitochondria to extract oxygen from blood is approximately three to five times greater in slow-twitch red than in fast-twitch white fibers. Training can double the mitochondrial mass, so it is possible for elite endurance athletes to have 10 times the muscle oxygen-extracting capacity in their trained muscles as sedentary people.[10] Several studies have demonstrated a high correlation ($r \cong 0.80$) between $\dot{V}_{O_2max}$ and leg muscle mitochondrial activity.[11,12] From these data it is apparent that both cardiac output and muscle mitochondrial capacities are important determinants of the upper limits of $\dot{V}_{O_2max}$.

There is a strong genetic component of $\dot{V}_{O_2max}$.[13-15] The famous exercise physiologist Per-Olaf Åstrand has stated that to become an Olympic-level endurance athlete requires choosing parents very carefully! Genetic studies typically show less variance in $\dot{V}_{O_2max}$ and muscle fiber type between monozygous twins than between dizygous twins. However, these studies also show that training is critical for success but that the ultimate ability to improve performance in response to an endurance training program depends on genetic factors.

Most studies have shown that intense endurance training will result in a maximum increase of approximately 20 percent in $\dot{V}_{O_2max}$.[16-18] However, greater increases are possible if the initial physical fitness of the subject is low.[19,20] Only certain types of exercise promote the cardiac alterations necessary for increased $\dot{V}_{O_2max}$. Maximal stroke volume can be increased in response to a volume overload induced by participation in sports such as running, cycling, and swimming. However, in pressure-overload sports, such as weight lifting, left ventricular wall thickness increases with no increase in left ventricular volume.[21,22]

### Factors Limiting $\dot{V}_{O_2max}$

The limiting factor of $\dot{V}_{O_2max}$ has been a source of debate for many years. Proposed limiting factors include cardiac output, pulmonary ventilation, lung diffusion, and oxygen utilization.

A basic experimental design for determining if oxygen supply or utilization is the limiting factor involves artificially increasing the supply of oxygen to the working muscle. If maximal oxygen consumption does not change, it implies that the ability of the tissues to utilize oxygen is the limiting factor. On the other hand, if $\dot{V}_{O_2max}$ increases with artificial increase in $O_2$ to the muscles, cardiac output probably is the limiting factor. The majority of such studies suggest that cardiac output is the limiting factor for maximal aerobic capacity. $\dot{V}_{O_2max}$ is increased if the rate of oxygen supply to the muscle is increased through induced erythrocythemia (blood doping) or breathing 100 percent oxygen during exercise.[23-25] Another technique for investigating this question is to vary the amount of active tissue requiring increased oxygen during exercise. It has been found that adding active arm work during maximal treadmill exercise (which increases the amount of tissue that requires oxygen) does not increase $\dot{V}_{O_2max}$.[26] This finding, too, suggests that $\dot{V}_{O_2max}$ is limited primarily by cardiac output.

Although many exercisers use expressions such as "I was winded" or "my wind gave out on me," there is little evidence that pulmonary function limits aerobic capacity at sea level in healthy individuals. The lungs have a very large reserve that enables them to meet almost all the body's requirements for gas exchange and the regulation of acid-base balance during heavy exercise. There is considerable direct and indirect evidence for this: (1) the alveolar and capillary surface areas of the system are approximately 140 and 125 $m^2$, respectively, and the alveolar-capillary diffusion distance is no more than a few microns thick, providing the lung with an extremely large diffusion capacity; (2) the low pulmonary resistance to blood flow allows pulmonary blood volume to increase during heavy exercise by three times the value at rest; (3) during exercise, the ventilation-perfusion ratio increases four to five times that during rest; (4) the sigmoid shape of the oxyhemoglobin dissociation curve allows the maintenance of resting values of hemoglobin oxygen saturation even when $P_aO_2$ drops slightly; and (5) $P_aO_2$ changes very little during heavy exercise. This last statement strongly suggests that the lungs do not limit $\dot{V}_{O_2max}$, because $P_aO_2$ is probably the best indicator of lung function.[3,27]

Dempsy and Fregosi[27] presented evidence that the lungs may be limiting in some elite male endurance athletes, but no such evidence has been presented for elite female athletes. In their subjects, $P_aO_2$ dropped as low as 65 mmHg, and there was a significant widening in the difference between alveolar oxygen partial pressure ($P_{AO_2}$) and $P_aO_2$. They hypothesized that there was a diffusion limitation as well as increased airway impedence at high levels of ventilation in these athletes.

### $\dot{V}_{O_2max}$ as Predictor of Endurance Performance

If $\dot{V}_{O_2max}$ were the only predictor of endurance performance, then endurance contests could be decided in the laboratory by research scientists who administer treadmill tests rather than on the track, on the road, or in the swimming pool. However, $\dot{V}_{O_2max}$ is only one factor that determines success in endurance events. There is a high negative correlation between $\dot{V}_{O_2max}$ and finishing time in the marathon among women distance runners with varying amounts of experience.[28] This relationship does not exist when the sample is homogeneous (i.e., the runners are of the same ability level).[29,30] For example, Grete Waitz and Derek Clayton had $\dot{V}_{O_2max}$ values of 73 and 69 $mL \cdot kg^{-1} \cdot min^{-1}$, respectively, measured after they set world records for the women's and men's marathons. Yet, Clayton's time was over 15 minutes faster than Waitz's. Other factors, such as the ability to continue exercising at a high percentage of $\dot{V}_{O_2max}$, lactic acid clearance capacity, and performance economy, are also important and are probably the factors that determine success when aerobic capacities are similar.

A high $\dot{V}_{O_2max}$ is a prerequisite to performing at elite levels in endurance events. The minimum values for elite female endurance athletes are approximately 65 $mL \cdot kg^{-1}$ for runners and cross-country skiers, 55 to 60 $mL \cdot kg^{-1}$ for swimmers, and 60 $mL \cdot kg^{-1}$ for cyclists. The evidence for a minimum aerobic capacity requirement is circumstantial:

1. All elite endurance athletes have high aerobic capacities. Even though $\dot{V}_{O_2max}$ is a poor predictor of performance among athletes at the same level of competition, the variance in maximal aerobic power between them is small.
2. Oxygen consumption increases as a function of velocity in all endurance events. Although athletes vary somewhat in their efficiencies, the variance between them is small.

However, even though a high $\dot{V}_{O_2max}$ is critical to achieving superior levels of endurance, it is not the only requirement for success.

### Mitochondrial Density

While $\dot{V}_{O_2max}$ is the best measure of cardiovascular capacity and the ability to reach a high intensity during endurance exercise, mitochondrial density is a better predictor of endurance capacity. Endurance is the ability to sustain a particular submaximal level of physical effort. Davies and co-workers[31,32] showed that cytochrome oxidase activity (which is directly dependent upon mitochondrial mass) had a correlation coefficient of 0.92 with running endurance but only 0.70 with $\dot{V}_{O_2max}$. With training, $\dot{V}_{O_2max}$ increases by less than 20 percent in most individuals, yet the ability to sustain a given submaximal exercise intensity may increase severalfold. Endurance performance in sports such as cycling, running, swimming, and cross-country skiing requires the athlete to perform at a high intensity and to maintain that intensity for a prolonged period. Increased mitochondrial density may be the key factor that allows some athletes to run, cycle, or swim at high velocities longer than others, even though their maximal oxygen uptakes are similar.

Endurance training results in an increased mitochondrial density in fast-twitch and slow-twitch muscle fibers, and this probably plays a major role in improving endurance.[33-35] There are several possible mechanisms for this: (1) increased mitochondrial mass may increase fat utilization during exercise and thus spare muscle glycogen, and (2) it may improve the muscles' lactic acid clearance capacity and thus allow the athlete to exercise at a higher intensity.[33,36]

A fundamental purpose of energy metabolism during exercise is to generate ATP at a level commensurate with the requirements of the exercise intensity. If this is not accomplished, the athlete fatigues very quickly. The *rate* of ATP formation is critical. Even though fat provides the most energy per gram, carbohydrate, principally in the form of muscle glycogen, is the most important fuel for high-intensity endurance exercise because it provides the most ATP per liter of oxygen. Thus, carbohydrate provides ATP more quickly than does fat.[37]

There are at least two problems associated with the use of carbohydrates during endurance exercise: (1) the supply of carbohydrates is limited; and (2) the rapid use of carbohydrates during high-intensity exercise results in a rate of lactic acid production in excess of its rate of clearance, and this accumulation of lactic acid may interfere with muscle contraction and energy metabolism.[38,39] Increasing muscle mitochondrial mass may help the body cope with both of these problems.

It has been known for many years that the glycogen content of muscle is an important factor in determining endurance capacity.[40] When glycogen is depleted, fatigue results. During sustained exercise, muscle glycogen is the muscle's principal source of carbohydrate.[36] In addition, the rate of glycogen utilization increases as a function of exercise intensity. It is very important, then, for the athlete to conserve glycogen in order to maintain the intensity of exercise at the desired level. Endurance training, which results in an increased mitochondrial mass, increases the capacity of the muscle to oxidize fats.[41] This slows the rate of glycolysis and the catabolism of glucose and glycogen. Thus, glycogen is spared and fatigue delayed.

The increased mitochondrial mass accompanying training may also increase the muscle's ability to remove lactate through oxidation. For more than 50 years, lactic acid has been thought of by many as a metabolic pariah. However, recent work using radioactive tracer methodology has demonstrated that lactate is an important substrate during exercise.[36,39] These studies have shown that (1) during sustained exercise both lactate production and removal occur within active muscle and that most lactic acid produced during exercise is oxidized; (2) during endurance exercise, the turnover and oxidation rates of lactate exceed those of glucose; (3) lactate production during both rest and exercise is not necessarily associated with muscle anaerobiosis; and (4) training mainly affects the rate of lactate removal rather than its production.

The effects of the increased mitochondrial mass with training are complex but elegant. Glycogen is the critical fuel for endurance exercise, but its use increases the risk of its own depletion and lactic acid accumulation due to an excess of lactic acid production over clearance. The increased mitochondrial mass that results from training prevents lactic acid accumulation by providing the muscles with an increased capacity for lactic acid oxidation and prevents glycogen depletion by allowing an increased use of fats as fuel.

Training is probably not as important as genetics for obtaining a high mitochondrial mass in the muscles required for endurance exercise. Studies of successful male endurance athletes have shown that they tend to have a high percentage of slow-twitch muscle fibers in the muscles required for their sport; a high mitochondrial density is a characteristic of these fibers.[41,41] However, recent evidence presented by Tesch and Karlsson suggests that the greater percentage of slow-twitch fibers in the active muscles of endurance athletes may be an adaptive response.[43] As discussed, $\dot{V}_{O_2max}$ and mitochondrial density are not mutually exclusive because of the positive relationship between the two (i.e., athletes whose muscles have a high mitochondrial mass also have high $\dot{V}_{O_2max}$ values).

## Performance Efficiency

Although exercise intensity is the most important determinant of metabolic rate, individual differences in performance efficiency can be responsible for the difference between winning and losing. When power output can be measured accurately, efficiency can be calculated with the following equation:[44]

**(Eq. 5-3)**

$$\text{Efficiency} = \frac{\text{Change in power output}}{\text{Change in caloric equivalent of } O_2 \text{ consumption (100)}}$$

Obviously, efficiency is decreased by energy lost as heat, wasted movement, and mechanical factors such as wind resistance and friction. The efficiency of walking and cycle ergometry is slightly less than 30 percent.[44,45] It is probable that the efficiency of running, cycling, swimming, and cross-country skiing at competitive exercise intensities is less than that. High-intensity exercise is not performed at a steady rate, so $\dot{V}_{O_2}$ does not account for all of the ATP supplied during exercise; a portion is supplied through anaerobic glycolysis. Consequently, efficiency cannot be accurately calculated even when power output can be measured. However, from a practical point of view, the relative change in efficiency can be estimated by measuring the effects on oxygen consumption of factors such as wind resistance, mechanical aids (e.g., toe clips in cycling and wax in cross-country skiing), and technique. However, a fundamental problem is determining how much of the variance is accounted for by mechanical factors (i.e., technique) and physiologic factors (i.e., mitochondrial density). For example, if one runner appears to be more efficient than another, it is difficult to say whether the greater efficiency is due to a more efficient running style or to a superior lactic acid clearance capacity.

Other than metabolic considerations, technique is probably the most important factor affecting performance efficiency. In swimming, developing optimum hydrodynamics through the use of strokes that employ efficient propulsive force and that minimize drag may contribute almost as much to success as improving the physiologic aspects of endurance.[46] Likewise, the frequent use of "skating" in cross-country skiing has revolutionized the sport. Efficient runners are thought to have a lower vertical component in their technique and efficient cyclists pedal smoothly at high revolutions per minute without engaging muscle groups that do not contribute to pedaling speed.[47,48] Wind resistance is also a factor in running and cycling and can be modified by techniques such as drafting and by wearing clothing that enhances aerodynamics.

## Body Composition

The importance of body composition for endurance varies with the sport. For example, in distance running, in which the effects of gravity play a relatively greater role than in swimming or cycling, athletes tend to be leaner and the variance in body fat among elite performers tends to be less.[49–52] Typical fat percentages for female endurance athletes are shown in Table 5–1. Although the data are limited, as might be expected, all categories of female endurance athletes tend to be leaner than sedentary women of the same age. Swimmers tend to have more body fat than runners, cyclists, and cross-country skiers.

Tanaka and Matsuura[50] reported that anthropometric factors accounted for 20 to 40 percent of the variance in male distance runners, which is comparable to that portion of the variance accounted for by maximal oxygen consumption. However, it is important to remember that correlation coefficients describe relationships and do not necessarily indicate that one factor causes another. These investigators did not study female athletes. Most studies have found that female distance runners average 16 percent fat, although levels as low as 6 percent have been reported. Christensen and Ruhling[28] have found that female marathon runners continue to become leaner the longer they par-

**Table 5–1.** BODY COMPOSITION OF ELITE FEMALE ENDURANCE ATHLETES

| Sport | Percent Fat | Researchers |
|---|---|---|
| Distance running | 15.2 | Wilmore and Behnke[79] |
| Distance running | 16.9 | Wilmore et al.[52] |
| Distance running | 15.3 | Christensen and Ruhling[28] |
| Cross-country skiing | 21.8 | Rusko et al.[80] |
| Cross-country skiing | 16.1 | Sinning et al.[81] |
| Cycling | 15.4 | Burke[17] |
| Swimming | 18.1 | Tittle and Wutscherk[82] |
| Swimming | 17.8 | Farmosi[83] |
| Swimming | 13.7 | Dessein[84] |
| Swimming | 15.6 | Meleski et al.[85] |
| Swimming | 16.6 | Malina et al.[49] |

ticipate in the sport—novice marathon runners were found to have 18 percent fat, experienced marathoners had 16.3 percent, and elite marathoners had 15.3 percent. The average body fat percentage of a young adult woman in the United States is 25 percent.

In running, cycling, and cross-country skiing, excess fat increases the energy cost of exercise, but the ideal lower limit of body fat is not known. The 40 to 60 percent difference between men and women in $\dot{V}_{O_{2}max}$, expressed in liters per minute, is reduced to less than 10 percent when the value is expressed per kilogram lean body mass.[53] So, on the surface it appears that extremely low levels of body fat are desirable. On the other hand, world distance running records have been set by women with greater than 15 percent fat. In addition, extremely low levels of body fat in female endurance athletes (along with the training and dietary habits necessary to achieve low body fat) may affect other aspects of physiology, such as endocrine and reproductive function, as well as bone metabolism. These problems are discussed elsewhere in this volume.

It is possible that the higher percentage of body fat found in female swimmers compared with that of other endurance athletes may be an advantage. When swimming at comparable velocities, women demonstrate a lower body drag than men (probably due to their greater amounts of subcutaneous fat), which makes women more efficient at the sport. Obviously, the ideal fat percentage of the female swimmer is also affected by the optimum body size and shape, functional capacity, and stroke mechanics of the athlete. Rennie and coworkers[54] have hypothesized that women could swim faster than men if they could develop comparable physical capacities. This seems more plausible when one considers that there is a 10 percent difference in the world record time between men and women in the 1500 meter run and only a 6 percent difference between them in the 400 meter swim. Top women swimmers today are swimming faster than did 1972 Olympic champion Mark Spitz.

## SEX DIFFERENCES IN ENDURANCE PERFORMANCE

Women's performance times are 6 to 15 percent longer than those for men in most endurance sports (Table 5–2).[55,56] However, there is considerable variance in performance in specific events. In the 400 meter swim, the difference between the men's and women's world record is slightly more than 6 percent, while the difference in the 80 km run is almost 44 percent. Although men rode longer distances in the 1984 Olympic cycling road race competition (79.2 km for women and 190.2 km for men), the average velocity of the winning man was only 5 percent faster than that of the winning woman. It is difficult to determine true sex differences from performance comparisons because some of these events, such as the 80 km run, are not contested very often by women. Likewise, when scrutinizing the literature, it is difficult to summarize and quantify physiologic sex differences, because physically fit male subjects often were compared with sedentary female subjects.

Body size and composition are probably the most important factors determining the sex differences in endurance performance. Greater size provides a greater power output capacity. Men tend to have more muscle mass, both in relative and absolute terms, while women tend to have more fat. Obviously, greater lean body mass is an asset, whereas greater fat weight is a hindrance. Although muscle fiber composition is similar between the sexes, both fast- and slow-twitch muscle fibers tend to be larger in men.[57]

**Table 5–2.** COMPARISON BETWEEN MALE AND FEMALE GOLD MEDAL ENDURANCE PERFORMANCE TIMES IN THE 1984 OLYMPICS

| Event | Performance Time | |
| --- | --- | --- |
| | *Males* | *Females* |
| **Athletics (Track and Field)** | | |
| 800 m run | 1:43.00 | 1:57.60 |
| 1500 m run | 3:32.53 | 4:03.25 |
| Marathon | 2:09.21 | 2:24.52 |
| **Canoeing** | | |
| 500 m | 1:47.84 | 1:58.72 |
| **Swimming** | | |
| 200 m freestyle | 1:47.44 | 1:59.23 |
| 400 m freestyle | 3:51.23 | 4:07.10 |
| 200 m butterfly stroke | 1:57.04 | 2:06.90 |
| 200 m breaststroke | 2:13.34 | 2:30.38 |
| 200 m backstroke | 2:00.23 | 2:12.38 |

Absolute maximal oxygen consumption ($L \cdot min^{-1}$) is more than 40 percent greater in the average man than in the average woman. However, this difference is reduced to approximately 20 percent when $\dot{V}_{O2max}$ is expressed per kilogram body weight and to less than 10 percent when expressed per kilogram lean body weight.[58] Although excess fat is a handicap to women endurance athletes, it does not appear to account for all of the differences in performance. Cureton and Sparling[59] added extra weight to men in an attempt experimentally to equalize fat masses. Although they were able to completely abolish the differences between men and women in relative $\dot{V}_{O2max}$, there remained sex differences in distance run in 12 minutes, maximum treadmill run time, and running efficiency of 30, 31, and 20 percent, respectively, after the experimental intervention. They estimated that fat percentage accounts for 74 percent of the sex differences in running performance, while the higher $\dot{V}_{O2max}$ of men (relative to lean body mass) accounted for 20 percent.

The average man has a larger heart size and heart volume than the average woman (in both absolute and relative terms), and this results in a greater stroke volume during maximal exercise and contributes to the sex differences in $\dot{V}_{O2max}$. Even though women have a higher relative heart rate during exercise, it is not enough to compensate for their lower stroke volume. The resultant smaller cardiac output of women contributes to their lower aerobic capacity. Both the amount and concentration of hemoglobin are higher in men, thus giving their blood greater oxygen-carrying capacity. Women average about 13.7 g Hb/dL, where men average 15.8 g Hb/dL. The difference is attributed to the stimulating effect of androgens on hemoglobin production and to the effects of menstrual blood loss and differences in dietary intake.[3] (See Chapter 7.)

Of the other major factors that may account for individual differences in endurance performance, there do not seem to be any substantial sex differences. Most studies show that there are no sex differences in the percent of $\dot{V}_{O2max}$ sustained during exercise.[60,61] In addition, although there is some disagreement among researchers, there do not seem to be any appreciable sex differences in performance efficiency in either running or cycling.[62] To date, there have been no definitive studies on sex differences in lactate production and clearance rates, or in the lactate inflection point (sometimes incorrectly referred to as the anaerobic threshold). There do not appear to be any substantial sex differences in temperature regulation capacity between the sexes when a serious attempt has been made by the researchers to use subjects of equal fitness. Finally, there do not seem to be any sex differences in the ability to improve $\dot{V}_{O2max}$ through training, nor in the ability to improve endurance performance through interval and continuous exercise programs.[63]

Ullyot[64] hypothesized that the higher body fat of women could be an advantage during marathon and ultramarathon endurance events, because it may provide women with a greater capacity for fat metabolism. This was based on the empirical observation that many women runners do not seem to "hit the wall" (exhibit sudden extreme fatigue that is probably related to glycogen depletion) during marathon running as do most male runners. A study by Costill and associates[65] did not support this hypothesis. They showed that in equally trained subjects during a 1-hour treadmill run, the capacity to use fat as fuel was similar in men and women.[65] In addition, they demonstrated that muscle succinate dehydrogenase and carnitine palmitoyl transferase activities were higher in the men, suggesting that the muscle mitochondrial density in the male subjects may have been greater.

## TRAINING FOR ENDURANCE

Training is an adaptive process. Unfortunately, athletes often forget this simple fact and attempt overzealous training programs with no real thought as to how their bodies will respond to them. Consequently, they often overtrain and either fail to improve at a desirable rate or become injured.

Selye[66] formulated a theory of stress adaptation, which has tremendous implications for conditioning endurance athletes. Selye called his theory the general adaptation syndrome (GAS). He described three processes involved in the response to a stressor: (1) alarm reaction, (2) resistance development, and (3) exhaustion. In the alarm reaction, the body mobilizes its resources. During exercise, this phase of GAS is characterized by an increased cardiac output, redistribution of blood to active muscle, and an increased metabolic rate. The resistance development stage, which can also be called the adaptive stage, occurs when fitness is increased and is the purpose of the endurance training program. The athlete must exercise at a threshold intensity in order to obtain an adaptive response. This threshold is individual and is much higher in elite athletes than in sedentary people. When a stress cannot be tolerated, the athlete enters the stage of exhaustion. This stress can be either acute or chronic. Symptoms of acute exhaustion include fractures, sprains, and strains, while chronic exhaustion is characterized by stress fractures, staleness, and emotional stress. Based on GAS, the basic purpose of the training program is to train hard enough to get an adaptive response and improve fitness but not so hard as to become injured.

The body adapts specifically to the stress of exercise.[67] While this obviously implies that athletes should develop the type of fitness required in their sport as a whole (i.e., runners should run and weight lifters should lift weights), the training program should also reflect the various components of the activity. For example, if a runner or cyclist must go up hills in competition, then she should include hill-running or -cycling in her program.

The varying force requirements encountered during exercise are met by recruiting the number of motor units needed to perform the task. Because a motor unit is trained in proportion to its recruitment, it is critical that the motor units that will be used in competition be trained regularly.[68] Therefore, a runner who hopes to run repeated 6-minute miles in competition must include a portion of her training at race pace or faster in order to condition the motor units that will be recruited during the race. The frequency of different types of training depends upon the relative importance of their target motor units. So, while repeated short sprints may be the central component of a 100-meter runner, they would be much less valuable for a distance runner.

## Components of Overload

The amount of overload (training stimulus) in the training program can be varied by manipulating four basic factors: intensity (speed), volume (number of repetitions), du-

ration (distance of each repetition), and rest (rest between repetitions). There is an interaction among all of these factors: a change in any factor affects the others. For example, if the intensity (speed) is increased, volume and duration will probably have to be decreased and rest increased. The application of each factor depends on factors such as experience, time of year, health, goals, and environment.

Intensity is perhaps the most critical of the basic overload factors. As discussed, the optimum intensity during endurance exercise is tied to carbohydrate metabolism. If the intensity is too great, lactic acid production exceeds clearance capacity, the athlete fatigues very quickly, and recovery is more difficult. In addition, valuable glycogen stores are rapidly depleted. However, if the pace is too slow, then the athlete does not perform up to potential and probably loses the race or does not reach the desired level of physical conditioning.

There have been numerous attempts by researchers to identify physiologic markers of the ideal exercise intensity. These markers include blood lactate, heart rate, ventilation, perceived exertion, and percentage of maximum effort. During graded exercise (exercise in which the intensity increases gradually toward maximum), there is an exercise intensity above which blood lactate levels rise very rapidly. Some researchers have called this lactate inflection point the "anaerobic threshold."[69] According to this theory, lactic acid is produced to compensate for an inadequate supply of oxygen. This results in disproportionate increases in the concentration of blood lactic acid and pulmonary ventilation. As discussed, isotope tracer studies have shown that lactate accumulation during exercise is due to an excess of lactate production over clearance rather than to a sudden onset of anaerobic metabolism. The anaerobic threshold theory is based upon observations of blood lactate concentrations during exercise. However, blood lactate concentrations provide no information about how fast it is produced or cleared by the tissues. While controversy continues to surround this topic, the majority of evidence indicates that the anaerobic threshold theory is fallacious. However, under certain circumstances (i.e., when the athletes are rested and are consuming a diet with constant proportions of carbohydrates, fats, and proteins), the lactate inflection point can accurately predict performance in endurance events and can be correlated with physiologic factors easier to measure, such as heart rate and ventilation.[69-72] However, even though these measures can be used to predict performance, this does not necessarily mean that they can accurately predict the ideal training intensity.

Does this mean that the great "anaerobic threshold debate" is nothing more than nitpicking? If the athlete on the field does not really care about the mechanism of lactate kinetics, why not use some of the tools of the anaerobic threshold theory even though its theoretical foundations are unsound? The answer is that the relationships between lactate inflection, heart rate, ventilation, and perceived exertion break down under a variety of circumstances, which could severely damage the athlete's progress and possibly lead to injury.[73,74] For example, glycogen depletion causes the lactate inflection point (the exercise intensity at which the blood lactate concentration abruptly increases) to shift to the right (to a greater percentage of maximum). Using the lactate inflection point as a marker for determining exercise intensity could cause athletes to train harder at a time when they are glycogen depleted and possibly more susceptible to injury. Costill and Miller[75] have shown that heavy training on consecutive days leads to progressive glycogen depletion unless the athletes consume a diet composed of 70 percent carbohydrate. Most athletes have a great deal of difficulty staying on such a diet due to family dietary habits and inadequate knowledge of nutrition. So it is likely that the lactate inflection point is an unreliable guideline for the athlete in training.

The best programs are those that work the athlete through a range of distances and intensities according to the requirements of the sport. Rather than using esoteric physiologic markers, such as lactate inflection point, athletes should use three simple measures that are based on the desired outcome of the program: exercise heart rate, percentages of race pace, and perceived exertion. Exercise heart rate helps the athlete select a pace that is proportional to oxygen consumption. Training at various percentages of race pace (submaximal and supramaximal paces) will effectively and systematically train motor units that are recruited at varying exercise inten-

sities. Perceived exertion helps the athlete adjust the training program in response to injury, illness, glycogen depletion, overtraining, and environmental stress.

The program should consist of two basic components: over-distance training and interval training. The purpose of over-distance training (long, slow distance) is to increase or maintain $\dot{V}_{O_2max}$ and to increase tissue respiratory capacity (by increasing muscle mitochondrial density). As discussed, mitochondrial density is better correlated with endurance capacity than is $\dot{V}_{O_2max}$ and is probably the major beneficiary of over-distance conditioning. Because of the principle of specificity, it is important that a segment of this distance training be conducted close to race pace.

Interval training involves periods of intense exercise interspersed with rest. The nature of the interval training program varies with the distance of competition. Athletes involved in the shorter, faster races will tend to use shorter, more intense intervals than those involved in longer, slower races. The benefits of interval training are that it increases $\dot{V}_{O_2max}$ (by increasing maximal cardiac output) and mitochondrial density (to a lesser extent than over-distance training does), teaches pace, builds speed, and improves lactate removal.

## Principles of Training

Nine principles of endurance training are listed in Table 5-3. They are explicit instruc-

**Table 5-3.** PRINCIPLES OF ENDURANCE TRAINING

1. Train all year round.
2. Get in shape gradually.
3. Listen to your body.
4. Begin with over-distance training before progressing to interval training.
5. Cycle your training: Incorporate load, peak, and recovery cycles.
6. Do not overtrain; rest the day before competition.
7. Train systematically.
8. Train the mind.
9. Put sport in its proper perspective.

Modified from Noakes.[56]

tions for applying the general adaptation syndrome to the training of endurance athletes and will result in improved performance with a minimum risk of injury.

The first principle is to train all year round. Athletes lose a tremendous amount of fitness through deconditioning. They are much more susceptible to injury if they try to get in shape rapidly during the competitive season. The next principle is related to the first: Get in shape gradually. The athlete should give her body time to adapt to the stress of exercise. Overzealous training leads to injury and overtraining.

"Listen to your body," the third principle, is familiar to anyone who has ever read a book or article on exercise. While the expression is a bit weathered, it is true nevertheless. The athlete should not adhere to her preplanned program too dogmatically. Sometimes her body needs rest more than exercise. Most studies show that the absolute intensity is perhaps the most important factor in improving fitness. An overtrained athlete is typically not recovered enough to train at the optimal intensity, in which case a few day's rest sometimes will allow her to recover enough to train more intensely. On the other hand, she should still try to follow a structured program.

Endurance athletes should train first for distance and only later for speed. This is the fourth training principle. Soft tissues require a great deal of time to adjust to the rigors of training, with ligaments and tendons adjusting very slowly to the stresses of exercise.[76] It is important to prepare the body for heavy training, or injury may result.

The fifth training principle suggests that athletes should cycle the volume and intensity of their workouts. The practice of alternating between hard and easy training days is an application of cycle training (also called periodization of training). Cycle training allows the body to recover more fully and to train hard when hard training is required. Athletes should incorporate base and peak cycles (workouts) into the competitive strategy. These cycles are groups of workouts practiced to gradually improve fitness (base) or increase sharpness for competition (peak). Base or load cycles are characterized by high volume with varying intensity, whereas peak cycles employ low volume and high-intensity workouts with plenty of rest. Peak cycles are designed to produce maximum performance. The base or load cycle is the foundation for peak performance. However, peak fitness can be maintained for only a short period of time; every peak is gained at the price of deconditioning. Both cycles are important. The successes of the peaks make the hard work of the base period seem worthwhile.

One of the most difficult training principles to adhere to is "do not overtrain," because it contradicts the work ethic that is ingrained in so many athletes. It is important for the athlete to think of conditioning for endurance events as a multiyear process. Adaptations to training take place very gradually. Excessive training tends to lead to overtraining and overuse injuries rather than accelerated development of fitness. It is important that athletes avoid excessive competition because numerous studies have shown that considerable muscle damage occurs during long-distance races, as indicated by extremely elevated levels of plasma creatine phosphokinase measured in athletes after races.[77] Competing too frequently results in an inability to recover, which decreases the overall level of conditioning.

The seventh training principle tells the athlete to train systematically. The athlete should plan an approximate workout schedule for the coming year (or even the next 4 years), month, and week. Of course, she should not be so rigid that she cannot change the program owing to unforeseen circumstances. The important thing is that she apply the stresses of exercise in a manner that will produce a consistent increase in fitness. Three things that will help her workouts become more systematic are coaching, training partners, and a training diary. Coaching helps the athlete meet her competitive goals. A good coach is knowledgeable and experienced and can keep her from repeating common training mistakes made by others; the coach will also help motivate the athlete. Training partners are important for motivation and competition. The training diary will help the athlete to formulate her goals and to keep track of which training techniques work and which do not.

Training the mind is as important as training the body. Successful athletes believe in themselves and their potential; they have goals and know how to achieve these goals.[78] In endurance training in particular, the athlete must be patient and be content with continuous small improvements over many years.

Finally, sports should be put in their proper perspective. Too often, athletes think of themselves solely as runners, cyclists, or swimmers rather than as human beings who participate in those activities. Although sports are important, the athlete must also have time for her family and other aspects of life that are important to her.

## SUMMARY

The determining factors of endurance performance include maximal oxygen consumption, mitochondrial density, performance efficiency, and body composition. Maximal oxygen consumption is the body's maximum ability to transport and use oxygen and is largely determined by the cardiac output capacity. It can be improved by about 20 percent through training, so a high initial value is critical for success in endurance events. Mitochondrial density is highly correlated to endurance capacity and provides the athlete with a high oxidative capacity and the ability to use fats as fuel during exercise. Efficiency is determined by physiologic factors such as mitochondrial density, but also by mechanical factors such as technique and wind resistance. The importance of body composition for endurance varies with the sport. In sports such as running, cycling, and cross-country skiing, additional fat increases the energy cost of exercise, but the ideal lower limit of body fat is not known. In long-distance swimmers, a slightly higher than normal fat percentage decreases drag in the water and provides insulation against the cold.

While sex differences exist in endurance performance, the relative changes that occur with training and the basic underlying mechanisms that determine performance are the same in men and women. Women trail men by 6 to 15 percent in most endurance sports, but there is considerable variance in performance in specific events. It is difficult to summarize and quantify physiologic sex differences reported in the literature because physically fit male subjects were often compared with sedentary female subjects.

Training is an adaptive process. It is important that athletes not become involved in overzealous training programs that often lead to injury. The body adapts specifically to the stress of exercise, so the training program should also reflect the various components of the activity. The amount of overload in the training program can be varied by manipulating four basic factors: intensity, volume, duration, and rest, with intensity being the most important for achieving high levels of performance. The best measures of intensity during training are exercise heart rate, percentages of race pace, and perceived exertion. Endurance athletes should use a combination of interval and over-distance training techniques.

## References

1. MacFadden B: MacFadden's Encyclopedia of Physical Culture. MacFadden Publications, New York, 1928, p 1092.
2. American College of Sports Medicine: Encyclopedia of Sport Sciences and Medicine. MacMillan, New York, 1971.
3. Brooks GA, and Fahey TD: Exercise Physiology: Human Bioenergetics and its Applications. MacMillan, New York, 1984.
4. Braunwald E, Ross J, and Sonnenblick EH: Mechanism of contraction of the normal and failing heart. N Engl J Med 277:794, 1967.
5. Bhan A, and Scheuer J: Effects of physical training on cardiac myosin ATPase activity. J Physiol 228:1178, 1975.
6. Scheuer J, and Tipton CM: Cardiovascular adaptations to physical training. Ann Rev Physiol 39:221, 1977.
7. Stromme SB, and Ingjer F: The effect of regular physical training on the cardiovascular system. Scand J Soc Med 29 (Suppl):37, 1982.
8. Zeldis SM, Morganroth J, and Rubler S: Cardiac hypertrophy in response to dynamic conditioning in female athletes. J Appl Physiol 44:849, 1978.
9. Barnard J, Edgerton VR, Furukawa T, et al: Histochemical, biochemical, and contractile properties of red, white, and intermediate fibers. Am J Physiol 220:410, 1971.
10. Gohil K, Jones DA, Corbucci GG, et al: Mitochondrial substrate oxidation, muscle composition, and plasma metabolite levels in marathon runners. In Knuttgen HG, Vogel GA, and Poortmans J (eds): Biochemistry of Exercise. Human Kinetics, Champaign, IL, 1982, p 286.
11. Booth FW, and Narahara KA: Vastus lateralis cytochrome oxidase activity and its relationship to maximal oxygen consumption in man. Pflugers Arch 349:319, 1974.
12. Ivy JL, Costill DL, and Maxwell BD: Skeletal muscle determinants of maximal aerobic power in man. Eur J Appl Physiol 44:1, 1980.
13. Bouchard C, and Lortie G: Heredity and endurance performance. Sports Med 1:38, 1984.
14. Klissouras V, Pirnay F, and Petit J-M: Adaptation to maximal effort: Genetics and age. J Appl Physiol 1:195, 1976.

15. Komi PV, and Karlsson J: Physical performance, skeletal muscle enzyme activities, and fiber types in monozygous and dizygous twins of both sexes. Acta Physiol Scand 462(Suppl):462, 1979.

16. Kearney JJ, Stull GA, Ewing JL, et al: Cardiorespiratory responses of sedentary college women as a function of training intensity. J Appl Physiol 41:822, 1976.

17. Burke EJ: Physiological effects of similar training programs in males and females. Res Q 48:510, 1977.

18. Hanson JS, and Nedde WH: Long-term physical training effect in sedentary females. J Appl Physiol 37:112, 1974.

19. Hickson RC, Bomze HA, and Holloszy JO: Linear increase in aerobic power induced by strenuous exercise. J Appl Physiol 42:372, 1977.

20. Lewis S, Haskell WL, Wood PD, et al: Effects of physical activity on weight reduction in obese middle-aged women. Am J Clin Nutr 29:151, 1976.

21. Schaible TF, and Scheuer J: Response of the heart to exercise training. In Zak R (ed): Growth of the Heart in Health and Disease. Raven Press, New York, 1984, p 381.

22. Longhurst JC, Kelly AR, Gonyea WJ, et al: Echocardiographic left ventricular masses in distance runners and weight lifters. J Appl Physiol 48:154, 1980.

23. Ekblom B, Goldbarg AN, and Gullbring B: Response to exercise after blood loss and reinfusion. J Appl Physiol 33:175, 1972.

24. Gledhill N: Blood doping and related issues: A brief review. Med Sci Sports 14:183, 1982.

25. Fagraeus L: Cardiorespiratory and metabolic functions during exercise in the hyperbaric environment. Acta Physiol Scand 92(Suppl 414):1, 1974.

26. Thiart BF, and Blaauw JH: The $\dot{V}_{O_2}$max and the active muscle mass. South African Journal for Research in Sport, Physical Education and Recreation 2:13, 1979.

27. Dempsy JA, and Fregosi RF: Adaptability of the pulmonary system to changing metabolic requirements. Am J Cardiol 55:59D, 1985.

28. Christensen CL, and Ruhling RO: Physical characteristics of novice and experienced women marathon runners. Br J Sports Med 17:166, 1983.

29. Costill DL, and Winrow E: Maximal oxygen intake among marathon runners. Arch Phys Med Rehab 51:317, 1970.

30. Pollock ML: Submaximal and maximal working capacity of elite distance runners. Part 1. Cardiorespiratory aspects. Ann NY Acad Sci 301:361, 1977.

31. Davies KJA, Packer L, and Brooks GA: Biochemical adaptation of mitochondria, muscle, and whole-animal respiration to endurance training Arch Biochem Biophys 209:538, 1981.

32. Davies KJA, Maguire JJ, Brooks GA, et al: Muscle mitochondrial bioenergetics, oxygen supply, and work capacity during dietary iron deficiency and repletion. Am J Physiol (Endocrinol Metab) 5:E418, 1982.

33. Holloszy JO: Adaptation of skeletal muscle to endurance exercise. Med Sci Sports 7:155, 1975.

34. Gollnick PD, and King DW: Effect of exercise and training on mitochondria of rat skeletal muscle. Am J Physiol 216:1502, 1969.

35. Baldwin K, Klinkerfuss G, Terjung R, et al: Respirator capacity of white, red, and intermediate muscle: adaptive response to exercise. Am J Physiol 22:373, 1972.

36. Donovan CM, and Brooks GA: Training affects lactate clearance not lactate production. Am J Physiol 244:E83, 1983.

37. Hill TL: Free Energy Transductions in Biology. Academic Press, New York, 1977.

38. Gollnick PD, Bayly WM, and Hodgson DR: Exercise intensity, training, diet, and lactate concentration in muscle and blood. Med Sci Sports Exerc 18:334, 1986.

39. Brooks GA: The lactate shuttle during exercise and recovery. Med Sci Sports Exerc 18:360, 1986.

40. Bergstrom J, and Hultman E: A study of the glycogen metabolism during exercise in man. Scand J Clin Invest 19:218, 1967.

41. Gollnick PD, and Saltin B: Hypothesis: Significance of skeletal muscle oxidative enzyme enhancement with endurance training. Clin Physiol 2:1, 1983.

42. Saltin B, Henriksson J, Hygaard E, et al: Fiber types and metabolic potentials of skeletal muscles in sedentary man and endurance runners. NY Acad Sci 301:3, 1977.

43. Tesch PA, and Karlsson J: Muscle fiber types and size in trained and untrained muscles of elite athletes. J Appl Physiol 59:1716, 1985.

44. Gaesser GA, and Brooks GA: Muscular efficiency during steady-rate exercise: effects of speed and work rate. J Appl Physiol 38:1132, 1975.

45. Donovan CM, and Brooks GA: Muscular efficiency during steady-rate exercise. II. Effects of walking speed on work rate. J Appl Physiol 43:431, 1977.

46. Holmer I: Energy cost of the arm stroke, leg kick, and whole stroke in competitive swimming style. J Appl Physiol 33:105, 1974.

47. Margaria R, Cerretelli P, and Aghems P: Energy cost of running. J Appl Physiol 18:367, 1963.

48. Faria IE: Applied physiology of cycling. Sports Med 1:187, 1984.

49. Malina RM, Muellere WH, Bouchard C, et al: Fatness and fat patterning among athletes at the Montreal Olympic Games, 1976. Med Sci Sports Exerc 14:445, 1982.

50. Tanaka K, and Matsuura Y: A multivariate analysis of the role of certain anthropometric and physiological attributes in distance running. Ann Hum Biol 9:473, 1982.

51. Fleck SJ: Body composition of elite American athletes. Am J Sports Med 11:398, 1983.

52. Wilmore JH, Brown CH, and Davis JA: Body physique and composition of the female distance runner. Ann NY Acad Sci

53. Sady SP, and Freedson PS: Body composition and structural comparisons of female and male athletes. Clin Sports Med. 3:755, 1984.

54. Rennie DW, Pendergast, DR, and di Prampero PE: Energetics of swimming in man. In Clarys JP and Lewillie L (eds): Swimming II. Baltimore: University Park Press, 1975, p 97.

55. International Olympic Committee: Games of the XXIIIrd Olympiad Los Angeles 1984 Commemorative Book. Salt Lake City: International Sport Publications, 1984.

56. Noakes T: Lore of Running. Cape Town: Oxford University Press, 1985.

57. Wells CL, and Plowman SA: Sex differences in athletic performance: biological and behavioral. Phys Sports Med 11(8):52, 1983.

58. Sparling PB: A meta-analysis of studies comparing

maximal oxygen uptake in men and women. Res Q. 51:542, 1980.

59. Cureton KJ, and Sparling PB: Distance running performance and metabolic responses to running in men and women with excess weight experimentally equated. Med Sci Sports Exerc 12:288, 1980.

60. Davies CTM, and Thompson MW: Aerobic performance of female marathon and male ultra-marathon athletes. Eur J Appl Physiol 41:233, 1979.

61. Conley DL, Krahenbuhl GS, Burkett LN, et al: Physiological correlates of female road racing performance. Res Q 52:441, 1981.

62. Pate RR, and Kriska A: Physiological basis of the sex difference in cardiorespiratory endurance. Sports Med 1:87, 1984.

63. Eddy DO, Sparks KL, and Adelizi DA: The effects of continuous and interval training in women and men. Eur J Appl Physiol 37:83, 1977.

64. Ullyot J: Women's secret weapon. In VanAaken E: VanAaken Method. World Publications, Mountain View, CA, 1976.

65. Costill DL, Fink WJ, Getchell LH, et al: Lipid metabolism in skeletal muscle of endurance-trained males and females. J Appl Physiol 47:787, 1979.

66. Selye H: The Stress of Life. McGraw Hill, New York, 1976.

67. Henry FM: The evolution of the memory drum theory of neuromotor reaction. In Brooks GA (ed): Perspectives on the Academic Discipline of Physical Education. Human Kinetics Publishers, Champaign, IL, 1981.

68. Edgerton VR: Mammalian muscle fiber types and their adaptability. American Zoology 18:113, 1976.

69. Davis JA: Anaerobic threshold: review of the concept and directions for future research. Med Sci Sports Exerc 17:6, 1985.

70. Farrell PA, Wilmore JH, Coyle EF, et al: Plasma lactate accumulation and distance running performance. Med Sci Sports 11:338, 1979.

71. Kumagai S, Tanaka K, Matsuura Y, et al: Relationships of the anaerobic threshold with the 5 km., 10 km., and 10 mile races. Eur J Appl Physiol 49:13, 1982.

72. Conconi F, Ferrare M, Ziglio PG, et al: Determination of the anaerobic threshold by a non-invasive field test in runners. J Appl Physiol 52:869, 1982.

73. Hughes EF, Turner SC, and Brooks GA: Effects of glycogen depletion and pedaling speed on "anaerobic threshold." J Appl Physiol 52:1598, 1982.

74. Brooks GA: Anaerobic threshold: review of the concept and directions for future research. Med Sci Sports Exerc 17:22, 1985.

75. Costill DL, and Miller JM: Nutrition for endurance sport: carbohydrate and fluid balance. International Journal of Sports Medicine 1:2, 1980.

76. Tipton CM, Matthes RD, Maynard JA, et al: The influence of physical activity on ligaments and tendons. Med Sci Sports 7:165, 1975.

77. Strachan AF, Noakes TD, Kotzenberg G, et al: Creative protein levels during long-distance running. Br Med J 289:1249, 1984.

78. Fahey TD: Getting Into the Olympic Form. Butterick Publishing, New York, 1980.

79. Wilmore JH, and Behnke AR: An anthropometric estimation of body density and lean body weight in young women. Am J Clin Nutr 23(26):7, 1970.

80. Rusko H, Hara M, and Karvinen E: Aerobic performance capacity in athletes. Eur J Appl Physiol 38:151, 1978.

81. Sinning WE, Cunningham LN, Racaniello AP, et al: Body composition and somatotype of male and female Nordic skiers. Res Q 48:741, 1977.

82. Tittle K, and Wutscherk H: Sportanthropometrie. Johann Ambrosius Barth, Leipzig, 1964, pp 1–126.

83. Farmosi I: Az úszónök testalkatának és teljesítményének összefüggése. In Lásló N (ed): A Sport és Testnevelés Idöszerü Kérdései—23. Sport, Budapest, 1980, p 77.

84. Dessein M: Studie van enkele zwemtechnisch gebonden componenten en in het bijzonder van somatische karakteristieken. Licentiaat. Katholieke Universitait te Leuven, Leuven, 1981, p 66.

85. Meleski BW, Shoup RF, and Malina RM: Size, physique and body composition of competitive female swimmers 11 through 20 years of age. Hum Biol 54:609, 1982.

# CHAPTER 6

# Bone Concerns

EVERETT L. SMITH, Ph.D.

The skeleton is a dynamic tissue, constantly changing to perform its two functions: providing structural support and acting as a mineral reservoir. Two homeostatic mechanisms act on plasma calcium and skeletal mineral simultaneously: hormones and mechanical stress. The structural support function of the skeleton permits movement and protects vital organs. As a reservoir, the skeleton responds to changes in hormone levels and helps to maintain blood calcium at about 9.8 mg/dL (Table 6–1).[1] Because of the skeleton's dual role, structural integrity is jeopardized when the demands on the reservoir are too high. When dietary calcium is inadequate, calcium is mobilized from the bone to maintain serum calcium. If the inadequacy is chronic, calcium will be pulled continually from the bone reservoir, resulting in a net loss of calcium and phosphorus. Mechanical stress through weight bearing and muscle contraction plays a significant role in maintaining skeletal structural integrity, as bone mineral content adapts to the mechanical stresses applied. Under balanced conditions, the hormonal and mechanical homeostatic mechanisms maintain both skeletal integrity and serum calcium. With aging, however, multiple factors (involving diet, hormonal levels, and mechanical stress) commonly precipitate bone involution, resulting in bone that is more susceptible to fracture and osteoporosis.

Hormones and mechanical stress interact in maintaining body and skeletal functions (Fig. 6–1). If stress to specific skeletal segments or to the skeleton as a whole is reduced, bone mass declines. The mobilization

**Table 6–1.** SERUM CALCIUM HOMEOSTATIS

| Condition | Hormonal Response | Metabolic Adaptation to Condition |
|---|---|---|
| Low serum calcium | Increased PTH | Increased fractional calcium absorption. Decreased renal excretion of calcium. Increased active form of vitamin D. Increased bone resorption. |
| High serum calcium | Decreased PTH Increased calcitonin | Decreased fractional calcium absorption. Increased renal excretion of calcium. Decreased active form of vitamin D. Decreased bone resorption. |
| Decreased gonadal function | Decreased gonadal hormones | Decreased fractional calcium absorption. Increased sensitivity of bone to PTH. |

*From Smith and Raab,[1] with permission.

of calcium from bone increases serum levels, decreases parathyroid levels and 1,25-(OH)$_2$ vitamin D, and thus decreases calcium absorption in the intestinal tract and increases calcium elimination from the kidneys. Long-term inactivity can significantly reduce bone mass and threaten the integrity of skeletal structure. Thus, skeletal integrity can be jeopardized by poor diet or inactivity.

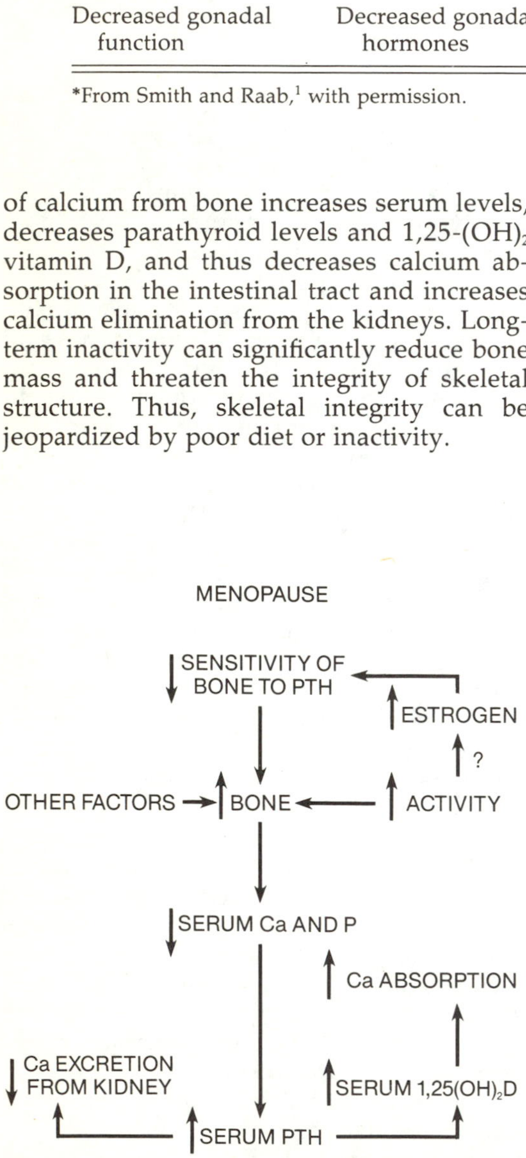

*Figure 6–1. Serum calcium homeostasis. Hormonal system is designed to maintain serum calcium within a 3 percent range for the individual (population normal values approximately 8.9 to 10.4 mg/dL). (From Smith and Raab,[1] with permission.)*

## INCIDENCE AND COST OF OSTEOPOROSIS

Osteoporosis is a major public health problem, affecting more than 20 million people in the United States. Osteoporosis causes 1.3 million fractures at a cost of 3.8 billion dollars each year.[2] Bone loss occurs primarily on the endosteal surface, with some loss on the periosteal surface. In conjunction with this decreased bone mass, the internal structure of bone also changes. Osteons are decreased in size and increased in number. Micropetrosis increases with lacunae filled by calcium depositions. These anatomic changes, in addition to the decreased bone mineral content, contribute to a greater fracture potential. Peak bone mass is reached at about age 35 in both men and women. After age 35, women lose up to 1 percent per year, and they may lose as much as 4 to 6 percent per year during the first 4 to 5 years after menopause. Men maintain bone mass until about age 50, after which they lose approximately 0.4 to 0.5 percent per year. Both peak bone mass and rate of loss are involved in the likelihood of developing osteoporosis.

## EFFECTS OF CALCIUM INTAKE

Matkovic and colleagues[3] evaluated the relationship of calcium intake and bone mass by comparing two Yugoslavian populations, one with high (947 mg/day) and one with low (424 mg/day) calcium intake. The two groups were otherwise similar in heredity and environment. The high-calcium group had a significantly greater skeletal mass at maturity and a lower fracture incidence in old age. The two groups lost bone mineral content at a similar rate; therefore, the greater incidence of fractures in the low-calcium group was attributed to lower peak bone mass.

## MECHANISM OF EXERCISE BENEFITS

Although the specific level and magnitude of physical activity has not been clearly delineated, data from our laboratory indicate that 40 to 50 minutes of aerobic weight-bearing exercise, 3 to 4 days per week, are adequate for skeletal maintenance.[4] While evidence is accumulating that physical activity stimulates bone formation, research on the mechanisms by which bone is affected by mechanical stress is still in its early stages.

In 1892, Wolff[5] hypothesized that increased weight bearing compresses and bends the long bones, increases mineral content, and consequently strengthens bones, making them less liable to fracture under similar loads. Weight bearing (gravity) and muscle contraction are the major mechanical forces on bone, which is affected by both hypodynamic and hyperdynamic states. Bone mass increases with greater weight bearing or muscle contraction or both and decreases with immobilization or weightlessness. The degree of bone change is proportional to the difference in magnitude and frequency of the mechanical stimulus from normal. The habitual stimulus to weight-bearing segments (legs and spine) is much greater than that to the non–weight-bearing areas (rib cage, arms, and skull). For example, the impact of the heel during walking (1.2 to 1.5 times body weight) is much greater than the stress applied by the muscular movements in the arm swing during acitivities of daily living. Therefore, the calcaneus is normally under greater stress than the radius, so when both bones are free of stress (as in the case of the astronauts in space), more bone is lost from the calcaneus than from the radius.[6,7] Although bone mass plays a significant role in determining bone strength, it is not the sole determinant. The geometric structure of the tissue, determined by habitual stresses, collagen orientation, ligaments, and muscle tone, is also important.

Numerous models of the mechanism by which bone responds to mechanical forces have been proposed. Bassett[8] indicated that bone functions as a piezoelectric crystal, generating an electric charge in proportion to the forces applied to the bone. Bone matrix is removed from areas of positive charge (convex surface) and laid down in areas of negative charge (concave surface). Carter[9] hypothesized that mechanical forces produce microfractures, which stimulate osteoclastic remodeling coupled with osteoblastic activity. Increased hydrostatic pressure may be another stimulus to osteoclastic and osteoblastic activity. Whereas dynamic loading produces hypertrophy, static loading of bone produces little or no hypertrophy.[10] For a bone to hypertrophy, an isotonic stimulus must exceed a threshold magnitude and frequency. Lanyon[11] demonstrated that both the rate and magnitude of strain influenced bone remodeling. He monitored bone mineral in the radii of sheep under artificial stimulation. No change occurred with strain magnitude less than that of the animal's normal walking load. With higher strain magnitude and normal strain rates, periosteal bone deposition increased slightly on both convex and concave surfaces. When both magnitude and rate were higher than in normal walking, periosteal bone increased substantially. Thus, bone, like muscle, requires a specific magnitude and rate of stimulus in order to stimulate hypertrophy. Within a normal range of stimulus specific to the individual's activities and genotype, bone neither atrophies nor hypertrophies. Beyond this range bone will change, as shown in Figure 6–2.[9] Increased hypertrophy with increased stress will occur only to a point. Severe repetitive loading may result in fatigue damage such as that seen in the metatarsals, calcaneus, tibia, and femur of some soldiers and distance runners. Fatigue damage may also occur in untrained persons who increase their activity levels more rapidly than the bone can adapt. Although muscles get stiff and sore, microfractures generally produce only transient minor pain until the damage is severe. At the other end of the spectrum, bone atrophies with lessened mechanical stress due to bedrest and weightlessness.

## EFFECTS OF INACTIVITY

Donaldson and associates[12] observed three men for 30 to 36 weeks of bedrest, and Hulley and colleagues[13] observed five men for 24

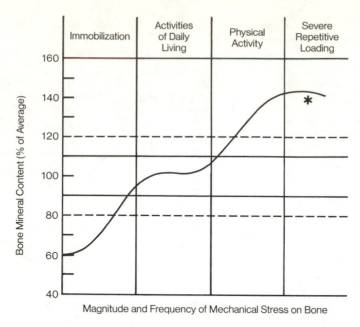

*Point at which the magnitude and duration of the load approach the elastic limits of the bone and osteoclast activity is greater than osteoblast.

**Figure 6–2.** *Effect of mechanical loading on bone mineral content. (Adapted from Carter.[9])*

to 30 weeks of bedrest. Calcium balance was negative throughout bedrest, with 0.5 to 0.7 percent of total body calcium lost per month. In the weight-bearing calcaneus, bone loss was magnified; 25 to 45 percent was lost after 36 weeks. After remobilization, calcium balance became positive within a month, and bone mineral was regained at a rate similar to the rate of loss, reaching beginning levels in about 36 weeks. Krolner and Toft[14] observed a 0.9 percent per week loss from the lumbar spine in individuals at bedrest for an average of 27 days because of a disk protrusion. Physicians who treat patients with back pain should pay attention to this fact before they commit patients to long-term bedrest. In the average woman, the usual decline in activity is more gradual and less severe than that of a patient at bedrest, but extended over years the resultant bone loss is significant and often results in osteoporosis. Human studies of disuse are rare, but a number of animal studies have been performed.

Kazarian and Von Gierke[15] immobilized 16 rhesus monkeys in full body casts for 60 days. The immobilized bone had fewer and smaller trabeculae, smaller trabecular plates, thinner trabecular surfaces, and reduced cortical thickness compared with bones of con-

trol animals. Remodeling occurred in the trabeculae of the femoral neck, which "corresponded in position and curvature to the lines of maximum compressive stress," so that only those trabeculae necessary for structural integrity were retained. The compressive strength of the immobilized bones was two to three times less than that in control animals. Significant cortical bone loss rates were observed at the sites of muscle and tendon attachments.

Young[16] and Niklowitz[17] and their co-workers investigated changes in the tibias of monkeys during 7 months of immobilization and up to 40 months of recovery and remobilization. Remodeling was obvious within 1 month of immobilization. After 10 weeks, they observed endosteal resorption, subperiosteal loss, striations in the cortex (indicative of resorptive cavities), surface erosion in the juxta-articular areas (patella and femoral condyles), and thin, irregular external lamellar bone. The medullary cavity widened and during 6 months of immobilization bone mineral content decreased 23 to 31 percent and bending stiffness 36 to 40 percent. Normal bending properties were restored within 8½ months of recovery and remobilization, but bone mineral content did not return to normal even after 15 months. New primary Haversian systems were generated during that time, and by 40 months the cortex contained many secondary and tertiary osteons and approached normal bone mineral content.

## EFFECTS OF EXERCISE

Increased activity correspondingly induces bone hypertrophy. For example, male tennis players have a 34.9 percent greater humerus mineral content in their playing arm than in their nonplaying arm.[18] A Milwaukee Brewers pitcher we measured had 40 percent greater humerus bone mass in his throwing arm. Participants in other sports similarly experience bone hypertrophy.

Various researchers have examined the effects of mechanical forces on bone in animal models. Chamay and Tschantz[19] removed a small segment of the radius in dogs and then allowed the animals to walk on the weakened limb, increasing muscle tension and weight bearing on the remaining intact ulna. Periosteal bone apposition occurred on both cortices, particularly on the concave cortex. After 9 weeks, the ulna had hypertrophied 60 to 100 percent.

In a similar experiment, Goodship and colleagues[20] removed an ulnar diaphysis from young swine. Using strain gauges, they found that following surgery compressive strains on the radial shaft were 2 to 2.5 times normal. After 3 months, the cross-sectional area of the radius on the surgical side had hypertrophied to equal the sum of the cross-sectional areas of the ulna and radius on the normal limb, with the compressive strain similar to or less than that of the control limb.

Recent studies have applied more precisely quantified stress to bone. Rubin and Lanyon[21] applied mechanical loads, using a pneumatically operated device, to rooster ulnae isolated from muscular stress. Bone mass decreased if no load was applied, remained fairly constant at a small dynamic loading (4 cycles/day of normal magnitude), and hypertrophied at a normal magnitude loading for 36 cycles/day. The hypertrophy from 1800 cycles/day of normal magnitude was no different than that from 36 cycles/day. This shows that increasing the number of stimuli beyond a certain point does not further increase bone growth. It is likely that bone, like muscle, hypertrophies primarily in response to the force of the stress, rather than to the number of weaker stresses that are applied to it.

Increased exercise has been used as a mode of increasing skeletal stress in animals. Saville and Whyte[22] found both bone and muscle hypertrophy in rats run on a treadmill. Woo and associates[23] found increased femoral mass and bone strength in exercising pigs run on a treadmill for 12 months.

Numerous studies support the efficacy of physical activity for increasing bone mineral content in athletes. Dalen and Olsson[24] reported that 15 cross-country runners (aged 50 to 59) had greater bone mineral content than did 24 sedentary control subjects of similar ages. The greatest difference appeared in the radius and ulna, followed by the head of the humerus, calcaneus, and femoral shaft, ranging from 19 to 13 percent. Differences in other sites, while ranging from 6 to 9 percent, were not significant.

In a study by Jacobson and co-workers,[25] bone mineral content of the radius, lumbar spine, and metatarsus was measured, using both single and dual photon absorptiometry in collegiate female athletes and sedentary women aged 18 to 22. Eleven varsity tennis players and 23 varsity swimmers were compared with 46 control subjects. The college tennis players demonstrated 16 percent greater bone mineral content in the playing arm versus the nonplaying arm. The swimmers showed no significant difference between the left and right radius bone mineral content. The tennis players had a significantly greater bone mineral content in the spine than did the control subjects and the swimmers. No significant difference in lumbar vertebral bone density existed between the controls and the swimmers. Radius and metatarsus bone contents were significantly greater in both the swimmers and the tennis players than in the controls. This study emphasizes that bone hypertrophy is specific to the areas stressed.

Aloia and associates[26] measured total body calcium determined by total body neutron activation analysis in 30 male marathon runners aged 30 to 50 and in 16 age-matched control subjects. The marathon runners demonstrated a significantly greater total body calcium of 11 percent compared with that of a control group. In conjunction with the total body calcium, Aloia also measured total body potassium. A 7 percent greater potassium content was observed in the marathoners, indicating a greater muscle mass in the runners than in the controls.

In a recent report by Brewer and colleagues,[27] premenopausal women aged 30 to 49 years were studied. The investigators measured the bone density of the midphalanx of the fifth finger, the os calcis (by x-ray densitometry), and the distal and midshaft radius (by single photon absorptiometry) in 42 marathon runners and 38 sedentary women. The marathoners had significantly greater bone mineral content at the midradius and midphalanx, but significantly less in the os calcis. The sedentary women, however, were an average of 8 kg heavier. There was a significant positive correlation between age of the marathon runners and bone mass at the os calcis, one-tenth distal radius, and one-third distal radius.

Nilsson and co-workers[28] measured the bone mineral content in 24 weight lifters (all men), 21 professional ballet dancers (8 men and 13 women), and controls. They used the gamma absorptiometry method to measure at the proximal end of the tibia and fibula, at the shaft of the radius and ulna, and at the distal ends of the radius and ulna in the weight lifters and controls. Only the proximal tibia and fibula were measured in the dancers. The weight lifters averaged 28 percent greater bone mass in the tibia and fibula than the controls, whereas the dancers averaged 25 percent greater bone mass in the tibia and fibula (male 23 percent, female 28 percent). The weight lifters had 19 percent greater bone mass at the proximal radius and ulna and 38 percent greater mass at the distal end. The weight lifters were heavier than the controls, who were significantly heavier than the dancers.

In a report by Block and associates,[29] the spine trabecular and spine integral (cumulative cortical and trabecular bone in L1 and L2 on 18 5 mm–thick contiguous CT scans) bone mineral content was evaluated in 18 male control subjects and 28 men involved in regular vigorous exercise. The 28 exercising men had participated in strenuous exercise for at least 2 years. The control group did not participate in any organized exercise program at the time of the study. The spine tra-

becular mineral density was 14 percent greater in the exercise group than in controls. The total integral bone mineral content of L1 and L2 of the physically active group was 11 percent greater than in the control group. Block indicated that the type of physical activity may also be important in bone mineral mass content. Those who performed both aerobic and weight-training activities had the greatest bone mass, followed by the group performing only weight training and then the group performing only aerobic activity. All three groups showed a significantly greater bone mass than the controls.

White and colleagues[30] determined the effects of 6 months of exercise in recently postmenopausal women. Twenty-seven women (mean age 56) walked, 25 (mean age 57) participated in aerobic dance, and 21 (mean age 55) maintained normal activities of daily living. Bone mineral content and width of the distal radius were measured by single photon absorptiometry. White reported a significant decline of bone mineral content of the radius in both the control subjects and the walking subjects during the 6-month period. However, no significant decline was observed in the aerobic dancers.

Changes in the lumbar vertebrae of 13 women (mean age 61) participating in an 8-month exercise program, for 1 hour twice per week, were studied by Krolner and co-workers.[31] Dual photon absorptiometry was used to measure the bone mineral content of the lumbar spine and forearm. At the program's end, exercisers had gained 3.5 percent in lumbar spine bone mineral content and sedentary women lost 2.7 percent. Bone mineral content of the forearm, however, did not differ significantly between the two groups. This implies that exercise strengthens only the bones that are stressed by that activity.

Smith, Reddan, and Smith[32] studied radius bone mineral in 12 exercising (mean age 83) and 18 nonexercising women (mean age 82) over a 3-year period. Exercising women increased bone mineral content 2.29 percent, while controls lost 3.29 percent. A third group, which did not exercise but received calcium (750 mg) and vitamin D (400 IU) supplements, gained 1.58 percent. This suggested that dietary supplements are helpful in maintaining bone, but not as beneficial as exercise.

In a report by Smith and associates,[4] middle-aged women were studied to determine if bone involution could be prevented by exercise. Eighty-six women (mean age 50) participated in an exercise program 3 days per week, 45 minutes per day; and 62 women (mean age 51) who did not change their activity patterns served as controls. The two groups did not differ significantly in height or weight. The exercise group loss was significantly less than that of the control group for the radius and ulna bone mineral content, for width and bone mineral content divided by width of the radius and ulna, and for the left humerus bone mineral content divided by width. The greatest difference between groups was in the ulna, followed by the radius, and finally the humerus.

Although a variety of studies have attempted to correlate bone and muscular strength in humans, the measurement sites have frequently been chosen for convenience rather than based on the dynamics of muscle and bone interactions.

Lanyon and Rubin[10] demonstrated that bone responds to stress and strain when dynamically, but not isometrically, stressed at the same magnitude. Early investigations found that grip strength and bone mineral content had little correlation. Grip strength is produced by forearm musculature, which most often is stressed isometrically. In the more dynamically stressed humerus, one would expect a better correlation of bone mass and muscle strength. As expected, tennis players show a greater increase in humeral bone mass than in radial or ulnar bone mass.[33]

Aloia and co-workers[34] studied calcium balance (by total body neutron activation) and radius bone mineral in 18 postmenopausal women. Nine women entered an exercise program and nine did not change their activity level. Total body calcium increased 20 g in the exercise group and decreased 20 g in the sedentary group. This difference was not reflected by any significant change in the bone mineral content of the radius.

Sixty-eight healthy normal postmenopausal white women were studied in 1986 by Sinaki and colleagues.[35] The women had no unusual dietary patterns and did not take therapeutic doses of calcium, vitamin D, or estrogen. Bone mineral content in the second, third, and fourth lumbar vertebrae and the strength of the back extensor muscles were measured. Lumbar bone mineral density correlated significantly with back extensor strength ($r = 0.34$, $p = 0.004$). Back extensor strength decreased significantly with age. Bone mineral content correlated significantly also with weight, height, age, and physical activity level.

## EFFECTS OF EXCESSIVE EXERCISE

Whereas exercise is associated with an increase in bone density,[25] *excessive* exercise leading to amenorrhea has recently been associated with a *decrease* in bone density.[36–38] Investigators have found that unlike hyperprolactinemic, anorexic, and premature menopausal women, amenorrheic athletes do not show a significant decrease in cortical (radius) bone mineral content. However, the amenorrheic athletes do lose a significant amount of vertebral bone mineral content.[36–38]

In one study, eleven hypothalamic amenorrheic women involved in variable degrees of "vigorous" exercise programs had an approximately 20 percent lower vertebral bone mineral content than age-matched controls.[36] Radial bone mineral was found to be only slightly less than that of the controls.

In a more recent study, Marcus and associates[38] compared amenorrheic (one to seven years) and eumenorrheic elite distance runners. Subjects ran between 56 and 160 km/week. Whereas forearm (radial) mineral density was normal in both the amenorrheic and eumenorrheic groups, spine density was significantly lower in the amenorrheic group. Marcus noted that the amenorrheic elite athletes in his study had significantly greater spine bone mineral content than the eight less active amenorrheic athletes in Cann's earlier study. It is worth noting, however, that the amenorrheic athletes consumed significantly less calcium than the eumenorrheic athletes.

Drinkwater and colleagues[37] also measured vertebral and radial bone mass in 14 eumenorrheic and 14 amenorrheic athletes. Subjects were matched for age, height, weight, sport, and training regimens, although the amenorrheic athletes ran more total miles per week (41.8 versus 24.9). There were no significant differences between the groups in radial bone density, but vertebral density was significantly lower in the amenorrheic group. (See Chapter 10 for additional discussion of this topic.)

Although Schwartz and co-workers[39] have suggested that the cause of athletic amenorrhea may be an entirely different endocrinologic entity than other hypothalamic amenorrheas, the resultant decrease in estrogen levels may have the same effect on bone. Circulating levels of estrogen have been found to be reduced to the same level as in hyperprolactinemic and ovarian failure groups.[36] Other factors that may affect bone loss are extreme thinness,[40] low calcium intake, and overloading the bone with extreme amounts of exercise.

We need more studies to help us understand the precise mechanisms that produce exercise-induced amenorrhea and the resultant physiologic effects. Meanwhile, it is best to recommend regular exercise that stresses the entire skeletal system appropriate to the individual's needs and physiologic response.

The National Institutes of Health Consensus Development Conference on Osteoporosis has stated that major factors in prevention of osteoporosis are estrogen replacement therapy for postmenopausal women, adequate calcium intake (1000 mg/day for premenopausal women and 1500 mg/day for postmenopausal women), and moderate physical activity.[2]

## SUMMARY

Bone is a dynamic tissue performing two functions: providing structural support and acting as a mineral reservoir. Two homeostatic mechanisms act on bone at the same time: hormones and mechanical stress.

Researchers have evaluated the relationship of weight-bearing and non–weight-bearing forces on bone to bone mass and bone strength. Bone adjusts locally to support the structural demands of weight-bearing and muscular activity. Inactivity results in bone involution, whereas increased activity induces bone hypertrophy. Subjects at bedrest or in weightless conditions lose bone rapidly. Conversely, athletes have greater bone mineral than their sedentary counterparts. Exercise intervention slows or reverses bone loss in middle-aged and elderly women. Bone response is specific to the area stressed, as seen in the selective hypertrophy of the dominant arm in tennis players. Very intense levels of exercise coupled with amenorrhea may reduce skeletal mass, especially in the spine.

More research is needed to understand the precise mechanisms by which exercise affects bone, and the optimum type and intensity of physical activity for preventing osteoporosis.

## References

1. Smith EL, and Rabb DM: Osteoporosis and exercise. In Åstrand PO, and Gumby G (eds): Proceedings, Second Acta Medica Scandinavica International Symposium: Physical Activity in Health and Disease. Almqvist and Wiksell Trycheri, Uppsala, Sweden, 1986, pp. 149–56.
2. National Institutes of Health: Consensus Development Conference on Osteoporosis. Vol 5, No 3. Government Printing Office, pub No 421-132:4652, Washington, DC, 1984.
3. Matkovic V, Kostial K, Simonovic I, et al: Bone status and fracture rates in two regions of Yugoslavia. Am J Clin Nutr 32:540, 1979.
4. Smith EL, Smith PE, Ensign CJ, et al: Bone involution decrease in exercising middle-aged women. Calcif Tissue Int 36:S129, 1984.
5. Wolff J: Das Gesetz der Transformation der Knochen. A. Hirschwald, Berlin, 1892.
6. Vogel JM, and Whittle MW: Bone mineral changes: the second manned skylab mission. Aviat Space Environ Med 47:396, 1976.
7. Smith MC, Rambaut PC, Vogel JM, et al: Bone mineral measurement—experiment M078. In Johnston RS, and Dietlein LF (eds): Biomedical Results from Skylab. National Aeronautics and Space Administration, Washington, DC, 1977, p 183.
8. Bassett CA: Biophysical principles affecting bone structure. In Bourne GH (ed): The Biochemistry and Physiology of Bone, ed 2. Vol III. Academic Press, New York, 1971, p 1.
9. Carter DR: Mechanical loading histories and cortical bone remodeling. Calcif Tissue Int 36S:19, 1984.
10. Lanyon LE, and Rubin CT: Static vs. dynamic loads as a stimulus for bone remodeling. J Biomech 15:767, 1984.
11. Lanyon LE: Bone remodeling mechanical stress and osteoporosis. In DeLuca HF, Frost HM, Jee WSS, et al (eds): Osteoporosis: Recent Advances in Pathogenesis and Treatment. University Park Press, Baltimore, Maryland, 1981, p 129.
12. Donaldson, CL, Hulley, SB, Vogel JM, et al: Effect of prolonged bed rest on bone mineral. Metabolism 19:1071, 1970.
13. Hulley SB, Vogel JM, and Donaldson CL: Effect of supplemental calcium and phosphorus on bone mineral changes in bed rest. J Clin Invest 50:2506, 1971.
14. Krolner B, and Toft B: Vertebral bone loss: an unheeded side effect of therapeutic bed rest. Clin Sci 64:537, 1983.
15. Kazarian LE, and Von Gierke HE: Bone loss as a result of immobilization and chelation: preliminary results in macaca mulatta. Clin Orthop Rel Res 65:57, 1969.
16. Young DR, Niklowitz WJ, and Steele CR: Tibial

changes in experimental disuse osteoporosis in the monkey. Calcif Tissue Int 35:304, 1983.

17. Niklowitz WJ, Bunch TE, and Young DR: The effects of immobilization on cortical bone in monkeys (m. nemestrina). Physiologist 26 (Suppl):S115, 1983.

18. Jones HH, Priest JS, Hayes WC, et al: Humeral hypertrophy in response to exercise. J Bone Joint Surg 59A:204, 1977.

19. Chamay A, and Tschantz P: Mechanical influences in bone remodeling: experimental research on Wolff's law. J Biomech 5:173, 1972.

20. Goodship AE, Lanyon LE, and McFie H: Functional adaptation of bone to increased stress. An experimental study. J Bone Joint Surg 61:539, 1979.

21. Rubin CT, and Lanyon LE: Regulation of bone formation by applied dynamic loads. J Bone Joint Surg 66a:397, 1984.

22. Saville PD, and Whyte MP: Muscle and bone hypertrophy: positive effect of running exercise in the rat. Clin Orthop Rel Res 65:81, 1969.

23. Woo SLY, Kuei SC, Amiel D, et al: The effect of prolonged physical training on the properties of long bone: a study of Wolff's Law. J Bone Joint Surg 63A:780, 1981.

24. Dalen N, and Olsson KE: Bone density in athletes. ACTA Orthopaed Scand 45:170, 1974.

25. Jacobson PC, Beaver W, Grubb SA, et al: Bone density in women: college athletes and older athletic women. Journal of Orthopaedic Research 2:328, 1984.

26. Aloia JF, Cohn SH, Babu T, et al: Skeletal mass and body composition in marathon runners. Metabolism 27:1793, 1978.

27. Brewer V, Meyer, BM, Keeler MS, et al: Role of exercise in prevention of involutional bone loss. Med Sci Sports Exerc 15(5):445, 1983.

28. Nilsson BE, Andersson SM, Havdrup TU, et al: Bone mineral content in ballet dancers and weight lifters. In Mazess RB (ed): Proceedings Fourth International Conference on Bone Measurement. Washington, DC, NIH Pub No 80-1938, 1980, p 81.

29. Block J, Genant HK, Black D, et al: Greater vertebral bone mineral in exercising young men. Western J Med 145:39, 1986.

30. White MK, Martin RB, Yeater RA, et al: The effects of exercise on the bones of postmenopausal women. Int Orthop 7:209, 1984.

31. Krolner B, Toft B, Nielsen SP, et al: Physical exercise as prophylaxis against involutional vertebral bone loss: a controlled trial. Clin Sci 64:541, 1983.

32. Smith EL, Reddan W, and Smith PE: Physical activity and calcium modalities for bone mineral increase in aged women. Med Sci Sports Exerc 13(1):60, 1981.

33. Montoye HJ, Smith EL, Fardon DF, et al: Bone mineral in senior tennis players. Scandinavian Journal of Sports Science 2:26, 1980.

34. Aloia JF, Cohn SH, Ostuni JA, et al: Prevention of involutional bone loss by exercise. Ann Intern Med 89:356, 1978.

35. Sinaki M, McPhee MC, Hodgson SF, et al: Relationship between bone mineral density of spine and strength of back extensors in healthy postmenopausal women. Mayo Clin Proc 61:116, 1986.

36. Cann CE, Martin MC, Genant HK, et al: Decreased spinal mineral content in amenorrheic women. JAMA 251(5):626, 1984.

37. Drinkwater BL, Nilson, K, Chesnut CH, et al: Bone mineral content of amenorrheic and eumonorrheic athletes. N Engl J Med 311(5):277, 1984.

38. Marcus R, Cann, C, Madvig P, et al: Menstrual function and bone mass in elite women distance runners. Ann Intern Med 102:156, 1985.

39. Schwartz B, Cumming DC, Riordan E, et al: Exercise induced amenorrhea: A distinct entity? Am J Obstet Gynecol 141:662, 1981.

40. Linnell SL, Stagger JM, Blue PW, et al: Bone mineral content and menstrual regularity in female runners. Med Sci Sports Exerc 16(4):343, 1984.

# CHAPTER 7

# Nutrition for Sports

GABE MIRKIN, M.D.

With the exception of iron and calcium, nutrient requirements for female athletes are the same as those for their male counterparts. Women suffer far more frequently than men from deficiencies of iron and calcium. Ten percent of healthy, white, middle-class female adolescents are iron deficient, while 5 percent have iron-deficiency anemia.[1] Athletes are at greater risk than nonathletes for developing iron deficiency,[2] which, even in the absence of anemia, can limit athletic endurance.

Hypoestrogenic female athletes are at increased risk of developing osteoporotic bone fractures.[3] In addition to hormone replacement, the prevention and treatment of this condition should include ingestion of adequate amounts of calcium.

A proper diet can help female athletes to maximize performance. However, many athletes have nutritional misconceptions that hinder performance rather than help it. For example, many athletes incorrectly believe that a high-protein diet improves performance and increases muscle size and strength, that vitamin requirements are significantly greater for athletes, that fluid requirements during exercise should be dictated by thirst, and that salt tablets should be taken in hot weather.[4,5] All of these myths will be refuted in this chapter.

In 1967, the women's world record for the marathon was 3:15:22, set by Maureen Wilton of Toronto, Canada. By 1985, the world record was lowered to 2:21:06 by Ingrid Kristiansen of Norway. The fantastic improvement in world records in all sporting events is due primarily to superior training methods, but it is also due to improved knowledge about nutrition. In the late 1960s, it was common for athletes to eat high-protein diets, to reduce their intake of food on the days before competition, to ingest no food or liquids during competition, and to eat only a limited amount of food after competition. Today knowledgeable athletes follow none of these old regimens.[6]

This chapter will review some of the basic physiologic principles that serve as the foundation for advising athletes how to use nutrition to improve sports performance.

## NUTRIENTS

Humans require approximately 46 nutrients to be healthy. An essential nutrient is one that cannot be produced by the body in adequate amounts and, therefore, must be supplied by the diet (Table 7–1). Lack of an essential nutrient can impair performance, but taking large amounts of any specific nutrient has not been shown to improve performance.

Athletes can improve their performances in competition by following sound scientific nutritional practices. A brief discussion of basic principles of nutrition will precede the sections on the application of such principles to athletic competition.

**Table 7–1.** ESSENTIAL NUTRIENTS

Water
Linoleic acid
8 or 9 amino acids
13 vitamins
Approximately 21 minerals
Glucose (for energy)

**Carbohydrates.** Carbohydrates are composed of sugars. They can be monosaccharides, such as glucose and fructose in fruit; disaccharides, such as lactose in milk or sucrose in candy; and polysaccharides, such as starch in a potato or fiber in celery.

Before carbohydrates can be absorbed, they must first be hydrolyzed into one or more of the following four sugars: glucose, fructose, galactose, and mannose. Of these sugars, only glucose circulates beyond the portal system. The other three are converted to glucose by hepatocytes before they can reenter the circulation (Fig. 7–1).

Circulating glucose can be used by all cells as a source of energy. Glucose that is not used immediately can be stored as glycogen only in the liver and muscles. When these tissues are saturated with glycogen, excess glucose is then converted to fat. Liver glycogen can yield glucose to the circulation, where it subsequently can be used by other tissues. On the other hand, the glucose from muscle glycogen can be utilized only by that particular muscle.

**Proteins.** Fifteen percent of ingested protein is hydrolyzed to amino acids and polypeptides in the stomach, while the remaining protein undergoes hydrolysis in the small intestine. These metabolites are actively transported into intestinal epithelial cells. Once there, most of the polypeptides are hydrolyzed to form amino acids, which are then absorbed into the general circulation.

The main functions of proteins are to form structural components, enzymes, hormones, neurotransmitters, antibodies, transport molecules, and clotting factors. Protein can also be a source of energy. As much as 10 percent of energy during exercise can come from protein, with more than half coming from one amino acid, leucine. Since leucine represents only a small fraction of the amino acids in ingested protein, the leucine that is used for energy must come from a source other than ingested protein. It also does not come from muscle sources of leucine. Most of the leucine that is used for energy is formed de novo. The nitrogen for the newly formed leucine comes from other branched-chain amino acids (isoleucine and valine), and most of the carbon comes from glucose and other amino acids.

Before amino acids can be used for energy, deamination or transamination must occur to

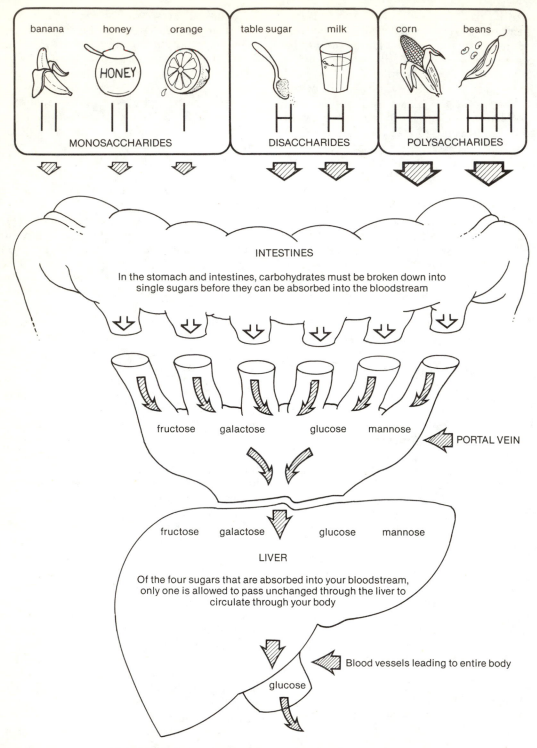

banana    honey    orange

HONEY

MONOSACCHARIDES

table sugar    milk

DISACCHARIDES

corn    beans

POLYSACCHARIDES

INTESTINES

In the stomach and intestines, carbohydrates must be broken down into single sugars before they can be absorbed into the bloodstream

fructose    galactose    glucose    mannose

PORTAL VEIN

fructose    galactose    glucose    mannose

LIVER

Of the four sugars that are absorbed into your bloodstream, only one is allowed to pass unchanged through the liver to circulate through your body

Blood vessels leading to entire body

glucose

All carbohydrates eventually end up as glucose before they can circulate through your body.

**Figure 7–1.** *Sugar circulation. All carbohydrates are sugars bound together. They can be single sugars, as in fruit and honey; two sugars bound together, as in milk and table sugar; and hundreds and thousands of sugars bound together, as in corn and beans.*

**Table 7-2.** GLYCEROL AND FATTY ACIDS

| | | | | |
|---|---|---|---|---|
| C-C-C-C· · ·C-C-COOH<br>\|<br>C-C-C-C· · ·C-C-COOH --------→<br>\|<br>C-C-C-C· · ·C-C-COOH | C-OH<br>\|<br>C-OH<br>\|<br>C-OH | + | C-C-C· · ·C-C-COOH<br><br>C-C-C· · ·C-C-COOH<br><br>C-C-C· · ·C-C-COOH | |
| TRIGLYCERIDE --------------------→ | GLYCEROL | + | FATTY ACIDS | |

remove the nitrogen. Athletic training can double the levels of important transaminases, such as SGOT and SGPT, and this increases significantly the body's ability to utilize leucine and other amino acids for energy.

**Fats.** More than 95 percent of the fat in foods is in the form of triglycerides. Fat is separated from other foodstuffs in the stomach, but it is not degraded until it is emulsified (dispersed in water) by bile salts in the small intestine. The fat globules are then hydrolyzed by pancreatic lipase into monoglycerides, free fatty acids, and glycerol (Table 7-2), which enter the epithelial cells lining the intestines. Once there, the monoglycerides are hydrolyzed to form glycerol and fatty acids. Then, triglycerides are formed again, are combined with cholesterol and phospholipids, and are covered with a lipoprotein coating to form chylomicron particles, which pass through the lymphatic system into the general circulation. Short-chain fatty acids can be absorbed directly into the circulation. Excess fat is stored primarily in fat cells and muscles.

## ENERGY STORAGE

Only fats and carbohydrates are stored for future use as an energy source. The human body cannot store extra protein. Fat stores energy in the most economical way, as it provides 14 times as much energy per given weight as stored liver glycogen, which must be stored with other liver tissue. One pound of stored fat will yield 3500 kcal, whereas 1 pound of liver contains only enough glycogen to yield 250 kcal. This great disparity in energy storage is explained by the fact that fat occupies 85 percent of the space in fat cells, while liver glycogen is diluted by other cellular elements and occupies less than 15 percent of the space in liver cells.

The body of the average athlete contains only enough stored fat to support exercise for 119 hours, enough stored muscle glycogen for 1½ hours, and enough stored liver glycogen for 6 minutes. Table 7-3 shows how limited the stores of carbohydrates are and how extensive the fat stores are.

**Comparing women and men.** At the same level of fitness, the average woman has 7 to 10 percent more body fat than the average man. For example, top female marathon runners have 12 to 20 percent body fat, compared with 5 to 10 percent for their male counterparts.

Muscles use primarily fats and carbohydrates as their energy sources. At rest, muscles use mostly fats for energy. During exercise, muscles use more carbohydrates, with a higher percentage of carbohydrates and a lower percentage of fat being used as the intensity of the exercise is increased. In spite of their increased percentage of body fat,

**Table 7-3.** MAXIMAL BODY STORAGE CAPACITY FOR CARBOHYDRATES AND FATS[7]

| Storage Site | Weight of Tissue (grams) | Available Energy (kilocalories) |
|---|---|---|
| Muscle glycogen | 125–300 | 500–1200 |
| Liver glycogen | 50–100 | 200–400 |
| Body fat | 6000–15,000 | 50,000–140,000 |

women use the same percentage of fat as men through all intensities of exercise. For example, at race pace for the marathon, top male and female runners have been shown to derive the same 50 percent of their energy from fat,[8] and top female athletes have not demonstrated greater endurance than male athletes.

In running events from 100 to 1500 meters, world records for women are 7 to 10 percent slower than those for men.[9,10] In running events from 1500 meters to the marathon, world records for women are 13 to 15 percent slower than those for men.[11] The extra fat that most women carry slows them down during running. However, having extra fat is an advantage during swimming. Penny Dean of California set the world's record for men *and* women for a single crossing of the English Channel in 7 hours and 40 minutes (in 1978), and Cynthia Nichols of Canada set the record for a double crossing at 19 hours and 12 minutes (in 1977). Their extra fat may well be the reason for their great endurance swimming performances. It is likely that the insulating properties of fat, rather than the glycogen-sparing effect, gave them an advantage. Loss of body heat is a major problem in distance swimming. Furthermore, having extra fat raises a swimmer higher out of the water and reduces drag (see Chapter 5).

## ENDURANCE

Endurance is the ability to continue exercising muscles for an extended period of time. To continue exercising, muscles require energy, the major sources of which are triglycerides and glycogen in muscles and triglycerides and glucose in blood.

The main advantage of fats is that the body can store vast amounts. The main advantage of carbohydrates is that they can be utilized under anaerobic conditions. Fat metabolism always requires oxygen. As exercise intensity increases, the percentage of energy derived from muscle glycogen also increases. Much of the exercise during most competitive events is done at maximum or near-maximum intensity. The limiting factor for exercising at an intensity greater than 70 percent of $\dot{V}_{O_2max}$ is the amount of glycogen that muscles can store.[12]

**"Hitting the wall": Depletion of muscle glycogen.** *Muscle endurance* depends on the adequacy of muscle glycogen stores. Depletion of muscle glycogen causes pain and fatigue and causes an athlete to lose much of her strength and to have difficulty coordinating muscle movements. Athletes refer to this as *"hitting the wall,"* a common occurrence in marathon runners after they have raced more than 18 miles. The more glycogen that can be stored in a muscle, the longer it can be exercised.

**"Bonking": Depletion of liver glycogen.** *Brain endurance* depends on circulating glucose. More than 98 percent of the energy for the brain is derived from blood glucose, which depends on hepatic glycogen stores for maintenance. When the blood concentration of glucose falls to low levels, the athlete may feel very tired and can suffer from a syncopal episode or seizures or both. Athletes refer to this as *"bonking."* Bicyclists who do not eat during endurance races may experience this after 4 or more hours of cycling.

## INCREASING ENDURANCE

An athlete can improve endurance by using training methods and dietary manipulations that increase muscle glycogen storage and decrease muscle glycogen utilization by increasing fat utilization.[13]

**Training to increase endurance.** To improve the ability of muscles to store increased amounts of glycogen[13] and utilize increased amounts of fat (and less glycogen),[15] athletes use a training technique called *depletion.* They exercise until muscle glycogen has been nearly depleted (Table 7–4). This causes muscle cells to increase production of glycogen synthetase, which increases glycogen synthesis and, in turn, glycogen storage.[14]

After the athlete eats, her muscles fill with glycogen, and this reduces production of glycogen synthetase. Therefore, the effects of depletion training are short-lived, and deple-

**Table 7–4.** AVERAGE TIMES FOR MUSCLE DEPLETION IN ELITE ATHLETES

| | |
|---|---|
| Marathon runner | 1½–2½ hr |
| Bicycle racer | 4–6 hr |
| Cross-country skier | 10–12 hr |

tion training should be repeated at frequent intervals. However, athletes usually do not perform depletion training more frequently than once a week, because depletion of muscle glycogen leads to increased utilization of muscle protein for energy. This damages the muscle, delays recovery, and limits the amount of intense training the athlete can accomplish.

Many recreational athletes do not appreciate the importance of depletion training and enter marathons before they have put this training technique to adequate use. As a result, they have inadequate muscle glycogen stores to enable them to run the necessary distance.

## UTILIZING FAT INSTEAD OF GLYCOGEN

In addition to depletion training, other techniques that have been promoted to decrease glycogen utilization by muscles during exercise include eating a high-fat diet for several days prior to competition, taking nutritional supplements, and taking sympathomimetic agents.

At least one study showed that eating a high-fat diet for several days prior to competition will increase muscle utilization of fat.[16] However, endurance was not improved by this technique.[16,17] It is not unusual for blood glucose concentrations to fall as low as 30 mg/dL during vigorous exercise. Eating a high-fat diet does not reduce muscle glycogen utilization or prevent development of hypoglycemia (with or without symptoms) during exercise.[17]

There is no evidence that taking large amounts of any vitamin, mineral, protein, or carbohydrate will cause muscles to use increased amounts of fat.[18]

Claims have been made that carnitine supplements enhance endurance. Carnitine is a protein that transports fat into mitochondria, where fat is catabolized for energy. However, there is no evidence that any supplement will increase mitochondrial fat content enough to increase fat utilization. Myocytes and hepatocytes synthesize large amounts of carnitine from lysine and methionine, and human myocytes contain enough carnitine to support fat metabolism even under extreme exercise conditions.[19] The fact that most athletes include meat, fish, or chicken—rich sources of carnitine—in their diets provides

another reason why athletes do not need carnitine supplements.

Caffeine raises blood triglyceride levels by increasing catecholamine production and sensitivity. Catecholamines increase triglyceride utilization by promoting free fatty acid release from adipocytes and uptake by myocytes. Taking caffeine prior to workouts has been shown to increase endurance in training sessions by increasing muscle utilization of fat,[20] but it has not been shown to increase endurance in competition. A possible explanation for this difference in responses is that caffeine may be effective in prolonging endurance only when endogenous catecholamine levels are low. In a laboratory setting, athletes may be relaxed and have low circulating levels of catecholamines. Raising catecholamines in this situation may enhance performance. However, prior to competition most athletes have very high levels of catecholamines. Raising their levels further may not help them and, indeed, may harm them. Large amounts of catecholamines can cause tremors and irritability.

## DIET AND ENDURANCE

Female athletes should follow the same nutritional principles as men, since their bodies process foods in the same ways. An athlete can increase her endurance by eating the right meals 3 days before, the night before, and several hours before competition.

**Food intake during the week before competition.** In 1939, Scandinavian researchers showed that eating a high-carbohydrate diet for several days before a competitive event increases muscle glycogen stores and endurance, while a low-carbohydrate diet decreases muscle glycogen stores and endurance.[21] In the mid-1960s, other investigators proposed a method of "carbohydrate loading" that was practiced by many endurance athletes throughout the world.[22,23]

1. Seven days prior to competition, the athlete performs a long depletion workout.
2. For the next 3 days, she keeps the glycogen content of her exercised muscles low by eating a low-carbohydrate diet.
3. For the next 3 days, she eats her regular diet plus extra carbohydrate-rich foods.

Athletes should not ingest extra carbohydrate for more than three consecutive days.

In that time, muscles and liver will be at their maximum capacity for storing glycogen, so no additional glycogen can be stored. Carbohydrates that cannot be utilized immediately are constored with almost three additional grams of water, making the muscles much heavier than usual.

Carbohydrate packing should not be used in events lasting less than 60 minutes because it will not be helpful and may even be harmful. The muscles of trained athletes are not depleted of glycogen in so short a period of time. Carbohydrate packing may *reduce* performance in events requiring great speed over short distances, since each gram of glycogen is stored with almost three additional grams of water, making the muscles much heavier than usual.

Few top athletes practice this 7-day regimen today because it can hinder performance. During the depletion phase, the athlete cannot train properly and usually is irritable and unable to perform mental tasks effectively. During the high-carbohydrate phase, the ingestion of vast amounts of carbohydrates has been reported to cause chest pain,[24] myoglobinuria, and nephritis.[25] However, these side effects are rare. Marked overeating raises blood lipid levels, and this can lead to occlusion of the coronary arteries in exercisers who already have significant arteriosclerosis. Furthermore, this regimen has not been shown to be more effective than simply reducing the workload and ingesting some extra carbohydrates.[26]

As a result of all of these concerns, most top athletes in endurance sports avoid the low-carbohydrate phase and modify the high-carbohydrate phase. The runner can maximize muscle glycogen by a combination of reducing her workload and eating a regular diet that contains at least 55 percent of its calories from carbohydrates.[27] The 7-day carbohydrate packing regimen thus becomes a 4-day program:

1. Four days prior to competition, the athlete exercises intensely.
2. For the next 3 days, she reduces her workouts markedly and eats a carbohydrate-rich diet.

**Eating the night before competition.** On the night before a competitive event, many athletes eat a high-carbohydrate meal. The primary purpose of this meal is to increase muscle glycogen stores (Table 7–5). The pre-

**Table 7–5.** PRIMARY FUNCTION OF MEALS BEFORE AN AFTERNOON COMPETITION

Supper (the day before): To increase muscle glycogen stores
Breakfast: To increase hepatic glycogen stores

game meal cannot serve this function, since it takes at least 10 hours to replenish muscle glycogen stores.[28]

It is controversial whether muscle glycogen storage is promoted more by ingestion of starch or monosaccharides and disaccharides. One recent study showed that a high-monosaccharide and -disaccharide diet caused more muscle glycogen to be stored than did a high-starch diet.[29] Based on these findings, ingestion of simple sugars on the evening prior to competition does not seem to hinder performance and may actually help it. However, more research is needed to resolve this question.

**Eating the meal before competition.** The major function of the precompetition meal is to maximize hepatic glycogen (see Table 7–5). Serum glucose is sufficient to support brain function for only 3 minutes. To prevent hypoglycemia, hepatocytes must release glucose constantly. However, there is enough glycogen in hepatocytes to last only 12 hours when the athlete is at rest.[30] Obviously, during exercise, liver glycogen is depleted much faster than that.

*Timing of meal.* To maximize hepatic glycogen stores, the precompetition meal should be ingested 3 to 5 hours before competition. If the meal is eaten more than 5 hours before competition, the hepatocytes will be depleted of a considerable amount of stored glycogen and will have less than maximal glycogen stores when the athlete starts competition. If the athlete eats less than 3 hours prior to competition, she may develop hypoglycemia because of postprandial hyperinsulinemia. Blood glucose levels rise after meals, causing insulin levels to rise also and to remain elevated for more than 2 hours. High blood insulin levels during exercise can cause hypoglycemia and increased muscle glycogen utilization, which can tire the athlete prematurely.

At rest, blood glucose levels as low as 25 mg/dL usually cause a deterioration in brain function and loss of consciousness. However, physically fit individuals can usually tolerate such levels during exercise without developing any symptomatology at all,[31] even though they are using up their muscle glycogen stores at an accelerated rate[32] and will feel fatigue sooner than usual.[33]

**Composition of meal.** A high-carbohydrate precompetition meal has not been shown to increase endurance more than a high-fat one. The precompetition meal should not contain a large amount of monosaccharides or disaccharides, both of which cause significant hyperglycemia and resultant hyperinsulinemia. Except for this avoidance, the athlete can eat foods she likes, as long as she suffers no discomfort and has an empty stomach by the time she starts to exercise (Table 7–6).

Theoretically, fat and protein are poor choices for the precompetition meal. Fat delays stomach emptying, and the urea and ketones released by the catabolism of protein can promote diuresis. However, no controlled studies have demonstrated adverse effects from fat or protein in precompetition meals, and many athletes can tolerate high-fat and high-protein precompetition meals without having their performances hindered.

**Eating before exercising.** Provided that the exercise is not too intense and the amount of food eaten is not too great, most exercisers will not suffer from abdominal pain or discomfort when they eat prior to exercising. In most who do develop pain, the cause is rarely found. It is speculated that the pain is due to stomach muscle spasms, which result from ischemia caused by the shunting of blood from the stomach muscles to the exercising muscles.[34] During exercise, gastric motility increases[35–37] and splanchnic blood flow decreases.[38]

Recently, a drug company has advertised that

> Taking fructose before exercise compared to glucose, results in a much lower rate of muscle glycogen depletion, because fructose does not cause a rapid rise in either blood sugar or insulin.[39]

However, there is no evidence that eating fructose prior to exercising offers any advantage over eating nothing at all, and there is evidence that eating fructose is less advantageous than eating nothing at all. It is true that fructose ingestion may cause a *lower* rise than glucose in blood glucose and insulin levels.[40,41] However, eating fructose does cause an increase in circulating glucose and insulin levels, whereas eating nothing does not; fructose ingestion also causes a greater rate of muscle glycogen utilization, compared with eating nothing.[42,43] The fact that fructose costs 15 times as much as glucose offers an added disadvantage.

**Eating during competition.** It is not necessary for most conditioned athletes to eat during events that last less than 2 hours. However, athletes can benefit from eating during events lasting longer than that. The ability of exercising muscles to utilize ingested carbohydrates in place of muscle glycogen is dependent on conditioning. The higher the level of fitness, the better able the athlete is to utilize ingested carbohydrates during exercise.[44]

In contrast to ingestion of food before exercising, ingestion of food *during* exercise does not cause significant pancreatic output of insulin. At rest, eating causes hyperglycemia, which promotes insulin release. However, during exercise, muscles remove glucose so rapidly from the circulation that blood levels of glucose rarely rise high enough to induce significant insulin release from the pancreas.[45] Insulin-induced hypoglycemia caused by eating during intense exercise does not occur.[46]

Almost any food can be used for energy. When taken during exercise, glucose has not been shown to be more effective than table food in prolonging endurance. Studies com-

**Table 7–6.** EXAMPLES OF PRECOMPETITION MEALS THAT PASS RAPIDLY FROM THE STOMACH

---

**Breakfast #1**

Breakfast cereal with milk
A few small pieces of fruit
Toast with butter
1 cup of coffee
1 glass of milk
No more than ½ glass of orange juice

**Breakfast #2**

Pancakes (no maple syrup)
A small pat of jelly
Breakfast cereal
Milk or coffee
Glass of water
½ glass of fruit juice or a small piece of fruit

---

paring glucose with fructose offer conflicting results. One study showed that neither glucose nor fructose is better than placebo in reducing muscle glycogen utilization.[37] Another study showed a greater muscle glycogen–sparing effect by fructose.[47] A third study showed that ingested glucose spares muscle glycogen, whereas ingested fructose does not.[48]

Any maneuver that causes muscles to increase the rate at which they utilize fat for energy theoretically should help to conserve muscle glycogen and prolong endurance. However, neither eating a fatty meal nor taking glycerol has been shown to prolong endurance.[49]

On the other hand, maltodextrin glucose polymer solutions (Exceed, made by Ross Laboratories of Columbus, Ohio, and MAX, made by Coca Cola) appear to enhance endurance in events lasting longer than 2 hours.[50] The polymers in these drinks are composed of five glucose molecules. They offer the distinct advantage of supplying many calories at a low osmotic pressure, thereby not delaying absorption and resultant glucose utilization significantly. In events lasting less than 2 hours, athletes who have maximally filled their muscles with glycogen prior to competition do not appear to benefit from taking any form of carbohydrate during exercise.[51] However, for events lasting longer than 2 hours, researchers at Ball State University recommend taking 50 to 60 percent glucose polymer solution 20 to 30 minutes after the start of competition and a slightly less-concentrated solution at 20- to 40-minute intervals thereafter.[52]

## DRINKING DURING COMPETITION

Although most fit athletes do not gain any advantage from eating during competition in events lasting less than 2 hours, they can always benefit from keeping themselves adequately hydrated. Competitive runners and swimmers can lose approximately 1½ liters of fluid during an intense 1-hour workout. Although athletes exercising in warm, humid environments can see their sweat and appreciate their obvious fluid loss, those exercising in water sports may not be able to perceive that this loss has occurred.

**Dehydration and "heat cramps."** As the athlete becomes progressively more dehydrated, her blood volume decreases. There may not be an adequate volume of circulating blood to carry heat from exercising muscles to the skin, where the heat can be dissipated, and, at the same time, to carry oxygen to heavily exercising muscles. Reduced cutaneous blood flow will raise body temperature, and this will impair performance. The decreased blood volume can also limit the amount of blood that flows to the most heavily exercising muscles. The resultant hypoxia can cause sustained painful muscle contractions, known as heat cramps.[53]

**Women may need less fluid than men.** Earlier studies showed that men have better tolerance than women for exercising in the heat. However, these studies did not compare men and women exercising at comparable percentages of their $\dot{V}_{O_2max}$. More recent studies have shown that women are able to tolerate exercise in the heat as well as men, provided that they both have the same $\dot{V}_{O_2max}$.[54]

During exercise, women perspire less than men of the same fitness level,[54] but there is no evidence that women tolerate exercise in the heat better than men. Therefore, female athletes should take the same precautions as men to ensure that they are adequately hydrated during hot-weather exercise.

**When to drink.** The athlete should drink before she feels thirsty. By the time that she perceives thirst, she already will have lost 1 to 2 liters of fluid and will not be able to replace that deficit while she exercises. During intense exercise, it is impossible to absorb fluids as fast as they are lost. The maximum rate of gastric emptying is about 800 mL per hour. It is common for competing athletes to perspire as much as 2000 mL per hour.

Thirst is a late sign of dehydration during exercise because osmoreceptors in the brain will not signal a thirst sensation until the blood sodium concentration rises considerably. The primary mode of fluid loss during exercise is sweating. Sweat contains some sodium, although it is hypotonic in comparison to blood. As sodium is secreted into sweat, the serum sodium level rises more slowly than if water alone were lost. As a result, significant amounts of fluid are lost before hypernatremia develops enough to cause thirst. Therefore, on a warm day, the athlete should drink a cup of cool water just before she starts to exercise and every 15 minutes during exercise.

**What to drink.** Adequate hydration will usually prevent heat cramps and hyperthermia. Water is the preferred drink to be taken during exercise lasting less than 2 hours. Extra calories[55] and minerals[56] are usually not needed. With adequate dietary intake, the athlete will store enough hepatic and muscle glycogen to last 2 hours. A glucose concentration of more than 2.5 percent in a drink markedly slows water absorption.[57,58] Orange juice and most other fruit juices, as well as most sugar-containing drinks contain approximately 10 percent glucose, at which concentration sweet drinks taste best.

Drinks with low levels of minerals are absorbed slightly more quickly than pure water, but the difference is not significant. Mineral loss through sweat occurs so slowly that conditioned athletes rarely develop hyponatremia, hypokalemia, or hypocalcemia during exercise.[56] In fact, the opposite is more likely to occur. Serum sodium and potassium levels rise during exercise and do not fall unless the exercise is intense and prolonged. Increased serum sodium levels are due to the loss of sweat, which is hypotonic in relation to blood. Increased serum potassium levels are due to release of potassium from myocytes, preventing overheating of muscles during exercise. Blood calcium levels usually are not altered during exercise. Magnesium levels in blood decrease slightly during exercise, but this is due primarily to cellular uptake of magnesium and not to a significant loss of magnesium from the body.[59,60]

**Optimal temperature of drinks.** Cold drinks are absorbed faster and are less likely to cause abdominal pain than warm ones.[58] Fluid is absorbed almost immediately once it reaches the intestines. Cold drinks cause stomach muscles to contract and to squeeze the fluid into the intestines more rapidly than warm drinks.

## EATING AND DRINKING AFTER COMPETITION

Much of postcompetition tiredness is due to depletion of muscle glycogen stores. Recovery from vigorous exercise depends on muscle glycogen replenishment.[61] It makes no difference whether such replacement is accomplished by eating simple sugars or complex carbohydrates.[62,63] Carbohydrate intake in athletes averages around 250 grams per day. This is far too little to afford maximal glycogen replacement. It takes at least 600 grams per day of carbohydrate for maximum compensation. Therefore, it is important for athletes to eat carbohydrate-rich meals *after* competition.[64]

In events such as gymnastics, track and field, wrestling, and swimming, athletes may be scheduled to compete in several events on the same day. It is very important for them to drink immediately after they finish each event. Even if they rehydrate completely (as evidenced by a return to normal weight), it will still take 4 to 5 hours for the water to redistribute among the body fluid compartments.[65]

## PROTEIN REQUIREMENTS

Protein requirements are based on body mass and are increased by reduced caloric intake. Protein requirements are 0.8 g/kg body weight per day and do not increase significantly with exercise.[66-68] When adjusted for weight, protein requirements are the same for men and women.

Taking extra protein will not increase muscle size or strength.[69] The sole stimulus to make a muscle stronger is to exercise that muscle against resistance. This stimulus is so strong that muscles can be enlarged and strengthened by proper resistance training, even if a subject is fasting or losing weight and if all of her other muscles are becoming smaller.[70]

It does not take much *extra* protein to supply amino acids for enlarging muscles. An athlete with an excellent strength-training program may gain 1 pound of muscle in a week. Since muscle is 72 percent water, 1 pound of muscle contains only about 100 grams of protein. However, the loss of efficiency in high-quality protein utilization is around 30 percent and in poorer-quality protein around 60 percent. Therefore, to build 100 grams of extra protein, the athlete must consume 130 grams of high-quality protein ($1.3 \times 100$) or 160 grams of lower-quality protein in a week. This is accomplished by eating the equivalent of only 2 cups of corn and beans per day.

Taking extra protein can harm an athlete. Since the body cannot store extra protein, the excess is catabolized into ammonia and organic acids, much of which is excreted in the urine. These compounds act as diuretics and, during exercise in hot weather, can cause dehydration and increase the risk of heat stroke.[71]

Ingesting excessive amounts of protein can also increase calcium requirements by increasing urinary loss.[72] While this is probably of little significance to most women, it may accelerate bone loss in hypoestrogenic female athletes. Taking extra protein can also cause loss of appetite and diarrhea.

## VITAMINS

Sixty million Americans, or 37 percent of the adult population, take vitamin supplements.[73] More women (42 percent) than men (31 percent) take vitamins, presumably because they are more health conscious than men. Three out of four Americans think that taking extra vitamins will give them more energy.[74] One out of five believes that lack of vitamins causes arthritis and cancer,[75] and one out of 10 does not know that vitamin requirements can be met without taking supplements.[76] Although 10 percent may seem like a small part of the population, this figure signifies that 24 million Americans believe that they have to take vitamin supplements to be healthy.

**Mechanism of function.** A vitamin is an organic compound that the body requires in small amounts for health. While the exact mechanisms of function for several vitamins are not completely understood, much is known about the function of the B vitamins, which are parts of enzymes. Because the enzymes containing these vitamins are required in only small amounts, they catalyze reactions without being depleted.

The B vitamins enter the cells that are to use them. Such cells produce apoenzymes, which combine with the vitamins to form holoenzymes. Cells produce only limited amounts of apoenzymes, leaving unbound B vitamins in excess. The Recommended Dietary Allowances (RDAs) for B vitamins, determined by the Food and Nutrition Board (FNB) of the National Research Council of the National Academy of Sciences, "are the levels of intake . . . to be adequate to meet the known nutritional needs of practically all healthy persons."[77] It also represents the amount of B vitamins that will saturate the apoenzymes of the target cells.[77] Ingesting more vitamins catalyzes no more reactions, because cellular apoenzymes are the limiting factor.

To help your patients understand why excess dosages of B vitamins are not needed, you can use the following analogy offered by Herbert and Barrett.[78] Consider the human body to be like a traffic intersection. Many cars (chemical reactions) pass through the intersection, but only one police officer (vitamin) is necessary to direct traffic. Bringing in many police officers (excess vitamins) will not cause more cars (chemical reactions) to pass through the intersection.

**Vitamin needs of female athletes.** The diets of athletes who take in more than 2000 calories per day usually supply vitamins in amounts greater than their RDAs.[79] People who try to control their weight usually restrict their intake of food, and this can lead to an intake of vitamins that is less than the RDA. However, the RDAs are set so far above minimum requirements that dieters rarely develop signs or symptoms of vitamin deficiency, even if they do not meet the RDAs.[80]

Prolonged exercise can increase requirements for thiamin, niacin, riboflavin, and pantothenic acid beyond their RDAs.[81] These four vitamins catalyze the reactions that convert carbohydrates and protein to energy.[82] For example, heavy exercise can increase riboflavin requirements by as much as 17 percent,[81] but the total daily needs for riboflavin can be met by drinking three glasses of milk. The total needs for all four "energy" vitamins can be met by eating a varied diet that contains more than 2000 calories per day, as all four of these vitamins are found in meat, fish, chicken, milk, and whole grains.

Although the refining process removes thiamin, niacin, riboflavin, and pantothenic acid from flour, most manufacturers routinely add these vitamins in order to comply with interstate shipping laws. Thus, athletes who eat breads made from refined flour rarely need supplements containing these "energy vitamins."

**Vitamin C and colds.** Some athletes take large doses of vitamin C in the hope that it will help to protect them from developing upper respiratory infections. However, virtually all double-blind studies on the subject show that vitamin C does not prevent colds.[83]

**Vitamins and birth control pills.** It remains controversial whether women who take oral contraceptives require vitamin supplementation.[84-86] A review of the literature shows that, on the average, women who take birth control pills have lower serum levels of riboflavin, pyridoxine, folacin, cyanocobalamin, and ascorbic acid and higher body levels of vitamin K.[86] However, their tissue levels[87] and blood levels[87,88] are still within the normal range. There is no evidence that such women are more likely to develop clinical symptoms of vitamin deficiency. Since birth control pills increase needs for these vitamins only a small percentage, if at all, it seems unlikely that vitamin requirements change appreciably because of oral contraceptive use.

**Vitamins and premenstrual syndrome (PMS).** Strength, speed, endurance, and coordination have not been shown to vary consistently throughout the menstrual cycle. Female athletes report greater perceived exertion premenstrually. PMS is discussed more thoroughly in Chapter 14.

Several investigators have suggested that nutritional factors play a role in PMS and have proposed dietary therapy for this syndrome. Pyridoxine has been touted as a treatment for PMS, because it is claimed to raise serotonin levels in the brain. High levels of serotonin are associated with mood elevation, low levels with depression.

Pyridoxine is a coenzyme for 5-hydroxytryptophan decarboxylase, which catalyzes tryptophan's conversion to serotonin. There is no evidence that PMS sufferers have low brain levels of serotonin or that giving extra pyridoxine will raise brain levels. Two studies showed that taking pyridoxine improves PMS symptoms,[89,90] while another showed no improvement.[91] Although many women consider pyridoxine, in any dosage, to be harmless, large doses of pyridoxine have been reported to cause neural toxicity.[92,93]

## MINERALS

The major minerals are listed in Table 7–7. Iron and calcium are the only supplements that healthy female athletes may need to take. An adequate diet can provide adequate amounts of all minerals, but many diets are deficient in these two.

**Iron.** As many as one out of every four female athletes is iron deficient.[94] Men and nonmenstruating women need about 12 mg of iron per day. The average man ingests adequate iron from dietary sources alone; the average woman ingests around 12 mg of iron

**Table 7-7. MINERALS**

| Major | Trace |
|---|---|
| Calcium | Fluorine |
| Phosphorus | Silicon |
| Chlorine | Vanadium |
| Potassium | Chromium |
| Sulfur | Manganese |
| Sodium | Iron |
| Magnesium | Cobalt |
| | Nickel |
| | Copper |
| | Zinc |
| | Selenium |
| | Molybdenum |
| | Tin |
| | Iodine |

per day. However, menstruating women need 18 mg of iron per day, the extra 6 mg needed to replace the iron that is lost through menstrual bleeding. Birth control pills reduce iron requirements, by decreasing menstrual blood loss and increasing iron absorption.[95]

Iron deficiency, even in the absence of anemia, can impair endurance. Approximately 40 percent of the iron in the body is in the iron reserves, such as the liver, bone marrow, and spleen. The rest is contained in hemoglobin. Iron-deficiency anemia does not occur until almost all the iron reserves are depleted. Iron deficiency reduces the concentration of alphaglycerophosphate oxidase in muscle, and this impairs glycolysis and leads to lactic acid accumulation in muscle and blood.[96] An increase in lactate causes a lowering of pH, and this reduces muscular endurance.[97] People who have iron deficiency, even without anemia, have a reduced rate of lactic acid clearance from the blood, and they tire earlier during exercise. Restoring their iron reserves to normal increases their endurance.[98]

The most accurate test for detecting iron deficiency is a microscopic examination of bone marrow for stained iron. However, obtaining marrow is painful, invasive, and expensive. A simple, noninvasive screening test for iron deficiency is the measurement of serum ferritin. Caution must be used in interpreting the results, since inflammation anywhere in the body can raise ferritin levels. A person who has an inflammatory proc-

**Table 7–8.** FOODS THAT CONTAIN APPROXIMATELY 250 MG CALCIUM

1 glass milk
1 cup yogurt
1½ cups cottage cheese
1½ cups ice cream
1½ oz hard cheese
2 oz sardines with bones
4 oz canned salmon with bones

ess may have normal serum ferritin levels, despite iron deficiency.

Up to 30 percent of heme iron, found in meat, fish, and chicken, is absorbed, while less than 10 percent is absorbed from nonheme iron sources. Acidity enhances iron absorption from nonheme sources but not from heme sources. Thus, eating an orange with spinach enhances iron absorption from the spinach, but taking vitamin C with meat does not increase absorption of iron from meat. On the other hand, alkalinity, fiber, and tannins reduce iron absorption from both heme and nonheme sources. For example, taking antacids, eating fibrous vegetables, and drinking tea and coffee decrease iron absorption from all sources.

Because of the high prevalence of iron deficiency among female athletes and because of its detrimental effect upon performance, I recommend that all female athletes eat meat, fish, or chicken daily, and, if they do not, I recommend supplementation with 30 to 60 mg/day of elemental iron. Although such doses may harm people who have hereditary disorders in iron absorption, such as hemochromatosis and porphyria, normal people are extremely unlikely to develop toxicity.[99]

**Calcium.** Estrogen, exercise, and dietary calcium all help to prevent osteoporosis. Of the three, estrogen appears to be the most important.

Exercise can enlarge bones and increase bone density.[100] The bones in the racquet-holding arm of a tennis player are larger and denser than those in the other arm. However, exercise will not maintain bone density effectively in women who lack estrogen. For example, exercise-associated amenorrhea is associated with decreased bone density,[101] and estrogen replacement helps to maintain bone density in hypoestrogenic women.[102]

Nevertheless, adequate calcium intake is essential for maintenance of bone density. Increasing dietary calcium can improve calcium balance in women who lack estrogen.[103] Hypoestrogenic women require 1500 mg of calcium per day to maintain zero calcium balance, whereas euestrogenic women require 1000 mg to do so.[104] However, estrogen is far more effective than dietary calcium in maintaining bone density.[105] Hypoestrogenic, amenorrheic women who do not have a contraindication to estrogen replacement therapy should be treated with estrogen and, if dietary calcium is inadequate, calcium supplements.

The best dietary sources of calcium are dairy products and soft-boned fish, such as canned salmon and sardines (Table 7–8). Dairy products provide 72 percent of dietary calcium for the average American.[106] Those who do not meet their calcium requirements from diet alone should take calcium supplements (Table 7–9), unless they are predisposed to nephrolithiasis.

The Food and Drug Administration has found significant amounts of lead in some samples of bone meal and dolomite.[107] Dolomite is most frequently harvested from

**Table 7–9.** CALCIUM CONTENT IN 600 MG SUPPLEMENT

| Content of Pill | Mg | % Calcium | Number of Pills Required to Ingest 1 Gram |
|---|---|---|---|
| Calcium carbonate | 240 | 40 | 4 |
| Calcium lactate | 78 | 13 | 12 |
| Calcium gluconate | 54 | 9 | 18.5 |
| Calcium phosphate (dibasic) | 171 | 28 | 6 |

shells of shellfish at the bottom of harbors. Dolomite taken from polluted harbors can contain toxic amounts of lead, mercury, arsenic, and other heavy metals. Bone meal also may contain significant amounts of toxic metals, since it usually comes from the bones of older animals.[108] With aging, toxic metals accumulate in the bones of all animals, including humans. Because dolomite and bone meal are usually sold as food supplements rather than drugs, manufacturers are not required by the government to list the heavy metal content of their products. Therefore, labels on packages containing these products do not list their heavy metal content.

**Sodium.** Most people do not need to consume extra sodium when they exercise. The requirement for sodium for people at rest is 0.2 grams per day. With prolonged exercise in very hot weather, the maximal requirement for sodium is approximately 3 grams per day. The average American diet contains between 6 and 18 grams of sodium chloride per day, of which 40 percent is sodium (2.4 to 7.2 grams). Manufacturers add sodium chloride to foods as a preservative, and some people add sodium chloride to foods to improve the taste. Athletes who try to limit sodium intake by avoiding salty-tasting foods and by adding no sodium to foods still take in about 3 grams of sodium each day.

Sodium chloride tablets should not be given routinely to exercising athletes. Besides being unnecessary, they can cause gastric irritation, nausea, and, in very large doses, potassium deficiency.[110]

Sodium deficiency can occur in healthy people because of inadequate intake of sodium or excessive use of diuretics. It can also occur in people with hormonal or renal defects. Any exerciser who feels tired and weak or develops painful muscle cramps should have serum levels of sodium measured. If present, hyponatremia requires a thorough evaluation to determine the cause (e.g., diabetes insipidus, diabetes mellitus, water intoxication, and so on).

Many women who experience premenstrual fluid retention as part of premenstrual syndrome (PMS) may benefit from dietary sodium restriction at the times of symptoms during each cycle. Despite anecdotal reports of the success of this regimen, no scientific studies have assessed its effectiveness.

**Potassium.** Potassium deficiency is an extremely rare condition in trained athletes.

The kidney and sweat glands are highly efficient in conserving potassium in response to low body levels. Even with prolonged exercise in very hot weather, potassium needs can be met by an intake of only 3 to 4 grams per day.[109] However, potassium deficiency can occur as the result of potassium restriction and sodium loading.[110]

The only way that one researcher could create a low-potassium diet for athletes and still provide enough calories for exercise was to feed them candy and little else throughout the day. Even then, the athletes did not develop potassium deficiency.[111] Almost all foods are rich in potassium. Since potassium is found primarily within cells, any food that contains cells also contains potassium.

Hypokalemia always requires a thorough evaluation to determine the cause. Potassium deficiency can be caused by drugs, such as diuretics and corticosteroids, and certain foods, such as licorice. Prolonged diarrhea and vomiting also can cause potassium deficiency (Table 7–10). With diarrhea, potassium is lost in the stool. With vomiting, loss of hydrogen ions causes a metabolic alkalosis, which increases potassium loss in the urine to conserve renal hydrogen ions.

Bulimia can present in athletes as weakness and tiredness with laboratory evidence of potassium deficiency. If blood samples show reduced potassium levels and 24-hour urine collections contain increased amounts of potassium, suspect vomiting as the cause.

**Trace minerals.** Humans require approximately 14 trace minerals in small amounts. There is no evidence that athletes need trace mineral supplements, with the exception of iron, because trace mineral deficiencies are extremely rare in healthy athletes.

Some lay publications for athletes claim incorrectly that trace mineral deficiencies are common causes of fatigue in athletes. They argue that repeated harvesting of crops depletes the soil of essential minerals. When the soil in a certain region is deficient in a

**Table 7–10.** MECHANISM BY WHICH VOMITING CAUSES HYPOKALEMIA

Loss of hydrogen ions
Raised blood pH
Renal hydrogen retention
Renal potassium loss

mineral, the plants and animals that grow in that region will suffer from a deficiency of that mineral also. That may have been possible in the past, but it is extremely unlikely to occur now. Although it is possible that some soils lack certain minerals, our transportation system is so extensive and efficient that very few Americans eat foods grown only in a single locality. It is impossible for all soils to be deficient in the same single mineral.

Oral contraceptive agents may reduce slightly requirements for copper and raise those for zinc, but there is no evidence that the latter is enough to require supplementation. Women who take birth control pills have higher serum levels of copper and lower levels of zinc than those who do not take such pills.[112,113] Estrogen is thought to raise serum copper levels by increasing serum ceruloplasmin levels.[114] The mechanism by which oral contraceptives lower serum zinc levels is not known.[115]

## THE ATHLETE'S DIET

Of course, your patients cannot become great athletes just by altering their diets. They have to choose their parents wisely and train harder than their competitors. From the foregoing discussion, it is obvious that they can get all the nutrients their bodies need from the foods they eat. With the possible exceptions of iron and calcium, a female athlete's requirement for nutrients is the same as it is for male athletes. The only supplements that are required commonly are iron and calcium. Taking large doses of vitamin and mineral supplements can be toxic. Adverse side effects have been reported from large doses of even the relatively harmless water-soluble vitamins, such as niacin, pyridoxine, and folic acid. To help your patients perform sports more effectively, you should recommend that they eat a varied diet that is rich in carbohydrates and that they follow the rules for eating and timing foods and drinks that are outlined in this chapter.

Several lay books claim that a high-fiber, low-fat diet will improve athletic performance. There is no evidence to support this. In fact, one study showed that exercisers who ate a diet that contained 10 percent fat had the same improvement in $\dot{V}_{O_2max}$ as those who obtained 45 percent of their calories

from fat.[116] Nevertheless, you may want to recommend restricting dietary fat, saturated fat, and cholesterol because it may help to reduce a woman's chances of developing coronary artery disease and certain types of cancers in the future.

Taking into account that foods have nutrients in different combinations and that foods in similar groups have similar nutrient content, the Department of Agriculture developed a simple plan for eating a varied diet that will supply all nutrients. The four food groups are

1. Fruits and vegetables
2. Grains and cereals
3. Milk and milk products
4. High-protein foods, which include meat, fish, fowl, and beans

The athlete should make sure that she eats a wide variety of foods from all four groups each day.

## SUMMARY

With the exception of iron and calcium, nutrient requirements for female athletes are the same as those for their male counterparts and can be met by consuming foods that contain energy sources that are adequate to maintain exercise. Iron deficiency, even in the absence of anemia, can impair endurance. Amenorrhea can be associated with exercise and can increase calcium requirements.

Endurance can be enhanced by maximizing muscle and liver glycogen stores by reducing the volume of training 3 days before competition, eating a high-carbohydrate meal on the night before competition, and by eating an easily absorbed meal 3 to 5 hours prior to competition. Maintaining adequate hydration, even before experiencing thirst, will also improve endurance. The rate of recovery following intense exercise can be hastened by eating extra carbohydrates soon after exercising.

Protein requirements do not increase significantly during exercise, and taking extra protein does not increase muscle mass. Vitamin supplementation is not necessary, since requirements can be met through diet. Healthy athletes do not need to increase their intake of sodium, potassium, or trace minerals because the body can usually compensate for increased loss or decreased intake by increasing retention.

# References

1. Cook JD, Clement AF, and Smith NJ: Evaluation of the iron status of a population. Blood 48:449, 1976.
2. Smith NJ, Stanitski CL, Dyment PG, et al: Decreased iron stores in high school female runners. Am J Dis Child 139:115, 1985.
3. Lloyd T, Triantaflou SJ, Baker ER, et al: Women athletes with menstrual irregularity have increased musculoskeletal injuries. Med Sci Sports Exerc 18(4):374, 1986.
4. Wolf EMB, Wirth JC, and Lohman TG: Nutritional practices of coaches in the big ten. The Physician and Sportsmedicine 7:113, 1979.
5. Grandjean AC, Hursh LM, Majure WC, et al: Nutrition knowledge and practices of college athletes. Med Sci Sports Exerc 13(2):82, 1981.
6. Mirkin GB, and Shangold MM: Sports Medicine. JAMA 254(16):2340, 1985.
7. Davison AJ, Banister E, and Tauton J: Rate limiting processes in energy metabolism. In Taylor AW (ed): Application of Science and Medicine to Sport. Charles A Thomas, Springfield, IL, 1975, p 105.
8. Costill DL, Fink WJ, Getchell LH, et al: Lipid metabolism in skeletal muscle of endurance-trained males and females. J Appl Physiol 47:787, 1971.
9. Dyer KF: Making up the difference. Some explanations for recent improvements in women's athletic performance. Search 16(9):264, 1985.
10. Dyer KF: The trend of the male-female differential in various speed sports 1936–84. J Biosoc Sci 18:169, 1986.
11. Costill DL: Inside Running. Basics of Sports Physiology. Benchmark Press, Indianapolis, 1986, p 154.
12. Hultman E: Studies on muscle metabolism of glycogen and active phosphate in man with special reference to exercise and diet. Scand J Clin Lab Invest 19:94, 1967.
13. Mirkin GB: Food and nutrition for exercise. In Bove AA, and Lowenthal DT (eds): Exercise Medicine: Physiological Principles and Clinical Applications. Academic Press, New York, 1983.
14. Karlsson J, Nordesjo LO, and Saltin, B: Muscle glycogen utilization during exercise after physical training. Acta Physiol Scand 90:210, 1974.
15. Koivisto V, Hendler R, Nadel E, et al: Influence of physical training on the fuel-hormone response to prolonged low-intensity exercise. Metabolism 31:192, 1982.
16. Maughan RJ, Williams C, Campbell DM, et al: Fat and carbohydrate metabolism during low-intensity exercise: Effects of the availability of muscle glycogen. Eur J Physiol 39:7, 1978.
17. Miller JM, Coyle EF, Sherman WM, et al: Effect of glycerol feeding on endurance and metabolism during prolonged exercise in man. Med Sci Sports Exerc 15:237, 1983.
18. Askew EW: Role of fat metabolism in exercise. Clinics in Sports and Medicine 3:605, 1984.
19. Askew EW, Dohm GL, Weiser PC, et al: Supplemental dietary carnitine and lipid metabolism in exercising rats. Nutr Metab 24:32, 1980.
20. Ivy JL, Costill DL, and Fink WJ: Influence of caffeine and carbohydrate feedings on endurance performance. Med Sci Sports Exerc 11:6, 1979.
21. Christensen EH, and Hansen O: Hypoglykamie, Arbeitsfahigkeit und Ermudung. Scand Arch Physiol 81:172, 1939.
22. Hultman E: Studies on muscle metabolism of glycogen and active phosphate in man with special reference to exercise and diet. Scand J Clin Lab Invest 19:94, 1967.
23. Astrand PO: Something old and something new—very new. Nutr Today 3(2):9, 1968.
24. Mirkin GB: Carbohydrate loading: a dangerous practice. JAMA 223:1511, 1973.
25. Banks WJ: Myoglobinuria in marathon runners: possible relationship to carbohydrate and lipid metabolism. Ann NY Acad Sci 301:942, 1977.
26. Sherman WM, Costill DL, Fink WJ, et al: The effect of exercise-diet manipulation on muscle glycogen and its subsequent utilization during performance. Int J Sports Med 2:114, 1981.
27. Costill DL, Sherman M, Fink W, et al: The role of dietary carbohydrates in muscle glycogen resynthesis after strenuous running. Am J Clin Nutr 34:1831, 1981.
28. Piehl K: Time course for refilling of glycogen stores in human muscle fibers following exercise-induced glycogen depletion. Acta Physiol Scand 90:297, 1974.
29. Roberts KM, Noble EG, Hayden DB, et al: The effect of simple and complex carbohydrate diets on skeletal muscle glycogen and lipoprotein lipase of marathon runners. Clini Physiol 5:41, 1985.
30. Hultman E, and Nilson LH: Liver glycogen in man: Effect of different diets on muscular exercise. In Saltin B, and Pernow B (eds): Muscle Metabolism During Exercise. Plenum, New York, 1971, p 143.
31. Felig P, Cherif A, Minagawa A, et al: Hypoglycemia during prolonged exercise in normal men. N Engl J Med 306:895, 1982.
32. Costil DL, Coyle E, Dalsky G, et al: Effects of elevated plasma FFA and insulin on muscle glycogen usage during exercise. J Appl Physiol 43:695, 1977.
33. Karlsson J, and Saltin B: Diet, muscle glycogen and endurance performance. J Appl Physiol 31:203, 1971.
34. Fogoros RN: Runners' trots. Gastrointestinal disturbances in runners. JAMA 243:1743, 1980.
35. Nielsen AA: Roentgenological examinations of the motility of the stomach in healthy individuals during rest and motion. Acta Radiol 1:379, 1921.
36. Helebrandt FA, and Tepper RH: Studies on the influence of exercise on the digestive work of the stomach. Am J Physiol 107:355, 1934.
37. Fordtran JS, and Saltin B: Gastric emptying and intestinal absorption during prolonged severe exercise. J Appl Physiol 23:331, 1967.
38. Clausen JP: Effect of physical training on cardiovascular adjustments to exercise in man. Physiol Rev 57:779, 1977.
39. American Health, April, 1985, p 27 (advertisement).
40. Decombaz J, Sartori D, Arnaud MJ, et al: Oxidation and metabolic effects of fructose or glucose ingested before exercise. Int J Sports Med 6:282, 1985.
41. Koivisto VA, Karvonen S-L, and Nikkila EA: Car-

bohydrate ingestion before exercise: comparison of glucose, fructose and sweet placebo. J Appl Physiol 51(4):783, 1981.

42. Hargreaves M, Costill DL, Fink WJ, et al: Effect of pre-exercise carbohydrate feedings on endurance in cyling performance. Med Sci Sports Exerc 19(1):33, 1987.

43. Bjorkman O, Sanlin K, Hagenfeldt L, et al: Influence of glucose and fructose ingestion on the capacity for long-term exercise in well-trained men. Clin Physiol 4:483, 1984.

44. Krzentowski G, Pirnay F, Luyckx AS, et al: Effect of physical training on utilization of a glucose load given orally during exercise. Am J Physiol 246:E412, 1984.

45. Ivy JL, Costill DL, Fink WJ, et al: Influence of caffeine and carbohydrate feedings on endurance performance. Med Sci Sports Exerc 11:6, 1979.

46. Koivisto VA, Harkonen M, Karonen S-L, et al: Glycogen depletion during prolonged exercise: influence of glucose, fructose or placebo. J Appl Physiol 58(3):731, 1985.

47. Levine L, Evans WJ, Cadarette BS, et al: Fructose and glucose ingestion and muscle glycogen use during submaximal exercise. J Appl Physiol 55(6):1767, 1983.

48. Bjorkman O, Sahlin K, Hagenfeldt L, et al: Influence of glucose and fructose on the capacity for long-term exercise in well-trained men. Clin Physiol 4:483, 1984.

49. Miller JM, Coyle EF, Sherman WM, et al: Effect of glycerol feeding on endurance and metabolism during prolonged exercise in man. Med Sci Sports Exerc 15:237, 1983.

50. Coyle EF, Hagberg JM, Hurley BF, et al: Carbohydrate feeding during prolonged strenuous exercise can delay fatigue. J Appl Physiol 55(1):230, 1983.

51. Flynn MG, Costill DL, Hawley JA, et al: Influence of selected carbohydrate drinks on cycling performance and glycogen use. Med Sci Sports Exerc 19(1):37, 1987.

52. Sherman WH, and Costill DL: The marathon: dietary manipulation to optimize performance. Am J Sports Med 12(1):44, 1984.

53. Mirkin GB, and Shangold MM: Muscle cramps during exercise. JAMA 253(11):1634, 1985.

54. Eddy DO, Sparks KL, and Adelizi DA: The effects of continuous and interval training in women and men. Eur J Appl Physiol 37:83, 1977.

55. Hargreaves M, Costill DL, Cogan A, et al: Effects of carbohydrate feeding on muscle glycogen utilization and exercise performance. Med Sci Sports Exerc 16:219, 1984.

56. Costill DL, Cote R, Fink WJ, et al: Muscle water and electrolyte distribution during prolonged exercise. Int J Sports Med 3:130, 1981.

57. Costill DL, and Saltin B: Factors limiting gastric emptying during rest and exercise. J Appl Physiol 37:679, 1974.

58. Fordtran JS, and Saltin B: Gastric emptying and intestinal absorption during prolonged severe exercise. J Appl Physiol 23:331, 1967.

59. Wolfswinkel JM, Van Der Walt WH, and Van Der Linde A: Intravascular shift in magnesium during prolonged exercise. South Afr J Sci 79:37, 1983.

60. Refsum HE, Meen HD, and Stromme SB: Whole blood serum and erythrocyte magnesium concen-

trations after repeated heavy exercise of long duration. Scand J Clin Invest 32:123, 1973.

61. Costill DL, Sherman WM, Fink WJ, et al: Role of dietary carbohydrate in muscle glycogen resynthesis after strenuous running. Am J Clin Nutr 34:1831, 1981.

62. Costill DL, and Miller JM: Nutrition for endurance sport: Carbohydrate and fluid balance. Int J Sports Med 1:2, 1980.

63. Williams C, Patton A, and Brewer J: Influence of diet on recovery from prolonged exercise. Proc Nutr Soc 44:28A, 1985.

64. Costill DL, Sherman WM, Fink, WJ, et al: The role of dietary carbohydrate in muscle glycogen resynthesis after strenuous running. Am J Clin Nutr 34:1831, 1982.

65. McCutcheon ML: The athlete's diet: A current view. J Fam Pract 16:529, 1983.

66. Consolazio CF, Johnson HL, Nelson RQ, et al: Protein metabolism of intensive physical training in the young adult. Am J Clin Nutr 28:29, 1975.

67. Wilson HEC: The influence of work on muscular metabolism. J Physiol (London)75:67, 1932.

68. FAO/WHO: Energy and protein requirements. A report of a joint ad hoc expert committee, serial number 522. FAO/WHO, Rome, 1973, p 5.

69. Marable NL, Hickson JF, Jr, Korsland MK, et al: Urinary nitrogen excretion as influenced by a muscle-building exercise program and protein intake variation. Nutrition Reports International 19:795, 1979.

70. Goldberg AL, Etlinger JD, Goldspink PF, et al: Mechanism of work-induced hypertrophy of skeletal muscle. Med Sci Sports Exerc 7(3):185, 1975.

71. Serfass RC: Nutrition for athletes. Contemporary Nutrition 12:1, 1977.

72. Anand CR, and Linkswiler HM: Effect of protein intake on calcium balance of young men given 500 mg calcium daily. J Nutr 104:695, 1974.

73. The Gallop Study of Vitamin Use in the United States: Survey VI, Vol I. The Gallop Organization, Princeton, NJ, 1981, p 1.

74. US Department of Health, Education and Welfare, Food and Drug Administration, Bureau of Foods: Consumer nutrition knowledge survey: report II, 1975. Government Printing Office, Washington, DC, 1976.

75. National Analysts, Inc: A study of health practices and opinions. Contract number FDA 66-193. National Technical Information Service, Springfield, VA, 1972.

76. Herbert V: Nutrition Cultism: Facts and Fictions. George F. Stickly Co, Philadelphia, 1980, p 145.

77. Food and Nutrition Board: Recommended Dietary Allowances, ed 9. National Academy of Sciences, Washington, DC, 1980, p 1.

78. Herbert V, and Barrett S: Vitamins and "Health Foods": The Great American Hustle. George F. Stickly Co, Philadelphia, 1981, p 6.

79. Short SH, and Short WR: Four-year study of university athlete's dietary intake. J Am Diet Assoc 82:632, 1983.

80. Hickson J, Schrader J, and Cunningham L: Female athletes' energy and nutrient intakes. Fed Proc 42:803, 1983.

81. Belko AZ, Obarzanek E, Kalkwarf HJ, et al: Effects of exercise on riboflavin requirements of young women. Am J Clin Nutr 37:509, 1983.

82. Shills ME: Food and nutrition relating to work and environmental stress. In Goodhart RS, and Shills ME (eds): Nutrition in Health and Disease, ed 5. Lea and Febiger, Philadelphia, p 711.

83. Hodges RE: Food fads and megavitamins. In Hodges RE (ed): Nutrition in Medical Practice. WB Saunders, Philadelphia, 1980, p 293.

84. Prasad AS, Lei KY, and Moghissi KS: The effect of oral contraceptives on micronutrients. In Mosley WH (ed): Nutrition and Human Reproduction. Plenum Press, New York, 1978.

85. Smith JL, Goldsmith GA, and Lawrence JD: Effects of oral contraceptive steroids on vitamin and lipid levels in serum. Am J Clin Nutr 28:371, 1975.

86. Webb JL: Nutritional effects of oral contraceptive use. J Reprod Med 25:150, 1980.

87. Shojania M: Oral contraceptives: effects on folate and vitamin $B_{12}$ metabolism. CMA 126:244, 1982.

88. Roe DA, Bogusz S, Sheu J, et al: Factors affecting riboflavin requirements of oral contraceptive users and nonusers. Am J Clin Nutr 35:495, 1982.

89. Day JB: Clinical trials in the premenstrual syndrome. Curr Med Res Opin 6(Suppl 5):40, 1979.

90. Abraham GE, and Hargrove JT: Effect of vitamin $B_6$ on premenstrual symptomatology in women with premenstrual tension syndromes: A double-blind cross-over study. Infertility 3:155, 1980.

91. Stokes J, and Mendels J: Pyridoxine and premenstrual tension. Lancet 1:1177, 1972.

92. Schaumberg H, et al: Sensory neuropathy from pyridoxine abuse. A new megavitamin syndrome. N Engl J Med 309:445, 1983.

93. Vasile A, Goldberg R, and Kornberg B: Pyridoxine toxicity: report of a case. J AOA 83(11):790, 1984.

94. Margen S, and King J: Effect of oral contraceptive agents on the metabolism of some trace minerals. Am J Clin Nutr 28:392, 1975.

95. de Wijn JF, De Jongste JL, Mosterd W, et al: Hemoglobin, packed cell volume, serum iron and iron-binding capacity of selected athletes during training. Nutr Metab 13:129, 1971.

96. Finch CA, Miller LR, Inamdar AR, et al: Iron deficiency in the rat, physiological and biochemical studies on muscle dysfunction. J Clin Invest 58:447, 1976.

97. Finch CA, Gollnick PD, Hlastala MP, et al: Lactic acidosis as a result of iron deficiency. J Clin Invest 64:129, 1979.

98. Nilson K, Schoene RB, Robertson HT, et al: The effects of iron repletion on exercise-induced lactate production in minimally iron-deficient subjects. Med Sci Sports Exerc 13(2):92, 1981.

99. Finch CA, and Monsen ER: Iron nutrition and the fortification of food with iron. JAMA 219:1462, 1972.

100. Aloia JF: Exercise and skeletal health. J Am Geriatr Soc 29:104, 1981.

101. Drinkwater B, Nilson K, Chesnut CH, et al: Bone mineral content of amenorrheic and eumenorrheic athletes. N Engl J Med 311:277, 1984.

102. Shangold MM: Causes, evaluation and management of athletic oligo/amenorrhea. Med Clin North Am 69:83, 1985.

103. Recker RR, Saville PD, and Heaney RO: Effect of estrogen and calcium carbonate on bone loss in postmenopausal women. Ann Intern Med 87:649, 1977.

104. Heaney RP, Recker RE, and Saville PD: Menopausal changes in calcium balance performance. J Lab Clin Med 92:953, 1978.

105. Riis B, Thomsen K, and Christiansen C: Does calcium supplementation prevent post-menopausal bone loss? A double-blind, controlled clinical study. N Engl J Med 316(4):173, 1987.

106. Marston RM, and Welsh SO: Nutrient content of the U.S. food supply. National Food Review 25:7, 1984.

107. Advice on limiting intake of bonemeal. FDA Drug Bull 12(1):5, April, 1982.

108. Roberts HJ: Potential toxicity due to dolomite and bonemeal. South Med J 76(5):556, 1983.

109. Lane HW, Roessler GS, Nelson EW, et al: Effect of physical activity on human potassium metabolism in a hot and humid environment. Am J Clin Nutr 31:838, 1978.

110. Talbot NB, Richie RH, and Crawford JD: Metabolic Homeostasis: A Syllabus for Those Concerned with the Care of Patients. Harvard University Press, Cambridge, 1959, p 32.

111. Costill D: Muscle water and electrolytes during acute and repeated bouts of dehydration. In Parizkova J, and Rogozkin VA (eds): Nutrition, Physical Fitness and Health. University Park Press, Baltimore, 1978, p 106.

112. Prasad AS, Oberleas D, Lei KY, et al: Effect of oral contraceptive agents on nutrients: I. Minerals. Am J Clin Nutr 28:377, 1975.

113. Schenker JG, Hellerstein S, Jungreis E, et al: Serum copper and zinc levels in patients taking oral contraceptives. Fertil Steril 22:229, 1971.

114. Carruthers ME, Hobbs CB, and Warren RL: Raised serum copper and caeruloplasmin levels in subjects taking oral contraceptives. J Clin Pathol 19:498, 1966.

115. Prasad AS, Moghissi KS, Lei KY, et al: Effect of oral contraceptives on micronutrients and changes in trace elements due to pregnancy. In Moghissi KS, and Evans TN (eds): Nutritional Impacts on Women Throughout Life with Emphasis on Reproduction. Harper and Row, New York, 1977, p 160.

116. Kosich D, Conlee R, Fisher AG, et al: The effects of exercise and a low-fat diet or a moderate-fat diet on selected coronary risk factors. In Dotson C, and Humphrey J (eds): Exercise Physiology: Current Selected Research Vol 2, AMS Press, New York, 1986, p 173.

# PART II

# Developmental Phases

# CHAPTER 8

# The Prepubescent Female

ODED BAR-OR, M.D.

Recent years have seen an increasing interest in the physiologic responses of children to exercise. Such interest reflects the greater participation—and success—of prepubescents and adolescents in elite sports, as well as the recognition that physical exercise is relevant to the health of the nonathletic child.

Although prepubescent athletes of both sexes engage in elite sports, it is primarily the females who have become extremely successful at the national and international levels. Such success is particularly apparent in gymnastics, figure skating, and swimming, in which prepubescents have been performing at levels that, a decade or two ago, were not considered feasible even for adults.

To achieve such excellence, many female athletes have to practice as much as 4 to 6 hours per day and at high intensity. Such involvement and dedication has educational, psychosocial, medical, gynecologic, orthopedic, and physiologic consequences. These have become a focus of research for sports scientists of various disciplines.

Exercise-related research is oriented also toward the young nonathlete, healthy or ill. Study of the healthy child has been of interest, for example, to kinanthropometrists, who are interested in growth patterns and the interrelationships between morphologic and functional changes; to epidemiologists, who assess the possible relationships between habitual activity during childhood and the risk of chronic disease in later years; to motor behaviorists, who study motor learning and skill acquisition; and to physiologists, who seek answers to such maturation-

109

related issues as strength development, energy expenditure of locomotion, trainability, and thermoregulation.

The relevance of exercise to the ill child has also generated growing interest. Pediatric cardiologists and respirologists, for example, are using exercise for the assessment of children with such diseases as congenital heart defects, bronchial asthma, and cystic fibrosis; an exercise prescription is incorporated into the management of the child with diabetes mellitus, obesity, muscular dystrophy, cerebral palsy, and cystic fibrosis; and detrimental effects of exercise are studied in such conditions as aortic stenosis, dysrhythmia, primary amenorrhea, and epilepsy.

This chapter is meant to focus on the physiologic responses to exercise of the healthy prepubescent girl. Emphasis will be given to differences among prepubescents, adolescents, and young adults. Differences will also be pointed out between the responses to exercise of girls and boys. Whenever relevant, the implications to health of such differences will be pointed out.

It is assumed that the reader has some basic knowledge of exercise physiology. Additional information on pediatric exercise physiology can be found in monographs,[1-4] edited books,[5,6] and proceedings of the Pediatric Work Physiology Group.[7-15]

## PHYSIOLOGIC RESPONSE TO SHORT-TERM EXERCISE

Differences in the response to short-term exercise (less than a 15-minute duration) of prepubescent and older females are summarized in Table 8–1. Table 8–2 is a summary of gender-related differences in the response of prepubescents to short-term exercise. The following discussion will highlight those characteristics of the prepubescent girl that have a direct relevance to her physical performance.

### Submaximal Oxygen Uptake

Typically for young girls, oxygen uptake (calculated per body mass unit) while running or walking at any given speed is higher than in adolescent or adult females.[1,16-18] A 5.5-year-old girl, for example, who runs at 10 km per hour, consumes about 46 mL of oxygen per kg body weight per minute, compared with 37 mL$\cdot$kg$^{-1}\cdot$min$^{-}1$ in a 16-year-old adolescent.[1]

The implication of such a high metabolic cost is that, at any walking or running speed, a young girl operates at a higher percentage of her maximal aerobic power and will fatigue earlier than an older girl or a woman. This may be the main reason why young girls cannot compete on a par with their older counterparts in middle- and long-distance running. Such a difference is virtually nonexistent during cycling.[19-21] This suggests that the biochemical-to-mechanical energy transfer efficiency in muscles is not lower at a young age, but young girls have a more "wasteful" gait, which increases their mechanical output and metabolic demands during the gait cycle. No data are available on the age-related differences in the metabolic cost of swimming. The success of young girls in elite swimming would suggest, however, that a proficient young swimmer is not less economical in her style than her older counterpart.

### Maximal Aerobic Power

Throughout childhood and adolescence maximal aerobic power, as reflected by maximal oxygen uptake ($\dot{V}_{O2max}$), increases with age. The $\dot{V}_{O2max}$ of 5-year-old preschoolers is 0.80 to 0.90 L$\cdot$min$^{-1}$, compared with 1.1 to 1.5 L$\cdot$min$^{-1}$ and 1.6 to 2.2 L$\cdot$min$^{-1}$ for 10- and 16-year-old girls, respectively.[1,2] Calculated per kilogram body weight, however, there is little change in the $\dot{V}_{O2max}$ of girls up to the age of 10 to 11 years. During the second decade of life, $\dot{V}_{O2max}$ per kilogram decreases with age, such that it is approximately 4 to 6 ml mL$\cdot$kg$^{-1}\cdot$min$^{-1}$ lower at age 17 to 18 than at age 10 to 11.[1,2,22,23] It has been suggested that the lower $\dot{V}_{O2max}$ per kilogram in the pubertal girl is due to the decrease in blood hemoglobin concentration, secondary to menstrual blood loss. This, however, does not explain the drop in $\dot{V}_{O2max}$ per kilogram body weight even before menarche. One reason could be the increasing adiposity of many girls who approach puberty.[24-26] Decreasing aerobic power could also result from an age-related decrease in spontaneous habitual activity in the second decade of life.[26-30]

Although gender-related differences in maximal aerobic power are apparent primar-

**Table 8–1.** SOME PHYSIOLOGIC RESPONSES TO ACUTE EXERCISE: COMPARISON BETWEEN PREPUBESCENT GIRLS AND OLDER FEMALES

| Physiologic Function | Typical for Girls (Compared With Older Females) |
| --- | --- |
| $O_2$ cost of walking/running | Lower |
| $O_2$ uptake max, $L \cdot min^{-1}$ | Lower |
| $O_2$ uptake max, $mL \cdot kg^{-1} \cdot min^{-1}$ | Higher |
| Heart rate submax | Higher |
| Stroke volume submax | Lower |
| Cardiac output submax | Lower |
| Minute ventilation submax | Higher |
| Ventilatory equivalent submax and max | Higher |
| Peak anaerobic power, watt | Lower |
| Peak anaerobic power, $watt \cdot kg^{-1}$ | Lower |
| Mean anaerobic power, watt | Lower |
| Mean anaerobic power, $watt \cdot kg^{-1}$ | Lower |

ily after age 12 to 13 years, boys seem to have a somewhat higher $\dot{V}_{O2max}$ even at earlier ages.[1,2,26,31–33] In a study comparing the maximal aerobic power of 6- to 16-year-old girls and boys who were tested on the cycle ergometer, such gender-related differences were eliminated when $\dot{V}_{O2max}$ ($L \cdot min^{-1}$) was plotted against lean leg volume rather than against age.[32] A similar pattern was apparent among 8- to 16-year-old girls and boys when $W_{170}$ (i.e., the mechanical power at which they cycle when their heart rate is 170 beats per minute) was plotted against body cell mass.[34] It should be realized, however, that when $\dot{V}_{O2max}$ is divided by lean leg volume or lean body mass, preadolescent boys still have higher values than preadolescent girls.[26] A more precise determination of body composition is needed to tell whether gender-related differences in maximal aerobic power of prepubescents are fully explained by the mass of their exercising muscles.

**Table 8–2.** GENDER-RELATED COMPARISON OF THE RESPONSE OF PREPUBESCENTS TO ACUTE EXERCISE

| Physiologic Function | Girls' Response (Compared With Boys) |
| --- | --- |
| $O_2$ cost of walking/running | Similar |
| $O_2$ uptake max, $L \cdot min^{-1}$ | Somewhat lower |
| $O_2$ uptake max per kg body weight | Somewhat lower |
| $O_2$ uptake max per kg lean mass | Similar |
| Heart rate submax | Higher |
| Heart rate max | Similar |
| Stroke volume submax and max | Lower |
| Minute ventilation submax | Similar |
| Minute ventilation max | Somewhat lower |
| Peak anaerobic power, watt | Somewhat lower |
| Peak anaerobic power, $watt \cdot kg^{-1}$ | Lower |
| Mean anaerobic power, watt | Somewhat lower |
| Mean anaerobic power, $watt \cdot kg^{-1}$ | Lower |

## Anaerobic Power and Muscle Endurance

High-intensity muscle contractions that cannot be sustained for more than 20 to 30 seconds are dependent primarily on anaerobic energy pathways. Examples of "anaerobic" activities are short and long sprints in running, skating, and cycling, as well as short slalom in downhill skiing. Until recent years, this component of fitness received little attention, compared with maximal aerobic power and muscle strength. This reflected the paucity of reliable and valid laboratory tests for peak muscle power and local muscle endurance. Such tests are currently available, using cycle ergometers or isokinetic machines. These have been added to the Margaria step-running test,[35] which assesses peak muscle power but not muscle endurance. The following information has been obtained using the Margaria test and the Wingate anaerobic test.[36]

The ability of prepubertal girls and boys to perform anaerobic tasks is distinctly lower than that of adolescents and young adults. This was first shown for 8- to 73-year-old sedentary Italians: even when divided by body weight, the peak muscle power of the 8- to 10-year-old girls was only about 60 percent that of the 20-year-old women.[35] Similar results have been shown for Nilo-Hamitic and Bantu African,[37] British,[32] American,[38] and Israeli[2] populations. In the last, peak muscle power and muscle endurance of the arms and the legs were both lower in the young girls, even when corrected for differences in body weight.

The aforementioned pattern is in contrast to maximal aerobic power which, when calculated per kilogram body weight, is *higher* in the prepubescent girl than in the adolescent or adult female.

The mechanism for the low anaerobic performance of prepubescent girls is not known. In a recent study performed in my laboratory on adolescent girls and boys (Blimkie and associates, unpublished), lean muscle mass of the upper limb explained much of the variance in arm peak power and muscle endurance of the boys but not of the girls. Performance of both prepubescent girls and boys in the Margaria test, even when corrected for fat-free mass, is lower than that of adolescents and adults.[37] It is quite likely, therefore, that *qualitative* characteristics of the muscles,

and possibly their neural control, would explain the relative deficiency of anaerobic power in the prepubescent. Children of both sexes have lower maximal blood lactate concentration than do adolescents and adults. It has been reported for boys, but not for girls, that creatine phosphate and glycogen concentrations in the resting muscle and, in particular, the rate of glycolysis in the contracting muscle are low before puberty. (For more details, see reference 2.) Based on animal studies, a relationship has been suggested between muscle lactate production and circulating testosterone. Whether this applies also to humans—females or males—has yet to be shown. It can be assumed, however, that a low glycolytic capacity in prepubescents of both sexes is the main cause of their low anaerobic performance.

## Muscle Strength

Muscle strength, defined as the maximal force that can be exerted by a muscle or a group of muscles, is similar in girls and boys during their first decade of life.[26,39] Strength is growth-dependent.[26,39-41] However, it does not increase linearly with the growth in body mass or stature. In girls, the main increase in strength occurs during, a few months following, or even just before the "growth spurt" (i.e., the year during which body height velocity is at its peak). In contrast, the increase of strength in boys reaches its peak about 1 year *after* the growth spurt.[42,43] This difference, coupled with the earlier growth spurt in girls (about a 2-year difference), may explain why the greater muscle strength of boys is usually not evident before age 11 or 12 years.

## TRAINABILITY

Does a prepubescent girl respond to training in the same manner as an adolescent or an adult female? This question is of utmost relevance to the theory and practice of coaching, but should be of interest also to the pediatric physiotherapist and the physiatrist who wish to apply physiologic principles to rehabilitation.

To obtain definitive answers about trainability (i.e., the ability of body systems to adapt to repeated exercise stimuli) of different age-groups, one must conduct a longitudinal training study on these groups. Such a design must satisfy two conditions: (1) the *initial fitness level* of all groups must be similar and (2) the *training dosage* must be equated among the groups.

Unfortunately, neither condition can be adequately satisfied. First, one cannot assume that a 6-year-old girl who, for example, sprints 50 meters in 11.0 seconds has the same sprinting ability as a 16-year-old adolescent who runs at the same speed. A better approach might be to use a physiologic criterion for equating the initial fitness level. One cannot be sure, however, that a maximal aerobic power of 40 mL·kg$^{-1}$min$^{-1}$ in a 6-year-old girl denotes the same aerobic fitness as an identical value in a 20-year-old woman. It is also fairly difficult to equate training dosages. Can one assume, for example, that weight training at 70 percent of their maximal voluntary contraction represents the same physiologic strain in a girl and a woman?

Because of such methodologic constraints, conclusions about the trainability of young girls are not definitive. Some patterns, however, seem to emerge. According to several reports, when prepubescent girls take part in aerobic training, they respond with little or no increase in maximal oxygen uptake, even though their athletic ability may improve.[44-47] This is unlike the response to aerobic training of women, who increase their maximal oxygen uptake and improve their athletic performance. Only a few studies have suggested that prepubescent females do improve their maximal oxygen uptake in response to aerobic training.[48]

A major reason for the improvement of running performance in the absence of increased $\dot{V}_{O2max}$ is the training-induced improvement in running economy, which is manifested by a decrease in the $O_2$ cost of running. During adolescence, both aerobic power and running economy may improve with training.

Few studies are available on the trainability of muscle strength at different ages. Nielsen and co-workers[41] trained 249 7- to 19-year-old Danish girls for 5 weeks. One subgroup did isometric knee extension, another the "vertical jump," and the third practiced acceleration in sprints. As in adults, there was *specificity* in the responses: each subgroup improved most in the specific strength (but not sprinting) task at which it had been training. While the authors did not report the pubertal stage of the subjects, the younger girls (less than 13.5 years) improved more than the older ones. Likewise, 8-year-old German girls improved their isometric arm strength more than did adults when given a similar training stimulus.[49] Whether trainability of strength is related to the pubertal stage has yet to be shown.

## THERMOREGULATORY CAPACITY

Most research on the thermoregulatory characteristics of the exercising child is based on studies in boys. (For a review, see my article, reference 50.) Data are available, however, to suggest that girls are at a disadvantage, compared with women, when exposed to either hot or cold climates. Very little data are available to compare the responses to heat and cold of prepubertal girls and boys.

**Response to hot climate.** Table 8–3 is a summary of the morphologic and physiologic characteristics of prepubescent females,

**Table 8–3.** MORPHOLOGIC AND PHYSIOLOGIC CHARACTERISTICS OF PREPUBESCENT GIRLS AS RELATED TO THERMOREGULATION

| Characteristic or Function | Typical for Girls (Compared With Women) | Implication for Thermoregulation |
|---|---|---|
| O$_2$ cost of running/walking | Higher | High metabolic heat |
| Surface-to-mass ratio | Larger | Greater heat exchange with environment |
| Onset of sweating | Later | Greater reliance on convective heat loss |
| Sweating rate | Somewhat lower | Lower evaporative capacity |
| Blood flow, peripheral vs central | Higher | 1. Higher heat convection |
| | | 2. Lower venous return |

as related to their thermoregulatory capability. As discussed earlier, the smaller the girl, the higher her $\dot{V}_{O_2}$ per kilogram body weight at any given walking or running speed. As 75 to 80 percent or more of the chemical energy during muscle contraction is converted into heat, the metabolic heat load of the prepubescent girl is higher (by as much as 5 to 20 percent) than that of the adolescent or the adult, at equivalent walking or running tasks. Such a difference imposes a greater strain on the young, small girl's thermodissipatory system.

Another size-related difference is the larger skin surface area–per–mass ratio in the smaller individual. The rate of heat exchange between the body and the environment depends on this surface area. Therefore, when the environment is warmer than the skin, the smaller the girl the greater the heat gain (through conduction, convection, and radiation) per unit body mass. This difference in heat gain becomes particularly important in extreme climatic heat.

Evaporation of sweat is the main avenue for heat dissipation during exercise, especially in hot climates. When ambient temperature exceeds skin temperature, evaporation is the *only* available means of heat dissipation. Compared with women, prepubertal girls have a slow onset of sweating and a somewhat lower sweating rate while exercising in the heat,[51] which limit their capacity for evaporative cooling. This difference between prepubescents and adults seems to be even more apparent among males.

Girls were found to respond to exercise in the heat with a marked shift of blood from the central to the cutaneous vascular bed.[51] Although greater skin blood flow facilitates greater convection of heat from body core to the periphery (which, under certain climatic conditions, may compensate for a low sweating capacity), it also decreases the venous return and stroke volume.[51] The resulting decrease in maximal cardiac output is another explanation for the low ability of prepubertal girls to exercise intensively in hot climates. It should be added that, at any given exercise level, even when performed in neutral environments, cardiac output in young girls is somewhat lower than that of women.[52]

In summary, these geometric and physiologic characteristics suggest that a priori young girls would tolerate exercise in hot climates less effectively than adolescent or adult females. It has indeed been shown that, during extreme climatic heat, prepubescent girls had to terminate their prescribed walking task earlier than did young women.[51,53] In thermoneutral environments, on the other hand, there is no evidence that young age or small body size is detrimental to thermoregulation.[54]

**Response to cold climate.** In most land-based sports, the rate of metabolic heat production exceeds heat loss, even when the environmental temperature is low. Such is the case, for example, in skating and cross-country skiing. In other winter sports, such as downhill skiing or curling, the rate of heat production may not be high, but clothing usually prevents excessive heat loss. Hypothermia occurs not infrequently in such sports as mountain climbing, snowshoeing, and even long-distance running at low intensity. There is, however, no epidemiologic evidence that prepubescent girls are more prone to hypothermia in these events than are older females.

In contrast, small individuals are at a distinct disadvantage during water-based activities. When swimming at a speed of 30 meters per minute in 20.3°C water, 8-year-old girls (club swimmers) had a drop in core temperature of as much as 2.5 to 3.0°C and had to be taken out of the water within 18 to 20 minutes owing to marked thermal discomfort. Their 16- to 19-year-old clubmates swam for some 30 minutes, with hardly any drop in core temperature and with little or no thermal discomfort.[55] The reason for the cold intolerance of the younger girls was their large surface area per mass, which facilitated conductive heat loss (water having a heat conductivity at least 25 times that of air). The authors also found that the leaner girls had a greater heat loss than those who had a thicker insulative subcutaneous fat layer.

**High-risk groups for heat- or cold-related disorders.** Some girls are at a potentially high risk for such heat-related disorders as heat exhaustion or heat stroke, while others may be prone to hypothermia.

Evidence is available that girls with anorexia nervosa have a deficient thermoregulatory capability, both in the heat and in the cold.[56,57] Patients with cystic fibrosis are prone to heat-related disorders,[58] possibly because of their abnormal sweating pattern. Undernourished children are prone to both hypothermia and hyperthermia.[59] Obese individuals perform well and feel comfortable in cold climates but are less tolerant to exercise in the heat than their leaner counterparts. Such intolerance has been documented for college-age women, although the findings for prepubertal girls were inconclusive.[53]

*Hypohydration* may often lead to heat-related disorders. While data are not available regarding the effects of hypohydration on the thermoregulation and health of prepubescent girls, data on boys suggest that, for a given level of hypohydration, children have a greater rise in core temperature than do young adults.[60] Conditions in which exertion may induce heat-related disorders through hypohydration are *diabetes mellitus, diabetes insipidus, diarrhea,* and *vomiting.* Prepubescent boys[60] and girls (unpublished data from my laboratory), like adults, undergo "voluntary hypohydration" when they exercise for long periods (e.g., 1 to 2 hours), even when fluids are available to them ad libitum. One group of young girls who are prone to hypohydration is those who compete in judo and "make weight" prior to competition. In some states, where elementary school girls compete in wrestling, the same practice is probably followed.

*Lack of acclimatization* to exercise in the heat is perhaps the most important factor that predisposes an individual to heat-related disorders. Data suggest that 8- to 10-year-old boys take longer than adults to acclimatize to the heat.[61] No similar studies are available for girls, but it makes good sense to ensure that young female athletes are well acclimatized to the heat before they are expected to train hard and perform well in warm or humid climates.

As for hypothermia, a small, lean girl who is immersed in water is at a greater risk than a larger girl or one with thicker subcutaneous adipose tissue.

## GROWTH, PUBERTAL CHANGES, AND ATHLETIC TRAINING

Trained prepubescent and adolescent girls often have different morphologic and maturational characteristics from those of their untrained counterparts. A question often asked by coaches, physicians, and parents is whether training per se affects growth, development, and maturation. To obtain a definitive answer, one would need to launch a prospective study in which nonathletic prepubescent girls are randomly assigned to training and control groups and then followed until after puberty. Such a project has yet to be launched. Data available at present are based on cross-sectional comparisons between athletes and nonathletes and among athletes of various specialties, or on retrospective analyses. The few longitudinal studies lack proper controls.[62] The conclusions derived from such studies therefore are tentative at best and cannot prove causality between training and changes in growth, development, and maturation.

The following are general comments, based on such studies. (For detailed reviews, see Malina,[63] Malina and co-workers,[64] and Wells.[65]) Various female athletes, primarily gymnasts, figure skaters, and ballet dancers, mature later and are shorter than the nonathletic female population. Others, notably the swimmers, have little or no delay in maturation and are often taller than nonathletes.[62–64,66–68] These data might suggest that the above morphologic and maturational differences are caused by training. Such conclusions, however, ignore preselection and a possible bias in the drop-out pattern. It is likely, for example, that those girls with delayed puberty and short stature become preferentially attracted to such sports as gymnastics and figure skating, while the taller ones are more attracted to competitive swimming. A recent retrospective study[69] has shown that 8- to 14-year-old female gymnasts who were shorter than the nonathletic population had been shorter even prior to having joined the gymnastics program. Similarly, swimmers who, as a group, were taller than their nonathletic counterparts had been taller before training. It is also possible that, within a group of gymnasts, those females who mature early—and thus attain broad hips, relatively short legs, and higher body adiposity—drop out because of unfavorable changes in body mechanics.

Based on reports from the late 1970s and early 1980s, delayed menarche (defined as occurring after age 15 years) was particularly common among divers, figure skaters, gymnasts, and volleyball players.[63] Menarche is particularly delayed in those athletes who are engaged in high-dosage training. Delayed menarche in athletes seems also to correspond to delayed skeletal maturity.[63]

Several factors, singly or in combination,

have been suggested to link delayed menarche to physical training. Among these are a low percentage of body fat,[70,71] insufficient calorie intake in conjunction with "energy drain,"[62] onset of training prior to menarche,[66] large sibship,[72] and emotional stress of training and competition. It has also been suggested,[73] but has yet to be confirmed, that hormonal changes that are associated with chronic exercise may be a cause for delayed menarche. In one study,[62] low serum gonadotropins—LH, particularly—were found in premenarcheal ballet dancers. Other endocrinologic studies are based on postmenarcheal athletes (see reference 74 for details).

In a comprehensive review on menarche in athletes, Malina[63] presented a two-part hypothesis on the possible relationship between physical activity and delayed menarche. First is the preselection by body characteristics, in which the girl with a linear physique, long legs, and narrow hips (who is often also a late maturer) is attracted to sports and eventually is successful in them. Second is the "socialization process," in which early-maturing girls tend to interact socially in a nonsport environment with the appearance of pubertal changes. Conversely, the late maturers are more likely to find sports participation socially gratifying.

Indeed, preselection and the bias in dropping out from athletics may explain the late menarche of athletes as found in cross-sectional and retrospective analyses. One cannot ignore, however, the accumulating data on a more direct, possibly cause-and-effect, relationship between intense sports participation and secondary amenorrhea.

Although primary amenorrhea is a "normal" and common occurrence among athletes, one should not overlook the possibility that it might reflect gynecologic or other hormonal abnormalities. (For details of recommended investigations and of therapeutic approach, see Shangold in reference 75, as well as Chapter 9.)

## COEDUCATIONAL PARTICIPATION IN CONTACT AND COLLISION SPORTS

Should prepubescent girls compete with boys in contact (e.g., wrestling, basketball, soccer) and collision (e.g., football, ice hockey) sports? This issue has become highly controversial, attracting media attention, because of its medical, educational, and cultural implications. The following comments are not meant to address the psychologic, sociologic, or ethical aspects of this controversy but only some of the physiologic and medical aspects.

A major issue is the added risk to health that participants of either sex group may incur owing to mixed participation. The main potential cause for such added risk is a marked difference in body mass, strength, or skill among the participants. At age 9 to 12 years, body mass of girls is similar to, or even slightly greater than, that of boys. Body height at that age range is quite similar in boys and girls, and the difference in the strength of various muscle groups is only about 1 to 2 kg in favor of the boys.[43] This is to be contrasted with the increasingly greater muscle strength of males—particularly in the upper body—after puberty.[76] The attainment of such motor skills as throwing, kicking, catching, jumping, hopping, and skipping during the first year of life is similar in boys and girls. Throughout the prepubertal years, these and other motor skills seem to develop and improve at a similar pace in both sex groups.[77]

It should be realized that, at any given chronologic age around puberty, differences in body size and strength of early and late maturers *within* a gender group far surpass the *intergender* differences. Nor is there any evidence to suggest that prepubescent girls are less capable of learning sport skills, less agile, or have less stamina than boys.[77,78] While not addressing specifically the prepubescent girl, a recent review on orthopedic issues in the young female athlete[79] points out the emergence of "overuse injuries" during the teens. It rejects, however, the notion that girls are more prone to injury than boys.

Based on anthropometric and fitness-related considerations alone, therefore, prepubescent girls can compete successfully with boys in contact and collision sports, and with no undue risk to health. An early maturing girl, in point of fact, may have an edge over boys who are average maturers. It seems as though matching of prepubescent and circumpubescent opponents by body size and maturation level has more relevance to health than the separation into gender groups.

## SUMMARY

The physiologic responses to exercise in the prepubescent girl are of a similar pattern to those of the more mature female. There are, however, some age- or development-related differences in these responses. The submaximal $O_2$ cost during walking or running is higher in the young girl, which causes a lower "metabolic reserve" and early fatigability in endurance events. Likewise, anaerobic muscle power and local muscle endurance are markedly lower in prepubescents, who are therefore unlikely to compete successfully with their older counterparts in events such as jumping and sprinting. Girls are less-effective thermoregulators when exercising in the heat and in the cold. This has implications both to their performance and to their health. Girls with obesity and anorexia nervosa are at special risk for heat-related illness. Although more research is needed, it appears that the training-induced improvement in maximal aerobic power is low before puberty.

A causal relationship among training, growth, and maturation has yet to be established. It seems, however, that the delayed menarche in athletes may be in part a result of intense training.

While coeducational participation in contact and collision sports may be objected to on psychologic and societal grounds, there are no physiologic or medical reasons to ban such activities before puberty.

## References

1. Åstrand PO: Experimental Studies of Physical Working Capacity in Relation to Sex and Age. Munksgaard, Copenhagen, 1952.
2. Bar-Or O: Pediatric Sports Medicine for the Practitioner: from Physiologic Principles to Clinical Applications. Springer Verlag, New York, 1983.
3. Godfrey S: Exercise Testing in Children. Applications in Health and Disease. WB Saunders, Philadelphia, 1974.
4. Shephard RJ: Physical Activity and Growth. Year Book Medical Publishers, Chicago, 1982.
5. Smith NJ (ed): Sports Medicine for Young Athletes. American Academy of Pediatrics, Evanston, IL, 1983.
6. Boileau RA (ed): Advances in Pediatric Sport Sciences. Vol 1. Human Kinetics, Champaign, IL, 1984.
7. Bar-Or O (ed): Pediatric Work Physiology. Wingate Institute, Natanya, Israel, 1973.
8. Berg K, and Eriksson BO (eds): Children and Exercise IX. University Park Press, Baltimore, 1980.
9. Binkhorst RA, Kemper HCG, and Saris WHM: Children and Exercise XI. Human Kinetics, Champaign, IL, 1985.
10. Borms J, and Hebbelinck M (eds): Children and Exercise. Acta Paediatr Belg (Suppl 28):1, 1974.
11. Borms J, and Hebbelinck M (eds): Pediatric Work Physiology. Karger, Basel, 1978.
12. Ilmarinen J, and Valimaki I: Pediatric Work Physiology X. Springer Verlag, Berlin, 1983.
13. Lavallee H, and Shephard RJ (eds): Frontiers of Activity and Child Health. Pelican, Quebec, 1977.
14. Rutenfranz J (ed): Pediatric Work Physiology XII. Human Kinetics, Champaign, IL, 1986.
15. Thoren C (ed): Pediatric Work Physiology. Acta Paediatr Scand (Suppl 213):1, 1971.
16. MacDougall JD, Roche PD, Bar-Or O, et al: Maximal aerobic power of Canadian school children: prediction based on age-related cost of running. Int J Sports Med 4:194, 1983.
17. Robinson S: Experimental studies of physical fitness in relation to age. Int Z Angew Physiol Einschl Arbeitphysiol 10:251, 1938.
18. Skinner JS, Bar-Or O, Bergsteinovac, et al: Comparison of continuous and intermittent test for determining maximal oxygen intake in children. Acta Paediatr Scand (Suppl 217):24, 1971.
19. Bal MER, Thompson EM, McIntosh EH, et al: Mechanical efficiency in cycling of girls six to fourteen years of age. J Appl Physiol 6:185, 1953.
20. Girandola RN, Wiswell RA, Frisch F, et al: Metabolic differences during exercise in pre- and post-pubescent girls (abstract). Med Sci Sports Exerc 13:110, 1981.
21. Wilmore JH, and Sigerseth PO: Physical work capacity of young girls 7–13 years of age. J Appl Physiol 22:923, 1967.
22. Chatterjee S, Banerjee PK, Chatterjee P, et al: Aerobic capacity of young girls. Indian J Med Res 69:327, 1979.
23. Drinkwater BL, Horvath SM, and Wells CL: Aerobic power of females, ages 10 to 68. J Gerontol 30:385, 1975.
24. Forbes GB, and Amirhakimi GH: Skinfold thickness and body fat in children. Hum Biol 42:401, 1970.
25. Karlberg P, and Taranger J: The somatic development of children in a Swedish urban community. Acta Paediatr Scand (Suppl):258, 1977.
26. Sunnegardh J: Physical activity in relation to energy intake, body fat, physical work capacity and muscle strength in 8- and 13-year-old children in Sweden. Doctoral dissertation, University of Uppsala, Uppsala, 1986.
27. Huenemann RL, Shapiro LR, Hampton MC, et al: Teenagers' activities and attitudes toward activity. J Am Diet Assoc 51:433, 1967.
28. Ilmarinen J, and Rutenfranz J: Longitudinal studies of the changes in habitual physical activity of schoolchildren and working adolescents. In Berg K, and Eriksson BO (eds): Children And Exercise IX. University Park Press, Baltimore, 1980, 149.
29. Telama R: Secondary School Pupils' Physical Activity and Leisure-Time Sports. Vol III (in Finnish). Institute of Educational Research, University of Jyvaskyla, Report No 107, Jyvaskyla, Finland, 1975.
30. Verschuur R, and Kemper HCG: The pattern of daily physical activity. In Kemper HCG (ed): Growth, Health and Fitness of Teenagers (Medicine and Sport Science, Vol 20). Karger, Basel, 1985, 169.

31. Cooper DM, Weiler-Ravell D, Whipp BJ, et al: Growth-related changes in oxygen uptake and heart rate during progressive exercise in children. Pediatr Res 18:845, 1984.

32. Davies CTM, Barnes C, and Godfrey S: Body composition and maximal exercise performance in children. Hum Biol 44:195, 1972.

33. Yoshizawa S, Ishizaki T, and Honda H: Physical fitness of children aged 5 and 6 years. J Hum Ergol (Tokyo) 6:41, 1977.

34. Burmeister W, Rutenfranz J, Stresny W, et al: Body cell mass and physical performance capactiy ($W_{170}$) of school children. Int Z Angew Physiol Einschl Arbeitphysiol 31:61, 1972.

35. Margaria R, Aghemo P, and Rovelli E: Measurement of muscular power (anaerobic) in man. J Appl Physiol 21:1662, 1966.

36. Bar-Or O: The Wingate Anaerobic Test. Characteristics and applications (in French). Symbioses 13:157, 1981.

37. Di Prampero PE, and Cerretelli P: Maximal muscular power (aerobic and anaerobic) in African natives. Ergonomics 12:51, 1969.

38. Kurowski TT: Anaerobic power of children from ages 9 through 15 years. M. Sc. Thesis, Florida State University, 1977.

39. Asmussen E: Growth in muscular strength and power. In Rarick L (ed): Physical Activity, Human Growth and Development. Academic Press, New York, 1973, 60.

40. Clarke HH: Physical and motor tests in the Medford Boys' Growth Study. Prentice Hall, Englewood Cliffs, New Jersey, 1971.

41. Nielsen B, Nielsen K, Behrendt Hansen M, et al: Training of "functional muscular strength" in girls 7–19 years old. In Berg K, and Eriksson B (eds): Pediatric Work Physiology IX. University Park Press, Baltimore, 1980, p 69.

42. Beunen G, Malina RM, Van'Thof MA, et al: Timing of adolescent changes in motor performance. Symposium on Maturation and Growth, ACSM, Nashville, 1985.

43. Malina RM: Growth, strength and physical performance. In Stull GA (ed): Encyclopedia of Physical Education, Fitness and Sports: Training, Environment, Nutrition and Fitness. Brighton Publishing, Salt Lake City, UT, 1980, p 443.

44. Bar-Or O, and Zwiren LD: Physiological effects of increased frequency of physical education classes and of endurance conditioning on 9- to 10-year-old girls and boys. In Bar-Or O (ed): Pediatric Work Physiology. Wingate Institute, Natanya, Israel, 1973, p 183.

45. Gilliam TB, and Freedson PS: Effects of a 12-week school physical education program on peak $\dot{V}O_2$, body composition and blood lipids in 7 to 9 year old children. Int J Sports Med 1:73, 1980.

46. Mocellin R, and Wasmund U: Investigations of the influence of a running-training programme on the cardiovascular and motor performance capacity in 53 boys and girls of a second and third primary school class. In Bar-Or O (ed): Pediatric Work Physiology. Wingate Institute, Natanya, Israel, 1973, p 279.

47. Yoshida T, Ishiko T, and Muraoka I: Effect of endurance training on cardiorespiratory functions of 5-year-old children. Int J Sports Med 1:91, 1980.

48. Brown CH, Harrower JR, and Deeter MF: The effects of cross-country running on pre-adolescent girls. Med Sci Sports Exerc 4:1, 1972.

49. Rohmert W: Rechts-links-Vergleich bei isometrichem Armmuskeltraining mit verschiedenem Trainingsreiz bei achtjaringen Kindren. Int Z Angew Physiol Einschl Arbeitphysiol 26:363, 1968.

50. Bar-Or O: Climate and the exercising child—a review. Int J Sports Med 1:53, 1980.

51. Drinkwater BL, Kuppart IC, Denton JE, et al: Response of prepubertal girls and college women to work in the heat. J Appl Physiol 43:1046, 1977.

52. Bar-Or O, Shephard RJ, and Allan CL: Cardiac output of 10- to 13-year-old boys and girls during submaximal exercise. J Appl Physiol 30:219, 1971.

53. Haymes EM, Buskirk ER, Hodgson JL, et al: Heat tolerance of exercising lean and heavy prepubertal girls. J Appl Physiol 36:566, 1974.

54. Davies CTM: Thermal responses to exercise in children. Ergonomics 24:55, 1981.

55. Sloan REG, and Keatinge WR: Cooling rates of young people swimming in cold water. J Appl Physiol 35:371, 1973.

56. Davies CTM, Fohlin L, and Thoren C: Thermoregulation in anorexia nervosa patients. In Borms J, and Hebbelinck M (eds): Pediatric Work Physiology. Basel, Karger, 1978, p 96.

57. Wakeling A, and Russel GFM: Disturbances in the regulation of body temperature in anorexia nervosa. Psychol Med 1:30, 1970.

58. Kessler WR, and Andersen DH: Heat prostration in fibrocystic disease of the pancreas and other conditions. Pediatrics 8:648, 1951.

59. Brooke OG: Thermal insulation in malnourished Jamaican children. Arch Dis Child 48:901, 1973.

60. Bar-Or O, Dotan R, Inbar O, et al: Voluntary hypohydration in 10- to 12-year-old boys. J Appl Physiol 48:104, 1980.

61. Inbar O: Acclimatization to dry and hot environment in young adults and children 8–10 years old. Ed.D. dissertation. Columbia University, New York, 1978.

62. Warren MP: The effects of exercise on pubertal progression and reproductive function in girls. J Clin Endocrinol Metab 51:1150, 1980.

63. Malina RM: Menarche in athletes: a synthesis and hypothesis. Ann Hum Biol 10:1, 1983.

64. Malina RM, Meleski BW, and Shoup RF: Anthropometric, body composition, and maturity characteristics of selected school-age athletes. Pediatr Clin North Am 29:1305, 1982.

65. Wells CL: Women, Sport and Performance—A Physiological Perspective. Human Kinetics, Champaign, IL, 1985.

66. Frisch RE, Gotz-Welbergen AV, McArthur JW, et al: Delayed menarche and amenorrhea of college athletes in relation to age of onset of training. JAMA 246:1559, 1981.

67. Malina RM, Harper AB, Avent HH, et al: Age at menarche in athletes and non-athletes. Med Sci Sports 5:11, 1973.

68. Malina RM, Spirduso WW, Tate C, et al: Age at menarche and selected menstrual characteristics in athletes at different competitive levels and in different sports. Med Sci Sports 10:218, 1978.

69. Peltenburg AL, Erich WBM, Bernink MJE, et al: Biological maturation, body composition, and growth of female gymnasts and control groups of school girls

and girl swimmers, aged 8 to 14 years: a cross-sectional survey of 1064 girls. Int J Sports Med 5:36, 1984.

70. Frisch RE, Wyshak G, and Vincent L: Delayed menarche and amenorrhea in ballet dancers. N Engl J Med 303:17, 1980.

71. Vanderbroucke JP, van Leer A, and Valkenburg HA: Synergy between thinness and intensive sports activity in delaying menarche. Br Med J 284:1907, 1982.

72. Malina RM, Bouchard C, Shoup RF, et al: Age at menarche, family size, and birth order in athletes at the Montreal Olympic Games. Med Sci Sports 11:354, 1979.

73. Brisson GR, Volle MA, DeCarufel D, et al: Exercise-induced dissociation of blood prolactin response in young women according to their sports habits. Horm Metab Res 12:201, 1980.

74. Shangold MM: Exercise and the adult female: hormonal and endocrine effects. In Terjung RJ (ed): Exercise and Sport Sciences Reviews, Vol 12. Collamore Press, Lexington, MA, 1984, p 53.

75. Shangold MM: Gynecological concerns in young and adolescent physically active girls. Pediatrician 13:10, 1986.

76. Montoye HJ, and Lamphier DE: Grip and arm strength in males and females, age 10 to 69. Res Q Am Assoc Health Phys Ed 48:109, 1977.

77. Branta C, Haubenstricker J, and Seefeldt V: Age changes in motor skills during childhood and adolescence. In Terjung RL (ed): Exercise and Sport Sciences Reviews, Vol 12. Collamore Press, Lexington, MA, 1984, p 467.

78. Rarick GL, and Dobbins DA: Basic components in the motor performance of children six to nine years of age. Med Sci Sports 7:105, 1975.

79. Micheli LJ, and LaChabrier L: The young female athlete. In Micheli LJ (ed): Pediatric and Adolescent Sport Medicine. Little, Brown, Boston, 1984, p 167.

# CHAPTER 9

# Growth, Performance, Activity, and Training During Adolescence

ROBERT M. MALINA, Ph.D.

Adolescence is a period of transition from childhood to adulthood. It includes changes in the biologic, personal, and social domains that prepare the young girl for adulthood in her particular culture. Thus, the biologic changes that occur during puberty, or sexual maturation, do not occur in isolation; rather, they are related to other developmental events so that any consideration of this period of life must be done in a biosocial or biocultural context.

Biologically, adolescence may be viewed as beginning with an acceleration in the rate of growth (i.e., an increase in size, prior to the attainment of sexual maturity), then merging into a decelerative phase, and eventually terminating with the cessation of growth. The latter is most often viewed as the attainment of adult stature. Sexual maturity and growth are thus closely related. The events that constitute this phase of the life cycle include changes in the nervous and endocrine systems that initiate and coordinate the sexual, physiologic, and somatic changes; growth and maturation of the primary (ovaries, vagina, and uterus) and secondary (breasts and pubic hair) sex characteristics leading to menarche and reproductive function; changes in size, i.e., the adolescent growth spurt; changes in proportions, physique, and body composition; and changes in the cardiorespiratory system, among others. The two most prominent outward features of adolescence (excluding behavior) are accelerated growth and appearance of secondary sex characteristics, which appear, on the average, during the second decade of life. However, the neuroendocrine and other physiologic events underlying growth and pubertal change have been in progress for some time prior to the appearance of physical changes. The time span accomodating the growth spurt and puberty is thus wide. It can vary from 8 or 9 years through 17 or 18 years of age in girls, and in some cases may continue into the early 20s. There is variation among individuals in the time and rate at which the structural and functional changes occur; i.e., the changes do not begin at the same time and do not proceed at the same rate.

## THE ADOLESCENT GROWTH SPURT

### Body Size

From birth to adulthood, both height and weight follow a four-phased or double-sigmoid growth pattern: rapid gain in infancy and early childhood; slower, relatively constant gain in middle childhood; rapid gain during adolescence; and slow increase and eventual cessation of growth at the attainment of adult size. Most dimensions of the body—sitting height, leg length, shoulder and hip breadths, limb circumferences, muscle mass, and so on—follow a similar growth pattern. What varies is the timing, duration, and intensity of the adolescent growth spurt in each. For example, maximum growth in body weight occurs, on the average, after maximum growth in stature, while maximum growth in leg length occurs early in the growth spurt, prior to that for sitting height or trunk length.

### Body Composition

Lean body mass of girls, estimated from potassium-40[1] and body density,[2] increases from about 25 kg at 10 years to about 42 kg at 16 years of age, whereas muscle mass, estimated from creatinine excretion,[3,4] increases from about 12 kg at 9 years to 23 kg at 15 years. On the average, lean body and muscle mass increase only slightly in late adolescence to about 43 and 24 kg, respectively, at 17 to 18 years of age. The gain in lean body mass and muscle mass during female adolescence is not as intense as that in males, so that by late adolescence, females attain an average of about two thirds of the estimated

values reported for males. Peak velocities of growth in arm and calf muscles occur after peak height velocity (PHV), or maximum rate of growth in stature.[5]

Fatness also increases during adolescence, but estimates are highly variable.[3] Densitometric estimates increase from 24 percent body fat at 9 to 10 years to 28 percent at 16 years,[2] whereas estimates based on potassium-40 show little change in relative fatness between 10 and 18 years (22 to 23 percent).[1] These estimates are derived from cross-sectional samples and do not control for maturity status. At the time of the growth spurt, however, the rate of fat accumulation slows down in girls. This is especially apparent on the extremities, and some data even suggest a negative velocity for arm fat, i.e., loss of fat, coincident with PHV in girls.[5]

## MENARCHE

The age at menarche is perhaps the most commonly reported developmental milestone of female adolescence. It is, however, a rather late maturational event. Menarche occurs after maximum growth in stature, the average difference between age at menarche and age at PHV in a number of studies being about 1.2 to 1.3 years.

Median age at menarche for American girls in the United States Health Examination Survey is 12.8 years, and with in the United States sample, black girls attain menarche significantly earlier than white girls, 12.5 compared with 12.8 years.[6] Estimates for many European samples vary between 13.0 and 13.4 years, but lower ages at menarche occur in southern European populations.[7]

In contrast to population surveys of menarche, in which the average age for the population is estimated mathematically on the basis of the number of girls in each age group who have attained menarche, many studies of athletes and of the influence of training on the age at menarche use the retrospective method. This approach relies on the memory of the individual and thus has the limitation of error in recall.

## PHYSICAL PERFORMANCE AND ACTIVITY DURING ADOLESCENCE

Characteristics of the adolescent growth spurt and sexual maturation, and of interrelationships among indices of sexual, skeletal, and somatic maturity, are reasonably well documented. Changes in physical performance and activity are less well documented. The data are largely cross sectional, with but few longitudinal observations spanning the immediate prepubertal and pubertal years.

## Strength

Muscular strength improves linearly with age from early childhood through about 15 years of age in girls, with no clear evidence of an adolescent spurt.[4] After 15 years, strength improves more slowly. This pattern is in contrast to the marked acceleration of strength development during male adolescence, so that sex differences in muscular strength are considerable.

The relationship between strength development and the growth spurt and sexual maturation in girls is not as clear as in boys. Maximum strength development occurs, on the average, after peak height and weight velocity in boys, the relationship being better with weight than with height.[4] In girls, the apex of strength development occurs more often after PHV, but there is much variation. Peak strength gain precedes peak weight gain in more than one half of the girls in the Oakland Growth Study and follows peak weight gain in only about one fourth of the girls.[8] Thus, strength development in adolescent girls is not as meaningful an indicator of maturity as in adolescent boys.

Early-maturing girls are stronger than late-maturing girls of the same chronologic age.[9–11] The differences are most apparent between 11 and 15 years and reflect the larger body mass of early maturers. The differences between contrasting maturity groups, however, are reduced by 16 to 17 years of age. Early- and late-maturing girls thus attain comparable strength levels in later adolescence by apparently different routes. On the average, the early maturer shows rapid strength development through 13 years of age, and then continues to improve slightly. The late maturer, in contrast, improves in strength gradually between 11 and 16 years. The differences in strength between girls in contrasting maturity groups during adolescence, however, are not nearly as marked as those between early- and late-maturing boys.

## Motor Performance

Average performances of girls in a variety of motor tasks (dash, standing long jump, jump and reach, distance throw, and others) improve more or less linearly from childhood through about 13 or 14 years of age, followed by a plateau in the ability to perform some tasks and a decline in others.[12,13] In most tasks, the average performances of girls fall within one standard deviation of the boy's averages in early adolescence; but after 13 to 14 years of age, the average performances of girls are often outside the limits defined by one standard deviation below the boys' mean performance. Overhand throwing performance is an exception; few girls approximate the throwing performances of boys at all ages from late childhood on.[14]

Correlations between skeletal and sexual maturity and motor performance in girls are low and for many tasks are negative. The latter thus suggests that later maturation is more often associated with better motor performance in girls,[10,15,16] whereas the opposite is more often true in boys. For example, a comparison of high- and low-performance girls indicated that the superior performers were about 0.5 year less mature skeletally and 0.4 year delayed in menarche.[15] This trend is apparent in elite female athletes, i.e., skilled performers, who tend to be delayed in age at menarche and skeletal maturation.[17,18]

## Maximal Aerobic Power

Absolute maximal oxygen uptake (mL/min) has a growth pattern in girls similar to that for motor performance: it increases linearly with age from 7 years through 13 to 14 years in untrained girls and then declines slightly. In contrast, in untrained boys, it increases linearly with age through adolescence, so that by 16 years of age the difference between maximal oxygen uptake in untrained boys and girls is about 56 percent. When expressed relative to body weight $(mL \cdot kg^{-1} \cdot min^{-1})$, aerobic power declines with age from 6 through 16 years in untrained girls, but is more or less constant in untrained boys. The slope of the regression in girls declines from a value of 52.0 mL $\cdot kg^{-1} \cdot min^{-1}$ at 6 years of age to 40.5 mL $\cdot kg^{-1} \cdot min^{-1}$ at 16 years. Values for untrained boys at corresponding ages are 52.8 and 53.5

mL·kg$^{-1}$·min$^{-1}$, respectively, yielding a negligible sex difference of 1.5 percent at 6 years and a considerable difference of 32 percent at 16 years.[19] The sex difference in aerobic power per unit body weight at 16 years of age is probably related to sex differences in body composition. The aerobic power of girls per unit body weight is approximately 77 percent of the value for boys. This percentage is not too different from estimates of lean body and muscle mass in late adolescence; i.e., girls attain, on the average, only about two thirds of the values for boys. The increase in relative fatness associated with sexual maturation of girls probably contributes to the sex difference in aerobic power per unit body weight.

Aerobic power responds positively to training so that absolute and relative maximal oxygen uptakes are greater in trained than in untrained girls at all ages. The differences between trained and untrained girls are greatest during adolescence. It is also interesting to note that trained girls and boys differ by only 24 percent for absolute and 18 percent for relative oxygen uptake at age 16. These percentages should be contrasted to those for the relative differences between untrained 16-year-old boys and girls, 56 percent for absolute and 32 percent for relative oxygen uptake.[19]

Studies of aerobic power seldom control for maturity status of the subjects, and the few studies that do are largely limited to boys. Correlations between skeletal age and aerobic power are generally low,[19] but the association between body mass and skeletal maturity confounds the relationship. In a sample of Norwegian and West German girls, aerobic power per unit body weight changed only slightly in the years preceding peak height velocity, and declined after it.[20]

## Physical Activity Habits

Physical activity is a major component of the daily energy expenditure of individuals. Energy expenditure in free living children and youth is difficult to measure, and the few available studies are limited to rather small samples, narrow age ranges, and largely to boys.[21] Standardized questionnaires, interviews, and diaries are often used to estimate physical activity habits in large samples of youngsters usually 10 years of age and older.

The data, however, are largely descriptive and do not consider growth and maturity characteristics. Results of several surveys of European, Canadian, and American youth indicate a slight decline in time spent in physical activity by girls during adolescence.[21] In the United States survey,[22] for example, the average weekly time engaged in physical activity outside of school physical education was 11.5 hours in grades 5 and 6 (10 to 11 years), 12.5 hours in grades 7 through 9 (12 to 14 years), and 11.8 hours in grades 11 and 12 (15 to 17 years). Although the data suggest a trend, more specific changes with age cannot be examined. In a mixed-longitudinal sample of Dutch girls,[23] the average number of hours per week spent in physical activity with an average energy expenditure of 4 METS or more declined from 9.6 hours at 12 to 13 years to 8.1 hours at 17 to 18 years. The earlier adolescent years were not considered.

Intensity is a critical variable when considering physical activity. In the mixed-longitudinal Dutch study, 12- to 13-year-old girls participated, on the average, in only 4.0 and 5.0 hours per week in activities of medium (7 to 10 METS) and heavy (10+ METS) intensity, respectively. By 17 to 18 years, the corresponding hourly figures per week were 1.5 and 0.3, respectively.[23] Clearly, the majority of the activities of Dutch girls is of light intensity.

Given the type of data available, it is difficult to make inferences about activity habits during the adolescent growth spurt and sexual maturation, as well as about possible effects of rapid growth and maturation on activity habits. The figures do suggest, however, that most adolescent girls are not getting sufficient regular physical activity to maintain a high level of aerobic fitness.

## Significance of the Adolescent Plateau in Performance

Data relating the physical performance of girls to the timing of the growth spurt and sexual maturation are not extensive. A question that merits more detailed study is the relative flatness of the performance curves of girls during adolescence; i.e., their level of performance shows little improvement in many tasks after 13 to 14 years of age, and in some tasks it actually declines. Is this trend related primarily to biologic changes in female adolescence (e.g, sexual maturation, fat accumulation, physique changes) or is it related to cultural factors (e.g., changing social interests and expectations, pressure from peers, lack of motivation, limited opportunities to participate in performance-related physical activities)? It most likely reflects both biologic and cultural factors, and, with recent emphasis on and opportunity for athletic competition for young girls and wider acceptability of women in the role of an athlete, the overall age-related pattern of physical performance during female adolescence may change.

## INFLUENCE OF TRAINING ON THE TEMPO OF GROWTH AND MATURATION DURING ADOLESCENCE

Under adequate environmental conditions, the timing of the adolescent growth spurt and sexual maturation is genetically determined. However, these processes can be influenced by environmental factors. The delaying effects of chronic undernutrition are well documented. Socioeconomic variation in growth and maturation is evident in some societies but not in others.[7] Criteria of socioeconomic status, of course, vary from country to country, but data from industrialized countries indicate inconsistent trends in ages at PHV and menarche relative to indices of socioeconomic status. Another factor related to age at menarche is family size, i.e., number of children in the family. Girls from larger families tend to experience menarche later than those from smaller families, and this applies to athletes as well as nonathletes.[24] Although the estimated effects vary, the influence of family size on the age at menarche of athletes is well within the range of that for nonathletes.

Stressful life events are also significant. They are especially evident in the growth and maturation of youngsters experiencing disturbed home environments,[25] and in the "unusually 'fractured' curves of growth and pubertal development in girls translated to unfamiliar boarding schools at various times in puberty."[26] Studies of secular change in menarche suggest that the timing of this maturational event may be programmed by conditions early in life and not necessarily by those conditions that may be operating at or about the time of puberty.[27,28]

A question of concern, therefore, is the role of intensive training for sport and perhaps the stress of competition on the tempo of growth and sexual maturation during adolescence. It should be obvious that *physical activity is only one of many factors which may influence growth and maturation.* Regular physical training has no apparent effect on stature in growing youngsters and on skeletal maturation as commonly assessed in growth studies. It is, however, a significant factor in the regulation of body weight and composition and in the growth and integrity of skeletal and muscle tissues. The role of regular activity in the development of adipose tissue cellularity is not clearly established, although activity will function to reduce fatness. More active individuals generally show greater changes in association with training, but some training-associated changes are specific to the type of program followed.[29]

The influence of regular physical activity on the adolescent growth spurt and sexual maturation is not clearly established. However, since menarche tends to occur later in athletes than in nonathletes, and since athletes who begin training before menarche tend to have later ages at menarche than those who begin training after menarche, intensive training has been suggested as a factor which *may* delay menarche.[17] The menarcheal data are generally consistent with observations of breast and pubic hair development and skeletal maturity of young athletes engaged in figure skating, gymnastics, and track—i.e., they are delayed.[18] However, those training for sport at prepubertal ages are not necessarily representative of those who are successful at later ages and in turn constitute the samples of athletes upon whom most menarcheal data are based. Also, Title IX legislation has influenced sport opportunity for girls and women, and many now continue to train and compete through the college years. In the not too distant past, on the other hand, many young girls stopped training and competing at 16 or 17 years of age. The opportunity provided by Title IX most likely has influenced the composition of the female athlete population at the college level, particularly in swimming. The age at menarche in college-age swimmers in recent estimates[30,31] is considerably older than that of elite swimmers 10 or 15 years ago,[17] and this is in contrast to the advanced pubertal status and skeletal maturity often observed in age group swimmers.[18]

Frisch and colleagues,[32] although not the first to suggest that training may delay menarche, concluded that for every year a girl trains before menarche, her menarche will be delayed by up to 5 months. This conclusion is based on a correlation of +0.53 between years of training before menarche and age at menarche, a moderate correlation that accounts for only about 28 percent of the sample variance. This correlation obviously does not imply a cause-and-effect sequence; the association is more likely an artifact. The older a girl is at menarche, the more likely she would have begun her training prior to menarche, and conversely, the younger a girl is at menarche, the more likely she would have begun training after menarche or would have a shorter period of training prior to menarche.[30] It could also be that delayed maturation may have been a factor in the girl's decision to take up sport rather than the training causing the lateness.[17] Further, athletes as a group tend to be rather select, and other factors known to influence menarche are not considered in the analysis.

Nevertheless, two questions merit consideration. First, is regular, intensive prepubertal training for sport and regular competition sufficiently stressful to prolong the prepubertal state and in turn delay the adolescent growth spurt and sexual maturation? And second, does intensive training for sport and the stress of competition during the adolescent growth spurt and sexual maturation produce conditions that are sufficiently adverse to influence the progress and thus the timing of these maturational events?

The suggested mechanism for the association between training and delayed menarche is hormonal. It is suggested that intensive training and perhaps associated energy drain influence circulating levels of gonadotropic and ovarian hormones, and in turn menarche. Exercise is an effective means of stressing the hypothalamic-pituitary-ovarian axis, producing short-term increases in serum levels of all gonadotropic and sex steroid hormones.[33,34] Other factors also influence hormonal levels, e.g., diurnal variation,

state of feeding or fasting, emotional states, and so on, and these need to be considered. Further, virtually all hormones are episodically secreted, so that studies of hormonal responses based on single serum samples may not reflect the overall pattern. What is needed are studies in which 24-hour levels of hormones are monitored or in which actual pulses are sampled every 20 minutes or so in response to exercise. Otherwise, the evidence from the available studies on the hormonal response to exercise is inconclusive.

It should be emphasized that the data upon which the above suggestion is based are derived from samples of postmenarcheal women, both athletes and nonathletes, who are physiologically quite different from the developing girl. What is specifically relevant for the prepubertal or pubertal girl is the possible cumulative effects of hormonal responses to regular training. The hormonal responses are apparently essential to meet the stress that intensive activity imposes on the body. Do they have an effect on the hypothalamic center, which apparently triggers the change that initiates sexual maturation and eventually menarche? Such data are lacking at present.

Hormonal data for prepubertal or pubertal girls involved in regular training are limited, and the results are variable and inconclusive. Low gonadotropin secretion in association with only "mild" growth stunting, for example, has been reported in premenarcheal ballet dancers.[35] The dancers were delayed in breast development, menarche, and skeletal maturation, which would suggest a prolonged prepubertal state. However, they were not delayed in pubic hair development.

Lower plasma levels of estrone, testosterone, and androstenedione have been observed in 11-year-old prepubertal gymnasts than in swimmers of the same age and maturity status, but plasma gonadotropin and dehydroepiandrosterone-sulphate (DHEAS) levels did not differ in the two samples of prepubertal athletes. On the other hand, plasma levels of the seven hormones assayed did not differ between early pubertal (stage 2 of breast development) gymnasts and swimmers, although the latter were an average of 0.5 year older.[36] Both the prepubertal and early pubertal gymnasts had been training regularly for a longer period than the swimmers. The two groups of gymnasts had been training since 4.8 and 5.0 years of age, respectively, whereas the two groups of swimmers had been training since 7.2 and 8.0 years of age, respectively. The similar levels of DHEAS in the prepubertal gymnasts and swimmers suggests a similar stage of adrenarche, although the gymnasts had been training for a significantly longer period. This observation thus does not support the suggestion that training delays adrenarche and prolongs the prepubertal state.[37] Moreover, recent evidence does not support the view that secretion of adrenal androgens triggers sexual maturation.[38] Early childhood growth data for the two groups of athletes suggests physique differences. The gymnasts were shorter and lighter than Dutch reference data since 3 years of age, whereas the swimmers were taller and heavier than the reference data since 3 years of age. Midparental (height of mother and height of father, divided by 2) heights and weights were also less in the gymnasts than in the swimmers, and the groups did not differ in socioeconomic status.[36]

Changes in basal levels of hormones in association with training in young athletes may be significant. Similar basal levels of ACTH, cortisol, prolactin, and testosterone have been reported during a 24-week training season in small samples of premenarcheal and postmenarcheal competitive swimmers 13 to 18 years of age.[39] During the season, ACTH levels gradually increased, prolactin levels tended to increase, and testosterone levels decreased, whereas cortisol levels showed a variable pattern in the combined sample. As expected, basal estradiol levels differed between the premenarcheal and postmenarcheal swimmers, and both groups experienced a decrease in basal levels during the first 12 weeks of training, followed by a rise at 24 weeks. Basal levels of estradiol at the start of training and after 24 weeks of training did not differ in the premenarcheal swimmers, whereas the basal level after 24 weeks was lower than at the start of training in the postmenarcheal swimmers.[39]

A role for beta-endorphins in amenorrhea of runners and in turn delayed menarche in athletes has been postulated.[40] Administration of naloxone, an opiate receptor antagonist, to amenorrheic athletes, for example, results in a marked increase in luteinizing hormone (LH).[40] However, responses of normal prepubertal girls and boys to naloxone under basal conditions are different from those of adults.[41] Naloxone apparently does not have an effect on LH secretion in children. A study of the effects of naloxone during exercise conditions in children might be enlightening, but ethical concerns make collection of such data difficult.

A corollary of the suggestion that training delays menarche is that weight or body composition changes associated with intensive training may function to delay menarche, i.e., may delay maturation in young girls by keeping them lean. This in turn is related to the critical weight or critical fatness hypothesis that suggests that a certain level of weight (about 48 kg) or fatness (about 17 percent) is necessary for menarche to occur.[42] Accordingly, intensive, regular training functions to reduce and maintain fatness below the hypothesized minimal level, thereby delaying menarche. The critical weight or fatness hypothesis has been discussed at length by many authors,[43-46] and the evidence does not support the specificity of weight or fatness, or of a threshold level, as the critical variable for menarche to occur.

Since indicators of sexual maturity are reasonably well related to indicators of skeletal and somatic maturity during adolescence, it seems logical to consider the effects of training on other maturity indicators. If the hormonal responses to regular training are viewed as important influences on sexual maturation, one might expect them to influence skeletal maturation, especially near menarche, since epiphyseal capping and fusion are influenced by gonadal hormones among others. Training, however, is not associated with changes in the skeletal maturity of the hand and wrist in athletes of both sexes.[18]

The stress of training and competition as factors that influence biologic maturation needs more systematic and controlled study. There is a need for prospective studies in which youngsters are followed from prepubescence through puberty, in which several indicators of growth and maturity are observed, and in which training as well as other factors known to influence growth and maturation are monitored. Active youngsters of both sexes should be studied, as it is somewhat puzzling why one would expect training to delay the maturation of girls and not of boys, even though the underlying neuroendocrine processes are quite similar.

## EARLY TRAINING AND REPRODUCTIVE FUNCTION

Observations on elite athletes in a variety of sports indicate no significant effect of early training on subsequent reproductive function.[47-49] Disorders of pregnancy (e.g., toxemias), the duration and course of labor, and obstetrical complications are no more common in athletes than in nonathletes, and in some instances are less common in athletes. Age at marriage in athletes is generally close to the norm for the particular cultures in which they live. Among East German athletes, 80 percent of whom had been actively training for 10 years or more, mean ages at first parturition do not differ among athletes in several sports, although mean ages at menarche vary.[49] Thus, training during childhood evidently does not influence reproductive performance. If early training has an effect on menarche and subsequent menstrual function, it is apparently temporary.

Distributions of birth weights of infants born to formerly and currently active athletes are generally similar to those of the appropriate reference data.[47,49] Among 242 babies born to East German athletes, only 6.6 percent had birth weights less than 2500 grams,[49] and this corresponds to 6.0 percent and 5.4 percent of babies born to American white women, 20 to 24 and 25 to 29 years of age, in 1975.[50]

## SUMMARY

Variation in the timing, duration, and magnitude of the adolescent growth spurt is considerable. Adolescent gains in lean body mass and muscle mass in adolescent girls are not as great as in adolescent boys, so that by late adolescence, young adult women attain, on the average, about two thirds of the estimated values for young adult men. In contrast, absolute and relative fatness increases more in adolescent girls. Menarche is a relatively late pubertal event, occurring usually a year or so after maximum growth in stature during the adolescent spurt.

Strength, motor performance, and absolute maximal aerobic power improve during adolescence, but the average performance level tends to reach a plateau between 13 and 15 years of age. Trained girls have higher performance levels than do untrained girls, and girls who are delayed in sexual and skeletal maturity tend to be better performers.

Under adequate environmental circumstances, the timing of the growth spurt and sexual maturation is genetically determined, and the evidence suggesting that regular training delays maturation of girls is not convincing and needs more systematic and controlled study.

## References

1. Forbes, GB: Growth of the lean body mass in man. Growth 36:325, 1972.
2. Young CM, Sipin SS, and Roe DA: Body composition of pre-adolescent and adolescent girls. Density and skinfold measurements. J Am Diet Assoc 53:25, 1968.
3. Malina RM: Quantification of fat, muscle and bone in man. Clin Orthop 65:9, 1969.
4. Malina RM: Growth of muscle tissue and muscle mass. In Falkner F, and Tanner JM (eds): Human Growth, rev ed. Plenum, New York, 1986, p 77.
5. Tanner JM, Hughes PCR, and Whitehouse RH: Radiographically determined widths of bone, muscle and fat in the upper arm and calf from age 3–18 years. Ann Hum Biol 6:495, 1981.
6. MacMahon B: Age at menarche, United States. Vital and Health Statistics, Series 11, No 133, 1973.
7. Danker-Hopfe H: Menarcheal age in Europe. Yrbk Phys Anthropol 29:81, 1986.
8. Faust, MS: Somatic development of adolescent girls. Monogr Soc Res Child Dev 42(1): 1977.
9. Jones HE: Motor Performance and Growth. University of California Press, Berkeley, 1949.
10. Beunen G, Ostyn M, Renson R, et al: Skeletal maturation and physical fitness of girls aged 12 through 16. Hermes (Leuven) 10:445, 1976.
11. Carron AV, Aitken EJ, and Bailey DA: The relationship of menarche to the growth and development of strength. In Lavallee H, and Shephard RJ (eds): Frontiers of Activity and Child Health. Pelican, Quebec, p 139, 1977.
12. Branta C, Haubenstricker J, and Seefeldt V: Age changes in motor skills during childhood and adolescence. Exerc Sport Sci Rev 12:467, 1984.
13. Haubenstricker JL, and Seefeldt VD: Acquisition of motor skills during childhood. In Seefeldt V (ed): Physical Activity and Well Being. American Alliance for Health, Physical Education, Recreation and Dance, Reston, VA, 1986, p 41.
14. Malina RM: Growth, strength, and physical performance. In Stull GA (ed): Encyclopedia of Physical Education, Fitness and Sports: Training, Environment, Nutrition, and Fitness. Brighton Publishing, Salt Lake City, UT, 1980, p 443.
15. Espenschade A: Motor performance in adolescence. Monogr Soc Res Child Dev 5(1):1, 1940.
16. Beunen G, de Beul G, Ostyn M, et al: Age of men-

arche and motor performance in girls aged 11 through 18. Med Sport 11:118, 1978.

17. Malina RM: Menarche in athletes: a synthesis and hypothesis. Ann Hum Biol 10:1, 1983.

18. Malina RM: Biological maturity status of young athletes. In Malina RM (ed): Young Athletes: Biological, Psychological and Educational Perspectives. Human Kinetics, Champaign, IL, in press.

19. Krahenbuhl GS, Skinner JS, and Kohrt WM: Developmental aspects of maximal aerobic power in children. Exerc Sport Sci Rev 13:503, 1985.

20. Rutenfranz J, Andersen KL, Seliger V, et al: Maximal aerobic power affected by maturation and body growth during childhood and adolescence. Eur J Pediatr 139:106, 1982.

21. Malina RM: Energy expenditure and physical activity during childhood and youth. In Demirjian A (ed): Human Growth: A Multidisciplinary Review. Taylor and Francis, London, 1986, p 215.

22. Ross JG, Dotson CO, Gilbert GG, et al: The National Children and Youth Fitness Survey: after school physical education . . . physical activity outside of school physical education programs. J Phys Educ Rec Dance 56:77, 1985.

23. Kemper HCG, Dekker HJP, Ootjers MG, et al: Growth and health of teenagers in the Netherlands: survey of multidisciplinary longitudinal studies and comparison to recent results of a Dutch study. Int J Sports Med 4:202, 1983.

24. Malina RM: Competitive youth sports and biological maturation. In Seefeldt V (ed): CIC Symposium on the Effects of Competitive Sports on Children and Youth. Human Kinetics, Champaign, IL, in press.

25. Patton RG: Growth and psychological factors. In Mechanisms of Regulation of Growth, Report of the 40th Ross Conference on Pediatric Research. Ross Laboratories, Columbus, OH, 1962, p 58.

26. Tanner JM: Fetus into Man. Harvard University Press, Cambridge, MA, 1978, p 102.

27. Ellison PT: Morbidity, mortality, and menarche. Hum Biol 53:635, 1981.

28. Liestøl K: Social conditions and menarcheal age: the importance of early years of life. Ann Hum Biol 9:521, 1982.

29. Malina RM: Human growth, maturation, and regular physical activity. Acta Med Auxol 15:5, 1983.

30. Stager JM, Robertshaw D, and Miescher E: Delayed menarche in swimmers in relation to age at onset of training and athletic performance. Med Sci Sports Exerc 16:550, 1984.

31. Malina RM: Age at menarche in university athletes: pre- and post-Title IX comparisons. Med Sci Sports Exerc 18:S50, 1986.

32. Frisch RE, Gotz-Welbergen AV, McArthur JW, et al: Delayed menarche and amenorrhea of college athletes in relation to age of onset of training. JAMA 246:1559, 1981.

33. Terjung R: Endocrine response to exercise. Exerc Sport Sci Rev 7:153, 1979.

34. Shangold MM: Exercise and the adult female: hormonal and endocrine effects. Exerc Sport Sci Rev 12:53, 1984.

35. Warren MP: The effects of exercise on pubertal progression and reproductive function in girls. J Clin Endocrinol Metab 51:1150, 1980.

36. Peltenburg AL, Erich WBM, Thijssen JJH, et al: Sex hormone profiles of premenarcheal athletes. Eur J Appl Physiol 52:385, 1984.

37. Brisson GR, Dulac S, Peronnet F, et al: The onset of menarche: a late event in pubertal progression to be affected by physical training. Can J Appl Sport Sci 7:61, 1982.

38. Wierman ME, and Crowley WR Jr: Neuroendocrine control of the onset of puberty. In Falkner F, and Tanner JM (eds): Human Growth, rev ed. Plenum, New York, 1986, p 225.

39. Carli G, Martelli G, Viti A, et al: The effect of swimming training on hormone levels in girls. J Sports Med Phys Fitness 23:45, 1983.

40. McArthur JW, Bullen BA, Beitins IZ, et al: Hypothalamic amenorrhea in runners of normal body composition. Endocr Res Commun 7:13, 1980.

41. Fraioli F, Cappa M, Fabbri A, et al: Lack of endogenous opioid inhibitory tone in LH secretion in early puberty. Clin Endocrinol (Oxf) 20:299, 1984.

42. Frisch RE: Fatness of girls from menarche to age 18 years, with a nomogram. Hum Biol 48:353, 1976.

43. Malina RM: Adolescent growth and maturation: selected aspects of current research. Yearbook of Physical Anthropology 21:63, 1978.

44. Johnston FE, Roche AF, Schell LM, et al: Critical weight at menarche: critique of a hypothesis. Am J Dis Child 129:19, 1975.

45. Trussell J: Statistical flaws in evidence for the Frisch hypothesis that fatness triggers menarche. Hum Biol 52:711, 1980.

46. Scott EC, and Johnston FE: Critical fatness, menarche, and the maintenance of menstrual cycles. Journal of Adolescent Health Care 2:249, 1982.

47. Niemineva K: On the course of delivery of Finnish baseball (Pesapallo) players and swimmers. In Karvonen MJ (ed): Sport Medicine. Finnish Association of Sports Medicine, Helsinki, 1953, p 169.

48. Erdelyi GJ: Gynecological survey of female athletes. J Sports Med Phys Fitness 2:174, 1962.

49. Markër K: Frau und Sport. Johann Ambrosius Barth, Leipzig, 1983.

50. National Center for Health Statistics: Teenage childbearing: United States, 1966–1975. Monthly Vital Statistics Report, 26, No 5, 1977.

# CHAPTER 10

# Menstruation

MONA M. SHANGOLD, M.D.

Increased participation of women in sports has led to greater awareness of the menstrual cycle alterations that frequently accompany exercise and training. This raised consciousness has inspired more scientists to investigate the etiologic mechanisms responsible for such changes and has led many athletes to seek medical attention. Unfortunately, many other athletes still avoid physician consultation, usually because they fear they will be told to stop exercising. It is the responsibility of all physicians and other health professionals to advise exercising women about what is known regarding reproductive effects of exercise and to assist them in formulating therapeutic plans.

## PREVALENCE OF MENSTRUAL DYSFUNCTION AMONG ATHLETES

Oligomenorrhea (infrequent menses) and amenorrhea (absent menses) are more prevalent among athletes (10 to 20 percent)[1,2] than among the general population (5 percent) and are found more often in runners than in swimmers or cyclists[3] (Fig. 10–1). Among competitive athletes, the prevalence of amenorrhea has been reported to be as high as 50 percent.[3] However, the prevalence of menstrual dysfunction does not correlate with average weekly mileage, running pace, or number of years of training.[2,4] Bachmann and Kemmann[5] have reported that the prevalences of oligomenorrhea and amenorrhea among college students are 11 percent and 3 percent, respectively. However, this popula-

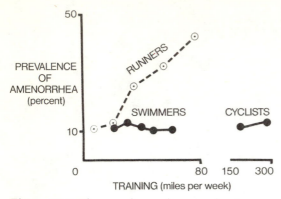

**Figure 10–1.** *The prevalence of amenorrhea in runners, swimmers, and cyclists, relative to training mileage. (From Sanborn,[3] with permission.)*

tion includes some athletes, for whom exercise and training contribute to the problem. The prevalence of menstrual dysfunction among college students is higher than that among the rest of the population because college students tend to experience more emotional stress than the general population and because many college students have not undergone full maturation of the hypothalamic-pituitary-ovarian axis, making them more susceptible to menstrual disorders. It is worth mentioning that the general population has previously been considered to be sedentary, but the rising numbers of exercising women will undoubtedly increase the percentage of exercising women in the general population and may raise the prevalence of menstrual dysfunction in this group.

Although it is tempting to presume that exercise itself is responsible for the higher prevalence of amenorrhea associated with it, many factors change simultaneously during the course of an athletic training program, making it difficult to isolate causal factors. The fact that amenorrheic runners have a higher incidence of prior menstrual irregularity[1,2] suggests that exercise alone may not be responsible for menstrual dysfunction in most cases (Fig. 10–2).

## REVIEW OF MENSTRUAL PHYSIOLOGY

A brief review of menstrual physiology follows, to facilitate the understanding of readers from diverse backgrounds. It is necessary to be familiar with the basic hormonal events of the menstrual cycle, in order to appreciate both the hormonal and menstrual alterations that accompany exercise and training. For more comprehensive reviews, the reader is referred to other publications.[6,7]

A normal menstrual cycle (counting from the beginning of one period to the beginning of the next period) lasts from 23 to 35 days. An ovarian **follicle** is the structure that contains an egg; a **corpus luteum** is what develops from a follicle after the egg has been expelled. The **follicular phase** is the portion of the ovarian cycle that extends from the first day of menstruation until ovulation; this corresponds temporally with the **proliferative phase** of the endometrial cycle. The **luteal phase** of the ovarian cycle extends from ovulation until the onset of the next menstrual period; this corresponds temporally with the **secretory phase** of the endometrial cycle. A normal luteal phase should approach 14 days, while a normal follicular phase may vary considerably in length. Thus, fluctuations in the length of the menstrual cycle of a woman who ovulates usually result from variations in the length of the follicular phase, or the time required for a follicle to enlarge and mature enough to undergo ovulation.

Throughout the menstrual cycle, the hypothalamus secretes gonadotropin-releasing hormone (GnRH), which is also referred to as luteinizing hormone–releasing hormone (LH-RH) or luteinizing hormone–releasing factor (LRF). This decapeptide is produced by cells in the arcuate nucleus of the hypothalamus; it promotes synthesis, storage, releasability, and secretion of both pituitary gonadotropins: follicle-stimulating hormone (FSH) and luteinizing hormone (LH). FSH promotes growth of the ovarian follicle and synthesis of estrogen from androgen precursors. LH stimulates ovarian androgen production, maintaining a supply of androgens available for conversion to estrogens.

In a normal menstrual cycle, a woman produces estrogen all the time and produces progesterone only after ovulation. Blood estrogen levels vary greatly throughout the cycle, being quite low during the early follicular phase and quite high during the late follicular phase. It is the high estrogen level in the late follicular phase that triggers ovulation. During the luteal phase, levels of both estrogen and progesterone are high.

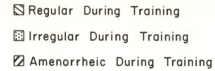

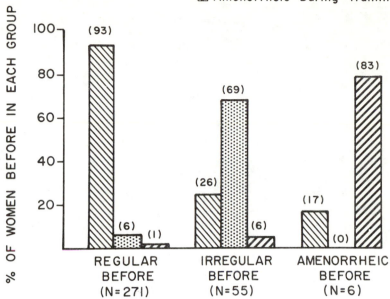

*Figure 10–2. Percent menstrual change during training for women with regular menses before training, irregular menses before training, and amenorrhea before training. Ninety-three percent of those women who had regular menses before training continued to have regular menses during training. (From Shangold,[2] with permission.)*

Estrogen stimulates the endometrium (the inner lining of the uterus) to proliferate; progesterone promotes maturation and stabilization of an estrogen-stimulated endometrium. It is the decline in the concentrations of estrogen and progesterone near the end of the menstrual cycle that results in menstruation, which is the desquamation of the endometrium (Fig. 10–3).

## MENSTRUAL DYSFUNCTION

With any insult to a woman's reproductive system, menstrual disturbance probably follows an orderly sequence of increasing severity: (1) luteal phase deficiency, (2) euestrogenic anovulation, and (3) hypoestrogenic amenorrhea. Thus, any condition that disturbs the delicate balance of carefully timed hormonal events needed for regular ovulation and menstruation usually produces luteal phase deficiency first. If the condition continues, euestrogenic anovulation will probably follow. If the condition continues

even longer, hypoestrogenic amenorrhea is likely to ensue. Many women do not seek attention when menstrual dysfunction is mild or of recent onset and may have hypoestrogenic amenorrhea by the time they first seek attention. Although progression of this sequence has not been documented in prospective studies, it is likely, nevertheless, and provides a useful model for understanding menstrual dysfunction.

## MENSTRUAL CYCLE CHANGES WITH EXERCISE AND TRAINING

The data collected from the surveys reported are derived from records of women who recorded only their menstrual patterns. Most, but not all, women who bleed at regular intervals have normal ovulatory and luteal function. More accurate information about menstrual cyclicity can be derived from basal body temperature records and hormonal measurements. By having 14 subjects record their basal body temperatures to

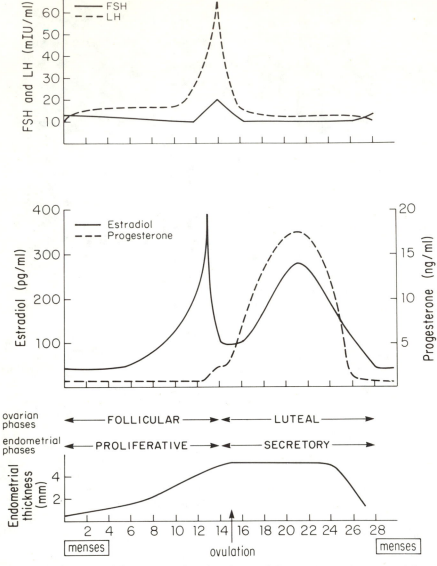

**Figure 10-3.** *Hormonal events of the menstrual cycle, phases of the ovarian and endometrial cycles, and endometrial height throughout the menstrual cycle.*

indicate that and when ovulation had occurred, Prior and co-workers[8] have shown in 48 menstrual cycles that even among athletic women with apparently regular menses, approximately one third have anovulation, one third have luteal phase deficiency, and one third have normal luteal function. This suggests that menstrual disturbance among exercising women may be more pervasive than has been appreciated.

In addition to the epidemiologic studies that demonstrate a higher prevalence of oligomenorrhea/amenorrhea among athletes than among sedentary women, several prospective investigations have demonstrated changes in menstrual cyclicity in individual women who trained. Each of these has studied a number of factors that vary during training, any of which may contribute to menstrual cycle alteration. It is usually very

## Table 10–1. FACTORS TO WHICH AN ATHLETE IS OFTEN SUBJECTED DURING TRAINING

1. Weight loss
2. Low weight
3. Low body fat
4. Dietary alterations
5. Nutritional inadequacy
6. Physical stress
7. Emotional stress
8. Acute hormone alterations
9. Chronic hormone alterations

difficult to separate the many contributory variables that change simultaneously during training, including body composition, physical and emotional stress, diet, and certain hormone levels (Table 10–1).

## Weight Loss and Thinness

Many women lose both weight and body fat when they begin to exercise regularly. Some attain and maintain very low levels of weight and fat. Simple weight loss and thinness may lead to amenorrhea, even in the absence of exercise. Shangold and Levine[2] have reported that amenorrheic runners are lighter than eumenorrheic (regularly menstruating) runners. Schwartz and associates[1] have demonstrated that amenorrheic runners were thinner and had lost more weight after initiating regular running.

Despite claims that women need a minimum amount of body fat in order to maintain regular menstrual cyclicity, this hypothesis remains unproven and suspect. If such a minimum amount of fat must be exceeded, the mechanism by which this functions also remains unproven. Adipose tissue produces and retains estrogen, but the amount of estrogen contributed by adipose tissue is negligible compared with the very large quantity produced by normal ovaries. Since muscle tissue contains aromatizing enzymes too, and since athletic women tend to have more muscle and less fat than sedentary women, aromatizing capability should be comparable in both groups. Thus, the mechanism by which thinness promotes menstrual dysfunction remains to be shown.

## Physical and Emotional Stress

Schwartz and colleagues[1] have shown that amenorrheic runners associate more stress with their exercise than do eumenorrheic runners. This supports the concept that the physical and emotional stress of both training and competition may be substantially greater than appreciated. Although regular exercise tends to relieve stress and anxiety, this action may be outweighed in busy women who are determined to incorporate a specific quantity of exercise into their daily schedules.

Warren[9] has demonstrated the complexity and interrelationship of the factors contributing to the development of menstrual dysfunction in two ballet dancers (Fig. 10–4). The dancer in the upper graph experienced no change in weight or body composition throughout the year in which she had three menstrual periods, each during an interval of inactivity. The dancer in the lower graph developed regular menses when she gained both weight and body fat, although she maintained her customary level of activity. She continued menstruating regularly, despite a loss of both weight and body fat that occurred during an inactive vacation interval. With no further loss of weight, she ceased menstruating altogether when she resumed her customary level of activity. It is likely that stress levels are higher during intervals of intensive dancing, compared with vacation intervals. Thus, activity, fat, weight, and stress must be considered variables in the changes observed.

## Dietary Factors

Many women who begin to exercise regularly alter their dietary patterns because they become more concerned about healthful living. Those who have been exercising regularly for a long time often eat differently from nonathletes. Schwartz and co-workers[1] reported that protein constituted a smaller percentage of the total caloric intake of amenorrheic runners compared with that of eumenorrheic runners and eumenorrheic nonrunners. These amenorrheic runners consumed more total calories than the other groups, however, so that equal quantities of protein were consumed by all three groups. Calabrese and colleagues[10] have demon-

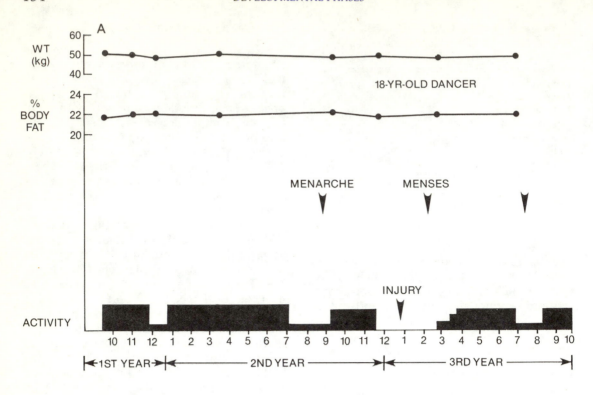

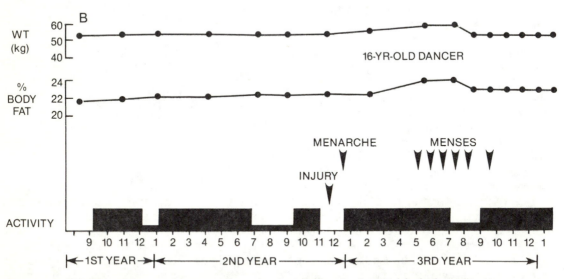

**Figure 10–4.** *Relationships among menses, exercise, weights, and calculated body fat values in two young ballet dancers. (From Warren,[9] with permission.)*

strated that professional and student ballet dancers consume fewer calories (1358 calories) than the recommended dietary allowance (RDA) (2030 calories) established by the National Research Council,[11] a figure in-

tended for an "average" woman, weighing 58 kg and exercising very little or not at all. Although the mean daily protein intake by these dancers (47.4 g) fell slightly below the RDA for "average-sized women" (50 g), this protein intake was adequate when based on the RDA of 0.8 g per kg[11] and the subjects' mean weight of 53.1 kg. Frisch and associates[12] have reported that a group of collegiate women who began athletic training prior to menarche consumed less fat (65 g) and protein (71 g) than a group who began training after menarche (95 g of fat and 92 g of protein), and that the former group also had higher incidences of oligomenorrhea and amenorrhea. It seems unlikely that these dietary differences contributed to menstrual dysfunction, though, since even the groups consuming less protein and fat appear to consume adequate amounts of these food components; the higher figures probably represent more of these food components than is desirable. Most people consume too much fat and would benefit from reducing their total daily fat intake to about 80 g, or approximately 30 percent of their total dietary calories. Very low levels of fat intake are difficult to attain, and such diets have been associated with insidious negative calcium balance.[13] Deficiencies of the fat-soluble vitamins, which require fat for absorption, have never been reported in people consuming low-fat diets, but such deficiencies remain a theoretical hazard.

Despite the suggestion that amenorrheic runners may consume inadequate cholesterol to produce sufficient estrogen, there remains no evidence that dietary cholesterol is necessary for hormone synthesis. The corpus luteum cannot make enough cholesterol de novo to synthesize adequate progesterone during a normal luteal phase, but the rest of the body can provide enough cholesterol to serve as precursor for adequate luteal progesterone production. Thus, more research is needed to explain whether the dietary differences between amenorrheic athletes and eumenorrheic women contribute to their menstrual differences and, if so, how this happens.

## HORMONAL CHANGES WITH EXERCISE AND TRAINING

### Acute Hormone Alterations With Exercise

Blood levels of several protein and steroid hormones increase transiently during continuous, aerobic exercise. The long-term effects of such repetitive, but brief, alterations remain unknown. Reported exercise-induced changes in gonadotropin levels are inconsistent and have been confused by the pulsatile nature of gonadotropin release. Circulating concentrations of prolactin,[14] estradiol,[15] progesterone,[15] and testosterone[14] rise during exercise and return to normal within an hour or two after cessation of exercise. Exercise-associated increments in ACTH, opioid peptides, melatonin, and cortisol are facilitated by training.[16,17] Since testosterone[18] and cortisol[19] increase also in anticipation of exercise, it is probable that psychologic factors contribute to the reported changes as well. Rebar and co-workers[20] have shown that dexamethasone suppression abolishes all effects of exercise on adrenal and gonadal hormones, including those in anticipation of exercise. Detailed review of the many studies of hormonal changes during exercise sessions, ranging in duration from a few minutes to the time required to complete a marathon, is beyond the scope of this chapter. For a more comprehensive review, readers are referred elsewhere.[21,22]

### Factors Influencing Hormone Levels

Plasma hormone levels represent a balance among production, metabolism, utilization, clearance, and plasma volume—all of which may change simultaneously during exercise. Levels of many hormones also are affected by episodic secretion, diurnal variation, state of sleep or wakefulness, state of feeding or fasting, dietary composition and caloric adequacy, temperature, body weight and composition, emotional factors, and body position. The hormonal response to exercise in any person is often influenced by the person's fitness, which affects the relative workload of any given activity and, in some cases, alters hormonal responsiveness during exercise. Difficulty in controlling these many variables during any specific investigation makes it even harder to interpret the observed exercise-induced changes in hormone levels.

### Chronic Hormone Alterations With Training

Shangold and associates[23] have observed one runner during 18 menstrual cycles in which she varied her weekly mileage. This woman had shortening of the luteal phase

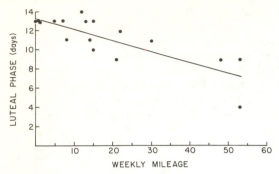

**Figure 10–5.** *Relationship between mileage run during the first 6 days of follicular phase and length of luteal phase, defined as the interval between the day of change in cervical mucus and onset of next menses, in 18 cycles. (y = 13.3 − 0.11x; r = −0.81; p <0.001). Point (1,13) represents three values. (From Shangold,[23] reproduced with permission of The American Fertility Society.)*

and lower progesterone levels in cycles of greater mileage (Figs. 10–5 and 10–6).

Prior and colleagues[24] have also reported luteal phase deficiency in two runners during several menstrual cycles of varying mileage. One of these two runners had a normal pregnancy when she stopped running, suggesting that exercise-induced luteal phase deficiency is a reversible phenomenon.

Similarly, Frisch and associates[25] observed a long-distance swimmer prior to, during, and after intensive training, with monitoring

of basal body temperature records, as well as blood and urine hormone measurements. She developed a luteal phase defect, followed by an anovulatory cycle, during intensive training. Three months after completion of a long-distance swim (the English Channel), she regained a normal, biphasic body temperature pattern. This confirms that the menstrual cycle alterations associated with intensive training occur in swimming as well as in running.

Menstrual and hormonal changes in two groups of untrained women were studied prospectively by Bullen and co-workers.[26] One group lost weight during a running pro-

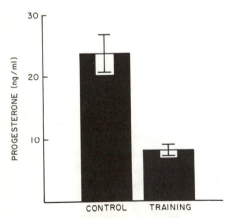

**Figure 10–6.** *Midluteal phase plasma progesterone concentrations obtained 3 to 7 days after change in cervical mucus (presumptive evidence of ovulation), comparing seven samples from three control cycles and seven samples from three training cycles. Bars indicate means plus standard errors (p <0.001). (From Shangold,[23] reproduced with permission of The American Fertility Society.)*

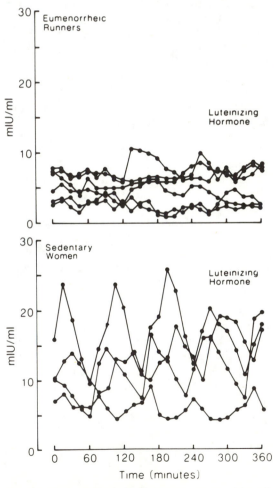

**Figure 10–7.** *Serum LH levels in samples obtained at 15-minute intervals over 6 hours in six eumenorrheic runners (upper) and four sedentary controls (lower). The studies were performed in the early follicular phase of the menstrual cycle (days 3 to 6). (From Cumming,[32] with permission.)*

gram of increasing mileage, and the other group maintained weight during the same program. The prevalence of menstrual dysfunction was high in both groups during intensive training, but was much higher in the weight-loss group. Ninety-four percent of the weight-loss group experienced menstrual disturbances, compared with 75 percent of the weight-maintenance group. Sixty-three percent of the weight-loss group experienced abnormal luteal function, and 66 percent of the weight-maintenance group did so. All subjects regained normal menstrual cyclicity within 6 months of termination of the study (and presumably training). As has been shown by Warren,[9] weight loss and exercise act synergistically in promoting menstrual dysfunction.

On the other hand, Russell and associates[27,28] found similar weights and body fat levels among athletic and inactive women, but found a correlation among strenuous exercise, anovulatory oligomenorrhea, and elevated levels of beta-endorphins and catechol estrogens. Although endogenous opiates are known to modulate pulsatile luteinizing hormone release in humans,[29] it is unlikely that circulating levels of these peptides correspond to the brain levels influencing hypothalamic secretion.

The fact that a generalized increase in "stress" hormones occurs with exercise and endurance training has been confirmed by Villanueva and colleagues,[30] who demonstrated increased cortisol production in both eumenorrheic and amenorrheic runners. Although the amenorrheic runners had higher levels of both serum cortisol and urinary cortisol, the differences between these two groups of runners were not statistically significant.

Boyden and associates[31] have provided a clue toward our understanding of the alterations in menstrual function associated with intensive exercise. They have shown that GnRH-stimulated LH levels in eumenorrheic women decrease with endurance training (distance running).

Cumming and co-workers[32] enhanced further our understanding of these changes when they reported that eumenorrheic runners (at rest) have lower LH pulse frequency, LH pulse amplitude, and area under the LH curve over 6 hours, compared with eumenorrheic sedentary women (Figs. 10–7 and 10–8). These investigators[33] then found that acute exercise reduces LH pulse frequency but does not change pulse amplitude or area under the 6-hour curve. These important findings suggest that acute exercise has an inhibitory effect on LH pulsatile release at the hypothalamic level in eumenorrheic runners, perhaps contributing to the observed alterations with training.

## CONSEQUENCES OF MENSTRUAL DYSFUNCTION

### Luteal Phase Deficiency

The only adverse condition definitely associated with luteal phase deficiency is infer-

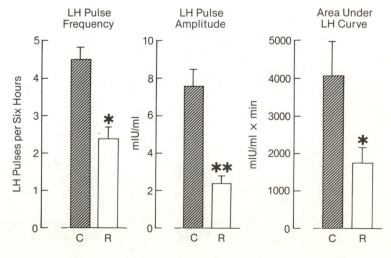

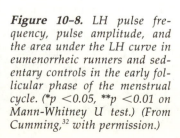

*Figure 10–8.* LH pulse frequency, pulse amplitude, and the area under the LH curve in eumenorrheic runners and sedentary controls in the early follicular phase of the menstrual cycle. (*p <0.05, **p <0.01 on Mann-Whitney U test.) (From Cumming,[32] with permission.)

tility. However, preliminary findings suggest that progesterone deficiency may also be associated with an increased breast cancer risk.[34]

## Anovulatory Oligomenorrhea

Chronic anovulation is associated with chronic, unopposed estrogen production, which leads to continuous endometrial stimulation and, as a consequence, increased risk of endometrial hyperplasia and adenocarcinoma. Although this association has been documented in women with polycystic ovary syndrome,[35-38] it has never been reported in athletes. It remains unknown whether anovulatory athletes carry the same, increased risk of developing endometrial hyperplasia and adenocarcinoma as nonathletes with chronic anovulation. Perhaps inadequate reporting or history-taking, or both, has led to the absence of such reports (i.e., gynecologists may not routinely elicit athletic histories, particularly when diagnosing cancer), or perhaps anovulatory athletic women do not maintain high enough estrogen levels long enough to induce hyperplasia or cancer. Until this question is answered, it seems reasonable to assume that the endometrium of the athlete responds the same as that of the nonathlete to estrogen stimulation. Thus, an increased risk of endometrial hyperplasia and adenocarcinoma should be presumed until it is disproved.

Recent studies have suggested that anovulatory women may also be at increased risk of developing breast cancer.[39] This preliminary report requires further confirmation. This suggestion, too, has not described the athletic habits of subjects. Thus, if chronic anovulation leads to an increased risk of breast carcinoma, it remains to be shown whether this increased risk includes anovulatory athletes.

Although Frisch and associates[40] have reported a lower prevalence of breast cancer among former college athletes compared with former college nonathletes, this report did not relate breast cancer prevalence to recent athletic participation. Thus, it remains to be demonstrated whether regular exercise has any effect on breast cancer risk.

Chronic anovulation usually leads to infrequent, heavy bleeding at unpredictable times. At best, this is an inconvenience, particularly to competitive athletes, and at worst, it may require hospitalization to control blood loss. Between these extremes, women with chronic, unopposed estrogen production may be iron-deficient or anemic. Either of these conditions can impair athletic performance, as can heavy bleeding during training or competition. The prevalence of heavy bleeding among athletes remains to be shown. As suggested earlier, it is possible that anovulatory athletic women do not maintain high enough estrogen levels long enough to induce sufficient thickening of the endometrial lining and consequent profuse bleeding. However, heavy, infrequent bleeding episodes are common among adolescents, even those who are athletes; it is probable that more mature athletes are subject to the same risk.

## Hypoestrogenic Amenorrhea

Several recent reports have demonstrated that athletes with hypoestrogenic amenorrhea have reduced bone density and increased risk of musculoskeletal injury, compared with eumenorrheic athletes.[41-47]

Cann and co-workers[41] were the first to bring this finding to our attention. They reported that women with hypothalamic amenorrhea, in many cases associated with exercise, had lower vertebral bone density than several other groups of eumenorrheic and amenorrheic women, including those with hyperprolactinemia and premature ovarian failure. This surprising, incidental finding led several other investigators to the same issue. It had been shown by others that exercise has a beneficial effect on bone density, as discussed in Chapter 6. In view of the higher prevalence of hypoestrogenic amenorrhea among athletes, it became important to resolve whether exercise is beneficial enough to compensate for an estrogen deficiency.

Rigotti and colleagues[42] reported that amenorrheic women with anorexia nervosa had lower radial bone density than eumenorrheic controls, and that those anorectics who reported a high physical activity level had a greater bone density than those who were less active. This suggested that physical activity offers some protection against bone loss induced by estrogen deficiency.

In a study by Drinkwater and co-workers,[43] lower vertebral bone density was found in amenorrheic athletes than in eumenorrheic athletes. However, these groups differed not only in their estrogen status but also in their calcium intake. Although the absolute values of calcium ingested by the groups were not significantly different, the amenorrheic group, but not the eumenorrheic group, consumed much less calcium than the amount recommended for hypoestrogenic women. Since estrogen enhances calcium absorption, hypoestrogenic women require an additional 500 milligrams of calcium daily, compared with that required by euestrogenic women. (It is recommended that euestrogenic women consume 1000 milligrams of calcium daily and that hypoestrogenic women consume 1500 milligrams daily.[48]) Thus, it is unclear whether the lower bone density of these amenorrheic athletes was caused by estrogen deficiency, calcium deficiency, or both.

Marcus and colleagues[44] also reported that eumenorrheic runners had greater vertebral bone density than eumenorrheic sedentary women, who had greater bone density than amenorrheic runners, who had greater bone density than amenorrheic sedentary women. This suggested that exercise is beneficial in increasing bone density, but not as beneficial as a normal estrogen level. Unfortunately, differences in calcium intake between some of these groups introduced another variable, as occurred in the Drinkwater study.[43] It remains difficult to separate estrogen, exercise, and calcium intake as variables in pinpointing causality in such studies.

It was demonstrated by Jones and associates[45] that radial bone density regresses in a linear fashion with increasing duration of amenorrhea, regardless of etiology, confirming that hypoestrogenic young women lose bone density in the same pattern as that observed for postmenopausal women.[49]

Warren and co-workers[46] have reported that ballet dancers have a higher prevalence of scoliosis and a greater incidence of fractures with increasing menarcheal age. They also found a higher incidence and longer duration of secondary amenorrhea among dancers with stress fractures. These findings suggest that menarcheal delay and prolonged intervals of hypoestrogenic amenorrhea may predispose ballerinas to scoliosis and stress fractures.

The suggestion of increased susceptibility to musculoskeletal injuries among amenorrheic athletes has been supported by the work of Lloyd and colleagues.[47] These authors reported that women who were injured during their running program were more likely to have had absent or irregular menses, were less likely to have used oral contraceptives, and had been running for more years than those running women who were not injured.

## DIAGNOSTIC EVALUATION OF MENSTRUAL DYSFUNCTION IN ATHLETES

I believe that all oligomenorrheic and amenorrheic athletes deserve a physical examination, including a pelvic examination, and some blood tests. Although most athletes with menstrual disturbances will be found to have no serious conditions, it is impossible to determine, without this assessment, whether the menstrual dysfunction is related to exercise or to some serious pathologic condition. A complete blood count, measurement of electrolytes and liver enzymes, and urinalysis are useful screening tests for the general population. However, because these tests have not proved cost-effective for patients in my practice who have only menstrual dysfunction, I no longer perform these tests routinely.

Menstrual disturbances may be caused by hyperprolactinemia, hypothyroidism, ovarian failure, and pregnancy. To detect these conditions, it is necessary to measure the following: serum prolactin, thyrotropin (TSH), thyroxine, triiodothyronine resin uptake, follicle-stimulating hormone (FSH), luteinizing hormone (LH), and beta–human chorionic gonadotropin (HCG) (Table 10–2). Hyperprolactinemia may result from a pituitary adenoma or microadenoma; it requires further evaluation and specific treatment. An elevated TSH level or a low thyroxine level indicates hypothyroidism, which also requires

**Table 10–2.** INITIAL DIAGNOSTIC EVALUATION OF OLIGOMENORRHEA/AMENORRHEA

1. History and physical examination
2. Prolactin, thyroid function tests, TSH, FSH, LH, HCG
3. Progesterone challenge test

further evaluation and specific treatment. Pregnancy, of course, requires further care. Ovarian failure requires at least counseling and possibly also further evaluation and treatment. In a patient younger than age 30, ovarian failure warrants a blood karyotype to detect the presence of a Y chromosome, which confers an increased risk of gonadal malignancy. In a patient older than age 30, no further evaluation is required. Most women who experience ovarian failure prior to age 45 should be treated with hormone replacement therapy to relieve vasomotor symptoms and prevent osteoporosis and atrophic vaginitis.

At the time of the initial examination and blood hormone evaluation, the patient should be given a prescription for a 5-day course of medroxyprogesterone acetate, which tests her endogenous estrogen level. If she experiences withdrawal bleeding after completion of the progestin trial, her endometrium had been stimulated by estrogen and requires progestin therapy for protection. If she has no withdrawal bleeding after the progestin trial, her endometrium had not been stimulated by estrogen, and the rest of her body probably also lacks sufficient estrogen.

## TREATMENT OF MENSTRUAL DYSFUNCTION IN ATHLETES

Even if no serious causative pathology is detected during the hormonal evaluation for menstrual dysfunction, treatment usually is indicated to prevent serious resultant pathology.

Because luteal phase deficiency is associated with no consequences other than infertility, this condition requires no treatment unless and until pregnancy is desired.

As discussed, euestrogenic anovulatory women are at increased risk of developing endometrial hyperplasia and should be treated with monthly progestin administration to protect the endometrium adequately. This can be effected by one of the following regimens: (1) medroxyprogesterone acetate 5 to 10 milligrams daily for 10 to 14 consecutive days of every month, (2) oral contraceptive pills, each containing 30 to 35 micrograms of ethinyl estradiol and 0.4 to 1.0 milligrams of progestin, or (3) clomiphene citrate to induce ovulation (Table 10–3).

**Table 10–3.** TREATMENT OF EUESTROGENIC OLIGOMENORRHEA

1. If not sexually active or using barrier contraception: monthly progestin therapy
2. If contraception needed or preferred: oral contraceptives
3. If fertility desired: clomiphene citrate

Ovulation induction should be reserved for only those women desiring pregnancy at the time of evaluation. The first two choices are acceptable for women who do not seek pregnancy now, regardless whether they are sexually active. Although oral contraceptive pills obviously provide contraception, medroxyprogesterone acetate does not, and this regimen requires individuals to use barrier contraceptive methods if they are sexually active.

Hypoestrogenic amenorrheic women require hormone replacement, primarily for skeletal protection, but also for urogenital protection. Such athletes should be treated with one of the following treatment protocols: (1) conjugated estrogens 0.625 to 0.9 milligrams daily on days 1 to 25 of every calendar month, and medroxyprogesterone acetate 5 to 10 milligrams daily on days 14 to 25 of every calendar month; (2) transdermal estradiol 0.05 to 0.10 milligram daily and medroxyprogesterone acetate 5 to 10 milligrams daily on days 1 to 12 of every calendar month; (3) oral contraceptive pills, each containing 30 to 35 micrograms of ethinyl estradiol and 0.4 to 1.0 milligrams of progestin; or (4) clomiphene citrate or human menopausal gonadotropins to induce ovulation (Table 10–4). Ovulation induction should be reserved for women desiring pregnancy at the time of evaluation. Oral contraceptive pills

**Table 10–4.** TREATMENT OF HYPOESTROGENIC AMENORRHEA

1. If fertility desired: clomiphene citrate
2. If contraception needed or preferred: oral contraceptives
3. If contraception and fertility not of concern: cyclic estrogen and progestin therapy
4. If very thin: weight gain?
5. If exercising very heavily: less exercise?

may be recommended to any hypoestrogenic amenorrheic athlete who does not desire pregnancy at the time of evaluation, regardless of whether she is sexually active; no additional contraceptive method is needed by athletes selecting this form of hormone replacement therapy. Those who select the more physiologic regimen of conjugated estrogens or transdermal estradiol and medroxyprogesterone acetate, separately, should be advised to use mechanical methods of contraception if they are sexually active.

The major advantages of taking oral contraceptive agents are convenience and contraception; the major disadvantages are their two most common side effects: breakthrough bleeding (bleeding on the days of pill ingestion) and amenorrhea (lack of withdrawal bleeding at the end of the hormone-containing pills in each package). These side effects are inconvenient but not serious; both can be alleviated by hormone manipulation. The low-dose oral contraceptive pills recommended are associated with much lesser side effects and complications than the higher doses prescribed commonly more than a decade ago; the low-dose preparations are also associated with a reduction in many disease risks, compared with the risk to the general population. Another advantage of oral contraceptives for athletes with menstrual dysfunction is the predictable bleeding and continued endometrial and skeletal protection, even if athletes experience fluctuations in their endogenous estrogen levels. Many athletes may produce enough estrogen to have withdrawal bleeding following progestin administration for several months and then produce too little estrogen to do so during the next few months. It is disturbing to many athletes to experience such fluctuations in their observed responses, and many experience psychologic benefit from the regularity and predictability of oral contraceptive therapy.

The major advantages of taking either progestin alone or estrogen and progestin as separate pills are the ingestion of more physiologic doses of medication and the likelihood of having predictable bleeding. Although the risks of exogenous hormone administration are much less than the risks of hormone deficiency, in my view, certain women should probably avoid estrogen and

**Table 10–5.** ABSOLUTE CONTRAINDICATIONS TO ESTROGEN THERAPY

1. Abnormal liver function
2. History of thromboembolic or vascular disease
3. Breast or endometrial carcinoma
4. Undiagnosed vaginal bleeding

others should definitely avoid it. Absolute contraindications to estrogen therapy are listed in Table 10–5; relative contraindications are listed in Table 10–6.

Many athletes have an aversion to exogenous hormone ingestion and do not comprehend the difference between physiologic replacement and pharmacologic therapy. It requires careful and concerned counseling to convince many of these women that hormone replacement therapy is advisable.

Although some of them may prefer to gain weight or to reduce training intensity or quantity, to see if menses return without hormone therapy, it is not recommended that these measures postpone for longer than 6 months the initiation of hormone replacement. A shorter trial is reasonable, particularly if the athlete herself makes this suggestion. I believe that the benefits of regular exercise far outweigh these potential reproductive hazards, which can and should be evaluated and treated if they develop.

Despite the demonstration by several investigators that exercise-associated menstrual dysfunction is often a reversible phenomenon, there is no evidence that it is reversible in *all* cases, nor is there any method of predicting when normal function will return, if ever. It is extremely unlikely that chronic, unopposed estrogen stimula-

**Table 10–6.** RELATIVE CONTRAINDICATIONS TO ESTROGEN THERAPY

1. Hypertension
2. Diabetes mellitus
3. Fibrocystic disease of the breast
4. Uterine leiomyomata
5. Familial hyperlipidemia
6. Migraine headaches
7. Gallbladder disease

**Table 10–7.** RECOMMENDATIONS
FOR FOLLOW-UP OF ATHLETES
WITH OLIGOMENORRHEA OR
AMENORRHEA

1. Annual history and physical examination
2. Annual prolactin, TSH, thyroid function tests, FSH, LH
3. Annual progestin challenge test
4. Hormone replacement therapy

tion of the uterus will cause hyperplasia or adenocarcinoma in less than 3 years. However, bone loss takes place at an accelerated rate as soon as a woman becomes hypoestrogenic, and a significant amount of bone will be lost within the first 3 years of hypoestrogenism. I believe that it is best to initiate hormone replacement therapy by the time 6 months have passed, for individuals experiencing oligomenorrhea and those with amenorrhea. I also believe that pelvic examination and blood evaluation should be repeated annually in all athletes with menstrual dysfunction, regardless of whether they are receiving hormone replacement (Table 10–7).

Many athletes claim that they prefer to be amenorrheic. However, there is an obvious difference between not wanting to menstruate on the day of an important competitive event and *never* wanting to menstruate at all. It is likely that most would prefer to have normal reproductive function, rather than amenorrhea, even if many are unwilling to admit this to themselves.

## EVALUATION AND TREATMENT OF PRIMARY AMENORRHEA

*Primary amenorrhea* refers to the condition in which menstruation has never occurred. *Secondary amenorrhea*, to which we have referred until now, refers to the condition in which menstruation had occurred in the past but subsequently has ceased. Because menarche is often delayed in athletic girls, as discussed thoroughly in Chapters 8 and 9, it is tempting to assume that menarcheal delay is related to exercise. However, this assumption is as dangerous as that for secondary amenorrhea. Serious pathologic conditions can easily be missed if they are not sought.

Any girl who has not developed any secondary sexual characteristics by the age of 13 should be examined and possibly evaluated further. The same should be done for any girl who has not begun to menstruate by age 16. Physical findings will direct appropriate testing for these problems. As shown in Table 10–8, the diagnostic evaluation of primary amenorrhea is similar to that for secondary amenorrhea, except for the greater emphasis in primary amenorrhea upon detection of a uterus.

Müllerian agenesis (which includes absence of the uterus) is the second most common pathologic cause of primary amenorrhea, second only to gonadal dysgenesis. If the presence of a uterus cannot be determined with certainty by pelvic examination, a pelvic sonogram should be performed to effect this. The third most common pathologic cause of primary amenorrhea is androgen insensitivity syndrome (testicular feminization). Thus, absence of a uterus requires further testing to distinguish between these two entities. The blood testosterone concentration should be measured, and a blood karyotype performed. Abnormal findings should be followed with appropriate testing, as indicated.

However, the most common cause of primary amenorrhea, particularly among athletes, is constitutional delay. If examination indicates good estrogen effect, the girl can be reassured that menarche is likely to occur soon spontaneously. Copious estrogenic cervical mucus usually indicates that spontaneous menarche will occur within 6 to 12 months. Hormone replacement therapy for euestrogenic or hypoestrogenic athletes is optional between the ages of 16 and 18, in

**Table 10–8.** DIAGNOSTIC
EVALUATION OF ATHLETES WITH
PRIMARY AMENORRHEA

1. History and physical examination
2. Prolactin, thyroid function tests, TSH, FSH, LH, HCG
3. Progesterone challenge test
4. If uterus not palpable on pelvic examination: sonogram
5. If uterus absent: testosterone, karyotype
6. If FSH high: karyotype

my view, but should not be postponed beyond the age of 18 because of the risk of osteopenia.

## SUMMARY

Athletes are more likely than sedentary women and girls to experience menstrual dysfunction and menarcheal delay. However, this greater susceptibility should not discourage young athletic girls from exercising intensely or frequently. The benefits of regular exercise far outweigh this potential hazard. Any woman who experiences oligomenorrhea or amenorrhea should be evaluated and probably treated. Any girl who has not experienced menarche by age 16 should be evaluated; treatment of menarcheal delay should be initiated by age 18.

## References

1. Schwartz B, Cumming DC, Riordan E, et al: Exercise-associated amenorrhea: a distinct entity? Am J Obstet Gynecol 141:662, 1981.
2. Shangold MM, and Levine HS: The effect of marathon training upon menstrual function. Am J Obstet Gynecol 143:862, 1982.
3. Sanborn CF, Martin BJ, and Wagner WW: Is athletic amenorrhea specific to runners? Am J Obstet Gynecol 143:859, 1982.
4. Wakat DK, Sweeney KA, and Rogol AD: Reproductive system function in women cross-country runners. Med Sci Sports Exerc 14:263, 1982.
5. Bachmann GA, and Kemmann E: Prevalence of oligomenorrhea and amenorrhea in a college population. Am J Obstet Gynecol 144:98, 1982.
6. Judd HL (guest ed): Reproductive endocrinology. Clin Obstet Gynecol 21(1):15, 1978.
7. Shangold MM: Menstrual irregularity in athletes: Basic principles, evaluation, and treatment. Can J Appl Sport Sci 7(2):68, 1982.
8. Prior JC, Cameron K, Ho Yuen B, et al: Menstrual cycle changes with marathon training: Anovulation and short luteal phase. Can J Appl Sports Sci 7(3):173, 1982.
9. Warren MP: The effects of exercise on pubertal progression and reproductive function in girls. J Clin Endocrinol Metab 51:1150, 1980.
10. Calabrese LH, Kirkendall DT, Floyd M, et al: Menstrual abnormalities, nutritional patterns, and body composition in female classical ballet dancers. The Physician and Sportsmedicine 11(2):86, 1983.
11. Recommended Dietary Allowances. Ed 9. National Research Council, Food and Nutrition Board, National Academy of Sciences, Washington, DC, 1980.
12. Frisch RE, Botz-Welbergen AV, McArthur JW, et al: Delayed menarche and amenorrhea of college athletes in relation to age of onset of training. JAMA 246:1559, 1981.
13. Godara R, Kaur AP, and Bhat CM: Effect of cellulose

incorporation in a low fiber diet on fecal excretion and serum levels of calcium, phosphorus, and iron in adolescent girls. Am J Clin Nutr 34:1083, 1981.
14. Shangold MM, Gatz ML, and Thysen B: Acute effects of exercise on plasma concentrations of prolactin and testosterone in recreational women runners. Fertil Steril 35:699, 1981.
15. Bonen A, Ling W, MacIntyre K, et al: Effects of exercise on the serum concentration of FSH, LH, progesterone and estradiol. Eur J Appl Physiol 42:15, 1979.
16. Carr DB, Bullen BA, Skrinar GS, et al: Physical conditioning facilitates the exercise-induced secretion of beta-endorphin and beta-lipotropin in women. N Engl J Med 305:560, 1981.
17. Carr DB, Reppert SM, Bullen B, et al: Plasma melatonin increases during exercise in women. J Clin Endocrinol Metab 53:224, 1981.
18. Cumming DC, and Rebar RW: Exercise and reproductive function in women. Am J Ind Med 4:113, 1983.
19. Hartley LH, Mason JW, Hogan RP, et al: Multiple hormonal responses to prolonged exercise in relation to physical training. J Appl Physiol 33:607, 1972.
20. Rebar RW, Bulow S, Stern B, et al: Patterns of endocrine response to exercise in normal and dexamethasone suppressed women. Sixty-fifth Annual Meeting, Endocrine Society, 1983, Abstract 464.
21. Shangold MM: Exercise and the adult female: Hormonal and endocrine effects. Exerc Sport Sci Rev 12:53, 1984.
22. Cumming DC, and Rebar RW: Hormonal changes with acute exercise and with training in women. Sem Reprod Endocrinol 3(1):55, 1985.
23. Shangold M, Freeman R, Thysen B, et al: The relationship between long-distance running, plasma progesterone and luteal phase length. Fertil Steril 31:130, 1979.
24. Prior JC, Ho Yuen B, Clement P, et al: Reversible luteal phase changes and infertility associated with marathon training. Lancet 2:269, 1982.
25. Frisch RE, Hall GM, Aoki TT, et al: Metabolic, endocrine, and reproductive changes of a woman channel swimmer. Metabolism 33:1106, 1984.
26. Bullen BA, Skrinar GS, Beitins IZ, et al: Induction of menstrual disorders by strenuous exercise in untrained women. N Engl J Med 312:1349, 1985.
27. Russell JB, Mitchell D, Musey PI, et al: The relationship of exercise to anovulatory cycles in female athletes: Hormonal and physical characteristics. Obstet Gynecol 63:452, 1984.
28. Russell JB, Mitchell DE, Musey PI, et al: The role of beta-endorphins and catechol estrogens on the hypothalamic-pituitary axis in female athletes. Fertil Steril 42:690, 1984.
29. Ropert JF, Quigley ME, and Yen SSC: Endogenous opiates modulate pulsatile luteinizing hormone release in humans. J Clin Endocrinol Metab 52:583, 1981.
30. Villanueva AL, Schlosser C, Hopper B, et al: Increased cortisol production in women runners. J Clin Endocrinol Metab 63:133, 1986.
31. Boyden TW, Pamenter PW, Standorth PR, et al: Impaired gonadotropin responses to gonadotropin-releasing hormone stimulation in endurance-trained women. Fertil Steril 41:359, 1984.
32. Cumming DC, Vickovic MM, Wall SR, et al: Defects

in pulsatile LH release in normally menstruating runners. J Clin Endocrinol Metab 60:810, 1985.

33. Cumming DC, Vickovic MM, Wall SR, et al: The effect of acute exercise on pulsatile release of luteinizing hormone in women runners. Am J Obstet Gynecol 153:482, 1985.

34. Cowan LD, Gordis L, Tonascia JA, et al: Breast cancer incidence in women with a history of progesterone deficiency. Am J Epidemiol 114:209, 1981.

35. Fechner RE, and Kaufman RH: Endometrial adenocarcinoma in Stein-Leventhal syndrome. Cancer 34:444, 1974.

36. Jafari K, Ghodratollah I, and Ruiz G: Endometrial adenocarcinoma and the Stein-Leventhal syndrome. Obstet Gynecol 51:97, 1978.

37. Coulam CB, Annegers JF, and Kranz JS: Chronic anovulation syndrome and associated neoplasia. Obstet Gynecol 61:403, 1983.

38. Dennefors BL, Knutson F, Janson PO, et al: Ovarian steroid production in a woman with polycystic ovary syndrome associated with endometrial cancer. Acta Obstet Gynecol Scand 64:387, 1985.

39. Gonzales ER: Chronic anovulation may increase post-menopausal breast cancer risk. JAMA 249:445, 1983.

40. Frisch RE, Wyshak G, Albright NL, et al: Lower prevalence of breast cancer and cancers of the reproductive system among former college athletes compared to nonathletes. Br J Cancer 52:885, 1985.

41. Cann CE, Martin MC, Genant HK, et al: Decreased spinal mineral content in amenorrheic women. JAMA 251:626, 1984.

42. Rigotti NA, Nussbaum SR, Herzog DB, et al: Osteoporosis in women with anorexia nervosa. N Engl J Med 311:1601, 1984.

43. Drinkwater BL, Nilson K, Chesnut CH, et al: Bone mineral content of amenorrheic and eumenorrheic athletes. N Engl J Med 311:277, 1984.

44. Marcus R, Cann C, Madvig P, et al: Menstrual function and bone mass in elite women distance runners. Ann Intern Med 102:158, 1985.

45. Jones KP, Ravnikar VA, Tulchinsky D, et al: Comparison of bone density in amenorrheic women due to athletics, weight loss, and premature menopause. Obstet Gynecol 66:5, 1985.

46. Warren MP, Brooks-Gunn J, Hamilton LH, et al: Scoliosis and fractures in young ballet dancers. N Engl J Med 314:1348, 1986.

47. Lloyd T, Triantafyllou SJ, Baker ER, et al: Women athletes with menstrual irregularity have increased musculoskeletal injuries. Med Sci Sports Exerc 18:374, 1986.

48. Heaney RP, Recker RR, and Saville PD: Menopausal changes in calcium balance performance. J Lab Clin Med 92:953, 1978.

49. Meema S, and Meema HE: Menopausal bone loss and estrogen replacement. Isr J Med Sci 12:601, 1976.

# CHAPTER 11

# Pregnancy

FREDERIK K. LOTGERING, M.D., Ph.D.

Exercise during pregnancy is a problem of potentially conflicting energy demands. Exercising muscles have a large and acute need of substrates, while the pregnant uterus, the placenta, and the fetus require a moderate, but uninterrupted, flow of oxygen and nutrients. If supply to the muscles is inadequate, working capacity will be reduced, whereas health or normal growth of the fetus may be affected when its requirements are not met. The remarkably effective physiologic adjustments through which the body copes with the combined demands of exercise and pregnancy will be discussed here. A more extensive review of the literature on this subject is given elsewhere.[1]

Before dealing with the physiology of exercise during pregnancy, it must be pointed out that present knowledge is limited for several reasons. First, maternal body weight, dimensions, and composition are subject to change throughout gestation and affect the baseline values of many physiologic variables. Second, these changes also affect the physiologic burden of a given workload. Third, the physiologic response of an individual to a given exercise regimen depends on both physical condition and motivation, which results in marked differences between individuals. Fourth, few studies on the subject of exercise during pregnancy can be considered well controlled for the aforementioned variables. Finally, for obvious ethical reasons, physiologic data on the effects of physical exercise on the uterine circulation and the fetus are derived mainly from animal studies.

## MATERNAL RESPONSES

### Oxygen Consumption

Oxygen consumption at rest increases during human pregnancy to a maximum value near term. This value is about 15 percent above that of nonpregnant controls,[2] but after subtracting the oxygen uptake of the uterus, the placenta, and the fetus, the maternal oxygen consumption is elevated only about 4 percent above that of nonpregnant controls. Enhanced cardiac and respiratory work is probably responsible for this slight increase in oxygen consumption, whereas the metabolic rate of the other maternal tissues is virtually unaffected.

Moderately strenuous bicycle exercise during the third trimester is associated with approximately 10 percent higher values of total oxygen consumption than during similar exercise in the nonpregnant state.[3] The amount of oxygen required for the exercise, as calculated by subtracting the oxygen consumption at rest from the total oxygen consumption during and following exercise, is unaffected by pregnancy.[2] This implies that pregnancy itself does not significantly affect the efficiency of non–weight-bearing exercise. However, when in late gestation leg weight is increased by edema, or body position on the bicycle changes, mechanical efficiency may be reduced and a slightly higher total energy output may be required to perform a given bicycle task. Obviously, when body weight increases progressively during pregnancy, the oxygen requirements of weight-bearing exercise tasks will also increase, and efficiency (task/energy expenditure) of such exercise will be markedly reduced.

Because every weight-bearing task requires a higher energy output during pregnancy than in the nonpregnant state, some training effect seems inevitable unless a more sedentary lifestyle is adopted. Two case studies[4,5] reported a 20 percent increase in maximal oxygen consumption in women who continued to exercise fairly strenuously during pregnancy. This figure compares favorably with the oxygen requirements associated with average pregnancy weight increase. One study, in which pregnant women participated in a mild training program, similarly demonstrated an increase in

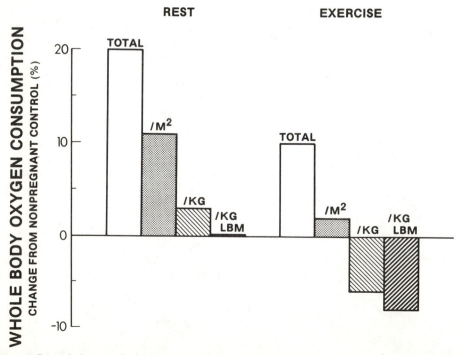

**Figure 11–1.** *Effect of changes in body composition during pregnancy on oxygen consumption at rest and during exercise. (From Lotgering,[1] with permission.)*

maximal oxygen consumption, whereas the sedentary controls showed a slight decrease.[6] In another study, a slight increase in maximal oxygen consumption of such a training program was observed in previously unfit women, but not in women who were more physically fit.[7] These observations suggest that the effect of training depends on the physical condition prior to training and the intensity of the program, similar to what is known about training in the nonpregnant state. In rats trained fairly strenuously only during pregnancy, the level of maximal oxygen consumption near term was increased 8 percent above that in the control animals, whereas training both before and during pregnancy resulted in 23 percent higher values.[8] The short gestational period and the small weight increase during pregnancy in rats are probably responsible for the limited effect of training during pregnancy on maximal oxygen consumption in this species. Although in humans training during pregnancy can be expected to have a more pronounced effect on maximal oxygen consumption, the best physical condition will be achieved when training is started prior to pregnancy.

In exercise studies, oxygen consumption is often standardized for body weight or surface area. Although this is useful when comparisons are made between subjects of comparable body composition, such standardization may be misleading when body composition changes during pregnancy. The main contributors to the body weight increase during gestation are the uterus, including the fetus, the placenta and the amniotic fluid, and the increased maternal plasma and interstitial fluid volumes. At rest, these changes are fairly represented by the changes in lean body mass. However, muscle mass, which determines the increase in oxygen consumption during exercise, is virtually unaffected by pregnancy. Consequently, although it is correct to normalize oxygen consumption at rest for the changes in (lean) body mass during pregnancy, when normalized for these changes the exercise-induced increase in oxygen consumption is falsely low. Figure 11–1 demonstrates the effect of normalization on the apparent oxygen consumption changes during exercise in pregnancy in a calculated example. The amount of oxygen used for exercise either should be represented by the absolute figure

in pregnancy or should be normalized for the lean body mass prior to pregnancy.[1]

## Physical Working Capacity

The performance of a weight-bearing task near term requires approximately 20 percent more energy than in nonpregnant individuals, as a result of increased body weight. The pregnancy weight increase, the physical condition prior to gestation, and the level of activity during pregnancy determine the extent to which improved condition, or increased maximal oxygen consumption, may compensate for these higher demands of exercise in pregnancy. However, working capacity is affected not only by the level of maximal oxygen consumption, but also by a variety of environmental, somatic, and psychic factors—including motivation. Consequently, it is difficult to interpret the observation that fatigue during a voluntary work bicycle test to exhaustion is reached slightly sooner in pregnant women than in controls.[9] By relating a given task or external workload to the physiologic burden of exercise, represented by the increase in heart rate or oxygen consumption, one can reduce the subjective element. When related to heart rate, physical working capacity during pregnancy at submaximal bicycle loads is either unaffected or only slightly reduced.

## Metabolism and Temperature

The plasma glucose concentration in pregnant women at rest is somewhat lower than in nonpregnant controls, but the glucose turnover rate is increased in the same proportion as body weight. This suggests that glucose utilization at rest is not affected by gestation. Because the respiratory quotient is similar in pregnant and nonpregnant women, the ratio of fats to carbohydrates used for combustion must also be virtually unaffected by pregnancy. During exercise the fall in plasma glucose concentration has been observed to be slightly more pronounced in pregnant women than in controls.[10] However, this does not seem to reflect any difference between pregnant and nonpregnant women in glucose utilization or in the balance of fats and carbohydrates used during exercise because the respiratory quotient during exercise is similar in pregnant women and postpartum controls.[3] This suggestion is further supported by the observation that the lactate concentrations during exercise in pregnant women are not different from those in postpartum controls.[11]

Although pregnancy is associated with hyperinsulinemia, increased peripheral insulin resistance protects against hypoglycemia during pregnancy, at rest and during exercise. In addition, glucagon secretion may be stimulated by the elevated concentrations of circulating catecholamines during exercise, and this will also contribute to maintaining normoglycemia during exercise. Although a transient increase in both catecholamines and glucagon has been reported in pregnant women following mild exercise,[12] it is unknown whether the response is quantitatively different from that in nonpregnant women. In pregnant women who have insulin-dependent diabetes, low-level exercise is safe and does not affect plasma glucagon or glucose concentrations,[13] but the response to more strenuous exercise has not been studied in such patients.

Despite the higher metabolism at rest during pregnancy, the increased production of heat remains in balance with heat loss, and core temperature is unaffected.[14] During moderate exercise the changes in core temperature are also similar in pregnant and nonpregnant women.[14] Increased skin temperature, body surface area, and respiratory rate may all contribute to the elimination of any excess heat produced during pregnancy. Although temperature regulation is adequate during moderate exercise in pregnancy, the effects of more strenuous exercise, high ambient temperature, and high humidity on temperature regulation have not been studied in pregnant women.

## Circulation and Respiration

During pregnancy, the systemic vascular resistance is markedly reduced because blood flow to the pregnant uterus increases severalfold and because the high levels of progesterone reduce the vascular tone. Possibly mediated through renin and angiotensin, the maternal circulation adjusts to this reduction in vascular resistance by increasing the blood volume. Near-term blood volume is approximately 50 percent above nonpregnant values. The increase in plasma volume is more pronounced than the increase in red

cell volume and results in a reduction in hemoglobin concentration. As a result of the reduction in vascular resistance and the increase in blood volume, stroke volume and cardiac output increase during pregnancy. This is accompanied by a reduction in mean systemic pressure and a slight increase in heart rate. Changes in the position of the body may markedly affect the circulatory dynamics by interference with venous return of blood to the heart, especially in late gestation. This is most pronounced in the supine hypotensive syndrome. If the supine position results in compression by the pregnant uterus of the inferior vena cava above the level of the kidneys, it may elicit a 50 percent reduction in cardiac output, as well as in heart rate and arterial blood pressure. Occlusion of the vena cava at a lower level will result in a less dramatic reduction in venous return but may still cause a decrease of up to 20 percent in cardiac output during third trimester human pregnancy.[15] When cardiac output is increased during exercise, positional changes may have even more pronounced hemodynamic effects.

Local metabolic changes are probably responsible for increasing the supply of blood to the exercising muscles, which results in reduced systemic vascular resistance. Simultaneously, cardiac output increases through an increase in both heart rate and stroke volume. The magnitude of the increase depends on the level and the duration of exercise. It has been observed that cardiac output during bicycle exercise is lower in women near term than in the postpartum period and that this is the result of reduced stroke volume despite increased heart rate.[16] Such a reduction in cardiac output response to exercise in late gestation has not been found in pregnant pygmy goats.[17] Differences in body position during exercise, rather than species difference per se, may be responsible for the observed difference in response. If the pregnant uterus partially obstructs the vena cava during exercise, cardiac output will decrease and the drop in stroke volume will be partly compensated by a further increase in heart rate.

Despite the reduction in systemic vascular resistance, the increase in cardiac output during exercise is associated with elevated systolic and mean arterial blood pressures. This pressure response to exercise has been reported to be slightly higher in pregnant women than in controls.[16] When plasma fil-

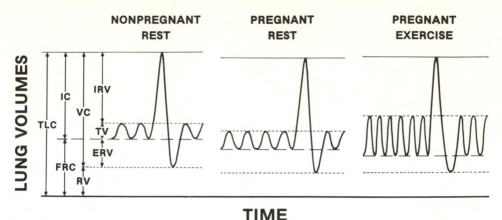

**Figure 11–2.** *Effects of pregnancy and exercise on respiratory volumes. TLC = total lung capacity, IC = inspiratory capacity, FRC = functional residual capacity, VC = vital capacity, RV = residual volume, IRV = inspiratory reserve volume, TV = tidal volume, and ERV = expiratory reserve volume.*

trate is forced across the capillary membrane in exercising muscles, apparent plasma volume drops and hematocrit increases by up to 20 percent,[18] and the increase in hematocrit may contribute to the increase in systemic vascular resistance during exercise. However, because both cardiac output and blood pressure responses to exercise are slightly enhanced during pregnancy, the reduction in peripheral vascular resistance during exercise must be of a similar magnitude in pregnant and nonpregnant women.

During normal pregnancy the sensitivity to vasopressors (e.g., angiotensin II) is reduced, whereas increased sensitivity to such vasopressors is one of the characteristics of gestational hypertension. It has recently been suggested that the pressure response to isometric exercise has predictive value for the development of hypertension later in pregnancy.[19] One should realize that in the presence of pregnancy-induced hypertension, exercise may further increase blood pressure to potentially dangerously high levels. In patients with heart disease, cardiac reserve is usually reduced by the limited ability to increase stroke volume, and heart rate is responsible for most of the increase in cardiac output during exercise in these patients.[20] Pregnancy will further reduce cardiac reserve because the increased blood volume tends to increase stroke volume. Consequently, in pregnant cardiac patients the capacity to perform exercise is reduced, and the risk of heart failure is increased.

The respiratory changes of pregnancy and exercise are summarized in Figure 11–2. Although the uterus elevates the diaphragm in late pregnancy, the tidal volume increases with gestational age and exercise intensity at the cost of the expiratory reserve capacity, and is higher than in nonpregnant controls.[2,3] Because the frequency of respiration is virtually unaffected by pregnancy, the respiratory minute volume increases with the tidal volume. During pregnancy, respiratory minute volume increases to a greater extent than does oxygen consumption,[3] and this relative hyperventilation is more pronounced at higher work intensities. As a result of the hyperventilation, both the arterial carbon dioxide tension and the bicarbonate concentration decrease during pregnancy, while the pH increases slightly and oxygen tension is unaffected. Exercise tends to change the respiratory blood gas values in the same direction, until lactate accumulation reduces the pH at high workloads. There is no evidence that pregnancy significantly affects the magnitude of these changes.[1] Although in healthy women respiratory ventilation does not limit the capacity to perform exercise, in pregnant patients with severe pulmonary disease exercise may be undesirable.

### Uterine Oxygen Consumption

Uterine blood flow increases with gestational age, in response to increased demands of, and hormonal stimulation by, the fetoplacental unit. Although the dilated uterine vascular bed is less sensitive to vasoconstrictive agents during pregnancy than in the nonpregnant state, it responds to sympathetic

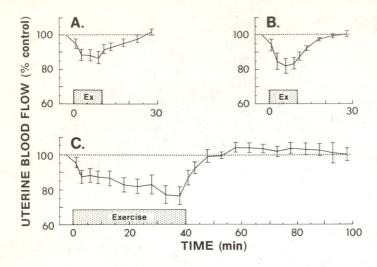

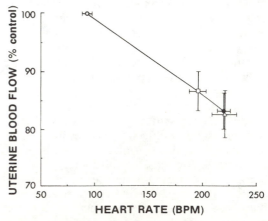

**Figure 11–3.** *Uterine blood flow response to three different exercise regimens in pregnant sheep. A, 10-minute exercise at 70 percent maximal oxygen consumption ($V_{O2max}$), B, 10-minute exercise at 100 percent $V_{O2max}$; C, 40-minute exercise at 70 percent $V_{O2max}$. (From Lotgering,[18] with permission.)*

stimulation and to circulating catecholamines and prostaglandins. It has been suggested that these stimuli are effective in causing the spontaneous fluctuations of up to 20 percent observed in uterine blood flow, as well as the larger reductions in response to various stresses.

Cardiac output is redistributed during exercise. This results largely from vasodilation in the exercising muscles, which is probably mediated by local metabolic factors, and from sympathetic- and catecholamine-mediated vasoconstriction in other tissues, including the splanchnic bed, the nonworking muscles, and the pregnant uterus. In the only human study of uterine blood flow during exercise in pregnancy, mild short-term bicycle exercise by women in the supine position caused a 25 percent reduction in flow.[21] This value was calculated from the disappearance of radioactive sodium injected into the uterine wall and, therefore, represents myometrial flow, rather than total uterine, or placental, blood flow. Further physiologic data on the uteroplacental blood flow response to exercise are derived from animal studies. Figure 11–3 demonstrates the changes in total uterine blood flow at different levels (percentage of maximal oxygen consumption) and durations of exercise in chronically instrumented pregnant sheep.[18] As shown in the figure, uterine blood flow decreases immediately at the onset of exercise, is significantly below control values throughout the exercise period, and returns to control values within 10 minutes of recovery. The reduction in uterine blood flow varies with the level

and the duration of exercise (Fig. 11–3),[18] and Figure 11–4 demonstrates that the uterine blood flow during exercise is inversely and linearly related to the increase in heart rate.[18] The maximal reduction in total uterine blood flow during exercise, reported in sheep and goats, is approximately 35 percent.[22–24] However, blood flow to the placental exchange area is reduced to a more limited extent, because during exercise blood is redistributed within the uterus, favoring the placental cotyledons at the expense of the myometrium.[24] This suggests either that the placental vasculature is less sensitive to the increased

**Figure 11–4.** *Relationship between heart rate and uterine blood flow in near-term sheep. O rest, = 10-minute exercise at 70 percent $V_{O2max}$; ● 10-minute exercise at 100 percent $V_{O2max}$, △ 40-minute exercise at 70 percent $V_{O2max}$. (From Lotgering,[16] with permission.)*

sympathetic activity during exercise than is the vascular supply of the uterine muscle or that the vasoconstriction is modified by local metabolic factors in the placenta.

Despite the marked reductions in uterine blood flow during exercise, oxygen consumption can be maintained by the pregnant uterus. The main compensatory mechanism is hemoconcentration. The increased hematocrit during exercise increases the oxygen content of the blood, and consequently the delivery of oxygen to the uterus is only slightly lower during exercise than it is at rest.[25] In addition, the pregnant uterus can compensate for reductions in oxygen delivery of up to 40 percent by increasing the extraction of oxygen from the blood, and this occurs also during exercise.[25]

## FETAL RESPONSES

### Oxygen Consumption and Blood Gases

The fetus requires a continuous and adequate supply of oxygen and nutrients for its metabolism and growth. Severe, acute interference with its supply is likely to cause hypoxic damage, while milder, more chronic reductions may result in suboptimal growth. However, physiologic variables such as oxygen consumption, oxygen tension, and heart rate may represent temporary adjustments, and they provide only limited information on the extent to which fetal tolerance is exceeded and damage may occur. Growth is a multivariable criterion and exhibits such large normal variation that retardation of growth cannot be detected accurately. Consequently, our possibilities to detect any such effects of exercise are limited.

During exercise the placental membrane transport characteristics are unaffected in sheep,[25] and the uptake of oxygen by the fetal umbilical circulation remains constant.[22] Apparently, by increased extraction of oxygen the fetal tissues compensate completely for the 10 percent reduction in umbilical blood flow observed during exhaustive exercise.[22] This suggests that the fetus is not in danger of hypoxia. However, one may question whether fetal oxygen requirements might increase during exercise as a result of the rise in body temperature, in which case unchanged fetal oxygen consumption would

imply relative hypoxia. Present knowledge of the regulatory mechanisms of fetal metabolism does not allow a definitive conclusion about this point.

Although uterine oxygen consumption is unaffected by exercise, several studies in exercising sheep have reported reductions of up to 25 percent in fetal arterial oxygen tension.[22,23] These blood gas values were falsely low, because they were not corrected for the fetal temperature changes in vivo.[25] Nonetheless, fetal oxygen tension does tend to decrease with increasing level and duration of exercise,[25] but the changes are smaller than previously reported. In near-term sheep run to exhaustion by 40 minutes of exercise at 70 percent $\dot{V}_{O2max}$, a maximal reduction of 11 percent, or 3 Torr, in temperature-corrected fetal arterial oxygen tension has been reported.[25] Simultaneously, fetal arterial oxygen content decreased by 1.5 mL/dL, from 5.8 mL/dL at rest, and carbon dioxide tension by 4.5 Torr, from 54.1 Torr, while pH was virtually unaffected. Theoretical considerations suggest that these changes are probably elicited mainly by the temperature and Bohr shifts of the oxyhemoglobin saturation curve and by the reduction in uterine blood flow.[1,25] Although the fetal oxygen tension was reduced slightly during exercise, it remained well within the accepted normal range throughout the exercise period, and recovery was fast and complete.[25] This suggests that the decrease in oxygen tension and content of the fetal blood during maternal exercise represents adaptation rather than damaging tissue hypoxia.

Certain conditions such as growth retardation, twin gestation, and pregnancy-induced hypertension may be associated with a reduced reserve in fetal oxygen supply, or even with overtly inadequate fetal oxygenation when the mother is at rest. Under such circumstances, the superimposed reduction in fetal oxygen tension during maternal exercise must be considered to be potentially harmful to the fetus.

Changes in maternal oxygen tension, as well as in glucose and catecholamine concentrations, are known to affect respiratory-like movements, or breathing movements of the fetus. Following bicycle exercise one group of investigators[26] observed an increase in the percentage of time spent breathing, with an increase in irregular movements and a decrease in periodic and apneic episodes, while another group[27] observed a variable response after mild treadmill exercise. Because respiratory-like movements are known to vary considerably with the activity state of the fetus, at present it is not clear whether the changes observed during exercise do relate to the stress of exercise per se or merely reflect differences in normal fetal behavioral states.

## Temperature and Metabolism

Fetal metabolism is relatively high, compared with that of the mother. Most of the heat produced by the fetus is transferred to the mother across the placenta, while a smaller proportion is transferred across the fetal skin, amniotic fluid, and uterine wall.[28] Because of limitations in heat transfer, fetal body temperature under normal resting conditions is approximately 0.5°C higher than that of the mother. Theoretical calculations suggest that maternal body temperature is the major determinant of fetal temperature, while changes in fetal metabolism or uterine blood flow are less important.[28]

Figure 11–5 demonstrates that fetal temperature is affected when maternal body temperature changes in response to exercise in sheep.[25] Because the fetus is surrounded by amniotic fluid and because transfer of heat is limited, the fetal temperature changes lag behind the relatively rapidly changing maternal temperature. This results in a smaller or reversed temperature gradient during the onset of exercise, and a larger gradient immediately following exercise. Because maternal body temperature is the major determinant of fetal temperature, the magnitude of the fetal temperature increase varies with the level and the duration of exercise, as well as with the temperature and the humidity of the environment. After prolonged (40-minute) exhaustive exercise at 70 percent $\dot{V}_{O_2max}$, the return of fetal temperature to normal may require as long as 1 hour.[25]

When the mother is at rest, the sheep fetus uses about 65 percent of the available substrates for basal metabolism and muscular activities, while 35 percent is used for growth. Quantitatively, glucose and lactate are the two most important substrates. Despite the reduction in uterine blood flow, uptake of glucose by the pregnant sheep uterus increases during exercise. This is largely the

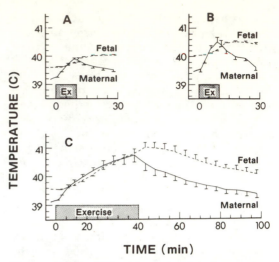

**Figure 11–5.** *Maternal and fetal temperature changes in response to three different exercise regimens. A, 10-minute exercise at 70 percent $\dot{V}_{O_2}max$; B, 10-minute exercise at 100 percent $\dot{V}_{O_2}max$; C, 40-minute exercise at 70 percent $\dot{V}_{O_2}max$. (From Lotgering,[25] with permission.)*

result of increased extraction, mediated by a larger maternal-to-fetal glucose gradient.[23] Although the fetal blood glucose concentration may increase during maternal exercise by up to 75 percent,[25] the fetal concentrations of insulin, glucagon, and growth hormone do not change significantly during moderately strenuous exercise.[29] This suggests that fetal glucose utilization is not markedly affected by maternal exercise.

Lactate metabolism at rest contributes approximately 25 percent to fetal oxidative metabolism, and the fetal lactate concentration is about twice that of the mother. When the maternal lactate concentration increases during prolonged exercise, the normal placental release of lactate into the maternal circulation is reversed[23] and the fetal lactate concentration may increase by up to 50 to 70 percent.[22,23,25] The absence of fetal acidosis suggests that the higher fetal lactate levels during maternal exercise result from altered placental lactate transport rather than from anaerobic fetal metabolism.

## Circulation

Fetal heart rate monitoring is a technique used in clinical obstetrics to detect "distress" and to predict outcome of the fetus. Empirically associated with fetal distress and poor fetal outcome are severe bradycardia (less than 100 bpm) and tachycardia (greater than 180 bpm), the loss of variability (bandwidth less than 5 bpm, zero crossings less than 2/min), and the presence of "late" or "unfavorable variable" decelerations. Accelerations and good variability of the heart rate are correlated with well-being and good outcome of the fetus. However, some physiologic variations, including fetal sleep states, may produce fetal heart rate patterns that resemble those of fetal hypoxic distress in some respects, while maternal body movements may cause large artifacts.[30] Consequently, fetal heart rate tracings may be difficult to interpret, and conclusions may be misleading.

The human fetal heart rate response to maternal exercise has been studied repeatedly since it was introduced as a clinical test for "uteroplacental insufficiency" in 1961.[31] In most of the early studies, measurements were made only before and after a period of mild or moderate exercise, rather than during the exercise period per se. Mean fetal heart rates following exercise were not significantly different from control values in most of these studies, and in most fetuses the heart rate pattern during recovery from exercise did not indicate distress.

More recently, three studies have reported fetal bradycardia during moderately strenuous exercise. In the first study,[32] transient bradycardia of 2 or 3 minutes' duration was found in three of the four fetuses studied, but recovery occurred during exercise. The second study[33] reported fetal bradycardia of about 90 bpm throughout most of the exercise period in 3 of the 19 women studied. In all three fetuses the heart rates returned to normal soon following exercise, with accelerations suggestive of fetal well-being in two of the three fetuses. The third study[34] reported on six fetuses, all of which had bradycardia and loss of heart rate variability throughout the exercise period. Three of these fetuses had an average heart rate of 50 bpm during the 13 minutes of exercise, which is suggestive of a life-threatening event. The other three fetuses had heart rates between 100 and 130 bpm. Onset and recovery of these changes was abrupt, and return to a normal accelerative heart rate pattern occurred within 1 minute following exercise. The abrupt nature of the return to a heart rate pattern that suggests fetal well-being,

following a prolonged period of fetal bradycardia suggestive of extreme fetal distress, is difficult, if not impossible, to explain physiologically. The presence of a normal heart rate pattern shortly after exercise and favorable fetal outcome in all of the aforementioned pregnancies is reassuring and demonstrates the unharmful nature of these findings.

Other recent studies[35–37] reported fetal heart rates following moderately strenuous exercise to be higher than during the control period. Although these observations were interpreted as compensatory tachycardia in two of these studies,[35,37] fetal arousal associated with accelerations, or increased fetal body temperature, may be the more likely explanations.

The fetal heart operates near the plateau of its Starling function curve. Consequently, most changes in fetal heart rate affect cardiac output almost directly. In animal experiments, fetal heart rates during and following exercise were found to be either unaffected[22,25] or slightly increased.[38] This suggests that fetal cardiac output in sheep is virtually unaffected by maternal exercise, and direct measurements of fetal cardiac output support this suggestion.[25] Fetal cardiac output, blood flow distribution, circulating blood volume, and hematocrit respond markedly to hypoxia and high fetal concentrations of circulating catecholamines, but all these variables are unaffected by maternal exercise.[25] In addition, although higher fetal norepinephrine levels during prolonged maternal exercise have been reported in one study,[38] other studies have not confirmed this observation.[25,39] The absence of pronounced changes in most measured fetal variables supports the view that maternal exercise is not a major hypoxic stress to the fetus.

## Outcome

Fetal outcome shows a wide variation because it is the result of a large number of variables, including genetic and socioeconomic factors, environmental factors, the nutritional and physical status of the mother, and so forth. Definitive conclusions regarding a single factor such as exercise should be based on large, well-controlled, prospective studies. At present, all studies on this subject have their limitations.

Most studies are retrospective and report either no change in pregnancy outcome or reduced birth weight. Two small prospective studies reported that outcome was unaffected by mild exercise programs during pregnancy.[6,40] The largest and best-controlled study presently available[41] used interview data to describe the level of exercise in 336 pregnant women. From this group of women only 29 continued to exercise at or above a conditioning level throughout pregnancy, including 6 of 15 women who were classified as having a high level of performance. The authors concluded that the level of exercise per se had no effect on pregnancy outcome, but that women who continued endurance exercise at or above preconceptual levels during pregnancy gained less weight (12.2 versus 16.8 kg), delivered earlier (274 versus 282 days), and had lighter-weight offspring (3009 versus 3577 g) and a higher incidence of low birth weight–for–gestational age infants (38 versus 11 percent) than did women who reduced their activities during pregnancy. Perinatal mortality and morbidity was low and not significantly different between the groups. These conclusions must be interpreted with care because they are based on interview data, and because the actual number of women (29) who continued to exercise throughout pregnancy was small. In addition, other factors (e.g., nutrition) may have affected the results in an uncontrolled fashion. Studies in laboratory animals have also not answered definitively the question of whether exercise during pregnancy does affect fetal growth.[1] The question of which mechanisms might cause any such effects must at present also remain unanswered. Although other, unconfirmed studies have reported a variety of adverse effects of maternal exercise, including teratogenic effects, the available evidence is insufficient to conclude that exercise of the mother does indeed affect the development of the fetus.[1]

## SUMMARY

The physiologic adaptations of a healthy mother and fetus seem to be adequate to deal with fairly strenuous and prolonged exercise during pregnancy without apparent damage. However, certain activities may be harmful to the mother or the fetus for reasons other than the exercise per se. In many sports the risk of trauma may be increased when joints and ligaments are more relaxed and body weight and position change during pregnancy. Such trauma may affect the uterus, placenta, or fetus directly, or indirectly by compromising the maternal circulation, respiration, or acid-base balance. Activities associated with altered inspired gas pressures, such as alpine sports and scuba diving, may carry an additional risk, as do low and high ambient temperatures. Certain obstetric conditions—e.g., multiple pregnancy, fetal growth retardation, and pregnancy-induced hypertension—as well as uterine contractions are also likely to increase the risk of exercise, and such conditions should be excluded before strenuous exercise is undertaken during pregnancy. Although the homeostatic mechanisms in mother and fetus are remarkably effective during exercise, pregnancy does not seem to be the best time to start vigorous training. A good physical condition prior to pregnancy will allow an active lifestyle throughout gestation and is the best possible guarantee for good fetal outcome. Advice with regard to exercise during pregnancy should be given on an individual basis and should take into account the somatic and psychologic demands, adaptability, and limits of the pregnant woman, her baby, and her sport.

## References

1. Lotgering FK, Gilbert RD, and Longo LD: Maternal and fetal responses to exercise during pregnancy. Physiol Rev 65:1, 1985.
2. Edwards MJ, Metcalfe J, Dunham MJ, et al: Accelerated respiratory response to moderate exercise in late pregnancy. Respir Physiol 45:229, 1981.
3. Knuttgen HG, and Emerson K: Physiological response to pregnancy at rest and during exercise. J Appl Physiol 36:549, 1974.
4. Dressendorfer RH: Physical training during pregnancy and lactation. The Physician and Sportsmedicine 6:74, 1980.
5. Ruhling RO, Cameron J, Sibley L, et al: Maintaining aerobic fitness while jogging through a pregnancy! A case study. Med Sci Sports Exerc 13:93, 1981.
6. Collings CA, Curet LB, and Mullin JP: Maternal and fetal responses to a maternal aerobic exercise program. Am J Obstet Gynecol 145:702, 1983.
7. Dibblee L, and Graham TE: A longitudinal study of changes in aerobic fitness, body composition, and energy intake in primigravid women. Am J Obstet Gynecol 147:908, 1983.
8. Wilson NC, and Gisolfi CV: Effects of exercising rats during pregnancy. J Appl Physiol 48:34, 1980.
9. Erkkola R: The physical fitness of Finnish primigravidae. Ann Chir Gynaecol Fenn 64:394, 1975.

10. Lehmann V, and Regnat K: Untersuchung zur körperlichen Belastungsfähigkeit schwangeren Frauen. Der Einfluss standardisierter Arbeit auf Herzkreislaufsystem, Ventilation, Gasaustausch, Kohlenhydratstoffwechsel und Säure-Basen-Haushalt. Z Geburtshilfe Perinatol 180:279, 1976.

11. Schweingel S, and Lauckner W: Untersuchungen zur körperlichen Leistungsfähigkeit im Verlauf der Schwangerschaft. Zentralbl Gynaekol 106:535, 1984.

12. Artal R, Platt LD, Sperling M, et al: Exercise in pregnancy. I. Maternal cardiovascular and metabolic responses in normal pregnancy. Am J Obstet Gynecol 140:123, 1981.

13. Artal R, Wiswell R, and Romem Y: Hormonal responses to exercise in diabetic and nondiabetic pregnant patients. Diabetes 34 (Suppl. 2):78, 1985.

14. Jones RL, Botti JJ, Anderson WM, et al: Thermoregulation during aerobic exercise in pregnancy. Obstet Gynecol 65:340, 1985.

15. Lotgering FK, and Wallenburg HCS: Hemodynamic effects of caval and uterine venous occlusion in pregnant sheep. Am J Obstet Gynecol 155:1164, 1986.

16. Morton MJ, Paul MS, Campos GR, et al: Exercise dynamics in late gestation: Effects of physical training. Am J Obstet Gynecol 152:91, 1985.

17. Dhindsa DS, Metcalfe J, and Hummels DH: Responses to exercise in the pregnant pygmy goat. Respir Physiol 32:299, 1978.

18. Lotgering FK, Gilbert RD, and Longo LD: Exercise responses in pregnant sheep: oxygen consumption, uterine blood flow, and blood volume. J Appl Physiol 55:834, 1983.

19. Degani S, Abinader E, Eibschitz I, et al: Isometric exercise test for predicting gestational hypertension. Obstet Gynecol 65:652, 1985.

20. Bruce RA, and Johnson WP: Exercise tolerance in pregnant cardiac patients. Clin Obstet Gynecol 4:665, 1961.

21. Morris N, Osborn SB, Wright HP, et al: Effective uterine blood-flow during exercise in normal and pre-eclamptic pregnancies. Lancet 2:481, 1956.

22. Clapp JF: Acute exercise stress in the pregnant ewe. Am J Obstet Gynecol 136:489, 1980.

23. Chandler KD, and Bell AW: Effects of maternal exercise on fetal and maternal respiration and nutrient metabolism in the pregnant ewe. J Dev Physiol 3:161, 1981.

24. Hohimer AR, Bissonnette JM, Metcalfe J, et al: Effect of exercise on uterine blood flow in the pregnant pygmy goat. Am J Physiol 246:H207, 1984.

25. Lotgering FK, Gilbert RD, and Longo LD: Exercise responses in pregnant sheep: blood gases, temperatures and fetal cardiovascular system. J Appl Physiol 55:842, 1983.

26. Maršál K, Löfgren O, and Gennser G: Fetal breathing movements and maternal exercise. Acta Obstet Gynecol Scand 58:197, 1979.

27. Platt LD, Artal R, Semel J, et al: Exercise in pregnancy. II. Fetal responses. Am J Obstet Gynecol 147:487, 1983.

28. Schröder H, Gilbert RD, and Power GG: Fetal heat dissipation: a computer model and some preliminary experimental results from fetal sheep. In Society for Gynecologic Investigation, 29th Annual Meeting, Dallas, TX, March 24–27, 1982, p 113.

29. Bell AW, Bassett JM, Chandler KD, et al: Fetal and maternal endocrine responses to exercise in the pregnant ewe. J Dev Physiol 5:129, 1983.

30. Paolone AM, Shangold M, Paul D, et al: Fetal heart rate measurement during maternal exercise—avoidance of artifact. Med Sci Sports Exerc (in press).

31. Hon EH, and Wohlgemuth R: The electronic evaluation of fetal heart rate. IV. The effect of maternal exercise. Am J Obstet Gynecol 81:361, 1961.

32. Dale E, Mullinax KM, and Bryan DH: Exercise during pregnancy: effects on the fetus. Can J Appl Sports Sci 7:98, 1982.

33. Artal R, Paul RH, Romem Y, et al: Fetal bradycardia induced by maternal exercise. Lancet 2:258, 1984.

34. Jovanovic L, Kessler A, and Peterson CM: Human maternal and fetal response to graded exercise. J Appl Physiol 58:1719, 1985.

35. Hauth JC, Gilstrap LC, and Widmer K: Fetal heart rate reactivity before and after maternal jogging during the third trimester. Am J Obstet Gynecol 142:545, 1982.

36. Collings C, and Curet LB: Fetal heart rate response to maternal exercise. Am J Obstet Gynecol 151:498, 1985.

37. Clapp JF: Fetal heart rate response to running in midpregnancy and late pregnancy. Am J Obstet Gynecol 153:251, 1985.

38. Palmer SM, Oakes GK, Champion JA, et al: Catecholamine physiology in the ovine fetus. III. Maternal and fetal response to acute maternal exercise. Am J Obstet Gynecol 149:426, 1984.

39. Hohimer AR, Bissonnette JM, Metcalfe J, et al: Effect of exercise on uterine blood flow in the pregnant pygmy goat. Am J Physiol 246:H207, 1984.

40. Sibley L, Ruhling RO, Cameron-Foster J, et al: Swimming and physical fitness during exercise. J Nurse Midwif 26:3, 1981.

41. Clapp JF, and Dickstein S: Endurance exercise and pregnancy outcome. Med Sci Sports Exerc 16:556, 1984.

# CHAPTER 12

# The Menopause*†

MORRIS NOTELOVITZ, M.D., Ph.D.

## THE MENOPAUSE IN PERSPECTIVE

The menopause is a natural phenomenon that usually lasts about 1 week—the duration of the last menstrual period. It is the biologic marker of the gradual but persistent decrease in ovarian steroidogenesis that precedes the cessation of menstruation by about 15 years and that postdates that event by a similar duration. This period of reproductive senescence is known as the climacteric. The differentiation between the "menopause" and the "climacteric" involves more than semantics, since it serves to illustrate that the midlife physical and psychologic needs of women extend over a 30-year continuum. There are two additional features of note: (1) the attenuation in endocrine function of the ovarian follicle affects many systems remote from the genital tract; and (2) the climacteric occurs at a time when certain age-related changes become apparent, hence the need to differentiate biologic- from chronologic-induced pathophysiology.

The date of the menopause can be accurately pinpointed: it is a retrospective diagnosis, a year of amenorrhea has to pass before the clinical diagnosis can be confirmed. The mean age of onset of the menopause in

*Supported by grants from National Institute on Aging R01 AG 00976, Nautilus Sports/Medical Industries, Inc.

†Although, as discussed at the beginning of this chapter, the period is more properly called the climacteric, the menopause is certainly the more commonly used term.

Western societies is 51 years.[1] The climacteric may be empirically but pragmatically categorized into three decades of clinical presentation and need (Fig. 12–1): the early climacteric (age 35 to 45), and premenopausal and postmenopausal periods (age 46 to 55), and the late climacteric (56 to 65).[2] Contrary to the theory promoting follicular depletion as the cause of the menopause, primordial follicles are frequently found in the ovaries of postmenopausal women but are unable to respond to stimulation of the pituitary gonadotropins—FSH and LH. The resultant alteration in ovarian function results in the dysfunctional uterine bleeding patterns that characterize this phase. As the climacteric progresses, the decrease in estradiol production results in the menopause and in a number of so-called hormone-dependent symptoms: hot flushes and changes in temperament, mood, and sleeping patterns. The late climacteric is often associated with conditions resulting from chronic estrogen deprivation—chronic atrophic vaginitis, the urethral syndrome, and urinary incontinence.

Although the conditions listed herein have an impact on an individual's quality of life, none is life-threatening. There are, however, two asymptomatic potential complications of the late climacteric that may have a serious adverse effect and that are responsible for much of the morbidity and mortality associated with older age in women: osteoporosis and atherogenic disease. In the United States over 300,000 women annually will fracture their hips owing to osteoporosis. Of this figure, approximately 12 to 20 percent will die as a result of factors directly attributable to their hip fracture;[3] only a third of the survivors will regain normal activity again.[4] Seventy to 80 percent of all hip fractures affect women. The total cost of osteoporosis (all forms) has been estimated to be 6.1 billion dollars in 1983.[5] This does not take into account the physical and psychologic pain suffered by these women. Cardiovascular disease accounted for 51 percent of all deaths in 1981. The resultant cost, including that of disability, amounted to an estimated 64.4 billion dollars in 1984.[6] Although there is no sudden escalation in coronary heart disease in the perimenopause, the loss of ovarian function does have an impact and is associated with an increase in the severity of the disease. For example, coronary heart disease presents more frequently as myocardial infarction or a fatal heart attack, rather than as

## THREE DECADES OF HEALTH NEEDS

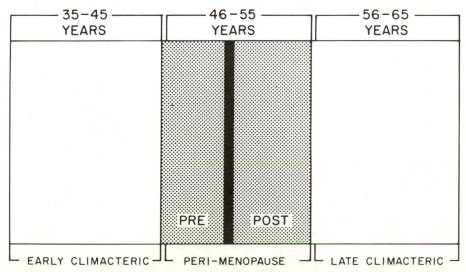

**Figure 12–1.** Diagrammatic representation of the menopause as a single event in the larger context of the climacteric. (From Notelovitz et al,[2] with permission.)

angina pectoris.[7] These conditions have a significant influence on the well-being of the fastest-growing age group in the United States: an estimated 1000 individuals join the ranks of the elderly every day.[8] A woman aged 65 can now expect to live an additional 18.8 years (14.5 years for men).[9]

Exercise can play an important role in ensuring an appropriate quality of mid- and later life, but in order to be maximally effective, it needs to be introduced as a premenopausal lifestyle; hence the emphasis on recognizing the climacteric as an important transitional phase in the pathogenesis of potentially preventable disease.

## OSTEOPOROSIS AND BONE HEALTH

Osteoporosis is preventable. It is a condition that is relatively uncommon in men and in black women, owing in part to their having a greater bone mass. Cohn and co-workers[10] examined the skeletal and muscle mass of normal black women and found that their total body calcium was 16.7 percent higher than that of age-matched white women. More than half of this difference (9.7 percent) was calculated to be due to a greater muscle mass in the black women. Thus, despite the complexity of bone physiology, there are two practical issues that need to be addressed: (1) women need to acquire as much bone as possible before the menopause, and (2) the rate at which bone is lost thereafter needs to be modulated. Exercise plays a pivotal role in that it is one of the few known means of stimulating new bone formation. Central to the entire issue is the fact that bone is a living tissue and needs to be treated as such.

## OSTEOGENESIS: A BRIEF OVERVIEW

Bone formation is dependent upon a five-stage cycle that results in "old" bone being removed and replaced with "new" bone. Normally, this process is coupled; the amount of old bone removed is replaced with an equal amount of freshly formed bone. Initiation of the cycle is dependent upon the recruitment and activation of osteoclasts. This activity usually takes place on the inner aspect of the bone's surface—the en-

dosteal layer—and results in the dissolution of bone mineral and collagen, and the formation of a cavity. Resorption ceases when the mean depth of the cavity reaches 60 $\mu$m (trabecular bone) and 100 $\mu$m (cortical bone) from the surface.[11] At this point, mononuclear cells lay down a highly mineralized collagen-poor bone matrix known as cement substance. It is from this surface that new bone is laid down by osteoblasts. These cells probably originate from bone marrow stromal cells (pre-osteoblasts), thereby sharing the ability of another cell type, the fibroblasts, to synthesize collagen.[11] The stimulus for osteoblast recruitment may be mechanical owing to humoral and/or locally produced substances (for example, human skeletal growth and other bone growth factors).[12]

The osteoblasts are responsible for the synthesis of collagen, which is the main component of newly formed bone matrix, or osteoid. The latter matures and is later mineralized by a process that is largely dependent on an adequate supply of calcium and phosphate and the formation of hydroxyapatite crystals.[10] At a microstructural level, numerous small crystallites of hydroxyapatite may be seen in intimate juxtaposition and in highly organized geometric arrangements with collagen fibrils.[11]

The elastic and tensile strength of bone is dependent in large measure on this combined interrelationship. Another very important determinant of the mechanical strength of bone is the orientation of the collagen fibrils in the bone matrix and the three-dimensional network of plates and bars found especially in trabecular bone (for example, in vertebrae), and to a lesser extent in cortical bone (for example, the radius). This results in a scaffold-like arrangement of vertical and horizontal trabeculae (Fig. 12–2). Interruption of this support system—for example, loss of horizontal trabeculae as a result of aging—can impair the structural integrity of the bone and result in fracture, even in the presence of a relatively normal amount of bone mineral.[13] This is of great importance when prescribing exercise for older women.

### Types and Rates of Bone Loss

There are two types of bone: cortical and trabecular bone. Cortical (compact) bone is found primarily in the appendicular skeleton

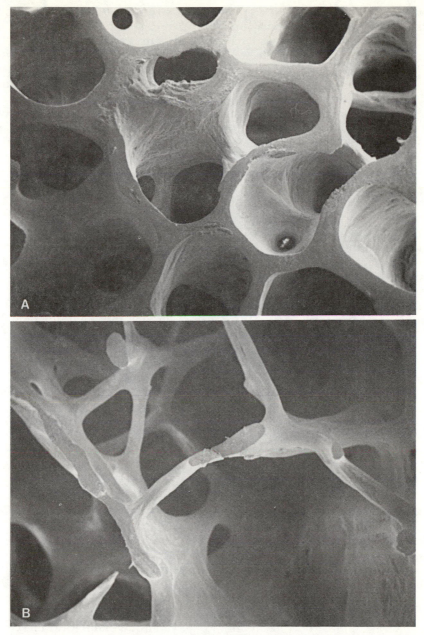

**Figure 12-2.** Scanning electron micrograph of an iliac crest biopsy from a normal subject and a woman with osteoporosis. A illustrates normal contiguous vertical and horizontal trabeculae, compared with the thinning, decreased number, and loss of continuity of the trabecular plates in osteoporosis (B). (From Dempster DW, et al: A simple method for correlative light and scanning electron microscopy of human iliac crest bone biopsies: qualitative observations in normal and osteoporotic subjects. J Bone Min Res 1(1):15, 1986, with permission.)

(for example, in the femur, tibia, and fibula of the lower limbs and in the humerus, ulna, and radius of the arms). Cortical bone constitutes 80 percent of the total skeleton but is metabolically less active than trabecular bone. About 10 percent of the cortical bone is remodeled each year. Trabecular (cancellous) bone is found in the axial skeleton, primarily in the vertebral bodies (70 to 95 percent), with lesser concentrations in areas such as the neck of the femur (25 to 35 percent) and the distal radius (5 to 20 percent). The remodeling process is far more active in trabecular bone, due in part to the architectural arrangement of the bone plates providing a larger exposed surface area for exchange with the extracellular compartment. Approximately 40 percent of trabecular bone is remodeled each year. It is because of this greater activity that vertebral osteoporosis occurs more frequently than hip (cortical-related) fractures. It may also account for the increased susceptibility of the vertebrae to the bone mineral loss noted in female long-distance runners.[14]

After longitudinal bone growth has been achieved, the bone mineral content and mass of bone further increase until about the age of 35 years, at which point the individual is said to have achieved her maximal cortical bone mass. From this age until onset of the menopause, it is considered normal for women to lose (as measured by single- and dual-photon absorptiometry) at least 0.12 percent of cortical bone per year; after the menopause and until age 65, the rate of bone loss increases to at least 1 percent per year, slowing down after age 65 to 0.18 percent per year. This "physiologic" bone loss averages out to a 25 percent decrease in cortical bone mass over a 30-year span from age 50 to age 80.[13] Trabecular bone accrual reaches its maximum during the mid- to late 20s and is followed thereafter by a linear loss of bone.[15] Others maintain that the trabecular bone loss pattern equals that of cortical bone, with a loss of at least 0.19 percent per year before the menopause and a loss of at least 1.1 percent thereafter. It has been estimated that 31.7 percent of trabecular bone is lost during the 50-year span between 30 and 80 years of age.[13] The greater the bone mineral content at bone mass maturity (maximum), the more an individual can afford to lose; this emphasizes the need to focus on the accrual of bone during the early climacteric (and even before) rather than on the treatment of a reduced bone mass in the postmenopausal period.

## How to Acquire More Bone

Mechanical force plays an important role in bone formation and function. What is not known, however, is how much exercise is needed and whether there is an optimal form of exercise for bone accrual. It is postulated[16] that there is a physiologic "band" of activity that is site specific: immobilization can lead to severe bone loss at some sites, whereas repeated loading at appropriate strain magnitudes can result in bone hypertrophy. The frequency and degree of activity is important. Repeated and prolonged exercise causes bone fatigue and microscopic fractures.[16] Given appropriate intervals between exercise, normal bone turnover will repair these microfractures and even strengthen the bone.[16] Excessive activity is known to have an adverse effect, with stress fractures a common reality in long-distance runners.[16]

**Gravity.** Bone mineral is lost with the inactivity of simple bed rest. The average rate appears to be 4 percent per month during the early phase of bed rest; although subjects with higher initial bone mass lose bone more rapidly than those with lower values, all immobilized patients seem to end up with a similar bone mass.[17] Lack of force on bones plays a major role in bone loss, with trabecular bone being more sensitive than cortical bone. Three hours a day of quiet standing has a partial effect in helping to restore bone mineral, while 4 hours of walking prevents the bone loss associated with 20 hours of bed rest.

Osteogenesis in long bones requires mechanical stress; when electrodes are placed on opposite sides of bone, bending results in a negative electrical potential on the concave side relative to the convex side.[18] The resulting piezoelectricity stimulates new bone cell growth. It is therefore not surprising that isometric or horizontal exercise—which does not "bend" bone and thereby stimulate this piezoelectricity—is not able to restore bone loss associated with immobilization.

**Systemic versus local effect.** It is important to differentiate the amount of exercise needed to maintain bone mass from that needed to increase it. This is well illustrated by a study that compared male professional tennis players with age-matched casual tennis players. The former group was found to have an overall greater bone mass; but in addition, the cortical thickness in the playing arm of the professional tennis players was 34.9 percent greater than in their nondominant arm. The same was found in female professional tennis players: cortical thickness in the dominant arm was 28.4 percent greater than in the control or nondominant arm.[19] Exercise thus seems to have both a systemic and a local effect and appears to be related to the type of exercise performed. When combined with the effect of gravity, weight-bearing activity is more osteogenic than weight-supporting exercises such as swimming.

**Age.** Age is yet another significant factor: bone mass accrual occurs more readily in "growing" than in "mature" bone.[20] Both animal experimentation and clinical experience have shown that the accumulation of appropriate mechanical damage can serve as a stimulus to bone hypertrophy. This requires exposure of adult bone to cyclic strain levels of 2000 microstrain or more.[21] However, there is an optimal level beyond which increasing strain levels will no longer enhance bone mass and may even have a negative effect.[21] Thus, the type and intensity of exercise prescribed must be tailored to the age of the individual.

**Exercise prescription.** In presenting an osteogenic exercise program, two additional criteria should be met: (1) the activity should be diverse and vigorous, but nonrepetitive;[22] and (2) the exercise program should be enjoyable, in order to ensure long-term compliance. In addition, a program that will simultaneously improve cardiovascular fitness would provide an added incentive and advantage. By extrapolating from animal data,[23] it has been suggested that aerobic exercise at an intensity associated with 65 to 80 percent of maximal heart rate is osteogenic.

## Exercise and Osteogenesis: Clinical Research

When interpreting the efficacy of a given program, the method of bone strength measurement needs to be considered. Most assessments are based on radiologic techniques, single- and dual-photon absorptiometry, and/or CT scanning. A qualitative improvement in bone strength resulting from aerobic exercise may also derive from an engineering rather than a biologic principle— an increase in bone width. Radial expansion of long bones is an important determinant of bone strength. The so-called cross-sectional moment of inertia (CSMI) is what determines bone's resistance to bending. Increase in the external diameter of the bone, brought about by increased periosteal (outer layer) new bone formation, can compensate for the inevitable loss in the quality of bone tissue that occurs with aging. A recent study investigated the effects of 6 months of walking or aerobic dancing on the bone mineral content of 73 early postmenopausal women. The exercising women had a significant increase in the CSMI when compared with the control group.[24] The bone mineral content of the walking group and the control group, however, was decreased.

Relatively brief exercise programs have been shown to have a positive effect on vertebral bone mineral. Sixteen healthy women (mean age $61 \pm 6$ years) participated in an exercise program that involved walking, running, and calisthenics for 1 hour twice weekly. At the end of 8 months, the vertebral bone mineral content (measured by dual-photon absorptiometry) increased by 3 to 5 percent, whereas in an age-matched control group it decreased by 2.7 percent. Simultaneously measured bone mineral content of the distal radius showed an average decrease of 3.5 percent.[23] The authors concluded that physical exercise inhibits and/or reverses bone loss from the lumbar vertebrae in normal women, but that the changes in the forearm were independent of these exercises.[25]

These results are divergent from another study that examined bone mineralization by x-ray densitometry (middle phalanx of the fifth finger and os calcis) and photon absorptiometry (distal and midshaft) in 42 normally menstruating marathon runners (mean age $37.7 \pm 0.82$ year) and 38 sedentary controls (mean age $39.6 \pm 1.0$ year). Mean values of the mineral content and the bone density of the marathon runners' radial midshaft and middle phalanx (representative of cortical bone) were significantly greater, but the mean density of the os calcis (trabecular bone) was higher in the physically inactive women.[26] Women with moderate exercise had greater cortical but less trabecular bone mineral contents, indicating that the increase in cortical bone through exercise comes at the "expense" of trabecular bone.

Although anatomically distinct, the metabolic functions of the cortical and trabecular bone compartments are shared—a gain in one compartment may be matched by a loss in another. These two studies raise the question: can you exercise too much, and if so will this result in a compromise of the trabecular skeleton? Women marathon runners whose activity was associated with exercise-induced amenorrhea were noted to have a reduced amount of trabecular bone in their lumbar vertebrae (as measured by dual-photon absorptiometry) with normal or minimally reduced cortical bone (as measured by single-photon absorptiometry and radiogrammetry).[14] This bone loss has been attributed to estrogen deficiency associated with decreased body fat, an observation that has been suggested by others.[27] The exercise-induced osteopenic effect cannot, however, be due to an estrogen deficiency alone. Calcium intake obviously plays a very important role. When reported, calcium intake was inadequate in most osteopenic groups, regardless of estrogen and exercise status. The menstruating marathon runners referred to previously[26] lost trabecular bone despite an intact hypothalamic pituitary ovarian axis; another study has shown that women with anorexia nervosa (all of whom were amenorrheic and obviously hypoestrogenic) and who were physically active had significantly greater bone mass than a similar group of inactive anorectics.[28]

Preliminary results from an ongoing study at the Center for Climacteric Studies comparing different forms of exercise in natural and surgically menopausal women reflect on some of the aforementioned issues—age, type and intensity of exercise, and an "intact" estrogen milieu. Bone mineral content in this study was measured by dual-photon absorptiometry of the total skeleton. Naturally menopausal women participating in aerobic (walking on a treadmill, riding a stationary bicycle) and muscle-strengthening (Nautilus) exercises, none of whom were receiving hormonal therapy, had significantly reduced bone loss over a 1-year period when compared with a control group that did not exercise. The controls lost 9.9 percent of their bone mineral content compared with 3.8 percent in the Nautilus exercise group and 0.5 percent in the bicycle-riding group. The treadmill subjects gained 0.4 percent.[29] In a parallel study involving surgically menopausal women (mean age $50.4 \pm 7.2$) receiving hormone replacement therapy (HRT), subjects receiving HRT alone maintained their bone mass, whereas those in a matched

**Table 12–1.** EFFECT OF EXERCISE AND HORMONE REPLACEMENT THERAPY ON BONE MASS IN POSTMENOPAUSAL WOMEN

| HRT* | Moderate Exercise (Aerobic) | Intense Exercise (Nautilus) | Effect on Bone Mass |
|------|------|------|------|
| no | yes | | 0 |
| no | | yes | − |
| yes | | yes | + |

*Hormone replacement therapy.
From Notelovitz et al,[29] with permission.

group training on Nautilus equipment three times a week (in addition to HRT) showed a significant 8 percent increase in their bone mineral content.[29] The duration, intensity, and frequency of exercise was approximately the same in all groups. It might be, as these studies suggest (Table 12–1),[29] that an estrogen-replete state is needed for an osteogenic effect in women involved in intense exercise programs and that more moderate levels of activity can conserve and maintain bone independent of the estrogen milieu. A question that still needs to be answered is whether older exercising postmenopausal women receiving estrogen replacement will have an osteogenic response similar to younger women.

**Exercise and calcium intake.** The precise mechanism whereby exercise stimulates new bone formation is not clearly established. Mechanical load, muscular activity, and gravity serve as an extracellular stimulus that is transmitted to bone cells to initiate their genetic program for growth and differentiation. Intermediaries include events such as the generation of piezoelectricity that stimulates cyclic nucleotide activity, prostaglandin synthesis, and other matrix-derived bone growth factors. What has been established, however, is that exercise is directly associated with the laying down of matrix on the remodeling surface of bone's trabeculae and cortices. The matrix is composed primarily of collagen. Chvapil and colleagues[30] showed that the amount and concentration of collagen in the femurs of adult rats increased with exercise but that no effect on the calcium content occurred. This experiment serves to illustrate a most important point: to benefit from exercise and its osteogenic stimulus, it is necessary to ensure an adequate supply of the substrate (mainly calcium) needed to mineralize and mature the newly formed bone. It is well known that fluoride therapy without simultaneous calcium supplementation will increase mineralization of the axial skeleton, but at the expense of the cortical bone and with an increase in hip fractures.[31] A similar situation may be true for exercise-induced osteogenesis, except that in this instance it is the cortical bone that benefits at the expense of the trabecular compartment. This may prove to be one of the reasons why the amenorrheic women reported by Drinkwater and associates[14] had lower spinal but not cortical bone mineral content when compared with the eumenorrheic controls. Although both groups met the current recommended dietary allowance of 800 mg of elemental calcium per day, the amenorrheic subjects fell short of the recommended amount needed to maintain calcium balance in low estrogen states (1500 mg of elemental calcium per day), whereas the eumenorrheic women exceeded the daily requirement of 800 mg.

### Established Osteoporosis

Exercise in women with established osteoporosis has to be modulated by the fact that pre-existing microfractures and discontinuity between the trabecular plates, especially in the axial skeleton, may be aggravated by weight-bearing exercise. Furthermore, even though individual fragments of the horizontal trabecular plates may be hypertrophied by exercise, the loss of their continuity, and hence structural integrity, will still deprive the bone from improving in strength in response to stress. Nevertheless, light to moderate exercise in older women has resulted in an improvement of the cortical bone mass. Smith and co-workers[32] designed an exercise program for older women (mean age 81 years) that oriented activity (1.5 to 3.0 METS in intensity) around a chair. One MET equals a maximal oxygen uptake of 3.5 ml per minute per kilogram, which is the average value of effort obtained on subjects during chair rest. Over a 3-year period, their exercise group demonstrated a 2.9 percent increase in midshaft radius bone mineral content, whereas a matched nonexercising control group showed a 3.29 percent decrease in their bone mineral content.

Inadequate attention is given to the prescription of exercise to women with established osteoporosis, most of whom will present to the physician during their late climacteric. A key issue is to discourage activities that involve flexion of the back. Long-term follow-up of patients with radiologically confirmed osteoporosis revealed recurrent fractures in 16 percent of women practicing back extension exercises, 89 percent in a flexion program, 53 percent in a combined extension and flexion regimen, and 67 percent in a nonexercising control group.[33] Posture is also important. Avoidance of activities that encourage flexion during sedentary activities, such as sewing, can prevent further stress to already weakened vertebrae.[34] Instruction should also be given to avoid back straining by twisting, lifting, and making sudden forceful movements. To remove the strain from the lower back when lifting or reaching lower objects, the large muscles of the legs (i.e., the hamstrings and quadriceps) should be used, by bending the knees and keeping the back vertical during these activities.

Walking is the safest form of exercise for women with osteoporosis. Also safe and effective are group activities such as square dancing, ballroom dancing, and folk dancing, as well as other activities such as riding a three-wheel bike or an exercycle. Swimming is an excellent exercise that allows patients to regain their confidence in being physically active, and at the same time allows them to increase the flexibility and mobility of their joints. Osteoporotic, or markedly osteopenic, women should be advised to avoid activities such as aerobic (jazz) dance classes that jar the spine and emphasize flexibility. In evaluating these women, care should be taken to test for balance and for orthostatic hypotension and to advise them about practical measures, such as the type of shoes they should wear.

## ATHEROGENIC DISEASE AND CARDIORESPIRATORY FITNESS

Premature cessation of ovarian function is said by some to increase the risk of myocardial infarction. Women who had a bilateral oophorectomy before age 35 were estimated to have a 7.2 times greater risk of being hospitalized for a myocardial infarction than age-matched normal premenopausal women.[35] This is consistent with other studies[7,36,37] that have observed high rates of coronary disease in women who experience an early menopause, but it is at variance with the opinions of others who cannot confirm this relationship.[38,39] Although the cardioprotective effect of the premenopausal milieu is still questioned, there is a general consensus that the postmenopausal period is associated with well-defined high-risk factors for atherogenesis: increased plasma cholesterol and decreased high-density lipoprotein (HDL) levels.[7] This is a biologic and not a chronologic event. A Swedish study compared women age 50 and older, some of whom were still menstruating while others had already reached the menopause; serum cholesterol and triglycerides were significantly higher in the postmenopausal group, and these levels increased with postmenopausal age.[40]

The pathogenesis of atherosclerosis is characterized by two factors: (1) endothelial desquamation with later smooth muscle cell proliferation and (2) cholesterol deposition within these cells. Inhibition of low-density lipoprotein (LDL) internalization and deposition in the smooth muscle cell by HDL cholesterol is said to be a key factor in the prevention and/or slowing down of the atherogenic process.[41] Exercise has a beneficial effect on the lipoprotein moiety, especially regarding the HDL cholesterol.[42]

Physical inactivity has also been linked to atherogenic disease. Men who are physically active have fewer stigmata of coronary heart disease, and when they do occur they are less severe and appear at an older age.[43] The same is true for women.[44] There are some who believe that physical inactivity per se is not a major risk factor,[45] but that it does contribute to the underlying adverse hemodynamic (e.g., hypertension) and metabolic changes (e.g., obesity, diabetes, hypercholesterolemia) associated with atherogenesis. The type, intensity, and duration of exercise linked to a potential decrease in coronary heart disease varies. There appears to be a threshold of activity that is needed in order to achieve a benefit. This has been estimated to be 300 kcal per day above normal daily activity, and requires 30 to 60 minutes of moderately intensive exercise per day.[46] There was earlier speculation that women,[47] especially older women, would not be able to achieve this goal and that they may indeed not be as trainable as men! This has since been disproved.

Based on the previous observations, there are two practical aspects of physical activity and cardiovascular health that can be objectively measured: (1) the response of biochemical parameters such as cholesterol and HDL cholesterol and (2) measures of physical fitness and exercise quantity—maximal oxygen uptake ($\dot{V}_{O_2max}$) and total exercise time.

## Lipids, Lipoprotein, and Exercise

The plasma lipoproteins are the means whereby endogenous synthesized lipids are transported in the circulation. They are classified according to their gravitational density into four basic classes: chylomicrons, very low-density lipoproteins (VLDL), LDL, and HDL. The latter are frequently subfractionated into $HDL_2$ and the more dense $HDL_3$. It is the $HDL_2$ cholesterol component that is higher in women[48] and that is inversely related to the development of coronary heart disease.[49] Exercise stimulates $HDL_2$ and is higher in male and female runners than in sedentary controls. In one illustrative study, for example, men had $HDL_2$ cholesterol values of 119 versus 53 mg/dL; in women the respective values for active and sedentary subjects were 218 versus 122 mg/dL.[48] The HDL-elevating effect of exercise is thought to be due to an increase in lipoprotein lipase, an enzyme responsible for the catabolism of triglyceride-rich lipoproteins. Lipoprotein lipase is found in greater concentrations in the skeletal muscle fibers (slow-twitch) of endurance athletes.[50]

In a cross-sectional study conducted at the Center for Climacteric Studies, an age- and menopause-related increase in serum cholesterol was noted.[51] The respective values were 170.5 ± 4.3 mg/dL (age 35 to 45); 203.2 ± 7.6 mg/dL (age 46 to 55 menstruating); 233.8 ± 5.9 mg/dL (age 46 to 55 nonmenstruating); 230.1 ± 6.9 mg/dL (age 56 to 65); and 238.8 ± 6.7 mg/dL (age 66 to 75). To determine if this endocrine- and age-related change would be improved by exercise, a group of 50 healthy women between the ages of 40 and 65 were invited to participate in a 12-week program of exercise, discussion sessions, or both. The discussion group served as the controls. Levels of serum cholesterol, triglycerides, total HDL, and $HDL_{2a}$ and $HDL_{2b}$ were monitored at baseline, at 6 weeks, and at 12 weeks. The exercise groups were instructed to walk-jog for 30 minutes (after a 15-minute warm-up session) and to pace their activity in order to maintain their heart rate at 70 to 80 percent of their predicted maximum heart rate. One exercise session was supervised by a group therapy leader, and the other two exercise sessions (per week) were repeated on their own. Cardiorespiratory function was determined at baseline and at 12 weeks, having subjects walk on a motorized treadmill until they declared fatigue or reached their predicted maximal heart rate. The exercising group had a significantly greater increase in $\dot{V}_{O2max}$, time spent on the treadmill, and time required to obtain 90 percent of maximal oxygen consumption (p <0.01), but did not show a statistically significant difference in the lipid or lipoprotein fractions at either 6 or 12 weeks.[52] This disappointing result was confirmed by Franklin and associates,[53] who exercised their subjects four times a week as part of a 12-week conditioning program. These discrepant results may be explained by the duration of the exercise program and intensity of the exercise. For example, it was only when the weekly running mileage of 22 women was increased from 3.5 miles to 44.9 miles (over a 7-month period) that mean HDL cholesterol increased from 53.5 to 58.5 mg/dL (p <0.01).[54]

Women (postmenopausal as well as other age groups) who engage in regular endurance exercise have higher HDL cholesterol levels than inactive women.[55–57] Postmenopausal long-distance runners and joggers had significantly greater levels of HDL cholesterol compared with a control group of relatively inactive women—79.8, 73.5, and 61.8 mg/dL, respectively. The lipid-lipoprotein profiles were minimally affected by exercise in a simultaneously studied group of exercising premenopausal women,[57] raising the issue of whether it is possible to make "normal," *more* normal.

In summary, the cardioprotective HDL cholesterol level improves only after at least 4 months of fairly strenuous activity (e.g., running 10 to 15 miles per week); at least 3 months of more moderate activity (e.g., walking 30 miles per week) is needed before a significant increase in HDL will occur.[48] As with men, exercise training in women lowers total cholesterol slightly or not at all.[53,54]

## Aerobic Power

With the advent of the "fitness craze," women have come into their own and have exploded the myth that women are "frail";* physical fitness in young women has now become socially acceptable. Until fairly recently, however, it was felt that exercise would not benefit middle-aged people and that the decline in cardiorespiratory function with aging would reduce the expected benefit from exercise.[47] Furthermore, it was postulated that menopause per se could be responsible for the decrease in aerobic power in women over the age of 50.[58,59]

As with men, there is an age-related decrease in cardiorespiratory fitness, but this is not related to the hormonal changes of the climacteric. One hundred sixty-three healthy sedentary women between the ages of 35 and 75 years had $\dot{V}_{O2max}$ testing after being screened for cardiovascular normalcy by a 12-lead ECG stress test and physical examination.[60] The $\dot{V}_{O2max}$ was elicited using a modified Balke treadmill procedure.[60] Each subject's $\dot{V}_{O2max}$ was directly measured using a Beckman Metabolic Measurement Cart. A decrement of 5.5 percent of $V_{O2max}$ occurred with each succeeding decade between ages 35 and 75 (Fig. 12–3). This observation approximates with the generalization that sedentary individuals have a $\pm 1$ percent loss of $V_{O2max}$ per year with age, especially after age 50. Women usually achieve maximal $\dot{V}_{O2}$ values in the decade 20 to 29 years; by age 50 to 65 years the values are decreased by almost 30 percent.[61] This loss of aerobic power is not related to the menopause per se. In a recent study, women age 45 to 55 had their $\dot{V}_{O2max}$ predicted by means of a submaximal bicycle ergometer test.[60] They were divided according to whether they were still menstruating. Their premenopausal or postmenopausal status was confirmed by hormonal analysis and by their menstrual

---

*"Frailty, thy name is woman."—Shakespeare, Hamlet I:ii, 146.

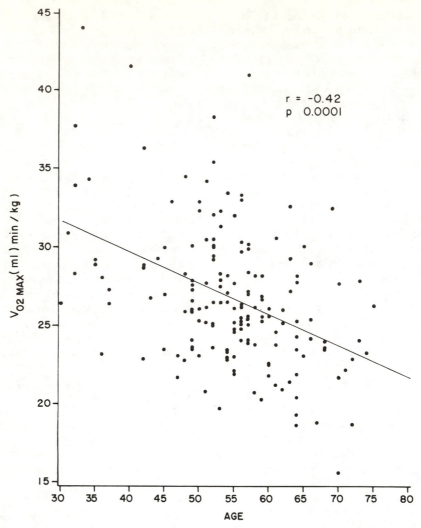

**Figure 12–3.** *Measured $\dot{V}_{O_2max}$ (mL/kg/min) in 163 healthy climacteric women. (From Notelovitz et al,[60] with permission.)*

pattern: postmenopausal women were required to have been amenorrheic for at least 1 year. As reflected in Table 12–2, serum LH and FSH were significantly higher in the postmenopausal women (p <0.0001), and the respective estradiol and estrone levels were significantly lower (p <0.0001). The premenopausal women were slightly younger (48.7 ± 0.4 year) than their postmenopausal peers (52.2 ± 0.4), but the difference was not statistically significant. No significant difference was found in the estimated $\dot{V}_{O_2max}$: 27.4 ± 6.3 mL·kg$^{-1}$·min$^{-1}$ for the premenopausal versus 26.3 ± 4.7 mL·kg$^{-1}$·min$^{-1}$ for the postmenopausal group (p >0.05).[60]

The observed decline in $\dot{V}_{O_2max}$ with age probably reflects a loss of functional capacity due both to a natural age-related deterioration and to a decrease in physical activity. The age-associated reduction in cardiorespiratory efficiency at *submaximal* exercise, however, is due primarily to weight gain rather than actual systems degeneration.[62] The rate of decline is slower in physically active men[63] and women.[58,64] This raises the issue of whether menopausal women can be efficiently trained. Premenopausal women (mean age 41 years) who trained for 9 weeks improved their $\dot{V}_{O_2max}$ by 12.1 percent, while similarly trained postmenopausal women (mean age 57 years) improved their $\dot{V}_{O_2max}$ by

**Table 12–2.** MEAN ESTIMATED MAXIMAL $O_2$ UPTAKE VALUES AND HORMONAL STATUS ($\pm$SD) OF PREMENOPAUSAL AND POSTMENOPAUSAL WOMEN AGE 46–55 YR

| Parameter | Premenopausal (n = 28) | Postmenopausal (n = 30) |
|---|---|---|
| Estimated $V_{O_2max}$ (mL·kg$^{-1}$·min$^{-1}$) | 27.4 ± 6.3 | 26.3 ± 4.7 |
| LH (mIU/mL) | 23.5 ± 3.6 | 62.8 ± 3.5 |
| FSH (mIU/mL) | 12.6 ± 2.6 | 55.7 ± 3.5 |
| Estrone (pg/mL) | 107.5 ± 11.5 | 62.9 ± 3.9 |
| Estradiol (pg/mL) | 146.2 ± 18.7 | 19.5 ± 3.5 |

From Notelovitz et al,[60] with permission.

19 percent.[65] This result has been confirmed by others,[66] including two studies conducted at the Center for Climacteric Studies. Moderate exercise (walk-jogging three times a week for 12 weeks) resulted in a significant increase in the maximal oxygen consumption, time on the treadmill, and the time to reach 90 percent of maximal oxygen consumption, when compared with age-matched female controls who did not exercise.[67] More recently, 63 postmenopausal women were evaluated over a 1-year period, during a structured program that involved three weekly 20-minute treadmill, ergometer, or Nautilus (muscle-strengthening) sessions. Two nonexercising groups were included: an age-matched nontreatment group and a slightly younger group on hormone replacement therapy. Aerobically trained subjects were exercised at a level between 70 to 85 percent of the maximal heart rate. Significant improvements in both $\dot{V}_{O_2max}$ and time on the treadmill were recorded and maintained only by the bicycle and treadmill groups (Tables 12–3 and 12–4).[68]

The anticipated degree of improvement in aerobic power is inversely related to the subject's initial level of fitness. The lower the degree of fitness, the greater the subsequent improvement. At all initial levels of fitness, the greater the intensity and frequency of the training program, the greater the improvement. For example, the postmenopausal women in Cowan and Gregory's study[65] had a 19 percent improvement in $\dot{V}_{O_2max}$ (from 12.6 mL·kg$^{-1}$·min$^{-1}$ to 15.0 mL·kg$^{-1}$min$^{-1}$) compared with a 10.7 percent improvement in the Gainesville study (from 26.9 mL·kg$^{-1}$·min$^{-1}$ to 29.8 mL·kg·$^{-1}$·min$^{-1}$).

An intriguing observation in both of these studies is the considerably greater improvement in total exercise time versus $\dot{V}_{O_2max}$. Cowan and Gregory[65] noted a 29.6 percent increase in total walking time; the respective values in the Gainesville study were 21.5 percent and 17.4 percent for the treadmill

**Table 12–3.** RESPONSE OF CLIMACTERIC WOMEN—MEAN AGE 56 YR—TO INTENSIVE STRUCTURED EXERCISE,[67] MEAN ($\pm$SD) MAXIMAL $O_2$ UPTAKE (mL·kg$^{-1}$·min$^{-1}$)

| Group | Age | n | Baseline | 3 Mo | 6 Mo | 12 Mo | % Difference Baseline vs 12 Mo |
|---|---|---|---|---|---|---|---|
| Nautilus | 59.3 ± 6.7 | 13 | 26.0 ± 5.2 | 26.1 ± 4.7 | 26.5 ± 4.0 | 26.2 ± 3.9 | 0.8 |
| Treadmill | 54.9 ± 6.9 | 10 | 27.1 ± 2.7 | 29.5 ± 2.8 | 30.5 ± 2.8 | 29.5 ± 2.4 | 8.9 |
| Ergometer | 55.9 ± 6.9 | 10 | 26.7 ± 4.7 | 28.9 ± 4.1 | 30.2 ± 4.1 | 30.0 ± 4.8 | 12.4 |
| Control | 62.0 ± 7.1 | 14 | 26.5 ± 4.7 | 26.1 ± 6.0 | 25.9 ± 5.9 | 26.2 ± 5.8 | −1.1 |
| Hormone | 48.4 ± 7.2 | 16 | 26.6 ± 3.9 | 26.3 ± 3.7 | 26.4 ± 4.2 | 25.1 ± 3.9 | −5.6 |

From Notelovitz et al,[68] with permission.

**Table 12–4.** RESPONSE OF CLIMACTERIC WOMEN—MEAN AGE 56 YR—TO INTENSIVE STRUCTURED EXERCISE,[67] MEAN ($\pm$SD) TOTAL EXERCISE TIME (MIN)

| Group | Age | n | Baseline | 3 Mo | 6 Mo | 12 Mo | % Difference Baseline vs 12 Mo |
|---|---|---|---|---|---|---|---|
| Nautilus | 59.3 ± 6.7 | 13 | 12.1 ± 3.2 | 12.2 ± 2.5 | 12.9 ± 2.4 | 12.5 ± 2.4 | 5.3 |
| Treadmill | 54.9 ± 6.9 | 10 | 12.5 ± 1.6 | 14.2 ± 2.1 | 15.2 ± 2.0 | 15.3 ± 2.1 | 21.5 |
| Ergometer | 55.9 ± 7.9 | 10 | 13.0 ± 3.1 | 14.1 ± 3.0 | 14.5 ± 3.0 | 15.2 ± 3.3 | 17.4 |
| Control | 62.0 ± 7.1 | 14 | 12.2 ± 3.3 | 11.6 ± 3.6 | 12.2 ± 4.0 | 12.1 ± 3.4 | −0.95 |
| Hormones | 48.4 ± 7.2 | 16 | 13.4 ± 2.4 | 12.6 ± 2.3 | 13.0 ± 2.3 | 12.3 ± 2.2 | −7.7 |

From Notelovitz et al,[68] with permission.

walkers and bicyclists, respectively. Premenopausal women exposed to the same exercise regimen had an improvement rate of 10.9 percent in total exercise time.[65] Since the heart rate and stroke volume response to exercise was appropriate in postmenopausal women, there is a possibility that the lesser percentage response in $\dot{V}_{O2max}$ compared with percentage improvement in exercise time might be accounted for by partially compromised lung ventilation, lung diffusion capacity for oxygen, and/or oxygen utilization by the tissues in the postmenopausal period.

The percentage gain in aerobic power from a number of different studies is summarized in Table 12–5. Values range from 8 to 30 percent. With only one exception, the duration of the training program was less than 14 weeks. The best improvement was obtained in programs whose duration of exercise exceeded 30 minutes in each session. The study that continued for 12 months demonstrated

**Table 12–5.** IMPROVEMENT OF MAXIMAL $O_2$ UPTAKE FOLLOWING AEROBIC TRAINING PROGRAMS IN WOMEN OVER AGE 50

| Author | n | Duration of Exercise per Session (min) | Frequency of Exercise per Week | Intensity of Exercise | Duration of Training Program (wk) | % Gain in Maximal $O_2$ Uptake |
|---|---|---|---|---|---|---|
| Kilborn[47] | 13 | 30 | 2–3 | 70%* | 7 | 8 |
| Adams and De Vries[98] | 17 | 50 | 3 | 85%† | 12 | 20.8 |
| Sidney et al[99] | 25 | 60 | 4 | HR 120–150/min | 7 | >30 |
| Sidney and Shephard[100] | 28 | 55 | 3 | 60–80%† | 14 | 17 |
| Cowan and Gregory[65] | 14 | 50 | 4 | 80%† | 9 | 18.9 |
| Notelovitz et al[68] | 10(T) | 20 | 3 | 70–85%† | 52 | 8.9 |
| | 10(E) | 20 | 3 | 70–85%† | 52 | 12.4 |

*$V_{O2max}$.
†Maximum heart rate.
T = Treadmill; E = Ergometer.
Adapted from Cowan and Gregory.[65]

that most of the improvement attained by 12 months had been achieved by 3 months of training. These results do not reflect the true potential of middle-aged women engaged in long-term intensive exercise programs, nor do they consider a most important practical real-life issue of exercise: compliance.

Exercise is good. According to a recent cross-sectional study,[69] active women had a cardioprotective effect of one decade when compared to sedentary women. The mean $\dot{V}_{O2max}$ of active 40- to 49-year-old women was higher than sedentary 30- to 39-year-old women; active 50- to 59-year old women had values similar to those of 40- to 49-year-old women. One way of encouraging women to exercise is to use cardiorespiratory fitness assessments as a means of demonstrating improvement in aerobic function before the physical benefits of exercise are appreciated. Bruce and colleagues[70] reported that 63 percent of their patients attributed a change in one or more risk factors for health habits to a graded exercise test. Persons with an abnormal result were motivated the most. Maximal oxygen uptake tests need to be performed in a specially equipped laboratory and are not suited to everyday clinical practice. Submaximal testing, on the other hand, is more ideally suited to the practicing physician. Several studies have shown that predicted maximum $\dot{V}_{O2}$ values (using bicycle ergometer) correlate well with observed maximal testing when corrected for age,[71,72] but none of these studies involve climacteric women. To test this relationship in postmenopausal women, 29 women (mean age 55.6 ± 9.1 years) participating in an ongoing exercise program had both a treadmill and an ergometry test.[60] The interval between the two tests was less than 1 month, and the order of testing was randomly selected. The measured $\dot{V}_{O2max}$ was 28.6 ± 4.9 mL·kg$^{-1}$·min$^{-1}$, and the predicted $\dot{V}_{O2max}$ 32.5 ± 5.3 mL·kg$^{-1}$·min$^{-1}$. When the latter result was calculated using the recommended Åstrand age correction factor, the mean predicted $\dot{V}_{O2max}$ was 23.4 ± 4.9 mL·kg$^{-1}$·min$^{-1}$. This correlated closely with the directly measured result (r = 0.789; Fig. 12–4).

Submaximal testing can thus be used both as a screen to determine the cardiorespiratory fitness of climacteric women and to monitor the response to prescribed exercise. Patients at high risk for cardiovascular dis-

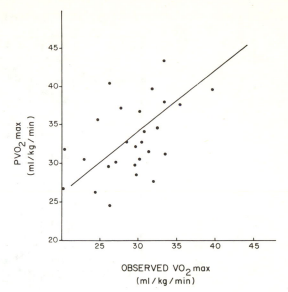

**Figure 12–4.** *Correlation between measured and predicted $\dot{V}_{O2max}$ in climacteric women. (From Notelovitz et al,[60] with permission.)*

ease and those classified as having fair to poor fitness (as measured by ergometry) require more detailed evaluation before embarking on a prescribed exercise program. A nomogram is also very useful (Figs. 12–5 and 12–6); when used together with age-adjusted tables listing cardiorespiratory fitness for women, potential exercise candidates obtained a good index of both their current fitness status and the goals they should reach (Table 12–6). Because postmenopausal women appear to show a greater response to a given exercise program in total exercise time than in maximum oxygen uptake, I believe that the total exercise nomogram may be used as the primary indicator of exercise response and improvement.

In view of the laziness inherent in most people, any program that can produce improved results for little effort is more likely to be successful and lead to a greater degree of compliance than a program that requires great effort and discipline. Schoenfeld and co-workers[73] examined the efficiency of walking with a backpack load as a method for improving physical fitness of sedentary men. They showed that it was possible to increase $\dot{V}_{O2max}$ from 15 to 30 percent by walking for 3 to 4 miles with a 3 kg or 6 kg backpack. To determine if load-bearing during

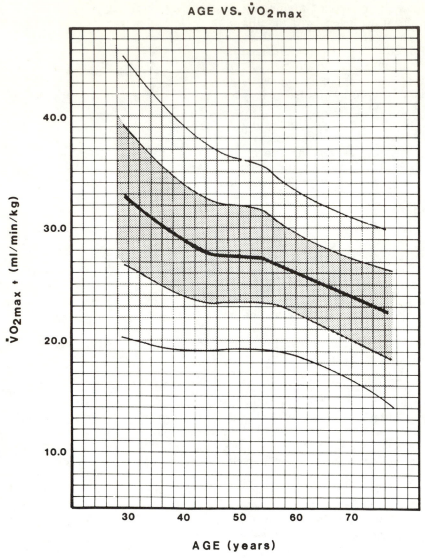

**Figure 12–5.** *Normative* $\dot{V}_{O_{2}max}$ *values for climacteric women. Mean* ± *1 and 2 SD for each age group. (From Notelovitz M, Fields C, et al: Unpublished data. Center for Climacteric Studies, Gainesville, FL, with permission.)*

treadmill walking would significantly affect the maximum aerobic capacity of normal healthy women aged 57 to 67 years, a "load-bearing" group of six women with a mean age of 61.2 years was compared with five non–load-bearing women with a mean age of 62.1 years. Each woman had a baseline $\dot{V}_{O_{2}max}$ test and then began a 12-week treadmill training program. Subjects were trained three times per week for 20 minutes each time, at 70 to 85 percent of maximal heart rate. Subjects in the load-bearing group carried a backpack with a 4 kg weight added to

it. At the conclusion of 12 weeks, subjects were retested for their $\dot{V}_{O_{2}max}$. There was no difference in the mean $\dot{V}_{O_{2}max}$ values of the two groups after training. However, the load-bearing group did exhibit a significant increase in $\dot{V}_{O_{2}max}$ when compared with their baseline results, whereas the non–load-bearing group did not. In addition, the load-bearing group had a mean increase of 2.09 minutes in treadmill time versus a 0.44 second improvement in the non–load-bearing group.[74] Prolongation of the period of training (to 6 months) led to a loss of this im-

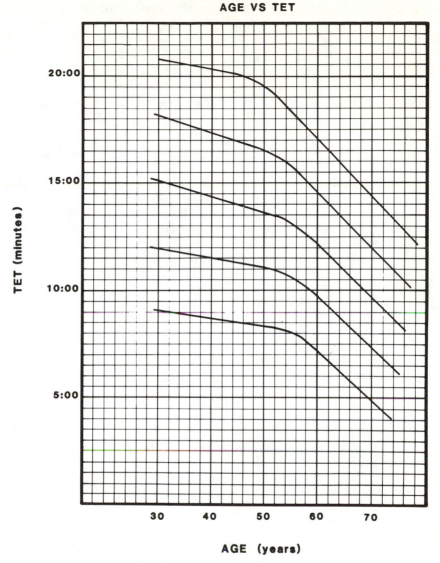

**AGE VS TET**

*Figure 12-6. Normative total exercise time (TET) values for climacteric women. Mean ± 1 and 2 SD for each age group. (From Notelovitz M, Fields C, et al: Unpublished data. Center for Climacteric Studies, Gainesville, FL, with permission.)*

**Table 12-6.** GUIDELINES FOR FITNESS ASSESSMENT BY $V_{O2max}$ ($mL \cdot kg^{-1} \cdot min^{-1}$) OF HEALTHY WOMEN AGE 30–70

| Age | Poor | Fair | Average | Good | Excellent |
|-----|------|------|---------|------|-----------|
| 30–39 | <20 | 20–27 | 28–33 | 33–44 | 45+ |
| 40–49 | <17 | 17–23 | 24–30 | 31–41 | 42+ |
| 50–59 | <15 | 15–20 | 21–27 | 28–37 | 38+ |
| 60–69 | <13 | 13–17 | 18–23 | 24–34 | 35+ |

Adapted from Exercise Testing and Training in Apparently Healthy Individuals: A Handbook for Physicians, published by the Committee on Exercise, The American Heart Association, Dallas, TX, 1972.

provement in treadmill time, and it is not clear whether load-bearing will really add to the efficacy of aerobic training, or will serve as a means of exercising less to achieve a similar or greater benefit!

## Strength Training

Several cross-sectional studies have shown a loss of muscle strength with age, beginning after the third decade of life and amounting to a decline of 16.5 percent or greater.[75] The loss is greater in women.[76] This loss of muscle tissue is related to a number of important metabolic activities. Tzanoff and Norris[77] maintain that the decrease in muscle mass may be wholly responsible for the age-related decrease in basal metabolic rate (BMR). The average $\dot{V}_{O_2max}$ of older men was 22 percent lower when compared with younger men; this difference decreased to only 8 percent when the values were expressed in terms of $mL \cdot kg^{-1}min^{-1}$ of muscle, as determined by 24-hour urine creatinine measurements. Increasing muscle mass can thus play an important role in determining energy expenditure: a 5 percent increase in the BMR of a 160-pound man results in an additional expenditure of 75 to 80 kcal per day, the equivalent of about 8 pounds of body fat per year. Muscle is also an important determinant of carbohydrate utilization. The rate of glucose removal from muscle is more rapid in physically active persons, and the amount of insulin needed significantly reduced.[78] This is reputed to be due to enhanced sensitivity of insulin receptors in skeletal (and adipose) tissue. Obesity and diabetes are two age-related changes that are prevalent in the late climacteric.

Weight training in women has shown that improvement in strength can be obtained with a loss of adipose tissue with relatively little muscle hypertrophy. These studies have involved young women or trained athletes, or both.[79,80] It is not known whether muscle strengthening exercises will enhance the metabolic function of postmenopausal skeletal muscle, and if so to what degree. However, extrapolation from data collected in male subjects suggests that accumulation of greater mass will lead to greater energy expenditure. Strength training does not improve cardiorespiratory function (see Table 12–2), a finding confirmed by studies done in middle-aged men.[81] Weight training stresses muscles far more than most aerobic exercises. It is safe to start an aerobic exercise program and then, many months later, to start lifting weights.

## Exercise and Osteoarthrosis

The articular cartilage that covers the bone ends in joints is rich in collagen and the mucopolysaccharide proteoglycan. This collagen layer acts as a barrier preventing the leakage of proteoglycan from the deeper layers into the joint space, and at the same time inhibits potential harmful enzymes in the synovial fluid from perfusing into the deeper cartilage.[82] Loss or damage of the cartilage layer leads to joint degeneration and the development of osteoarthritis.

Osteoarthritis is a highly prevalent disease: 86 percent of women over the age of 65 show radiologic evidence of the condition,[83] although only 25 to 30 percent of individuals with diagnosed osteoarthritis are symptomatic. There are conflicting opinions regarding the role of microtrauma to the joint surface in the pathogenesis of osteoarthritis. Impulse loading causes trabecular microfracture with subsequent healing by sclerosis, resulting in a stiffened bone that increases the stress on the articular cartilage with eventual damage to the cartilage and joint degeneration. These changes appear on roentgenogram as osteophytes, sclerosis of the subchondrial bone, cyst formation, and narrowing of the joint space.

Postmenopausal women have decreased amounts of collagen in skin and bone,[84] and it is most likely that the same is true for the collagen content of their articular surfaces. The collagen in the skin (and possibly also in the bone) of postmenopausal women is responsive to estrogen replacement. Although arthralgia is a common symptom in the late climacteric, a direct linkage between the menopause and joint disease has not been established. However, a recent study has demonstrated that noncontraceptive hormonal therapy does help some women with rheumatoid arthritis.[85] With the increased interest in jogging, the inevitable question arises, regarding whether damage to the musculo-skeletal-articular system exceeds the benefit of exercise. Lane and associates[86] recently studied female long-distance runners over age 50 and compared them with age-matched nonactive community controls. The female runners did have more sclerosis and spur formation in the weight-bearing areas of the spine and knees, but not in the hands. These changes were not found in men studied in the same and other investigations.[87]

Given the asymptomatic nature of these changes and the difficulty of extrapolating cross-sectional data into "real-life" terms, it cannot be concluded that jogging has an adverse affect on the joints of middle-aged women. Notice should be taken, however, of the absence of joint changes in age-matched and hormone-replete men and the possibility that an estrogen-primed articular surface (with an improved collagen content) might be similarly resilient to mechanical stress.

## EXERCISE AND WELL-BEING

Administration of exogenous estrogens to postmenopausal women is frequently associated with a mood-elevating effect. This is especially true for women receiving parenteral estrogen therapy. Exercise is also known to induce a state of well-being and, according to some studies, a reduction in symptoms such as depression and anxiety. The early work of Weber and Lee[88] demonstrated that vigorous activity in animals had a positive influence on psychologic measures and that this was probably due to alterations in brain neurotransmitter levels or to activity, or both.[89] Studies in humans have been less clear, and there are some who question that the "runner's high" really exists.[90]

Part of the controversy lies in the fact that much of the research has been conducted in nondepressed subjects. Greist and colleagues[91] demonstrated that aerobic exercise performed for 12 weeks reduced depression (in patients complaining of mild to moderate depression) to a greater degree than traditional psychotherapy. Additional advantages noted by the authors included persistence of a depression-free state when evaluated 12 months later, whereas half of the patients receiving psychotherapy returned earlier for additional treatment; less expense; and no need to use antidepressant medication.

One of the most distressing symptoms expressed by menopausal women is anxiety.

Vigorous physical activity reduces muscle tension and is also associated with a significant decrease in anxiety.[92] This effect was, however, noted only when the exercise was intense enough to provoke significant elevations in plasma epinephrine and norepinephrine[93] and did not occur if light to moderate exercise was performed.

Another common problem associated with the menopausal syndrome—insomnia—may be positively influenced by exercise. Healthy subjects who engaged in static exercise (e.g., contraction of a hand dynamometer at 40 percent of maximal level for 40 minutes, separated by a 10-minute rest at midsession) 2 hours before bedtime were shown to have a significantly reduced time to onset of sleep relative to nonexercise nights. The improvement in sleep was associated with increased slow-wave sleep and decreased movement time during sleep, factors that contribute to a "refreshing" sleep period.[94] In summary, although the chemical basis of the mood improvement induced by physical activity is not known, there is fairly strong evidence that acute and chronic vigorous exercise is associated with an improvement in affective states, especially in individuals who show signs of anxiety and moderate depression.

To evaluate the effect of exercise on psychologic well-being, preprogram and postprogram psychosocial measures were obtained by questionnaire and standardized tests in a group of healthy women (age 40 to 64 years) participating in a 12-week exercise program. Methods of evaluation included a self-report of physical activity, a somatization scale, the multidimensional health locus of control inventory, the Profile of Mood States Scale, and a social support questionnaire. The exercised group were required to walk-jog for 30 minutes three times a week for 12 weeks, and they were compared with matched women participating in discussion groups and a nonintervention control group. The only noted apparent benefit of exercise was a decrease in intake of stimulants (e.g., coffee) among exercisers, whereas there was an increase in intake among the nonexercisers. These results are similar to the report of Penny and Rust,[95] whose subjects participated in a walk-jog program involving 1½ miles of exercise twice a week for 15 weeks. Comparison of personality scales measured

**Table 12–7.** CHANGES IN PERCEPTUAL SPEED* ASSOCIATED
WITH CHRONOLOGIC AND BIOLOGIC AGING IN WOMEN

|  | Menstruating | | Nonmenstruating | | |
|---|---|---|---|---|---|
| Age range | 30–45 | 46–55 | 46–55 | 56–65 | 66–75 |
| Mean age | 40.9 ± 5 | 48.7 ± 0.4 | 52.2 ± 0.4 | 59.3 ± 0.5 | 68.5 ± 0.5 |
| N | 30 | 29 | 30 | 29 | 27 |
| Perceptual speed | 64.4 ± 2.1 | 61.1 ± 1.9 | 56.6 ± 1.8 | 55.3 ± 1.3 | 48.0 ± 2.6 |
| p <0.0001 | r = −0.41 | | | | |

*Seconds.
From Notelovitz et al,[51] with permission.

by the MMPI showed no difference from a control nonexercising group. Despite these negative results, discussions with individuals who exercised elicited commonly observed responses: "feeling better, enjoying social functions more, participating in more extracurricular activities, and not being tired at day's end."[95] I have noted these observations in discussion with subjects participating in an ongoing exercise study. The operative factors appear to be frequency, intensity and duration of exercise, and patience. The last is most important, as the benefits of exercise rarely occur before 10 weeks of training, the time when most individuals drop out of exercise programs.

Psychomotor speed is one well-recognized behavior that is slowed by aging. This is especially true for response speed that occurs in reaction time, performance of tasks that require the coordination of two simultaneous movements, writing speed, and simple tasks such as tapping in place.[96] Perceptual speed was evaluated in healthy aging women as part of a larger study examining age-related changes (Table 12–7), and a progressive decrease was noted with both chronologic and biologic aging.[51] The perceptual speed in 40-year-old menstruating women decreased from a mean value of 64.4 ± 2.1 seconds to 48.0 ± 2.6 seconds in 68-year-old women (p <0.0001; r = −0.41). An interesting observation was the decrease in the perceptual speed of menstruating and nonmenstruating women between the ages of 46 and 55. Although the menstruating women were slightly younger (mean age 48.7 ± 0.4 versus 52.2 ± 0.4 year), the perceptual speed was significantly lower than in the nonmenstruating group and similar to that of women 5 or more years since their menopause. Fur-

5 or more years since their menopause. Further analysis of these data revealed that within the groups physical fitness was positively correlated with perceptual speed. The greater the degree of fitness, the more functionally competent the individual.[51]

This raises the issue of whether exercise may prevent premature aging of the central nervous system and compensate for possible alterations in the neurohormonal milieu of postmenopausal women. A number of investigators have shown that people who exercise consistently have a faster reaction time and that this is related to generalized rather than specific exercise. For example, the reactive speed of fingers is improved in runners who primarily exercise their legs.[97] It is not clear whether this exercise-induced improvement is due to CNS processing time or motor speed. As with the psychologic response to exercise, CNS function (e.g., short-term memory) that is not impaired in a particular individual cannot be expected to be improved by exercise. With this caveat in mind, it is fair to conclude that "exercise seems to be one way for people to achieve maximal plasticity in aging, approximating full vigor and consistency of performance until life's end."[97]

## SUMMARY

The "menopause," an often-misused term, is actually the duration of a woman's final menstrual period. The 15-year time period leading up to and following this event is known more properly as the "climacteric."

Women lose a small percentage of bone as a natural phenomenon in the aging process. However, the greater the bone mineral content at bone mass maturity, the more one can afford to lose. Thus, women should be encouraged during, and even before, the early climacteric to accrue as much bone as possible, through an appropriate calcium intake and an osteogenic exercise program. Likewise, such practices can be used to avoid excessive bone loss during the climacteric.

For women who have osteoporosis, a regimen of walking may be the safest type of exercise program. These women should avoid exercises that emphasize flexion of the back.

The postmenopausal period has been associated with an increased plasma cholesterol level and a decreased HDL level—both risk factors for atherosclerotic disease. Physical activity in the form of a regular and long-term exercise program can increase HDL levels, as well as improving $\dot{V}_{O_2max}$, in perimenopausal women.

Exercise also adds to a feeling of well-being and may counteract clinical depression and anxiety experienced by some women in this stage of life.

## References

1. Jaszman LJB: Epidemiology of the climacteric syndrome. In Campbell S (ed): The Management of the Menopause and Postmenopausal Years. University Book Press, Baltimore, 1976, p 11.
2. Notelovitz M: Climacteric medicine and science: A societal need. In Notelovitz M, and van Keep P (eds): The Climacteric in Perspective. MTP Press Ltd, Lancaster, England, 1986, p 19.
3. Lewinnek G, Kelsey J, White A, et al: Significance and comparative analysis of the epidemiology of hip fractures. Clin Orthop 152:35, 1980.
4. Keene JS, and Anderson CA: Hip fractures in the elderly, discharge predictions with a functional rating scale. JAMA 248:564, 1982.
5. Cummings SR, Kelsy JS, Nevitt MC, et al: Epidemiology of osteoporosis and osteoporotic fractures. Epidemiol Rev 7:178, 1985.
6. Heart Facts, 1984. Dallas, American Heart Association, 1983, quoted in Intersociety Commission for Heart Disease Resources, Circulation 70:154A, 1984.
7. Gordon T, Kannel WB, Hjortland MC, et al: Menopause and coronary heart disease, Framingham Study. Ann Intern Med 89:157, 1978.
8. Council on Scientific Affairs: Exercise programs for the elderly. JAMA 252:544, 1984.
9. Health United States, US Dept of Health and Human Services, DHHS Pub No (PHS) 85-1232, 1984.
10. Cohn SH, Abesamis C, Yasumura S, et al: Comparative skeletal mass and radial bone mineral content in black and white women. Metabolism 26:171, 1977.
11. Parfitt AM: The cellular basis of bone remodelling: The quantum concept re-examined in light of re-

cent advances in cell biology of bone. Calcif Tissue Int 36:S37, 1984.
12. Katz JL, Yoon HS, Lipson S, et al: The effects of remodelling on the elastic properties of bone. Calcif Tissue Int 36:531, 1984.
13. De Deuxchaisnes C, Nagant: The pathogenesis and treatment of involutional osteoporosis. In Dixon AHJ, Russel RGG, and Stamp TCB (eds): Osteoporosis: A Multidisciplinary Problem. The Royal Society of Medicine. Academic Press, London, 1983, p 291.
14. Drinkwater BL, Nilson K, Chesnut III C, et al: Bone mineral content of amenorrheic and eumenorrheic athletes. N Engl J Med 311:277, 1984.
15. Riggs BL, Wahner HW, Dunn WL, et al: Differential changes in bone mineral density of appendicular and axial skeleton with aging: Relationship to spinal osteoporosis. J Clin Invest 67:328, 1981.
16. Editorial: Osteoporosis and activity. Lancet 2:1365, 1983.
17. Whedon GC: Interrelation of physical activity and nutrition on bone mass. In White PL, and Mondeika T (eds): Diet and Exercise: Synergism in Health Maintenance. American Medical Association, Chicago, 1982, p 99.
18. Basset CA, and Becker RO: Generation of electric potentials by bone in response to mechanical stress. Science 137:1063, 1962.
19. Jones HH, Priest JD, Hayes WC, et al: Humeral hypertrophy in response to exercise. J Bone Joint Surg 59A:204, 1977.
20. Carter DR: Mechanical loading histories of bone remodelling. Calcif Tissue Int 36:S19, 1984.
21. Lanyon LE: Functional strain as a determinant for bone remodelling. Calcif Tissue Int 36:S56, 1984.
22. Lanyon LE, and Rubin CT: Regulation of bone mass in response to physical activity. In Dixon AHJ, Russel RGG, and Stamp TCB (eds): Osteoporosis: A Multidisciplinary Problem. The Royal Society of Medicine. Academic Press, London, p 51, 1983.
23. Woo SLY, Kuei SC, Amiel D, et al: The effect of prolonged physical training on the properties of long bone. J Bone Joint Surg 63A:780, 1980.
24. Yeater RA, and Martin RB: Senile osteoporosis: The effect of exercise. Postgrad Med 75:147, 1984.
25. Krølner B, Toft B, Nielsen SP, et al: Physical exercise as prophylaxis against involutional vertebral bone loss: A controlled trial. Clin Sci 64:541, 1983.
26. Brewer V, Meyer BM, Keele MJ, et al: Role of exercise in prevention of involutional bone loss. Med Sci Sports Exerc 15:445, 1983.
27. Linnell J, Stager JM, Blue PW, et al: Bone mineral content and menstrual regularity in female runners. Med Sci Sports Exerc 16:343, 1984.
28. Rigotti NA, Nussbaum SR, Herzog DR, et al: Osteoporosis in women with anorexia nervosa. N Engl J Med 311:1601, 1984.
29. Notelovitz M, et al: Unpublished data, 1986.
30. Chvapil M, Bartos D, and Bartos F: Effect of long-term physical stress on collagen growth in the lung, heart and femur of young and adult rats. Gerontologia 19:263, 1973.
31. Inkovaara J, Heikinheimo R, Jarvinen K, et al: Prophylactic fluoride treatment and aged bones. Br Med J 3:73, 1975.
32. Smith EL, Reddan W, and Smith PE: Physical activity and calcium modalities for bone mineral in-

crease in aged women. Med Sci Sports Exerc 13:60, 1981.

33. Sinaki M, and Mikkelsen BA: Postmenopausal spinal osteoporosis: Flexion versus extension exercises. Arch Phys Med Rehabil 65:593, 1984.

34. Goodman CE: Osteoporosis: Protective measures of nutrition and exercise. Geriatrics 40:59, 1985.

35. Rosenberg L, Hennekens CH, Rosner B, et al: Early menopause and the risk of myocardial infarction. Am J Obstet Gynecol 139:47, 1981.

36. Szajderman B, and Oliver MF: Spontaneous premature menopause, ischemic heart disease and serum lipids. Lancet 1:962, 1963.

37. Robinson RW, Higano N, and Cohen WD: Increased incidence of coronary heart disease in women castrated prior to menopause. Arch Intern Med 104:908, 1959.

38. Heller RF, and Jacobs HJ: Coronary heart disease in relation to age, sex and the menopause. Br Med J 1:472, 1978.

39. Lindquist O, Bengtsson C, and Lapidus L: Menopausal age and risk of cardiovascular disease and death. Acta Obstet Gynecol Scand Suppl 130:37, 1985.

40. Bengtsson C, and Lindquist O: Menopausal effects on risk factors for ischemic heart disease. Maturitas 1:165, 1979.

41. Miller G, and Miller N: Plasma high density lipoprotein concentration and development of ischaemic heart disease. Lancet 1:16, 1975.

42. Haskell WL: The influence of exercise on the concentrations of triglyceride and cholesterol in human plasma. In Terjung RL (ed): Exercise and Sports Sciences Reviews. Collamore Press, Lexington, MA, 1984, p 205.

43. Paffenbarger RS, Hyde RT, Wing AL, et al: A natural history of athleticism on cardiovascular health. JAMA 252:491, 1984.

44. Salonen JT, Puska R, and Tuomilehto J: Physical activity and risk of myocardial infarction, cerebral stroke and death: A longitudinal study in eastern Finland. Am J Epidemiol 115:526, 1982.

45. Leon S: Exercise and risk of coronary heart disease in exercise and health. The American Academy of Physical Education Papers, No. 17. Human Kinetic Publishers, Champaign, IL, 1984, p 14.

46. Haskell WL, and Superko R: Designing an exercise plan for optimal health. Family and Community Health, May 1984, p 72.

47. Kilborn A: Physical training in women. Scand J Clin Lab Invest 28(Suppl 119):1, 1971.

48. Wood P, and Haskell W: The effect of exercise on plasma high-density lipoproteins. Lipids 14:417, 1979.

49. Goffman J, Young W, and Tandy R: Ischemic heart disease, atherosclerosis and longevity. Circulation 34:679, 1966.

50. Jacobs I, Lithell H, and Karlson J: Dietary effects on glycogen and lipoprotein lipase activity in skeletal muscle of men. Acta Physiol Scand 115:85, 1982.

51. Notelovitz M, Dougherty M, Resnick J, et al: The psychosocial and biologic adaptation to aging in women. Final Report NIA #R01 AG00796-03, 1982.

52. Busby J, Notelovitz M, Putney K, et al: Exercise, high density lipoprotein cholesterol and cardiorespiratory function in climacteric women. South Med J 78:769, 1985.

53. Franklin B, Buskirk E, Hodgson J, et al: Effects of physical conditioning on cardiorespiratory function, body composition and serum lipids in relatively normal weight and obese middle-aged women. Int J Obes 3:97, 1979.

54. Rotkis T, Boyden TW, Pamenter RW, et al: High density lipoprotein cholesterol and body composition of female runners. Metabolism 30:994, 1981.

55. Moore CE, Hartung GH, Mitchell RE, et al: The effect of exercise and diet on high-density lipoprotein cholesterol levels in women. Metabolism 32:189, 1983.

56. Vodak PA, Wood PD, Haskell WL, et al: HDL-cholesterol and other plasma lipid and lipoprotein concentrations in middle-aged male and female tennis players. Metabolism 29:745, 1980.

57. Harting GH, Moore CE, Mitchell R, et al: Relationship of menopausal status and exercise level to HDL cholesterol in women. Exp Aging Res 10:13, 1984.

58. Drinkwater B, Horvath S, and Wells C: Aerobic power of females ages 10 to 68. J Gerontol 30:385, 1975.

59. Plowman S, Drinkwater B, and Horvath S: Age and aerobic power in women: A longitudinal study. J Gerontol 34:512, 1979.

60. Notelovitz M, Fields C, Caramelli K, et al: Cardiorespiratory fitness evaluation in climacteric women: Comparison of two methods. Am J Obstet Gynecol 154:1009, 1986.

61. De Vries HA: Exercise and the physiology of aging. In De Vries HA: Exercise and Health. American Academy of Physical Education Papers, No. 17, Human Kinetics Publishers, Champaign, IL, 1984, p 76.

62. Zauner C, Notelovitz M, Fields CD, et al: Cardiorespiratory efficiency at submaximal work in young and middle-aged women. Am J Obstet Gynecol 150:712, 1984.

63. Dehn MM, and Bruce RA: Longitudinal variations in maximum oxygen intake with age and activity. J Appl Physiol 33:805, 1972.

64. Åstrand I: Aerobic work capacity in men and women with special reference to age. Acta Physiol (Scand) 49:45, 1960.

65. Cowan MC, and Gregory LW: Responses of pre- and postmenopausal females to aerobic conditioning. Med Sci Sports Exerc 17:138, 1985.

66. White MK, Yenter RA, Martin RB, et al: Effects of aerobic dancing and walking on cardiovascular function and muscular strength in postmenopausal women. J Sports Med 24:159, 1984.

67. Gill AA, Veigl VL, Shuster J, et al: A well-woman's health maintenance study comparing physical fitness and group support programs. Occ Ther J Res 4:286, 1984.

68. Notelovitz M, Fields C, Caramelli K, et al: Alternatives to hormone therapy. Presented at XIth World Congress of Obstetrics and Gynecology, October, 1985.

69. Profant GR, Early RG, Nilson KL, et al: Response to maximal exercise in healthy middle-aged women. J Appl Physiol 33:595, 1972.

70. Bruce RA, DeRouen TA, and Hossack KF: Pilot study examining the motivational effects of maximal exercise testing to modify risk factors and health habits. Cardiology 66:111, 1980.

71. Glassford RG, Baycroft GHY, Sedgwick AW, et al:

Comparison of maximal oxygen uptake values determined by predicted and actual methods. J Appl Physiol 20:509, 1965.

72. Cink RE, and Thomas TR: Validity of the Åstrand-Rhyming Monogram for Predicting Maximal Oxygen Uptake. Br J Sports Med 15:182, 1981.72.

73. Schoenfeld Y, Keven G, Shimoni I, et al: Walking. A method for rapid improvement of physical fitness. JAMA 243:2062, 1980.

74. Caramelli KE, and Notelovitz M: Effect of load-bearing during treadmill walking in women aged 57 to 67 years (abstr). Maturitas 6:95, 1984.

75. Fisher MB, and Birren JE: Age and strength. J Appl Psychol 31:490, 1947.

76. Montoye HJ, and Lamphiear DE: Grip and arm strength in males and females age 10–69. Res Q 48:109, 1977.

77. Tzanoff SP, and Norris AH: Effect of muscle mass decrease on age-related BMR changes. J Appl Physiol 43:1001, 1973.

78. Joman VR, Veikko AK, Deibert D, et al: Increased insulin sensitivity and insulin binding to monocytes after physical training. N Engl J Med 301:200, 1979.

79. Wells JB, Jokl E, and Bohanen J: The effect of intensive physical training upon body composition of adolescent girls. J Assoc Phys Mental Rehab 17:68, 1963.

80. Brown CH, and Wilmore JH: The effects of maximal resistance training on strength and body composition of women athletes. Med Sci Sports Exerc 6:174, 1974.

81. Hurley BF, Seals AA, Ehsani AA, et al: Effects of high-intensity strength training on cardiovascular function. Med Sci Sports Exerc 16:483, 1984.

82. Bullough PG: Pathologic changes associated with the common arthritides and their treatment. Pathol Ann 14:69, 1979.

83. Gordon T: Osteoarthritis in U.S. adults. In Bennett BH, and Wood PHN (eds): Population Studies in the Rheumatic Diseases. Excerpta Medica, New York, 1968, p 391.

84. Brincat M, Moniz CT, Studd JWW, et al: Skin thickness and skin collagen mimic an index of osteoporosis in the postmenopausal woman. In Christiansen C, Arnaud CD, Nordin BEC, et al (eds): Osteoporosis. Copenhagen International Symposium on Osteoporosis, June 3–8, 1984, p 353.

85. Vandenbroucke JP, Witteman JC, Valkenburg HA, et al: Non-contraceptive hormones and rheumatoid arthritis in perimenopausal and postmenopausal women. JAMA 255:1299, 1986.

86. Lane NE, Bloch DA, Jones HH, et al: Long-distance running, bone density and osteoarthritis. JAMA 255:1147, 1986.

87. Panush RS, Schmidt C, Caldwell JR, et al: Is running associated with degenerative joint disease? JAMA 255:1152, 1986.

88. Weber JC, and Lee RA: Effects of differing pre-puberty exercise programs on the emotionality of male albino rats. Res Q 39:748, 1968.

89. Olson EB Jr, and Morgan WP: Rat brain monoamine levels related to behavioral assessment. Life Sci 30:2095, 1982.

90. Levin DC: The runner's high: Fact or fiction? JAMA 248:24, 1982.

91. Greist JH, Klein MH, Eicchens RR, et al: Running as treatment for depression. Comp Psychiatry 20:41, 1979.

92. Morgan WP: Anxiety reduction following acute physical activity. Psychiatr Ann 9:36, 1979.

93. Morgan WP, Horstman DH, Cymerman A, et al: Facilitation of physical performance by means of cognitive strategy. Cog Ther Res 7:251, 1983.

94. Browman CP: Sleep following sustained exercise. Psychophysiology 17:577, 1980.

95. Penny GD, and Rust JO: Effect of a walking-jogging program on personality characteristics of middle-aged females. J Sports Med 20:221, 1980.

96. Spirduso WW: Exercise as a factor in aging motor behavior plasticity in exercise and health. American Academy of Physical Education Papers, No. 17, Human Kinetics Publishers, Champaign, IL, 1984, p 89.

97. Spirduso WW, and Clifford P: Replication of age and physical activity effects in reaction and movement time. J Gerontol 33:26, 1978.

98. Adams G, and De Vries H: Physiological effects of an exercise training regimen upon women aged 52 to 79. J Gerontol 28:50, 1973.

99. Sidney K, Shephard R, and Harrison J: Endurance training and body composition of the elderly. Am J Clin Nutr 30:326, 1977.

100. Sidney K, and Shephard R: Frequency and intensity of exercise training for elderly subjects. Med Sci Sports Exerc 10:125, 1978.

# PART III

# Special Issues and Concerns

# CHAPTER 13

# The Breast

CHRISTINE E. HAYCOCK, M.D.

Wearing a bra can provide two useful functions during exercise. Padding can be added to help prevent traumatic injuries, such as that from a hockey stick or an elbow. Well-designed bras can provide support and limit breast motion during exercise.[1,2] This can help reduce discomfort and impact of the breast against the anterior chest wall.

There is no evidence that free-swinging breasts are more likely to be damaged during exercise. However, women in primitive cultures who never wear bras do develop long pendulous breasts, whereas those in modern society who frequently wear bras are less likely to develop these changes.

## BREAST SUPPORT

In an effort to ascertain the injury potential for the female athlete in the early 1970s, two surveys were conducted in more than 300 physical education departments throughout the country. The first questionnaire, performed by Joan Gillette, A.T.C., and published in 1975[3] in *The Physician and Sportsmedicine*, asked for the numbers and types of injuries seen by coaches and trainers. I sent out a more detailed questionnaire to cover the 1974–1975 season, with more emphasis on the types of injuries rather than on just the numbers and associated sports. The results of the two surveys were combined and published in *JAMA* in 1976.[4] The surveys indicated that, in general, the types and numbers of injuries to these female athletes were essentially the same as to their male counterparts. Of particular interest to me was the fact that, of all injuries reported, those to the

181

breast were least common. Other studies have confirmed these findings.[5-7]

The results of the earlier surveys prompted me to undertake a third survey,[8] specifically asking if female athletes reported tenderness or soreness in their breasts, or injuries such as scratches from metallic parts or allergies to the materials in their bras. Thirty-one percent of the respondents indicated sore or tender breasts after exercise. Of these, 52 percent reported specific minor injuries to the breasts.

A study was undertaken by Gillette, Shierman, and Haycock[9] to ascertain what factors cause breast injury and discomfort. To determine if a bra is necessary to control breast motion, a test was instituted to measure breast movement during exercise. Twelve female athletes with different breast sizes were fitted with special supportive bras. They were encouraged to use these garments during athletic competition and to note how they compared in comfort and support with the bras they had been using previously. Most of the women felt that the bulky test bras provided better support than their own. The women who benefited the most had size B cups or larger. Five volunteers were filmed with a high-speed (100 frames per minute), 16 mm camera while walking and running on a treadmill and while jumping to simulate the motion of shooting a basketball into the hoop. A marker was placed on each nipple so that line studies made by tracing each frame could be drawn. Each marker was placed either on the bra or on the breast itself, since the athletes were filmed wearing their own bras, wearing the special bras, and with no bras.

The films showed that during running, the breast moves considerably up and down and during jumping, the breasts roll in a spiral motion (Fig. 13–1). Although the force of breast impact upon the chest wall was not measured, it was estimated to be between 60 and 80 foot pounds per square inch, with the largest breasts exerting the greatest force. Although both sets of bras limited motion, the specially fitted ones did the best job, corroborating the increased support and comfort reported by the athletes themselves.

These findings are consistent with the original expectations of the authors. The natural support of the breasts is minimal. The breast is composed mostly of adipose tissue. It is held in place by the skin and some deep

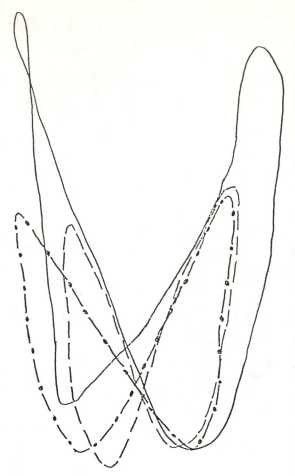

**Figure 13–1.** *The subject wore a size D cup. The solid line* represents the range of motion with no bra; the *dash-dot-dash line,* the subject's own bra, which had fairly good support; the dash line, the *specially fitted bra, showing the best support.*

fascial structures, which loosely attach the glands to the underlying muscles, blood vessels, and nerves. Cooper's ligaments do not support the breasts. They are merely connective tissue strands extending between the skin and the pectoralis fascia and separating the glandular structures.[8] As a result of this study, the following recommendations regarding sports bras can be made:[9]

1. A bra should be made of firm, mostly nonelastic material with good absorptive qualities (about 60 percent cotton plus about 40 percent synthetic materials) for fast drying and easy laundering. More elasticity provides less support.

2. It should be constructed to limit motion in all directions and provide firm sup-

port. There should be either no seams over the nipples or smooth seams that will not irritate.

3. Some provision should exist for insertion of padding, if indicated to reduce the risk of traumatic injury. Obviously, a bra intended only for use during running does not need these features.

4. All metal or plastic hooks or catches should be well covered to protect the wearer from skin irritation or abrasion.[8,10,11] Various types of bras have been studied.[12-16] In the most recent study, Dr. Deana Lorentzen of Utah State University at Logan[17] compared eight of the most popular bras currently on the market. Her findings were in agreement with the previous recommendations and also suggested adding an underwire. Many athletes prefer this type of bra, as do many larger-breasted women, regardless of their exercise habits.

## NIPPLE INJURY

"Runners' nipples" is a condition in which the nipples are irritated, abraded and/or lacerated[18-20] by the rubbing of clothing on the nipple during activity over a prolonged period of time. Any type of rough-surfaced cloth or seam can cause this problem. Male runners can wear Bandaids over their nipples to prevent this from happening to them. Female runners can wear well-designed bras to protect their nipples. An abrasion of the nipple can lead to infection.

Exposure to cold can damage the nipples, too. A combination of moisture from perspiration with evaporation and wind chill can lower nipple temperature to injure the nipples and cause soreness and sensitivity to touch and temperature change. The use of windbreaking material over the chest area helps prevent this type of injury. There is no treatment for cold injury to nipples, except for supportive measures. Athletes should be cautioned to prevent such injury by avoiding cold exposure.[21,22]

## TRAUMA

Blows to the breasts by field hockey sticks, pucks, elbows, kicks, and other objects certainly occur but seldom result in more than mild contusions. This superficial capillary damage may look significant but usually responds well to the simple application of cold for 10 to 20 minutes. Edema and ecchymosis gradually resolve within weeks.

A severe blow to the breast may cause a hematoma owing to subcutaneous bleeding from deeper vessels. Hemostasis usually is attained spontaneously, and most breast hematomas resolve spontaneously too. A breast hematoma should be evacuated only if accompanied by increasing pain, increasing size, or possible infection. If a fibrous nodule remains after resolution or evacuation of a hematoma, its removal may be necessary.

There is no evidence that trauma to the breast causes cancer.[23-25] However, breast injury usually leads to careful examination, and previously undetected masses are more likely to be appreciated as a result of more careful scrutiny.

## BREAST AUGMENTATION AND REDUCTION

Cosmetic surgery involving either augmentation or reduction of the breast can cause special problems. Following breast augmentation, a swimmer was unable to swim at her previous freestyle speed despite regaining all her previous skills and strength and regaining her previous backstroke speed. Her larger breasts increased her resistance against the water. She was able to accept this loss of speed because she felt an increase in her breast size from 32A to 34B more than compensated psychologically. However, a more competitive swimmer probably would not have been content to sacrifice speed for the emotional benefit of a more personally satisfying appearance.[26] Dr. K. Barthels of California showed that simulated augmentation of the breasts slowed swimmers with specific heights and weights but did not slow others.[27]

Athletes in contact sports probably should not undergo breast augmentation. Blunt chest trauma can cause rupture of the prosthesis, with resultant hemorrhage and deformity of the breasts.[28]

There are no studies to show whether a reduction in breast size improves swim speed in large-breasted swimmers, but this possibility has been suggested.[27] Theoretically, breast reduction might improve the performance of large-breasted athletes, particularly those in nonaquatic endurance sports. Several top track coaches feel that large-breasted women do not perform as well as small-breasted women in running events. This impression remains anecdotal and unconfirmed and, if real, may relate to carrying less fat weight as well as having altered contours and resistance factors.

## PREGNANCY

Physiologic breast enlargement during pregnancy has not been shown to hinder athletic performance, which usually declines during pregnancy, particularly for sports requiring speed. It is impossible to isolate the effects of breast enlargement, abdominal enlargement, weight gain, altered center of gravity, and hormonal changes in determining causal relationships. A good supporting bra is certainly useful to the pregnant exerciser.[29]

## PREMENSTRUAL CHANGES AND FIBROCYSTIC BREASTS

Many female athletes experience breast discomfort premenstrually. This may be reduced by wearing a supportive bra and by taking bromocriptine or danazol orally, if indicated. Premenstrual mastalgia may also occur in women who have fibrocystic changes. About 50 percent of women have some clinical evidence of this process. No specific therapy has proven effective, although some investigators have advocated reduction of methylxanthine consumption or administration of vitamin E or of danazol.[30-32] (See Chapter 14 for additional discussion.) A supportive bra is helpful for these women, too. In addition to wearing it during exercise, athletes with nocturnal discomfort may find it helpful to wear it while sleeping as well.

Any breast masses should be evaluated with mammography and probably also sonography. Diagnostic needle aspiration of breast cysts may be therapeutic. If a cyst resolves completely following aspiration, biopsy is not necessary. Persistence of a cyst following attempted needle aspiration requires excisional biopsy for diagnosis. All athletes should practice breast self-examination on a monthly basis. This is best performed at the end of menses, when palpable

physiologic changes from hormonal influence are minimal.

## EXERCISE FOLLOWING TRAUMA OR SURGERY

Appendix A discusses appropriate return to exercise following various types of breast surgery as well as trauma.

## SUMMARY

The subject of breast problems in the female athlete can at times be one of serious import to the participant, but usually it falls more into the category of a nuisance to performance, when size and resultant discomfort are a factor. Trauma and tumors are responsible for the more disturbing conditions.

The use of good supporting bras for the large-breasted athlete is certainly indicated and can make athletic events for these individuals more enjoyable. The role of cosmetic surgery is best relegated to the postathletic phase of life.

## References

1. Haycock C: Supportive bras for jogging. Med Aspects Hum Sexuality 14(3):6, 1980.
2. Haycock C: The female athlete and sportsmedicine in the 70's. J Florida M A 67(4):411, 1980.
3. Gillette J: When and where women are injured in sports. The Physician and Sportsmedicine 3(5):61, 1975.
4. Haycock C, and Gillette J: Susceptibility of women athletes to injury: myths vs reality. JAMA 236(2):163, 1976.
5. Whiteside PA: Men's and women's injuries in comparable sports. The Physician and Sportsmedicine 8(3):130, 1980.
6. Eisenberg I, and Allen WC: Injuries in a women's varsity athletic program. The Physician and Sportsmedicine 6(3):112, 1978.
7. Zelisko JA, Noble B, and Porter M: A comparison of men's and women's professional basketball injuries. Am J Sports Med 10(5):297, 1982.
8. Haycock C: A need to know: joggers breast pain. Response. The Physician and Sportsmedicine 7(8):27, 1979.
9. Haycock C, Shierman G, and Gillette J: The female athlete—does her anatomy pose problems? Proceedings of the 19th Conference on the Medical Aspects of Sports, AMA, 1978.
10. Haycock CE: Breast support and protection in the female athlete. AAHPER Research Consortium Symposium Papers 1(2):50, 1978.
11. Report: Female athletes need good bras. MD reports. The Physician and Sportsmedicine 5(15):15, 1978.
12. Bayne JD: Pro+ Tec Protective Bra. J Sports Med Phys Fitness 8(1):34, 1968.
13. Hunter L: The bra controversy: Are sports bras a ne-

cessity? The Physician and Sportsmedicine 10(11):75, 1982.

14. Gehlsen G, and Albohm M: Evaluation of sports bras. The Physician and Sportsmedicine 8(10):89, 1980.

15. Schuster K: Equipment update: jogging bras hit the streets. The Physician and Sportsmedicine 7(4):125, 1979.

16. Survey: Women marathoners describe bra needs. The Physician and Sportsmedicine 5(12):12, 1977.

17. Lorentzen D, and Lawson L: Selected sports bras: a biomechanical analysis of breast motion while jogging. The Physician and Sportsmedicine 15(5):128, 1987.

18. Levit F: Jogger's nipples. N Engl J Med 297(20):1127, 1977.

19. Cohen HJ: Jogger's petechiae. N Engl J Med 279:109, 1968.

20. Corrigan AB, and Fitch KD: Complications of jogging. Med J Aust 2(2):363, 1972.

21. Powell B: Bicyclist's nipples. JAMA 29(18):2457, 1983.

22. Adrian MJ: Proper clothing and equipment. In Haycock CE (ed): Sports Medicine for the Athletic Female. Medical Economics Book Div, Oradell, NJ, 1980, p 61.

23. Karon SE: Medical testimony in a trauma and breast cancer case, showing the direct and cross-examina-tions of the plaintiff's internist and the defendant pathologist. Med Trial Tech Q 13:361, 1967.

24. Stevens M: Traumatic breast cancer. Med Trial Tech Q 25(1):1, 1978.

25. Dziob JS: Trauma and breast cancer, or the anatomy of an insurance claim. RI Med J 63:37, 1980.

26. Levine NS, and Buchanan RT: Decreased swimming speed following augmentation mammaplasty. Plast Reconstr Surg 71(2):255, 1983.

27. Barthels KM: Discussion—decreased swimming speed following augmentation mammoplasty. Plast Reconstr Surg 71(2):257, 1983.

28. Dellon AL: Blunt chest trauma: evaluation of the augmented breast. J Trauma 20(11):982, 1980.

29. Shangold M: Gynecological and endocrinological factors. In Haycock C (ed): Sports Medicine and the Athletic Female. Medical Economics Book Div, Oradell, NJ, 1980.

30. Minton JP, Abou-Isaa H, Reiches, N, et al: Clinical and biochemical studies on methyl-xanthine related fibrocystic breast disease. Surgery 90:301, 1981.

31. Ernster VL, Mason L, Goodson WH, et al: Effects of caffeine-free diet on benign breast disease: a randomized trial. Surgery 91:263, 1982.

32. London RS, Sundaram GS, Schultz M, et al: Endocrine parameters and $\alpha$-tocopherol therapy of patients with mammary dysplasia. Cancer Res 41:3811, 1981.

# CHAPTER 14

# Gynecologic Concerns in Exercise and Training

MONA M. SHANGOLD, M.D.

CONTRACEPTION
DYSMENORRHEA
ENDOMETRIOSIS
PREMENSTRUAL SYNDROME
FERTILITY
STRESS URINARY INCONTINENCE
POSTOPERATIVE TRAINING AND
   RECOVERY
EFFECT OF MENSTRUAL CYCLE ON
   PERFORMANCE

Athletic women have many concerns about the effects of regular training upon various gynecologic conditions, the effects of various gynecologic conditions and their treatment upon exercise performance, and the effects of endogenous and exogenous hormones upon exercise and health parameters. Menstrual and hormonal changes associated with exercise and training have been discussed comprehensively in Chapter 10. This chapter will address what is known about other gynecologic concerns of the athlete, including contraception, dysmenorrhea, premenstrual syndrome, fertility, stress urinary incontinence, and cyclic changes in exercise performance.

## CONTRACEPTION

Although oral contraceptives have been reported to be the most popular form of contraception among American women,[1] two surveys have found that runners prefer diaphragm use.[2,3] In a survey of the 1841 women who entered the 1979 New York City Marathon, Shangold and Levine[2] reported that 37 percent of the 394 respondents were diaphragm users, while only 6 percent were oral contraceptive users. Jarrett and Spellacy[3] surveyed runners through a newspaper advertisement and found that 44 percent of the 70 respondents used diaphragms, while only 13 percent used oral contraceptives. Thus, based on these survey data, it seems that at the time of these studies runners preferred the diaphragm over any other form of contraception.

Many women are concerned about side effects and complications associated with oral contraceptive use, and such fears have undoubtedly limited the use of these agents. However, most of the reported and publicized side effects and complications were associated with higher-dose pills than are generally prescribed now. Studies have shown that the low-dose pills, each containing 30 to 35 micrograms of ethinyl estradiol, are much safer than the pills containing 50 or more micrograms of ethinyl estradiol, offering reductions in cardiovascular and thromboembolic risks. Many of the adverse effects of oral contraceptives on thrombosis, arterial disease, and lipid and carbohydrate metabolism are related to the progestin content of the pill.[4-8] As described in an excellent review article by Mishell,[9] despite the detrimental effects associated with steroid contraceptives, women who take these agents actually have reduced incidence of heavy bleeding, irregular bleeding, endometrial cancer, several types of benign breast disease, ovarian carcinoma, rheumatoid arthritis, and salpingitis, compared with women who do not take oral contraceptives.

Low-dose oral contraceptive agents were first introduced in 1973 and have grown in availability since then. They are probably used more widely now than at the time of the surveys cited. Progestin-only pills were first marketed in 1973 and were intended for those women for whom estrogen is contraindicated; these pills have a high incidence of break-through bleeding, and their use is rarely indicated. Oral contraceptive agents containing less than 30 micrograms of estrogen also have a high incidence of break-through bleeding and are poorly tolerated by most women as a result. Biphasic preparations were first introduced in 1982 and were followed by the introduction of triphasic preparations in 1984. In these pills, the doses of progestin, and occasionally of estrogen, are different on different days. These newest agents have not been proven to offer consistent advantages over the standard (monophasic) pills containing 30 to 35 micrograms of estrogen and seem to lead to more breakthrough bleeding and confusion at this time.

Because of the beneficial effects of endurance training upon some parameters affected adversely by oral contraceptives (e.g., coagulation, lipid metabolism, and carbohydrate metabolism), several investigators have studied the combined effects of exercise and oral contraceptives on these variables.

Oral contraceptives are associated with a number of changes in coagulation and fibrinolytic factors in both sedentary and trained women. Plasma plasminogen activator, which converts plasminogen to plasmin, is increased by oral contraceptive use and is further increased by exercise.[10] Huisveld and co-workers[11] reported that oral contraceptive users have increased total plasminogen and free plasminogen levels, increased factor XII and decreased C1-inactivator and increased factor XII–dependent fibrinolytic activity, higher activity levels of normal euglobulin fraction-fibrinolytic activity and extrinsic (tissue-type) plasminogen activator, and decreased urokinase-like fibrinolytic activator activity. Hedlin and associates[12] confirmed the increased fibrinolytic activity induced by exercise or oral contraceptive use or both, and they have also shown that exercise raises antithrombin III activity, whereas oral contraceptive use lowers it. In this study, the hemostatic change induced by oral contraceptives was offset by exercise. It is probable that exercise and training offset any net tendency toward increased coagulability induced by oral contraceptive use.

Powell and colleagues[13] demonstrated that several different oral contraceptive agents alter lipoprotein lipid levels adversely, raising total triglyceride, total cholesterol, and low-density lipoprotein (LDL) cholesterol significantly. However, the report by Gray and co-workers[14] showed that runners taking oral contraceptives have lipid profiles similar to those of runners taking no hormonal medication, suggesting that exercise may offset the adverse effects of oral contraceptive agents upon lipid levels.

In view of the many beneficial effects known about oral contraceptive use, it remains unclear why these agents are not chosen by more female athletes. It is likely that many avoid using them because of unfounded fears based on reported side effects of the higher dose oral contraceptive agents (containing 50 micrograms or more of estrogen). However, the weight gain, bloating, depression, and mood changes associated with higher dosages are uncommon with pills containing less than 50 micrograms of estrogen. The two major side effects associated with use of the lower dose agents are break-through bleeding (i.e., bleeding on the days of hormone ingestion) and amenorrhea (i.e., lack of withdrawal bleeding at the end of each hormone cycle). Each of these is a nuisance, but not of serious consequence. Break-through bleeding may resolve spontaneously within three cycles; if it does not, it may resolve with additional hormone therapy, either transiently or permanently. Amenorrhea rarely resolves spontaneously but usually resolves with transient or permanent ingestion of additional estrogen or less progestin.

Intrauterine contraceptive devices were associated with an increased prevalence of menorrhagia (heavy menstrual bleeding) and dysmenorrhea (painful menstruation), each of which could impair athletic performance. Since nearly all of these devices are no longer available, they are not discussed here.

The choice of an optimal contraceptive agent for any athlete rarely should be affected by exercise habits but should include consideration of medical history and lifestyle. Women who have coitus once weekly or less frequently probably should not take synthetic hormones daily for contraception, unless there is some other indication for their use (e.g., hormone deficiency or treatment of acne or hirsutism). It is reasonable for women who have coitus twice weekly or more frequently to use oral contraceptives, unless there is some contraindication to their use (see Tables 10–5 and 10–6.) Oral contraceptives have not been shown to alter athletic performance.

Mechanical methods of contraception are acceptable for all women who are motivated and reliable enough to use them. Diaphragms and condoms are more effective when used in combination with contraceptive foam or jelly. The sponge is no more effective than the diaphragm and has been reported to be associated with more local irritation and other side effects. The main disadvantages of mechanical (barrier) methods of contraception are their messiness, inconvenience, and disruption of sexual activity. Since athletes tend to be motivated and disciplined, these deterrents are usually considered minor. However, leakage of vaginal contraceptive jellies or foams during exercise may be uncomfortable. When added to vag-

**Table 14–1.** FIRST-YEAR FAILURE RATES OF BIRTH CONTROL METHODS

| Method | Lowest Observed Failure Rate* (%) | Failure Rate in Typical Users* (%) |
|---|---|---|
| Tubal sterilization | 0.4 | 0.4 |
| Vasectomy | 0.4 | 0.4 |
| Injectable progestin | 0.25 | 0.25 |
| Combined birth control pills | 0.5 | 2 |
| Progestin-only pill | 1 | 2.5 |
| IUD | 1.5 | 5 |
| Condom | 2 | 10 |
| Diaphragm (with spermicide) | 2 | 19 |
| Sponge (with spermicide) | 9–11 | 10–20 |
| Cervical cap | 2 | 13 |
| Foams, creams, jellies, and vaginal suppositories | 3–5 | 18 |
| Coitus interruptus | 16 | 23 |
| Fertility awareness techniques (basal body temperature, mucus method, calendar, and "rhythm") | 2–20 | 24 |
| Douche | — | 40 |
| Chance (no method of birth control) | 90 | 90 |

*Designed to complete the sentence: "In 100 users who start out the year using a given method and who use it correctly and consistently, the lowest observed failure rate has been _____."

†Designed to complete the sentence: "In 100 typical users who start out the year using a given method, the number of pregnancies by the end of the year will be _____".

(From Hatcher et al: Contraceptive Technology 1986–1987. Irvington, New York, 1986, with permission.)

inal secretions and semen, the volume of such discharge may be substantial and annoying during exercise. This problem may be remedied by placing a second, smaller diaphragm distal to the first, by inserting a vaginal tampon, or, preferably, by wearing a minipad.

Diaphragm use requires vaginal retention of the diaphragm for 6 to 8 hours following the last vaginal ejaculation. Some athletes may find it uncomfortable to exercise with a diaphragm in the vagina; such women may benefit from refitting with a slightly smaller diaphragm, which will provide equal contraceptive efficacy and greater comfort.

Failure rates for various contraceptive methods are listed in Table 14–1.[15]

## DYSMENORRHEA

Dysmenorrhea is caused by myometrial ischemia during myometrial contractions induced by prostaglandin $F_{2\alpha}$, which is produced by the endometrium. Synthesis of this chemical can be prevented by any of several prostaglandin synthetase inhibitors (Table 14–2).

Although many women have noticed less dysmenorrhea during exercise or training or both, most of these observations remain anecdotal and unsupported by well-controlled scientific studies. The nature of studies involving exercise as the independent variable and perception of pain as the dependent variable makes double-blinding impossible. Several theories have been proposed to explain the apparent reduction of pain by exercise and training. These hypotheses include the following: exercise-induced increase in pain-preventing endorphins, exercise-induced increase in vasodilating prostaglandins, and exercise-induced vasodilatation. The truth remains to be elucidated.

Athletes who experience dysmenorrhea should be treated with prostaglandin inhibitors. Exercise-induced relief from dysmenorrhea should not be expected, since responses are variable and unpredictable. Prostaglandin inhibitors often cause reduced menstrual blood loss as an additional benefit, because of the vasoconstriction caused by inhibition of vasodilating prostaglandins.

## ENDOMETRIOSIS

Endometriosis is a condition in which functioning endometrial tissue exists outside the endometrial cavity. Its most common symptoms are pain and infertility, although it may produce no symptoms. In a multicenter study, Cramer and associates[16] have reported that women who have exercised regularly since age 25 or younger and for more than 2 hours weekly have a decreased risk of developing endometriosis. Conditioning exercises such as jogging seemed most associated with this decreased risk.

Women who have endometriosis may be treated medically or surgically. Surgical treatment depends on the severity of disease and may include fulguration of endometriotic implants, resection of endometriotic tissue or cysts, or hysterectomy with bilateral salpingo-oophorectomy. Medical treatment is most effective with danazol, a derivative of testosterone having the expected androgenic and anabolic properties. Anecdotally, athletes treated with danazol for endometriosis have noticed improved performance, but this has not been investigated scientifically to date. In addition to androgenic side effects (Table 14–3), muscle cramps may occur with use of this drug.[17]

## PREMENSTRUAL SYNDROME

Premenstrual syndrome (PMS) is a condition in which women experience emotional and/or physical symptoms during the 3 to 5 days prior to the onset of menstruation. In some cases, it may last even longer. Symp-

**Table 14–2.** PROSTAGLANDIN INHIBITORS

| | |
|---|---|
| Aspirin | 650 mg every 4 hr |
| Naproxen | 500 mg, then 250 mg every 6–8 hr |
| Naproxen sodium | 550 mg, then 275 mg every 6–8 hr |
| Ibuprofen | 400 mg every 4–6 hr |
| Mefenamic acid | 500 mg, then 250 mg every 6 hr |

**Table 14–3.** SIDE EFFECTS OF
DANAZOL

Weight gain
Fluid retention
Fatigue
Decreased breast size
Acne
Oily skin
Deepening of the voice
Hirsutism
Atrophic vaginitis
Hot flushes
Muscle cramps
Emotional lability

toms may include anxiety, depression, mood swings, increased appetite, headaches, mastalgia, and edema and may vary in severity as well as in duration. The multitude and variability of symptoms in this syndrome have made it difficult to define this entity precisely, and this problem has led Magos and Studd to propose the following working definition for investigators and clinicians: "distressing physical, psychological, and behavioral symptoms, not caused by organic disease, which regularly recur during the same phase of the menstrual/ovarian cycle, and which disappear or significantly regress during the remainder of the cycle."[18]

Although the cause of PMS remains to be elucidated, it is probably related to hormone levels and/or changes at that time of the menstrual cycle. No laboratory tests can diagnose this condition, since no laboratory measurements have been shown to correlate with symptomatology during any given cycle or to vary between affected and unaffected individuals. The diagnosis of PMS is a historic one, made solely by reviewing a calendar record of when symptoms and menstruation occur. Those women whose symptoms occur solely premenstrually have PMS, and those whose symptoms occur randomly throughout the cycle do not. This seemingly clear picture is confused somewhat by the fact that some women who have symptoms throughout the cycle note a premenstrual exacerbation of symptomatology.

It has been reported that women who exercise are less likely to experience PMS and that women are less likely to experience

PMS when exercising regularly. Prior and colleagues[19] have shown that conditioning exercise decreases premenstrual symptoms. However, it is difficult to design controlled studies in which women are blinded to the fact that they are exercising. Thus, it remains difficult to isolate exercise as a variable and difficult to confirm that exercise prevents or relieves PMS symptoms. It is probable that the mood elevation and general feeling of well-being associated with exercise may play a role.

Optimal treatment of PMS remains to be determined. Although several drugs relieve symptoms, only a few of these have been shown to be more effective than a placebo. The high placebo response in this entity makes it difficult to evaluate the effectiveness of all treatments. Spironolactone has been shown to be more effective than a placebo[20] and is associated with very few side effects. Although pharmacologic doses of progesterone are prescribed by many clinicians to treat PMS, there is no evidence that PMS is caused by a progesterone deficiency or that progesterone therapy in physiologic doses is more effective than a placebo in treating it. Luteal phase deficiency is not associated with a more severe premenstrual syndrome than a normal luteal phase.[21] Progesterone in pharmacologic doses has been shown in only one study to be more effective than a placebo;[22] other studies have found this agent to be no more effective than a placebo.[23] A few studies showed bromocriptine to be more effective than a placebo in relieving some PMS symptoms, particularly mastodynia;[24] however, other studies have failed to confirm this.[24] Danazol has been reported to relieve PMS symptoms;[25,26] however, this has been tested in only one double-blind, controlled fashion to date. (The side effects associated with danazol are listed in Table 14–3.) A gonadotropin-releasing hormone (GnRH) agonist has been shown to relieve PMS symptoms, while inducing amenorrhea.[27] Since this drug and other analogs and antagonists of GnRH promote bone loss as a result of the hypoestrogenic state they induce,[28] these agents are not promising for long-term use in this condition. Alprazolam has also been shown to be more effective than a placebo in relieving the severity of several symptoms of PMS; its reported low incidence of side effects may make it a good choice for many women unresponsive to other therapies.[29] It remains to be shown whether any of these medications will affect athletic performance.

Despite claims to the contrary, there is no evidence that PMS is caused by any dietary deficiency or excess, or that dietary manipulation will consistently relieve symptoms. However, salt restriction may alleviate symptoms in some PMS sufferers and certainly will harm no one.

Athletes who are inconvenienced by significant PMS symptoms probably should be treated with spironolactone (25 to 100 milligrams daily). It may be reassuring for some of them to know that 75 percent of all women experience at least some premenstrual symptomatology, probably due to hormonal changes that reflect normal reproductive function (i.e., regular ovulation).

## FERTILITY

No studies to date have shown that infertility is more prevalent among athletes than among the general population. However, luteal phase deficiency, oligomenorrhea, and amenorrhea are more prevalent among athletes, and infertility is more prevalent among women who have these conditions. The definition of infertility includes a desire for pregnancy. Since many athletes are not actively seeking pregnancies at the time of intensive training, when they are most likely to experience menstrual dysfunction, these women technically are not infertile, even though their fertility, if tested, might be impaired. Many of these women resume having regular ovulatory menses when they decrease intensive training because competitive athletic goals become less important than having children. It is probable that transient infertility is associated with intensive training, but this has not been documented to date.[2]

Even if temporary infertility is associated with training, athletes who do not desire pregnancy should not presume that conception is impossible. As discussed in Chapter 10, reliable contraception should be used by even amenorrheic athletes who do not want a pregnancy. Many anecdotal reports of amenorrheic athletes with unsuspected and unwanted pregnancies support this recommendation. Hypothalamic-pituitary-ovarian

dysfunction can resolve spontaneously, and ovulation can occur prior to the first subsequent menstrual period. The cause of the amenorrhea in such cases changes from hypothalamic-pituitary-ovarian dysfunction to pregnancy, but the symptom of amenorrhea continues. Thus, the amenorrheic athlete may not detect an unplanned, unwanted pregnancy until it is advanced enough to produce a significant increase in abdominal girth.

## STRESS URINARY INCONTINENCE

Many women experience stress urinary incontinence during exercise. Involuntary urine leakage results when intravesical pressure is higher than intra-urethral pressure.

Although stress incontinence is most likely to occur in women who have an anatomic defect in the posterior urethrovesical angle, even women with normal anatomy can experience stress urinary incontinence when intravesical pressure increases enough. Physical activity involving a Valsalva maneuver increases intra-abdominal pressure. Because changes in intra-abdominal pressure are not always transmitted equally to both bladder and urethra, physical activities like running and jumping may raise intravesical pressure above intra-urethral pressure, leading to urine leakage during exercise.[30] Although stress urinary incontinence is more common during exercise than during rest, exercise-induced increases in intra-abdominal pressure are transient and do not produce chronic pressure alterations or anatomic abnormalities.

Genital prolapse includes several anatomic abnormalities marked by loss of support, including cystocele, urethrocele, rectocele, and uterine descent. These anatomic defects have been reported to be associated with prior trauma during vaginal delivery and with endogenous joint hypermobility.[31] Such joint laxity may predispose women to joint injury also.

Many women who have stress urinary incontinence may be able to control leakage by avoiding fluid ingestion for 3 hours prior to exercising and emptying their bladders immediately prior to exercising. However, they must be careful to avoid dehydration during prolonged exercise sessions lasting more than 1 hour. Such women should replace fluid loss immediately after cessation of exercise.

Many women who experience involuntary urine leakage may benefit from practicing Kegel exercises. These are done by contracting the pubococcygeus muscle at any time, or specifically during urination, thereby stopping the urinary stream. Women who lose urine during exercise may decrease their discomfort and embarrassment by wearing a mini-pad. No medication will alleviate this condition. Those who have anatomic defects and who cannot relieve their symptoms to a satisfactory degree by practicing Kegel exercises or wearing a mini-pad should consider surgical correction of the anatomic defect. Postoperatively, such women may be at increased risk of recurrence due to the pressure changes during exercise and to persistence of the endogenous tissue factors that caused the original problem. No studies are available to confirm or disprove this suspicion, but these women probably should be cautious when exercising postoperatively.

## POSTOPERATIVE TRAINING AND RECOVERY

The traditional recovery period following abdominal or other major surgery has been 6 to 10 weeks. Recommendations for recovery should be site- and sport-specific. However, athletes should aim to recover cardiovascular fitness as soon as possible, while avoiding excessive stress on the surgical site. As a general rule, postoperative avoidance of pain will lead to avoidance of injury or damage. Those who have greater strength in muscles far from the operative site can gain mobility early by using those muscles rather than the muscles near the operative site.

A surgical wound begins to heal immediately following closure. By the 21st postoperative day, the wound has gained nearly as much strength as it will ultimately have (although it will never be as strong as it was preoperatively). Based on the fact that it takes 21 days for a surgical wound to regain nearly all of its ultimate strength, it is probably reasonable for athletes to postpone submaximal resistance training that involves the operative site for 21 days following a surgical procedure. Lighter work can probably be done safely prior to this time, particularly if the wound is not stressed. Avoidance of pain

remains a reasonable goal for the exercising patient postoperatively, and exercises that do not cause pain are probably safe. Overzealous athletes should be cautioned to use moderation in training postoperatively and to notice subtle body perceptions of discomfort and fatigue.

Although there are no studies to indicate when exercise can be safely resumed following surgery, I propose the following guidelines for earliest safe resumption of exercise.

Following a dilatation and curettage or a first-trimester abortion, weight training and aerobic exercise, except water sports, may be resumed the same or the next day; water sports should be avoided until bleeding has ceased. Tampon use also should be avoided until bleeding has ceased.

Following a vaginal delivery or a second-trimester abortion, weight training may be resumed the same day; aerobic exercise, except water sports, may be resumed in 2 days; water sports may be resumed when bleeding has ceased. Tampon use should be avoided until bleeding has ceased.

Following a laparoscopy, aerobic exercise in and out of water and weight training may be resumed after 1 to 2 days.

Following a cesarean delivery or other abdominal surgery (requiring an incision), light aerobic exercise outside of water and light weight training may be resumed in 7 days; intense aerobic exercise (speed work), submaximal weight training, and water sports should be postponed until at least 21 days.

It must be emphasized that these are the earliest times I recommend resuming exercise postoperatively. Delays may enhance healing despite potential hindrance of training. Exercise should never be resumed if it causes pain.

## EFFECT OF MENSTRUAL CYCLE ON PERFORMANCE

Many investigators have studied the effect of the menstrual cycle on performance, including specific measurements of strength, speed, endurance, fatigability, perceived exertion, and cognitive, perceptual, and motor skills at different phases of the menstrual cycle, reflecting different levels and ratios of estrogen and progesterone. For a thorough review of these reports, the reader is referred elsewhere.[32] Findings of all these studies have been inconsistent and suggest that menstrual cycle phase does not have a significant effect on any of these parameters. Very few of such studies have been published in peer review journals. No reports substantiate any consistent effect of menstrual cycle phase on performance either.

It is rarely advisable or necessary to manipulate an athlete's menstrual cycle to enhance her performance. However, some women *do* perform better during the follicular phase than at other times, and others perceive or believe that they do. If such women are elite athletes, it may be appropriate to manipulate the menstrual cycle for special events of great importance; I believe that such manipulation should be reserved for world-class athletes (e.g., Olympic competition).

The simplest and least invasive method of manipulating an athlete's menstrual cycle involves administration of low-dose oral contraceptives for several months prior to the competitive event and continuing the hormone-containing pills until 10 days before the competitive event. She can expect to have withdrawal bleeding within 3 days of cessation of the pills. She should postpone restarting the pills (if she plans to do so) until the competitive event has passed. This plan will give her a predictable bleeding pattern during training and will leave her with low levels of both estrogen and progesterone at the time of the important event. For world-class athletes in their prime, this regimen can be repeated every few months for the events of great importance. It also provides hormonal protection to those athletes who are deficient in one or both hormones (estrogen and progesterone) during training, and it provides contraception to all athletes, regardless of menstrual status.

The only undesirable side effects associated with this plan are the potential risks of break-through bleeding during training and of impaired training during oral contraceptive use, in certain individuals. However, I believe these risks are small and are outweighed by the benefits of this plan.

An alternative method of management involves administration of only a progestin (e.g., medroxyprogesterone acetate) for 5 to 10 days, ending 10 days prior to the important event. This is most likely to be effective in women with chronic anovulation, and it

may produce undesirable bloating and a sensation of "heaviness," which may impair training. This method provides no contraception. As I have indicated, I prefer to prescribe low-dose oral contraceptives to athletes in need of menstrual manipulation.

## SUMMARY

Female athletes ask our advice about many gynecologic conditions for which studies are either lacking or inconclusive. To meet the needs of our patients, this chapter has reviewed the available literature and proposed recommendations based on what is known and on what I have learned from clinical experience. Until more data are available, it is hoped that these guidelines will help clinicians in caring for female athletes.

### References

1. Contraceptive Utilization, United States, 1976. US Department of Health and Human Services, Vital and Health Statistics, Series 23, No 7.
2. Shangold MM, and Levine HS: The effect of marathon training upon menstrual function. Am J Obstet Gynecol 143:862, 1982.
3. Jarrett JC, and Spellacy WN: Contraceptive practices of female runners. Fertil Steril 39:374, 1983.
4. Plunkett ER: Contraceptive steroids, age, and the cardiovascular system. Am J Obstet Gynecol 142:747, 1982.
5. Mann JI: Progestogens in cardiovascular disease: An introduction to the epidemiologic data. Am J Obstet Gynecol 142:752, 1982.
6. Kay CR: Progestogens and arterial disease—Evidence from the Royal College of General Practitioners' study. Am J Obstet Gynecol 142:762, 1982.
7. Wynn V, and Niththyananthan R: The effect of progestins in combined oral contraceptives on serum lipids with special reference to high-density lipoproteins. Am J Obstet Gynecol 142:766, 1982.
8. Spellacy WN: Carbohydrate metabolism during treatment with estrogen, progestogen, and low-dose oral contraceptives. Am J Obstet Gynecol 142:732, 1982.
9. Mishell DR: Noncontraceptive health benefits of oral steroidal contraceptives. Am J Obstet Gynecol 142:809, 1982.
10. Hedlin AM, Milojevic S, and Korey A: Plasminogen activator levels in plasma and urine during exercise and oral contraceptive use. Thromb Haemost 39:743, 1978.
11. Huisveld IA, Kluft C, Hospers AJH, et al: Effect of exercise and oral contraceptive agents on fibrinolytic potential in trained females. J Appl Physiol 56:906, 1984.
12. Hedlin AM, Milojevic S, and Korey A: Hemostatic changes induced by exercise during oral contraceptive use. Can J Physiol Pharmacol 56:316, 1978.
13. Powell MG, Hedlin AM, Cerskus I, et al: Effects of

oral contraceptives on lipoprotein lipids: A prospective study. Obstet Gynecol 63:764, 1984.

14. Gray DP, Harding E, and Dale E: Effects of oral contraceptives on serum lipid profiles of women runners. Fertil Steril 39:510, 1983.

15. Hatcher RA, Guest F, Stewart F, et al: Contraceptive Technology 1986–1987, 13th Revised Edition. Irvington, New York, 1986, p 102.

16. Cramer DW, Wilson E, Stillman RJ, et al: The relation of endometriosis to menstrual characteristics, smoking, and exercise. JAMA 255:1904, 1986.

17. Speroff L, Glass RH, and Kase NG: Clinical Gynecologic Endocrinology and Infertility. Williams and Wilkins, Baltimore, 1983, p 500.

18. Magos AL, and Studd JWW: The premenstrual syndrome. In Studd JWW (ed): Progress in Obstetrics and Gynaecology. Vol. 4, Churchill Livingstone, Edinburgh, 1984, p 334.

19. Prior JC, Vigna Y, and Alojado N: Conditioning exercise decreases premenstrual symptoms—A prospective controlled three month trial. Eur J Appl Physiol 55:349, 1986.

20. O'Brien PMS, Craven D, Selby C, et al: Treatment of premenstrual syndrome with spironolactone. Br J Obstet Gynaecol 86:142, 1979.

21. Ying Y-K, Soto-Albors CE, Randolph JF, et al: Luteal phase defect and premenstrual syndrome in an infertile population. Obstet Gynecol 69:96, 1987.

22. Dennerstein L, Spencer-Gardner C, Gotts G, et al: Progesterone and the premenstrual syndrome: A double-blind crossover trial. Br Med J 290:1617, 1985.

23. Sampson GA: Premenstrual syndrome: A double-blind controlled trial of progesterone and placebo. Br J Psychiatr 135:209, 1979.

24. Andersch B: Bromocriptine and premenstrual symptoms: A survey of double blind trials. Obstet Gynecol Surv 38:643, 1983.

25. Day J: Danazol and the premenstrual syndrome. Postgrad Med J 55 (Suppl 5):87, 1979.

26. Sarno AP, Miller EJ, and Lundblad EG: Premenstrual syndrome: Beneficial effects of periodic, low-dose danazol. Obstet Gynecol 70:33, 1987.

27. Muse KN, Cetel NS, Futterman LA, et al: The premenstrual syndrome: Effects of "medical ovariectomy." N Engl J Med 311:1345, 1984.

28. Abbasi R, and Hodgen GD: Predicting the predisposition to osteoporosis: Gonadotropin-releasing hormone antagonist for acute estrogen deficiency test. JAMA 255:1600, 1986.

29. Smith S, Rinehart JS, Ruddock VE, et al: Treatment of premenstrual syndrome with alprazolam: Results of a double-blind crossover clinical trial. Obstet Gynecol 70:37, 1987.

30. James ED: The behaviour of the bladder during physical activity. Br J Urol 50:387, 1978.

31. Al-Rawi ZS, and Al-Rawi ZT: Joint hypermobility in women with genital prolapse. Lancet 1:1439, 1982.

32. Brooks-Gunn J, Gargiulo J, and Warren MP: The menstrual cycle and athletic performance. In Puhl JL, and Brown CH (eds): The Menstrual Cycle and Physical Activity. Human Kinetics, Champaign, IL, 1986, p 13.

# CHAPTER 15

# Orthopedic Concerns

LETHA Y. HUNTER-GRIFFIN, M.D., Ph.D.

With the growth of women's athletics, many observers predicted an increase in the number and types of injuries occurring as women became more aggressive and competitive in sports.[1] Early injury studies of female athletes actually reported that a greater number of injuries were sustained by female than by male athletes.[2,3] However, this reflected a lack of adequate conditioning in women rather than any true physiologic weakness and predisposition to injury. As women became more serious in their sport participation, training and conditioning techniques improved, and injury rates decreased.[4] Recent studies surveying injury rates in conditioned female athletes demonstrate that their injury rates are no higher than those of their male counterparts.[5–7]

A review of injuries in professional and recreational athletes demonstrated sprains and strains to be the most common injuries, and the knee and ankle to be the most frequently traumatized areas in both men and women.[8] Injuries are more sport-specific than sex-specific; that is, injury types and rates are similar for men and women in the same sport, but differ for female athletes participating in different sports.[9]

**Table 15–1.** SPECIFIC SPORTS COMMONLY ASSOCIATED WITH ORTHOPEDIC INJURIES

| Injury | Sport |
| --- | --- |
| Shoulder subluxation | Swimming |
| | Throwing sports |
| Sprains | |
|     Thumb | Skiing |
|     Ankle | Running sports |
| |     Uneven ground (field hockey, soccer, softball, cross-country) |
| | Basketball, volleyball (one-foot landings) |
| | Ice skating |
|     Knee | Basketball, volleyball |
| Tendinitis | |
|     First dorsal compartment | Gymnastics (squeezing poles or bars) |
|     Achilles tendon | Track, basketball, skiing, iceskating, rollerskating |
|     Biceps | Tennis, other racquet sports, throwing sports |
| Lateral epicondylitis (tennis elbow) | Tennis, other racquet sports, throwing sports |
| Shin splints | Running |
| Impingements | |
|     Shoulder | Swimming,* throwing sports, racquet sports |
|     Ankle | Gymnastics, ballet, diving, iceskating |
|     Wrist | Gymnastics, crew, racquet sports |
| Low back pain | Gymnastics, diving, skating |
| Stress fractures (pars intra-articularis) | Running, gymnastics, iceskating, diving |

*In greater numbers than male counterparts.

There are, however, certain conditions that occur more commonly in women—in some cases owing to anatomic differences, in others owing to greater participation in specific sports. We have therefore elected to focus on conditions more prominent in women, and refer the reader to the many volumes already written on evaluation and treatment of athletic injuries for a discussion of such injuries as sprains, dislocations, fractures, and inflammation of muscle origins. Table 15–1 briefly lists some common musculoskeletal injuries and the women's sports that are most often associated with those injuries. This chapter concentrates on patella pain, impingement syndromes, Achilles tendinitis, shin splints, stress fractures, low back pain, bunions, and Morton's neuroma.

## PATELLA PAIN

### Anatomy of the Patella

The patella (a lens-shaped sesamoid bone, commonly called the kneecap) is completely surrounded by fascial extensions (retinaculum) of the quadriceps muscle—the vastus medialis, the vastus lateralis, the rectus femoris, and the vastus intermedius (Fig. 15–1). Fascial terminations of these muscle groups emerge at the patella, extend over it, and extend inferiorly from the patella to form the patella tendon, which inserts into the tibial tubercle. The patella sits in the distal femoral groove, which is formed by the joining of the medial and lateral femoral condyles. As the patella tracks in the femoral groove with knee flexion and extension, it is guided by this powerful quadriceps muscle group. Since the quadriceps muscle courses along the long axis of the femur while the patella tendon inserts into the tibial tubercle, patella excursion with activity is very much influenced by the tibial-femoral angle. This angle (the Q angle) is measured by drawing a line through the center of the quadriceps muscle and noting its intersection with a line drawn through the center of the tibial tuberosity (Fig. 15–2). Because the gynecoid pelvis of the woman is wider than the narrow an-

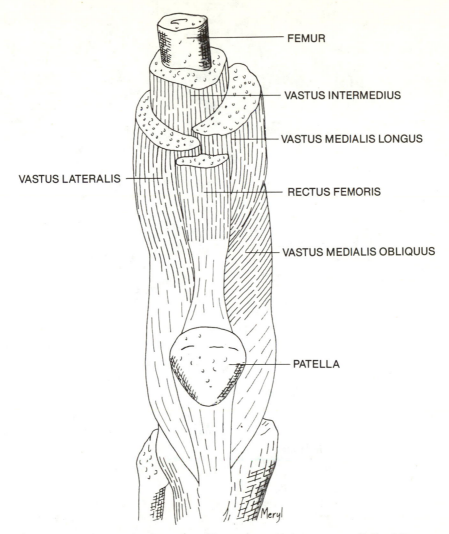

FEMUR

VASTUS INTERMEDIUS

VASTUS MEDIALIS LONGUS

VASTUS LATERALIS

RECTUS FEMORIS

VASTUS MEDIALIS OBLIQUUS

PATELLA

**Figure 15-1.** *The quadriceps muscles. Note the oblique course of the vastus medialis obliquus muscle. (From Scott WN, Nisonson B, Nicholas JA, et al: Principles of Sports Medicine. Williams and Wilkins, Baltimore, 1984, p. 274, with permission.)*

droid pelvis of the man, this angle is generally greater in women than in men and may explain the increase in patella tracking problems and patella pain in women (Fig. 15–3). In fact, patella pain is one of the most common complaints of female athletes.

Although the superior surface of the patella is flat, the inferior surface is composed of two facets intersecting at an angle and forming the V-like posterior aspect of the patella (Fig. 15–4). The medial facet is generally smaller than the lateral. The facets are lined with hyaline cartilage and articulate with the

hyaline cartilage-covered superior extensions of the femoral condyle, forming the patellofemoral joint (Fig. 15–5).

**Sources of Pain**

Forces across the joint have been the subject of much investigation, since patellofemoral pain is a common source of discomfort in many activities, especially in sports that require forced flexion-extension maneuvers (running), or multiple falls on the flexed knee (volleyball). Forces across the joint increase

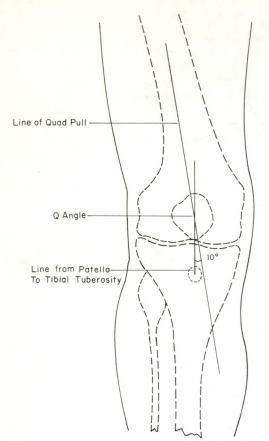

**Figure 15–2.** *The Q angle is an angle formed by the intersection of a line drawn longitudinally through the middle of the quadriceps and a line drawn from the middle of the patella to the center of the tibial tuberosity. (From O'Donoghue DH: Treatment of Injuries to Athletes, ed 4. WB Saunders, Philadelphia, 1984, p. 510, with permission.)*

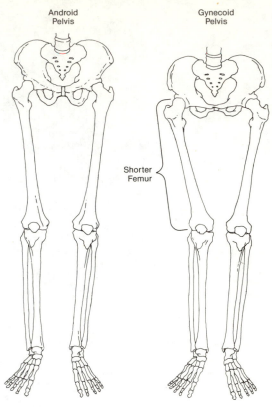

**Figure 15–3.** *Android pelvis and gynecoid pelvis. Note that the female (gynecoid) pelvis is wider, with a greater varus angle of the femoral neck, resulting in a greater valgus angle at the knee when compared with the typical male (android) pelvis.*

with increasing flexion of the knee (Fig. 15–6). Although some have theorized that increased ligamentous laxity contributes to an increase in patella dislocation and subluxation in women, this has not been objectively demonstrated.[10] In fact, review of knee anatomy in women who sustained multiple patella subluxations or dislocations revealed altered bony anatomy to be a significant contributing factor.[11] They generally had a shallow patellofemoral groove; the patella sometimes sat high in the groove and often was tipped laterally (Fig. 15–7).

Patella tracking in the patellofemoral groove may also be influenced by foot strike. Pronation of the foot increases the knee val-gus angle and may lead to an increase or at least an alteration in lateral patellofemoral forces (Fig. 15–8).

## Evaluating Patella Pain

In evaluating the athlete who complains of a painful knee, one must always consider the patella, along with the other structures within the knee, as a source of her pain. The athlete who sustains a traumatic patella dislocation with spontaneous relocation may not report that her "kneecap jumped out of joint" but may perceive only severe knee pain following her twisting injury. Similarly, an athlete who complains of give-way or locking of her joint may not have a mechanical locking of her knee from a torn meniscus or loose body, but may have pseudolocking or give-way on the basis of patella pain.

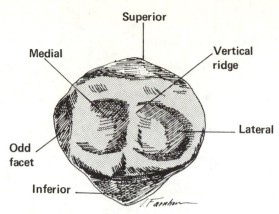

**Figure 15–4.** *Posterior aspect of the patella, illustrating the two patellar facets. (From Norkin and Levangie: Joint Structure and Function. FA Davis, Philadelphia, 1983, p. 321, with permission.)*

## Observation

The first step in evaluating the patella is to observe the knee: does the patella sit higher in the femoral groove than usual (patella alta), or is it lower (patella baja)? Athletes whose patellas sit higher in the femoral groove have a greater tendency to patella subluxation, whereas those with low-lying patellas may have increased forces across the patellofemoral joint, especially with repetitive flexion-extension activities.

Does the patella lie centrally in the femoral groove, or is it tipped laterally? The Q angle should be measured, and the quadriceps mechanism assessed. The development of the vastus medialis muscle should be noted, especially its more medial oblique fibers, known as the vastus medialis obliquus. An increased Q angle and poorly developed vastus medialis, especially the oblique fibers, are associated with an increased incidence of patella pain.

## Palpation and Manipulation

The retinaculum around the patella's medial, lateral, and superior borders should be palpated to check for tenderness. The athlete who has just sustained an acute patella subluxation or dislocation with spontaneous relocation will have a great deal of tenderness at the insertion of the vastus medialis on the medial border of the patella. In addition, she may have ecchymoses along the fibers of the

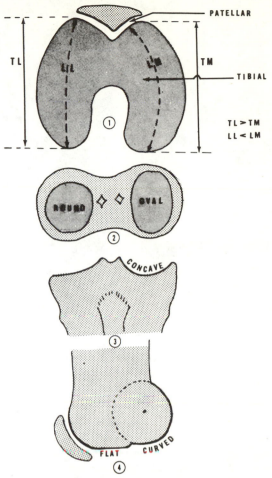

**Figure 15–5.** *Patellofemoral joint. 1, Femoral condyle surfaces of the right knee. TL = anteroposterior length of the lateral condyle; TM = length of the medial condyle. The length of the medial condyle (LM) is greater than the length of the lateral condyle (LL), because of its curved surface. 2, Superior surface of the right tibia. The lateral articular surface is rounded and the medial articular surface is oval. 3, The medial tibial articular surface is deeper and more concave than is the lateral. 4, Side view of the femur showing the flat anterior surface and the curved posterior surface. The two articulations are illustrated in part 1: the patellar surface in which the patella articulates with the anterior femur and the tibial surface then glides upon the tibia. (From Cailliet R: Knee Pain and Disability. FA Davis, Philadelphia, 1983, p. 2, with permission.)*

muscles, from having stretched or disrupted part of the fibers at the time of the subluxation or dislocation.

Next, the patella should be tipped medially, and the examiner should feel under the

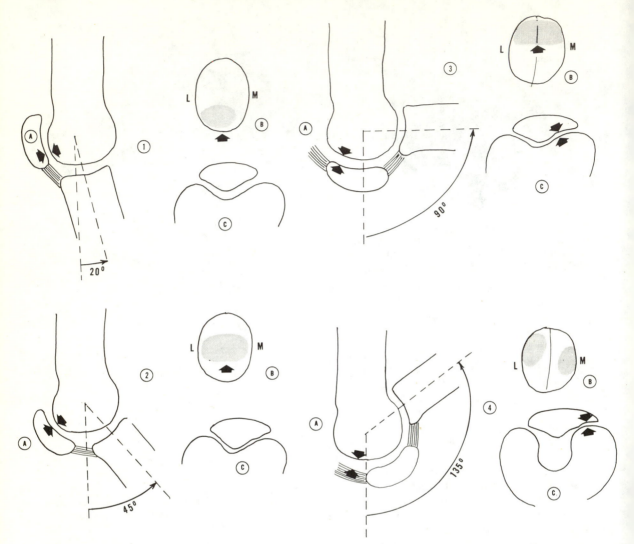

**Figure 15-6.** *Patellar contact areas with femoral condyles during knee flexion. 1, Knee flexed 20 degrees: 1A, Lateral view of the patellofemoral joint.* Arrows *depict site of contact. 1B, Area of contact of the patella (shaded area) (L = lateral, M = medial). 1C, Superior view showing patella within femoral condyles. At 20-degree flexion, there is contact symmetrically of the lateral condyle. 2, Knee flexed 45 degrees: Pressure site upon patella in broader central zone (2C). As in 1, there is symmetrical pressure of medial and lateral patellar facets. 3, Knee flexed 90 degrees: The patellar contact is broad contact of the superior area of medial and lateral facets (3B). In 3C, there is beginning to be more contact of medial facets. 4, Knee flexed 135 degrees (full flexion): The patellar facets contact both femoral condyles and the patella shifts (4C) so that the odd facet contacts the medial condyle more firmly. (From Cailliet R: Knee Pain and Disability. FA Davis, Philadelphia, 1983, pp. 88–89, with permission.)*

medial facet (Fig. 15–9). Athletes with patellofemoral stress syndrome or chondromalacia will experience pain with this maneuver. Then the examiner should place a hand firmly above the patella and ask the patient to contract her quadriceps (Fig. 15–10). In this maneuver, called an inhibition test, athletes with patellofemoral stress syndrome or chondromalacia will have give-way symptoms after beginning the contraction. This action mimics the give-way sensations reported by the women with these entities.

Next, one should palpate the patella tendon to check for its intactness and to examine

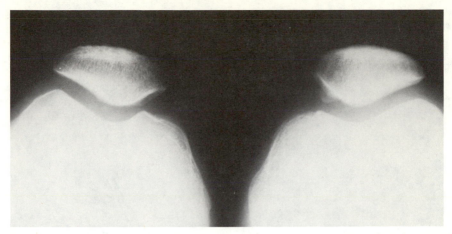

**Figure 15–7.** *Radiograph of laterally tipped patellas. Note the very short medial condylar flare and the elongated lateral flare, corresponding to the increased width of the lateral patella facet when compared with the medial one.*

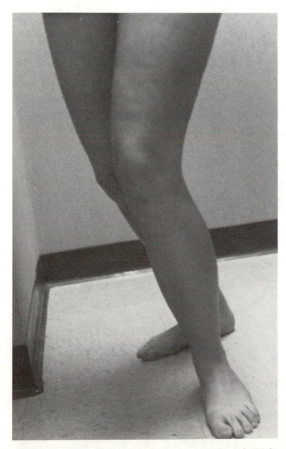

**Figure 15–8.** *As the foot goes into pronation, the valgus angle of the knee and lateral tracking of the patella are accentuated.*

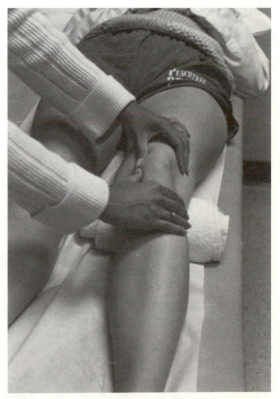

**Figure 15–9.** *Palpation of the medial patella facet. Patients with patellofemoral stress frequently have tenderness along the medial border of the patella at the retinaculum or under the medial facet of the patella.*

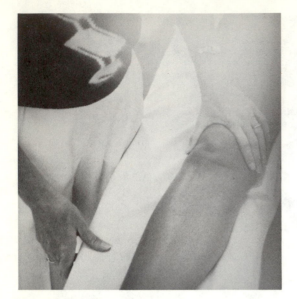

**Figure 15–10.** *In the inhibition test, the examiner applies pressure above the patella as the patient contracts the quadriceps muscle. This maneuver frequently reproduces the pain of the athlete with patellofemoral stress syndrome.*

for tenderness at its origin off the inferior surface of the patella or at its attachment to the tibia. In the very young patient (age 6 to 9 years), inflammation of the patella tendon at its origin off the inferior surface of the patella may be associated with irregularities of the lower patella apophyseal pole (Fig. 15–11). Similarly, irritation of the attachment of

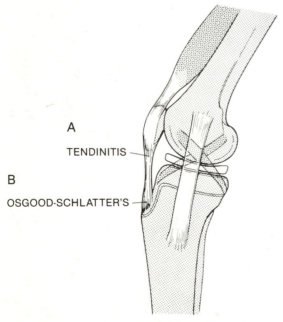

**Figure 15–11.** *A, The patient with patella tendonitis will have pain at the origin of the patella tendon. B, The patient with Osgood-Schlatter's disease (seen in the teenager with open growth centers) will have irritation at the insertion of the patella tendon into the tibial apophysis. (From Andrish JT: Knee injuries in gymnastics. In Weiker GG (ed): Gymnastics. Clin Sports Med 4(1):120, 1985, with permission.)*

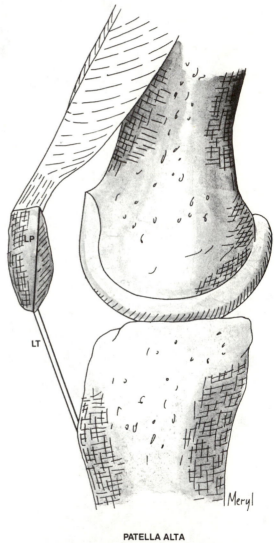

PATELLA ALTA

**Figure 15–12.** *Objective confirmation of patella alta is obtained by using a lateral radiograph and determining the length of the patella (LP) and the length of the patella tendon (LT). If the tendon length exceeds the patella length by 20 percent, then patella alta is present (i.e., LP/LT ≤ 0.8). (From Scott WN, et al: Principles of Sports Medicine. Williams and Wilkins, Baltimore, 1984, p. 312, with permission.)*

the patella tendon to the tibial apophysis during periods of its rapid growth (age 11 to 13 years) can result in its inflammation or apophysitis, a condition termed Osgood-Schlatter's disease (Fig. 15–11).

### Aspiration of Fluid

If there is fluid within the knee joint, it may be aspirated. A hemarthrosis, or blood in the knee, may result from a traumatic patella dislocation with spontaneous relocation, and this diagnosis should always be considered if a bloody aspirate is obtained, because, as previously indicated, the athlete who has had a spontaneous relocation of her patella may not have perceived her injury as a patella dislocation.

Yellow synovial fluid aspirated from the joint may indicate that the knee joint has been or is irritated, and this can occur with less traumatic patella subluxations or result from increased repetitive forces across the patellofemoral joint (patellofemoral stress syndrome) or from abnormalities of the hyaline cartilage of the retropatellar surface (chondromalacia).

### Radiographic Evaluation

Many different radiographic techniques have been designed to evaluate the patella and its relationship to the femur in the patellofemoral groove. The lateral radiograph of the knee taken at 50 degrees of flexion can be used to estimate the height of the patella and the relationship to the knee joint. The ratio of a line drawn longitudinally through the patella to a line drawn from the tip of the patella to the tibial tubercle measured on a lateral radiograph, with the knee in 50 degrees of flexion, can be used to estimate patella alta or baja. A ratio greater than 1.2 is indicative of patella alta (Fig. 15–12), whereas a ratio of less than 1.0 is associated with patella baja.

A view of the patella taken with the knee flexed to 30 degrees and the cassette held perpendicular to the radiograph tube is called a skyline view of the patella (Fig. 15–13). It is used to assess the patella's position in the femoral groove, as well as patella spurs or compromise of the height of the articular cartilage of the patellofemoral joint.

Another helpful study used to assess the intactness of the patellofemoral cartilage and the position of the patella in the femoral groove is computerized axial tomography done following injection of contrast material into the knee joint. The contrast material nicely coats the articular surface for visualization (Fig. 15–14).

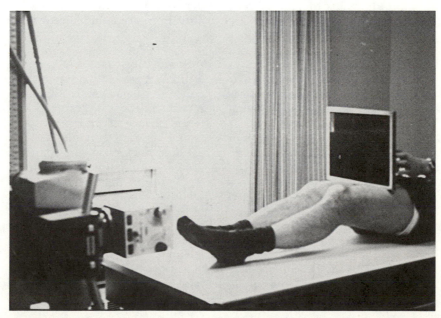

**Figure 15–13.** *Technique for obtaining skyline view of the patella. (From Hunter LY, et al: Common orthopedic problems of female athletes. In Frankel VH (ed): Instructional Course Lectures. American Academy of Orthopaedic Surgeons, CV Mosby, St Louis, 1982, p. 131, with permission.)*

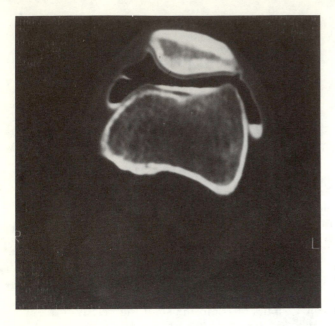

*Figure 15–14.* The patellofemoral joint as viewed by computed axial tomography after injection of contrast material into the knee joint.

## Acute Traumatic Patella Dislocation

### Diagnosis

If spontaneous relocation has not occurred, the diagnosis of a dislocation of the patella is obvious from observation. The patella typically lies lateral to the knee joint, and the injured athlete usually will hold her knee partially flexed because of pain. To confirm the diagnosis and make certain there are no fractures, a radiograph should be taken.

### Treatment

First, the intactness of the neurovascular structures should be assessed. After medication has been given to decrease pain (giving intravenous morphine as an analgesic is often extremely helpful), the examiner should gently extend the patient's leg while exerting a medial force on the patella. The patella will relocate with an audible sound, producing marked pain relief. A dislocated patella can sometimes be reduced on the field or court without medication, but it is usually wiser to radiographically document the diagnosis first.

Next, one should apply a compressive wrap with lateral pads to hold the patella medially. A soft knee immobilizer to support the knee and to keep it extended is usually used, as it is often easier to adjust than a cylinder cast. Knee extension should allow the vastus medialis fibers, which have been stretched, to heal.

The physician should instruct the athlete to ice and elevate the extremity and should place her on crutches, so that she bears only partial weight on the affected leg. If she develops a marked hemarthrosis over the next several days, it can be aspirated to increase her comfort and to decrease stretching of the already injured medial retinaculum.

### Arthroscopy

Some physicians recommend immediate arthroscopic examination of the joint to evacuate the hemarthrosis and to check for the presence of a chondral fracture off the posterior surface of the patella or the opposing lateral femoral condyle. Cartilage fractures are not recognized on routine radiographs unless the fracture extends into bone (an osteochondral fracture). Fracture fragments, whether cartilage alone or cartilage and bone, need to be removed, as they will become loose bodies that can intermittently catch in the joint, causing severe pain and locking.

Physicians who do not recommend immediate arthroscopy feel that the joint lining is so irritated following the injury that visualization of the joint is difficult. They feel that if an athlete develops loose body symptoms following patella dislocation, arthroscopy can be performed at that time. Most physicians follow the latter philosophy.

### Rehabilitation

Following a patella dislocation, the knee is kept wrapped with a lateral pad and immobilized in the extended position for approximately 3 to 6 weeks, to allow the torn medial retinaculum to heal. Isometric exercises can be done by the athlete while she is in the immobilizer. Some physicians will use muscle-stimulating units during this period to help strengthen the vastus medialis.

At the end of this time, short arc extension exercises, as well as functional strengthening activities such as bike-riding, can be started. If an exercise bike is used, the seat should be set as high as possible and tension kept on medium to low. If biking outdoors, a bike that has at least three gears, but preferably 5 or 10, should be used. The athlete should be instructed to use low gears (rapid pedaling at low tension) and to avoid hills. Again, seat height should be set so the athlete's knee is completely extended on the downstroke.

Short arc extension exercises are performed by placing a rolled towel beneath the knee, so that the exercise is begun at approximately 30 degrees of knee flexion. In a rhythmic fashion, the athlete performs multiple extensions from this flexed starting position (Fig. 15–15). Initially, no ankle weights should be used; as the athlete progresses in her exercise program, up to 5 pounds of weight may be added. Usually sets of 10 to 15 repetitions are done at one time, incorporated into a total strengthening program for the lower extremities. The partially flexed starting position and use of minimal weights minimize the forces over the patellofemoral joint, while the exercises increase quadriceps strength.

As rehabilitation proceeds, a lateral patella pad or one of the many braces designed for patella stabilization can be used. The braces typically incorporate a lateral pad to "force" the patella medially, or a horseshoe pad that completely envelops the patella (Fig. 15–16). These same braces may be used by the athlete when she returns to her sport. Following acute patella dislocation, however, it may be as much as 6 months before an athlete can fully participate in (pivotal) sports.

The athlete who sustains a patella dislocation is at greater risk for redislocation. A routinely performed quadriceps-strengthening program as well as brace support may be helpful in minimizing that risk. Athletes with recurrent patella dislocation may require operative procedures to help stabilize the patella. (See Surgery, under Patella Subluxation.)

## Patella Subluxation

Athletes whose patellas sit laterally or who have small, high-riding patellas (patella alta) are more predisposed to patella subluxation, that is, patellas that slide laterally with twisting movements of the knee (especially lateral twists or valgus stresses) but do not frankly dislocate, or come out of joint completely. Also, in principle, the greater the Q angle, the more easily the patella can slip laterally. Medial patella subluxation theoretically can occur, but practically is rarely found.

Chronic patella subluxation is not commonly found in teenaged or older athletes, as most girls with this condition find their athletic ability limited because of their patella pain, and therefore become interested in other activities.

### Symptoms

Athletes with patella subluxation may complain merely of knee pain with kicking, twisting, or running maneuvers. The whip kick or frog kick in swimming may be painful. Even though both patellas are high-riding, small, and easily subluxable, frequently only the dominant knee is symptomatic and so the athlete may not complain of pain in both knees. She may state that she has giveway episodes when going downstairs (an activity that increases patellofemoral forces) or may complain of locking or catching of her knee, symptoms typically associated with torn meniscal cartilage. She may not localize her pain to the patella and may never have experienced an episode of frank patella dislocation.

The pain experienced by the athlete with chronic patella subluxation may result from inflammation of the parapatellar retinaculum as it is stretched when the patella rides laterally, or may be secondary to abnormal forces on the hyaline cartilage surface of the patella. In fact, some women with chronic subluxable patellas may develop fibrillation or even fissuring of the hyaline cartilage, and

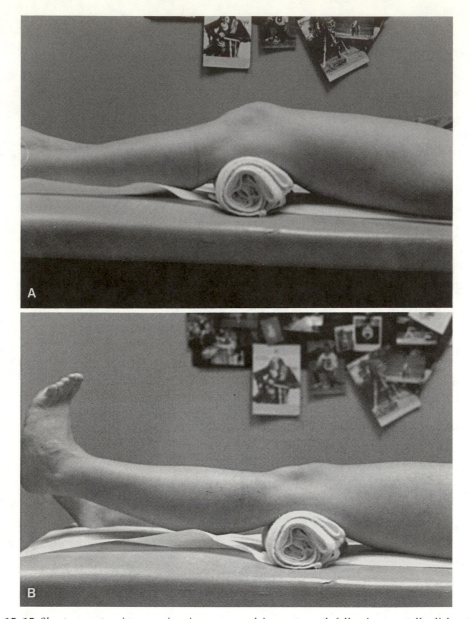

**Figure 15–15.** *Short arc extension exercises increase quadriceps strength following a patella dislocation.*

eventually have erosion and loss of the hyaline cartilage surface, and hence develop patellofemoral arthritis.

### History

The history from the athlete with subluxable patellas may reveal a sister, mother, grandmother, or even a male relative who has had knee problems. The predisposition

for patella symptoms is based on anatomic factors.

### Physical Examination

As indicated previously the patella is frequently small and high-riding. The vastus medialis obliquus may be poorly developed. In fact, the whole vastus medialis may be poorly developed.

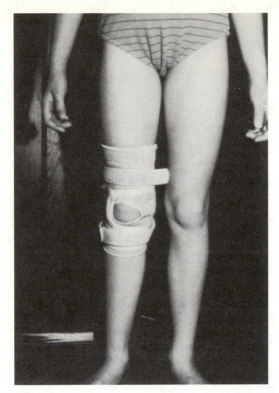

**Figure 15–16.** *An example of a patella-stabilizing brace. Note pad encircling the patella. (From Walsh WM, et al: Overuse injuries in girls' gymnastics. In Walsh WM (ed): The Athletic Woman. Clin Sports Med 3:841, 1984, with permission.)*

Women with patella subluxation frequently have an ectomorphic body type, with slender, poorly muscled lower extremities. The examiner observing active and passive knee flexion can see the patella riding laterally in the femoral groove.

Palpating the medial retinaculum or the medial facet of the patella will frequently cause discomfort. The athlete generally will be apprehensive if one moves her patella laterally. In fact, this sign is so characteristic of the patient whose patella subluxes or dislocates that it is felt to be diagnostic of this condition. Frequently, the examiner may be able to completely dislocate the patella by putting a direct lateral force on it with the knee in extension.

### Treatment

Treatment of the athlete with symptomatic chronic patella subluxation is difficult. Exercise to strengthen the quadriceps, especially the vastus medialis and particularly its oblique fibers, so that the patella will ride more medially in the patellofemoral groove, may be helpful. When the athlete is acutely symptomatic with pain, the anti-inflammatory agents, such as aspirin (two taken four times a day) or one of the other nonsteroidal anti-inflammatory drugs, may be helpful.

Intra-articular injection of steroids is not recommended in the young, as this may cause softening of the hyaline cartilage.

### Surgery

Operative procedures to better centralize the patella can be performed. Incising (releasing) the lateral retinaculum arthroscopically or with a small parapatellar lateral incision may help the patella to track more medially. Theoretically this weakens the pull of the vastus lateralis muscles on the patella. However, this procedure must be linked with a rehabilitation program designed to strengthen the vastus medialis muscles.

Other operative procedures transfer the bony attachment of the patella tendon more medially on the tibia. This decreases the Q angle and should better centralize the patella, preventing subluxation. Such a procedure may be combined with lateral retinacular release.

Care must be taken not to move the patella tendon attachment distally on the tibia, as this will increase patellofemoral forces and lead to patella cartilage softening or chondromalacia.

### Patellofemoral Stress Syndrome

Patellofemoral stress syndrome is very common, particularly in the teenaged female athlete. This diagnosis is used to describe a syndrome in which there is patella pain with activities that load the patellofemoral joint such as kneeling, kicking, running (especially downhill running), or sitting for a prolonged period of time with the knee acutely flexed. The syndrome does not include athletes with subluxable or dislocatable patellas.

### Symptoms

The athlete with patellofemoral stress syndrome may have symptoms similar to those of the athlete with patella subluxation. She may present with increasing aching discomfort in the knee, with or without associated effusion, or she may present with an acute episode of knee pain with locking or giving way. Effusions are more typically associated with patella subluxations or dislocations.

### Physical Examination

On physical examination, although she may have a patella that rides laterally in the patellofemoral groove, with an increased Q angle, a woman with patellofemoral stress syndrome is not apprehensive when the examiner tries to force her patella laterally. Moreover, although her patella may sit laterally in the patellofemoral groove, it is stable in its position, and the examiner will not have the feeling that it could be dislocated by being pushed too firmly laterally.

The athlete with patellofemoral stress syndrome will have a positive patella inhibition test; that is, she will experience pain if the examiner puts a hand firmly above the patella and asks the athlete to contract her quadriceps. This test increases patellofemoral forces, and hence, reproduces the athlete's pain and give-way episodes.

The examiner should note the degree of vastus medialis development, as frequently athletes with patellofemoral stress syndrome, like those with patella subluxation or dislocation, have a poorly developed vastus medialis. Hamstring tightness has also been reported to increase patellofemoral forces—when the athlete fully extends the knee, the tight hamstrings create a "bowstring" effect.

Note should be made of the footstrike in the athlete with patella pain. Check to see if the feet appear to have no arches, due to excessive inward rolling of the feet at the ankles. Most people who have "flat feet" have normal arches. Their feet appear to be flat because they pronate excessively. Their feet roll inward so much that the arches are not visible because they almost touch the ground. These people are at increased risk of developing patella pain during running.

Knee cap pain is most frequently caused by excessive lateral patellar tracking, which is increased by normal pronation and, more so, by excessive pronation. The patella is pulled laterally by three of the four quadriceps muscles. During running, the foot strikes the ground on the lateral part of the sole and rolls medially prior to toeing off (pronation). As the foot rolls medially, the tibia twists medially also. This can cause

pain, as the underside of the patella may rub against the medial aspect of the lateral condyle of the femur.

### Treatment

Treating the athlete with patellofemoral stress may be frustrating, as symptoms may be quite refractory to most treatment routines. Like other patella pain problems secondary to abnormal tracking, alteration of patella tracking is the fundamental principle in any treatment program.

Quadriceps-strengthening exercises, designed to minimize patellofemoral force while increasing quadriceps strength, are recommended. Short arc extensions and biking, as described under the treatment of the athlete following patella dislocation, are two ways of achieving this objective. Another is straight leg lifts, with minimal weights and maximal repetitions.

Devices that limit pronation are often useful in treating patella pain. Many track shoes have varus wedges (thicker heels medially than laterally). Special orthotics that fit in the shoe underneath the heel and part of the sole of the athlete's foot can be bought at many running shoe stores, and if that does not work, the injured exerciser can have custom-fitted orthotics made. To limit pronation, orthotics have a much thicker base underneath the medial heel than under the lateral aspect of the heel. For an orthotic to limit pronation effectively, it must be used in a shoe that has a tight counter to grip the heel and a saddle to keep the foot from slipping over the orthotic.

Icing the parapatellar area following exercise may be helpful to decrease inflammation, and hence, pain. Oral anti-inflammatory agents, either aspirin or another nonsteroidal drug, may be useful in the patient who is acutely symptomatic.

Braces like those previously described for use in athletes with patella subluxation or dislocation can also be helpful in altering patella tracking in patients with this syndrome.[12] In addition, there are patella straps or bands of material that fasten about the proximal tibia at the level of the patella tendon. Theoretically, these bands are designed to alter the resting length of the quadriceps-patella tendon unit, and hence, decrease the force this unit can generate at the patellofemoral joint, much like tennis elbow bands

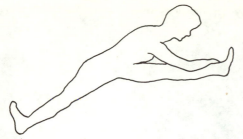

*Figure 15–17. Hamstring stretch. For stretching the left hamstring and the right side of the back, slowly bend forward from the hips toward the foot of the left leg from a sitting position with the legs spread. Keep the head forward and the back straight. Hold the stretch for 20 seconds. With repetitions, the stretch will become easier. Repeat the stretch with the opposite leg. (From Vinger and Hoerner: Sports Injuries. John Wright PSG, Boston, 1982, p. 237, with permission.)*

are thought to alter force generated by the wrist extensor mechanism, and hence, decrease the stress placed on the lateral epicondyle.

The athlete should be instructed to avoid prolonged knee flexion; i.e., she should not sit "Indian-style" for long periods of time, she should stretch her legs frequently while riding in a car, and so on. Her training routine should be reviewed to make certain she is not doing activities that maximally load the patellofemoral joint, such as stair-climbing or deep squats. If the hamstring muscles are tight, hamstring-stretching should be initiated. Slow stretches, as shown in Figure 15–17, are recommended.

### Prognosis

Although the patellofemoral stress syndrome may be associated with significant pain, which incapacitates the athlete, this overuse syndrome is not typically associated with any permanent impairment. Unlike chronic patella subluxation or multiple patella dislocations, patellofemoral stress syndrome infrequently results in chondromalacia or frank patellofemoral arthritis.[9]

### Patella Plica

Patella plica (also called synovial plica or patella shelf) is a normal developmental fold of tissue that sits retropatellarly. It is the em-bryonic remnant of the divisions in the knee.[13]

### Symptoms

The remnant is normally thin and filmy, but following multiple episodes of minimal trauma or one severe acute traumatic episode to the patellofemoral joint, this fold of tissue can become thickened. When the patella rides over this thickened fold, it can cause an audible "pop" and associated pain. The pain may be reported by the athlete as being diffuse, or as being definitely associated only with the "pop" and localized well along the medial side of the joint. She may feel a catching sensation as the patella tries to slide under the thickened fold.

Pain can be gradual in onset over days and weeks, as this tissue slowly thickens with multiple low levels of trauma, or it can be acute, especially if the athlete has had a knee-intense activity and the plica has acutely been irritated and thickened.

On physical examination, the athlete may have a small effusion. She will feel tenderness over the medial parapatellar area over the location of the plica. Moreover, an audible "pop" or snap can be felt as the knee actively extends, and this sound is accompanied by pain. Occasionally, the "pop" can also be produced by passive knee extension.

### Treatment

For the acutely symptomatic athlete, having her rest the knee in extension in a soft knee immobilizer for 5 to 10 days, and prescribing a nonsteroidal anti-inflammatory agent such as aspirin may decrease inflammation and resolve the symptoms completely.

Treatment of the athlete with chronic pain from a symptomatic plica is more difficult. Rest and anti-inflammatory agents can be tried. Exercises to alter patella tracking may also be helpful. In rare cases, excision of the patella plica must be done to relieve symptoms.

### Patella Pain: Summary

Patella pain is one of the most common musculoskeletal complaints in female athletes. It may result from repeated episodes of patella dislocation, from multiple patella subluxations, from patellofemoral stress syndrome, or from symptomatic patella plica. Diagnosis is made on history and physical examination. Altering patella tracking while decreasing acute inflammation is the basis of most treatment programs.

## IMPINGEMENT SYNDROMES

Impingement syndromes result when soft tissues are repetitively traumatized between bony prominences. For example, shoulder impingement refers to irritation of bursa and rotator cuff tissue, which becomes trapped between the humeral head and acromion with shoulder elevation if the humeral head is not firmly held in the glenoid fossa. Impingement syndromes commonly occur about the ankle, the wrist, and the shoulder, and are particularly common in women involved in gymnastics, racquet sports, swimming, throwing sports, ballet, diving, ice skating, and crew (see Table 15–1).

### Ankle Impingement

Impingement of soft tissues about the ankle may occur with either repetitive marked dorsiflexion, such as that seen with landings in gymnastics, or repetitive marked plantar flexion, such as occurs in dance, gymnastics, and diving. Athletes with anterior capsular impingement complain of pain in the region just lateral to the anterior tibial tendon as it crosses the ankle. The pain is increased with dorsiflexion activities, and may even be present only when performing this maneuver.

Posterior capsular pain may be harder to localize. The athlete describes her pain as posterior in the ankle, deep to the Achilles tendon. The pain is present when she rises to her toes, and in fact may prevent her from achieving a forced plantar flexed position. On palpation of her peroneal tendons, Achilles tendon, and posterior tibial tendon, no tenderness is found.

Ankle radiographs of the athlete with soft tissue ankle impingement appear normal, but occasionally athletes may demonstrate bony abnormalities (beaking of the tibia and talus anteriorly, and hypertrophy of the talar process posteriorly) (Fig. 15–18).

Treatment of most athletes with ankle impingement syndromes is conservative. Oral and/or local administration of anti-inflam-

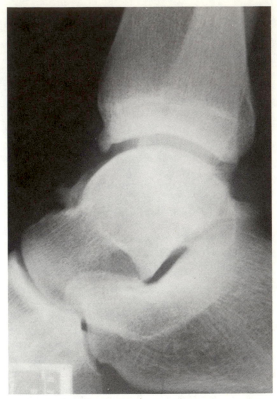

**Figure 15–18.** *Beaking of the anterior talar-tibial surface, secondary to multiple flexor impingements. With repetitions, the stretch will become easier. Repeat the stretch.*

matory agents, ice massage, ultrasound, electrical stimulation, and other physical therapy modalities may help diminish the inflammatory response. Use of an anterior ankle pad for anterior impingement, or a posterior pad to prevent hyperextension with posterior impingement may be helpful. The athlete should review her fundamentals, as alteration of technique may diminish symptoms; for example, "landing short" in gymnastics results in a hyperflexed position and may precipitate anterior capsulitis. In the rare athlete with excessive bony hypertrophy, surgical excision may be required.

### Wrist Impingement

Impingement of the palmar capsule of the wrist is not as common as that of the dorsal capsule. Dorsal capsular impingement may develop acutely if an athlete falls on an outstretched hand or absorbs a sharp impact on the dorsiflexed hand, such as might occur in a tumbling routine in gymnastics, in a poor angle of contact with a volleyball, or in improper baton handoff in track.

The athlete with dorsal impingement will complain of pain diffusely along the dorsal wrist structures. The pain is made worse with forced dorsiflexion. A fracture of the radius or navicular must be considered in the differential diagnosis of any athlete presenting with a painful wrist. The pain of dorsal capsulitis will not be limited to the snuffbox, as with navicular fractures, and the pain is more distal (centered over the radial-carpal junction) than that seen with a nondisplaced radial fracture. Radiographs are normal.

Rub-in analgesic cream and ice massage, as well as other physical therapy modalities, may be helpful. After acute pain subsides, strengthening exercises for the wrist extensors and flexors are recommended prior to returning to the sport. Chronic impingement pain—that is, pain that has been present at a low level of discomfort for several months—is more difficult to resolve than the pain of acute impingement. Similar treatment routines are used, however. Taping the wrist upon return to activity may be beneficial in the athlete with either an acute or a chronic wrist impingement.

## Shoulder Impingement

Shoulder impingement is commonly seen in swimmers and in athletes participating in throwing and racquet sports. The impingement syndrome results from a weakened rotator cuff, which allows upward migration of the humeral head in the glenoid, causing compromise of the humeral-acromial space. As this space becomes compromised, the tissues contained therein, those of the subacromial bursa, and the rotator cuff itself can become traumatized and inflamed. With greater inflammation, there is greater mass of tissue; and therefore, a vicious cycle of pain, swelling, more pain, and more swelling is established. Shoulder impingement is often associated with bicipital tendinitis, since the biceps tendon lies in the subcromial space and can be irritated as part of the syndrome.

The athlete with shoulder impingement complains of pain at the tip of the acromion or in the proximal arm. Frequently the pain radiates down the external rotators of the

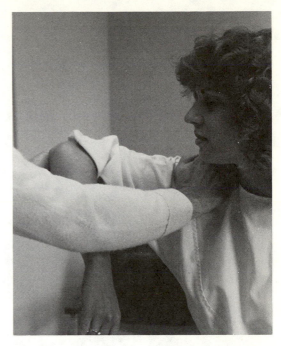

**Figure 15–19.** *To produce the impingement sign of the shoulder, the examiner holds down the acromioclavicular area while elevating the extremity at the elbow in a pronated, abducted, and forwardly flexed position. If this maneuver reproduces the pain of impingement it is called a positive impingement sign.*

shoulder. Tenderness can be elicited if the examiner places one hand on the patient's acromion, holding it down while elevating the arm in either forward or side flexion, mimicking the impingement process that occurs dynamically during sport. This maneuver is termed the "impingement sign" (Fig. 15–19).

No atrophy is generally found. The biceps tendon will be tender if it is involved in the impingement process. There is often tenderness over the acromioclavicular joint, especially if arthritis of this joint is present, as in the older patient who develops the impingement syndrome. Acromioclavicular arthritis is less common in the younger competitive athlete. Typically, external rotation strength is diminished over the opposite side, but abduction is possible.

Shoulder radiographs are usually normal in the young athletic individual with shoulder impingement. In the impingement syndrome of some athletes, one occasionally sees osteophytic spurring of the inferior surface of the acromion or sclerosis of the lateral

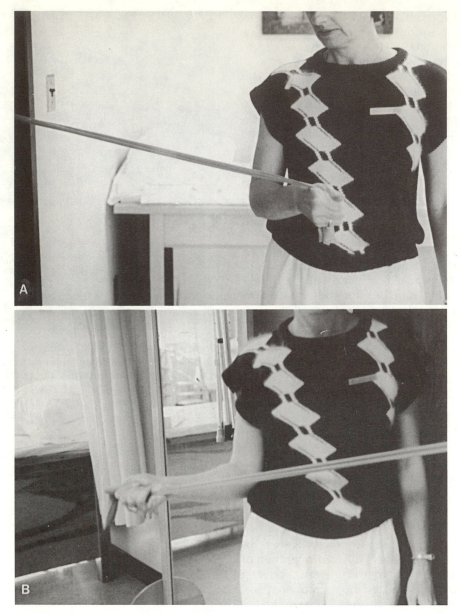

**Figure 15-20.** A, *Patient using rubber tubing to strengthen the internal rotators of the shoulder. Note that the elbow is held tightly to the side and the forearm is rotated internally to the abdomen, as the rubber tubing is affixed to the door. B, Patient demonstrating use of rubber tubing to strengthen external rotators of the shoulder. Again, the elbow is held tight to the side and the forearm is rotated externally against the resistance of rubber tubing affixed to the door.*

aspect of the humeral head from repetitive trauma.[14]

A treatment program for the athlete with an impingement syndrome may include temporarily avoiding any activity that requires the elbow to be raised above shoulder height, combined with physical therapy modalities and oral anti-inflammatory agents.

After the initial inflammatory response subsides, exercises to strengthen the rotator cuff muscles, to reinstitute proper mechanics of the shoulder, are advised. Many different exercise routines can be used to strengthen the rotator cuff. The simple exercises using rubber tubing attached to a door (Fig. 15-20) were adapted from the program initiated by the Naval Academy.[15] The athlete should be advised to review technique with her trainer or coach, as frequently impingement is precipitated by an alteration in form; e.g., in swimming, an increase in internal rotation of the arm at the shoulder may cause impingement of the tissues.

Chronic impingement syndromes are much more difficult to treat. Physical therapy modalities and oral anti-inflammatory agents can be tried. However, the key to improvement of symptoms is to reinstitute proper shoulder mechanics through a rotator cuff–strengthening exercise program. The athlete should be advised that such a program will take anywhere from 4 to 6 weeks, so she should not become discouraged. Controversy exists as to the role of injected steroids to diminish symptoms. The decision to use these should depend on the assessment of each individual case.

## OTHER COMMON CONDITIONS

### Achilles Tendinitis

Achilles tendinitis is the result of damage to the fibers of the Achilles tendon or to its tendon sheath. It can be seen in sports requiring repetitive ankle flexion and extension (e.g., track, basketball, soccer). It also occurs in athletes who wear boots, such as skaters and skiers, from the irritation of the boot on the tendon.

Acute Achilles tendinitis is usually characterized by pain that is exacerbated when the patient actively plantar flexes or resists passive dorsiflexion of the foot. Chronic Achilles tendinitis usually results in severe pain on first rising in the morning, which lessens with activity. It also generally causes considerable pain at the start of a workout, which lessens as the workout progresses.

When asked to localize her pain, the athlete will touch either the tendon behind the ankle or its insertion into the superior posterior tip of the calcaneus. If the examiner puts a hand over the patient's Achilles tendon, frequently crepitation can be heard as the athlete moves her foot from dorsi- to plantar flexion. The posterior ankle may appear swollen when compared with the opposite extremity. This swelling may be easier to assess if the patient stands facing away from the examiner or if she lies prone on the examining table.

### Treatment

Treatment requires resting the tendon. Sports that require running stress the Achilles tendon most, so the athlete is encouraged to substitute sports that use upper body motions, pedaling, swimming, or rowing. If walking is painful, crutches to assist ambulation, heel lifts to relax the Achilles tendon, or cast immobilization can be used. Cast immobilization, continuing for several weeks, should be required only in severe cases that are unresponsive to other treatment. Rarely, the athlete will require surgical release of the inflamed tendon sheath.

Oral anti-inflammatory agents, local anti-inflammatory creams, ice massage (rubbing the inflamed area with an ice cube), ultrasound, iontophoresis, or electrical stimulation can all be useful in decreasing acute inflammation. Glucocorticoid injections are not generally recommended because, if injected into the tendon itself rather than the tendon sheath, they may weaken the tendon by compromising the blood supply.

Stretching an injured tendon can delay healing, but once the acute inflammation has subsided, exercises to stretch as well as to strengthen the Achilles tendon are begun. Stretching can be done by standing on a slant board with the heel lower than the ball of the foot, by leaning against a wall (facing it) with the feet flat on the floor, or by using a towel under the ball of the foot to pull the foot gently into increasing dorsiflexion. Toe raises are an effective strengthening exercise.

After pain has completely disappeared with walking, stretching, and gently jogging, the athlete can gradually resume her running sport. Icing following activity for several months is recommended, and the athlete should always warm up well and stretch prior to sport.

### Shin Splints

"Shin splints" may be used as a general term to refer to any pain between the tibial tubercle and the ankle that is not a stress fracture or compartment syndrome. However, many physicians use the term to refer specifically to pain along the anteromedial aspect of the tibia at the origin of the posterior tibial muscle (Fig. 15–21).

Running on hard surfaces, running in inappropriate shoes, having weak lower leg muscles, and improper stretching have all

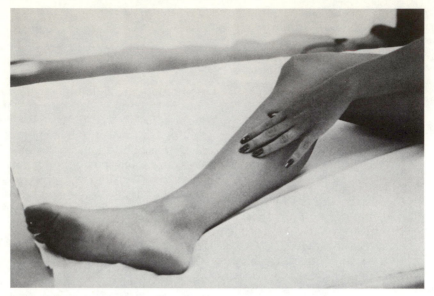

**Figure 15–21.** *Patient with shin splints demonstrating area of pain.*

been blamed for causing shin splints. Running on hard surfaces or in noncushioned shoes may increase stress on the longitudinal arch of the foot and, hence, indirectly on the posterior tibial muscle and tendon that help support this arch.

Diagnosis of shin splints is made by history and physical examination. Pain may initially increase with activity, usually improves as the activity proceeds, and may return following activity. The pain of shin splints is localized to a 2- to 4-inch area on the anteromedial aspect of the tibia at the origin of the muscle. Radiographs usually are negative, but occasionally some diffuse periosteal reaction at the posterior tibial muscle origin can be seen.

Shin splints must be differentiated from a stress fracture of the tibia. The pain of a stress fracture increases with activity and is relieved with rest. The athlete with a stress fracture of the tibia will have a very discrete area of pain on palpation of the tibia (see section on Stress Fractures, following).

As with other overuse syndromes, shin splints can be treated with rest, local and/or oral anti-inflammatory agents, physical therapy modalities (e.g., ultrasound and electrical stimulation), and ice massage (more effective than an ice bag). Stretching and strengthening exercises for the posterior tibial muscle, as well as the associated toe flexor muscles, are recommended. Support of the tendons by arch supports or taping may be beneficial.

In patients with chronic shin splints, slow return to sports may be advocated despite the persistence of mild symptoms, as long as the possibility of a stress fracture has been eliminated. The athlete should be very careful to warm up sufficiently and perform adequate stretching prior to beginning activity. If an activity causes severe pain, it should be discontinued. The athlete may be able to substitute another activity (e.g., changing from running to biking) until her symptoms improve sufficiently to permit return to her preferred sport.

**Stress Fractures**

When the rate of bone breakdown from activity (a normal process) is greater than the rate of bone formation (repair), a stress fracture may result. Stress fractures have been reported to occur more often in female than in male athletes.[16] The reason for this increased incidence may be a lack of conditioning or improper training technique, rather than a true predisposition to injury. A woman who fails to condition slowly and sensibly for her sport does not give her bone ample time to increase in cortical thickness to meet the mechanical demands of the activity.

Some investigators have tried to relate the low estrogenic secondary amenorrhea seen occasionally in competitive female athletes to osteoporosis and a higher incidence of stress fractures.[17,18] However, the only area of diminished bone content in these women has been in the cancellous bone of the vertebral bodies;[19] no change in the density of cortical bone has been found. Most stress fractures occur just proximal to the metaphysis, in the areas of cortical bone. Therefore, it is doubtful that their incidence is related to the low estrogen levels. More investigation needs to be done in this area.

In the few studies that have been reported, the most common location of stress fractures in women is the tibia;[20] also common are fractures of the fibula and metatarsals. Fractures of the pars interarticularis are a special type of stress fracture, as noted in the previous section on low back pain.

### Diagnosis

The pain of a stress fracture is typically restricted to a limited anatomic area. It is made worse with activity and may be relieved with rest. Radiographs are helpful in diagnosing stress fractures only if the pain has been present for a minimum of 2 to 3 weeks. Since stress fractures are really "microfractures," the fracture line itself is often not visible on the x-ray film. Radiographs do not demonstrate an abnormality until significant healing reaction of the periosteum (healing callus) is present.

To diagnose a stress fracture before a healing callus is visible radiographically, a bone scan can be done. This study will detect increased osteoblastic activity as soon as microfractures occur. Bone scans are particularly valuable in diagnosing intracapsular stress fractures, such as those of the femoral neck. In this location, bone has no periosteum. Hence, radiographs demonstrate no abnormality until intracortical healing takes place, and this takes longer than periosteal healing.

### Treatment and Exercise

In treating stress fractures, the primary consideration is to decrease the mechanical stress on the bone to allow healing to occur. Neither cast immobilization nor operative stabilization is generally required. For stress fractures of the lower extremity, the athlete should use a cane or crutch until she can bear weight on the extremity without pain.

Swimming and bicycling can be started early in the treatment of stress fractures. These activities will maintain cardiovascular endurance and muscle tone, but are non–weight-bearing activities and therefore do not stress bones of the lower extremities in the same manner as running and walking. Psychologically, the athlete will fare much better if she can participate in some sporting activity during her treatment course.

Because stress fractures heal at variable rates, it is better to advance activity as pain resolves rather than to establish routine time intervals for activity adjustment. When no pain results from walking long distances unassisted by crutches or cane, running can be attempted.

### Low Back Pain

Causes of low back pain have been listed as mechanical, neurologic, neoplastic, infectious, and metabolic. Mechanical causes, the most frequent in athletes, include nerve root impingement; repetitive microtrauma resulting in overuse syndromes such as tendinitis, fasciitis, and stress fractures; and some anatomic abnormalities. Most anatomic abnormalities, such as asymmetric lumbar or sacral facets, scoliosis, increased lumbar lordosis, and transitional vertebrae, do not usually result in back pain. However, unequal leg lengths (generally a difference of 1.5 cm or greater) may cause low back pain on a mechanical basis, especially in runners.

Athletes with mechanical low back pain may present with either an acute episode of severe low back pain, or with pain slowly increasing over several days or months. Pain associated with numbness or tingling of the lower extremities, or pain radiating from the back into the leg, implies nerve root impingement (neurologic back pain).

On physical examination, mild, moderate, or severe spasm of the paravertebral muscles may be found. Palpation of the low back region usually elicits pain. Reflexes, motor function, and sensation are normal in both lower extremities. Radiographs may be normal or show a lumbar list (curve) secondary to muscle spasm.

Most low back pain runs a 2- to 3-week course but is self-limited. If pain lasts longer

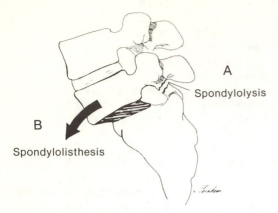

**Figure 15–22.** A, *Spondylolysis.* B, *Spondylolisthesis. (From Norkin and Levangie: Joint Structure and Function. FA Davis, Philadelphia, 1983, p. 151, with permission.)*

despite institution of conservative therapy with bed rest, muscle relaxants, anti-inflammatory agents, physical therapy modalities, and a graded exercise program, the athlete should be thoroughly evaluated to rule out the possibility of spondylolysis (a defect in the pars interarticularis, as in Figure 15–22), spondylolisthesis (forward slipping of one vertebra on an adjacent vertebra, also in Figure 15–22), disc herniation, infection, neoplasm, or metabolic disease. Most acutely symptomatic lumbar disc problems in athletes respond to conservative measures.

### Spondylolysis

Female gymnasts have been found to have a greater incidence of spondylolysis than the general population.[21] Defects in the pars interarticularis in the athletic population present an intriguing diagnostic problem: Is this defect a stress fracture resulting from repetitive hyperextension and flexion activities of the area, or is it a developmental abnormality? The youngest reported pars defect occurred in a 3½-month-old child. An increased incidence of the defect is seen between the ages of 5½ and 6½; by age 7, 5 percent of all white children have been found to have a pars defect.[22] A familial predisposition for this defect has been reported.

If initial radiographs demonstrate a well-established pars defect indicative of an older injury, return to athletics can follow a period of rest. A strengthening program should be instituted prior to returning to activity. Bent-knee sit-ups, walking, and swimming all help to develop abdominal and paravertebral muscles.

### Spondylolisthesis

Spondylolisthesis occurring in association with spondylolysis is most common in females between the ages of 9 and 13 years. Unlike spondylolisthesis in the adult, which tends to remain stable, spondylolisthesis in children can increase in severity during the years of rapid growth. Children known to have spondylolisthesis who complain of back pain should be examined carefully to note any progression of their slip.

There is disagreement over whether athletes with mild spondylolisthesis should return to contact sports: some authorities have suggested that they can do so if they are protected by a brace. Although this may be acceptable in a football lineman, female gymnasts would find it difficult to compete in such a restrictive device.

Rarely, the athlete with spondylolisthesis may have persistent significant pain following a treatment program consisting of resting, taking anti-inflammatory agents, and wearing a brace. Fusions are occasionally performed in these recalcitrant cases. A few athletes have even returned to their sport following fusions for spondylolisthesis, but contact sports are generally not recommended.

### Stress Fractures

In athletes with normal radiographs and persistent low back pain, the possibility of stress fracture must be entertained. A bone scan may be required to establish this diagnosis. If this is positive, resting from activities for a minimum of 3 to 4 months is recommended, and many physicians suggest immobilization in a spica or plastic orthosis.[23] Anti-inflammatory and muscle relaxing agents can be useful for symptomatic relief. A program of abdominal and back-strengthening exercises should be instituted prior to returning to athletics.

### Herniated Lumbar Disc

Athletes with nonradicular back pain unresponsive to conservative measures or with radicular back pain should be evaluated for possible herniated lumbar disc. In the athlete with radicular pain, careful neurologic examination may enable localization of the pain to a particular nerve root or disc level.

Initial treatment of the athlete with suspected disc herniation is similar to that for mechanical low back pain—initial rest and oral anti-inflammatory medications, followed by a program of strengthening paravertebral and abdominal muscles prior to return to sport. Muscle relaxing agents and physical therapy modalities may be helpful in diminishing pain secondary to muscle spasm.

In the athlete whose pain is unresponsive to such treatment over 2 to 3 weeks, or who has increasing neurologic complaints (increased weakness, muscle atrophy, decreased sensation in the lower extremities, absent reflexes, and so forth), further evaluation by CAT scan, magnetic resonance imaging or myelogram may be needed, and surgical decompression of the ruptured disc may have to be done. However, less than 30 percent of myelogram-proven ruptured discs need operative intervention.[24] Most improve with conservative measures.

### Vertebral Apophysitis

Another cause of back pain in the skeletally immature population is vertebral apophysitis, irritation of the growth centers of the vertebral body. Inflammation is felt to result from traction on the epiphysis (the growth center) from the anterior longitudinal ligament, as it is stretched in repetitive extension maneuvers that are a part of sports such as gymnastics, diving, and skating.

Rest often relieves symptoms, yet bony changes may persist. Prior to returning to sports, these youngsters should begin a strengthening and flexibility program for back and abdominal muscles. Symptoms determine when a child may resume full participation in sports.

### Bunions

The abnormal prominence of the inner aspect of the first metatarsal head, accompanied by bursal formation and resulting in lateral displacement of the great toe, is termed a bunion. Bunions appear to be more common in women, and hence, they are more common among female athletes than among male athletes. Many women have inflammation of the bursa overlying the medial prominence or flare of the great toe metatarsal head, without significant changes in the metatarsophalangeal joint. This bursitis is

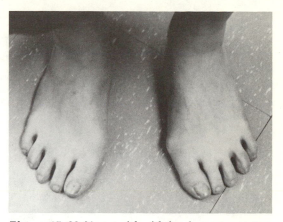

**Figure 15–23.** *Young girl with bunions on metatarsus primus varus.*

most prevalent in those with metatarsus primus varus (Fig. 15–23). Shoe alteration and protective pads to reduce pressure over the metatarsal flare are often helpful in diminishing symptoms. The problem is more difficult when the athlete has not only bursitis but also degenerative changes in the metatarsophalangeal joint, a condition seen in athletes involved in kicking sports.

The athlete with bunions must be careful when choosing shoes. They should have a sufficiently wide forefoot, yet be narrow enough in the heel to prevent the foot from sliding forward in the shoe. With forward slippage, the first ray is forced into a valgus position and pressure is exerted on the medial metatarsal head.

If pain persists despite all conservative treatment, bunionectomy can be performed, but great care must be taken to avoid altering foot mechanics disadvantageously by such a surgical procedure. Figure 15–24 demonstrates multiple stress fractures of the middle metatarsals in a long-distance runner, which occurred following a bunionectomy. Operative procedures should not be done purely for cosmetic reasons; they should be reserved for cases in which pain is unresponsive to conservative care.

### Morton's Neuroma

Pain between the second and third metatarsal heads, or between the third and fourth metatarsal heads, made worse by transverse compression of the forefoot, generally results from inflammation and scarring about the in-

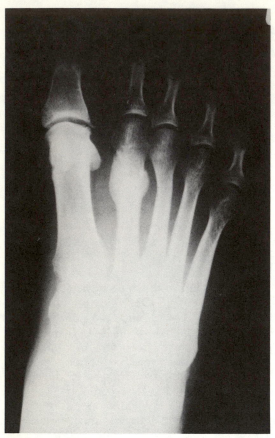

***Figure 15–24.*** *Runner who has had stress fractures of the second and third metatarsals following her bunionectomy procedure. The stress fracture of the second metatarsal is old and has a good healing reaction associated with it, whereas the stress fracture of the third metatarsal is new and no healing reaction is yet seen.*

terdigital nerve (i.e., Morton's neuroma). The patient may complain of numbness in the toes supplied by the compromised nerve. Swelling between the metatarsal heads at the site of the neuroma may also be noted.

The mechanism of development of this lesion is not clearly understood, but it appears to involve scarring of both the nerve and the supplying vessel.[25] It has been theorized that compression of the adjacent metatarsal heads creates repetitive trauma, which produces scarring.

In some cases, a metatarsal pad will alleviate symptoms. The athlete should be advised to wear wider shoes and place antiskid pads in the shoes to prevent forward migra-

tion of the foot in the shoe, causing transverse compression of the metatarsal heads.

If all these measures fail, excision of the neuroma may be performed, but the athlete should be warned that postoperative swelling of the foot can persist for 3 to 4 weeks following the procedure. She should plan resection of the neuroma for an appropriate time in her competitive season to permit an adequate recovery.

## SUMMARY

Over the last several decades, we have seen an increasing awareness of women's sports injuries. Since better conditioning programs have been instituted, the rate of injuries has diminished. When injuries do occur, whether acute traumatic injuries or chronic overuse syndromes, proper diagnosis and treatment should be instituted as soon as possible to help minimize the time lost from sport.

Frequently, sport substitution is possible, and therefore, a swimming athlete with an upper extremity injury may well be able to cycle or run to maintain her conditioning level, even though she cannot use her upper extremity until her injury heals. Similarly, a runner with patellofemoral stress syndrome may be able to cycle to increase the quadriceps muscle and yet not irritate her patellofemoral joint. Substitution of one aerobic sport for another is important to an athlete, because it allows her to maintain her conditioning level while allowing her injury to heal.

Guidelines for the athlete's return to exercise after orthopedic injury or surgery are discussed in greater detail in Appendix A.

## References

1. Albohm M: Equal but separate—insuring safety in athletics. JNATA 13(3):131, 1978.
2. Anderson J: Women's sports and fitness programs at the U.S. Military Acacemy. The Physician and Sportsmedicine 7(4):72, 1979.
3. Eisenberg I, and Allen W: Injuries in a women's varsity athletic program. The Physician and Sportsmedicine 6(3):112, 1978.
4. Clarke K, and Buckley W: Women's injuries in collegiate sports. Am J Sports Med 8(3):187, 1980.
5. Whiteside P: Men's and women's injuries in comparable sports. The Physician and Sportsmedicine 8(3):130, 1980.
6. Gillette J, and Haycock C: What kinds of injuries

occur in women's athletics? 18th Conference on the Medical Aspects of Sports, American Medical Association, 1977, p 18.

7. Shiveley RA, Grana WA, and Ellis D: High school sports injuries. The Physician and Sportsmedicine 9(8):46, 1981.

8. DeHaven K: Athletic injuries: Comparison by age, sport, and gender. Am J Sports Med 14(3):218, 1986.

9. Hunter L, Andrews J, Clancy W, et al: Common orthopaedic problems of the female athlete. American Academy of Orthopaedic Surgeons Instructional Course Lecture, Vol 31, 1982, p 126.

10. Bennett JB, and Tullos HG: Ligamentous and articular injuries in the athlete. In Morrey BF: The Elbow and its Disorders. WB Saunders, Philadelphia, 1985.

11. Hunter LY: Women's Athletics: The Orthopedic Surgeon's Viewpoint. Clin Sports Med 3(4):809, 1984.

12. Palumbo PM: Dynamic patellar brace: A new orthosis in the management of patellofemoral disorder. Am J Sports Med 9:45, 1981.

13. Boland A: Soft tissue injuries of the knee. In Nicholas J, and Hershman E: (eds): The Lower Extremity and Spine in Sports Medicine. CV Mosby, St Louis, 1986, p 938.

14. Cone R, Resnick D, and Danzig L: Shoulder impingement syndrome: radiographic evaluation. Radiology 150:29, 1984.

15. Regan K, and Underwood L: Surgical tubing for rehabilitating the shoulder and ankle. The Physician and Sportsmedicine 9(1):144, 1981.

16. Micheli L: Injuries to female athletes. Surgical Rounds 2:44, 1979.

17. Caldwell F: Light-boned and lean athletes: does the penalty outweigh the reward? The Physician and Sportsmedicine 12(9):139, 1984.

18. Mitchell D: Case presentation. In Bulletin of the Department of Gynecology and Obstetrics, Emory University School of Medicine, VI(1), 74–75, 1984.

19. Lutter J: Mixed messages about osteoporosis in female athletes. The Physician and Sportsmedicine 11(9):154, 1983.

20. Protzman R, and Griffis C: Stress fractures in men and women undergoing military training. J Bone Joint Surg 59-A(6):825, 1977.

21. Jackson D, Wiltse L, and Cirincrone R: Spondylolysis in the female gymnast. Clin Orthop 117:68, 1976.

22. Hoshina H: Spondylolysis in athletes. The Physician and Sportsmedicine 8(9):75, 1980.

23. Micheli L: Low back pain in the adolescent: differential diagnosis. Am J Sports Med 7(6):362, 1979.

24. Jackson D, and Wiltse L: Low back pain in young athletes. The Physician and Sportsmedicine 2:53, 1974.

25. Bossley C, and Cairney P: The intermetatarsophalangeal bursa: its significance in Morton's metatarsalgia. J Bone Joint Surg 62-B(2):184, 1980.

# CHAPTER 16

# Medical Conditions Arising During Sports

ARTHUR J. SIEGEL, M.D.

Things are not always what they appear to be. Athletes acquire an altered physiology from training, and as a result of those changes, basic laboratory tests that are abnormal for nonathletes may be normal for athletes. The medical literature is full of descriptions of medical conditions or illnesses in athletes that have subsequently been shown to be physiologic or normal responses to exercise. For example, athletic nephritis and athlete's anemia have been appropriately reclassified as pseudosyndromes. A physician who is unfamiliar with laboratory data in athletes may diagnose disease when none exists.

The following case history illustrates the complexities of medical conditions that may arise through intense sports activity:

A 21-year-old woman was brought to the emergency room scantly clad and comatose, having been found, unresponsive, by the roadside. Her blood pressure was 68/40, pulse 36 bpm and regular, respirations 8 and unlabored, temperature 96°F. Examination showed no evidence of head injury or other trauma. The chest was clear. The heart was markedly enlarged with an LV lift and pansystolic murmur with an S3 gallop. Abdominal examination was unremarkable. The extremities showed the appearance of muscle wasting with scant subcutaneous tissue and a height/weight ratio below the fifth percentile. Laboratory data included a hematocrit value of 30 percent, a urinalysis positive for protein and trace amounts of blood, and hyaline casts present in the sediment. Serum creatinine was borderline elevated at 1.7, liver and cardiac enzymes were two to three times normal with a CPK 10 times normal. Chest radiograph showed marked cardiomegaly without congestive heart failure. The ECG showed a first-degree AV block with voltage criteria for LVH, ST-segment changes consistent with early repolarization or acute ischemia.

This case illustrates the challenging differential that may arise during the acute evaluation of individuals—athletes or otherwise—with abnormal clinical examinations and laboratory data. Although this scenario might well fit an individual with an advanced stage of a debilitating illness (even AIDS), it is also entirely compatible with a nondisease state and might easily fit the description of an elite female marathon runner enjoying a nap after competition! Inability to arouse this patient with appropriate stimulation, or a marked elevation of body temperature, or both, might raise the possibility of severe heat injury or even heat stroke.

This sample case illustrates the importance of a working knowledge of the effects of endurance training on exercise physiology to assess specific conditions that may arise in athletes during sport as well as to differentiate true clinical problems from changes in laboratory data that may not indicate any underlying illness or dysfunction. A number of pseudosyndromes have been recognized in athletes, from the athletic heart syndrome to pseudonephritis, pseudoanemia, and pseudohepatitis. These are examples of abnormal laboratory findings which may result from strenuous training but not be connected to any underlying organ dysfunction.[1,2]

These pseudosyndromes must be differentiated from a range of medical complications that may arise in the athlete during prolonged strenuous exercise or competition, especially due to overexertion states. The purpose of this chapter is to examine both aspects of medical conditions arising during sports: true exercise-related illnesses, conditions, or risks; and the spectrum of pseudosyndromes or apparent disorders that may arise as a result of altered physiology through training.

## SCREENING THE ATHLETE FOR MEDICAL CLEARANCE

With an estimated 25 to 50 million young women engaging in sports activity, some basic concepts of medical clearance prior to sports participation justifiably arise. A sports-related questionnaire for athletes provides an opportunity for health screening with the purpose of identifying predisposing medical conditions that might lead to complications during sports participation. A sample questionnaire is included in Appendix 16–1, which addresses the major factors of sports injury as complications for young athletes and also screens for pre-existing medical conditions, medication allergies, and other possible complications. Such a medical checklist is useful in preventing problems during training and competition, such as exercise-induced asthma, anaphylaxis, and other conditions discussed in subsequent sections of this chapter. This gives the physician an opportunity to screen for areas of major concern such as possible familial heart disease, and also to practice prevention with regard to conditions such as sports-related anemia and oligomenorrhea, which commonly arise. A sample physical examination form for recording findings is given in Appendix 16–2, and a list of medical conditions disqualifying an individual for sports participation as provided through guidelines of the American Medical Association is found in Appendix 16–3. This focuses on acute conditions that should be evaluated prior to competitive sports participation. These sample materials are useful for identifying pre-existing medical conditions that may influence or affect sports participation, and they help prepare the athlete for safer training and participation. This focus is in contrast to subsequent discussion in the following sections of this chapter, which deal with conditions that may arise in previously healthy individuals during vigorous sports participation.

## GENERAL MEDICAL CONSIDERATIONS

Statistically, women differ from men in body composition. In general, women have less muscle mass than men, muscle comprising roughly 23 percent of a woman's total body weight compared with 40 percent in a man. Even fit women tend to have more body fat, 22 percent to 25 percent of ideal body weight, compared with 14 to 18 percent in men. Some exercise physiologists have speculated that this edge in percent of body fat might mean that women have a greater capacity for endurance training and performance.

Difference in body composition notwithstanding, all evidence points to identical patterns of physiologic adaptation for endurance training in women and men with respect to cardiovascular and musculoskeletal responses. Female athletes are as capable of achieving progressive increases in $\dot{V}_{O2max}$ as are male athletes, although muscular changes with progressive training in elite female athletes have been less well studied than they have in men.

## Heat Stress

Adaptation of the athlete to environmental stresses such as heat, cold, or altitude depends on specific physiologic responses, which may be different in women. The capacity to dissipate body heat generated during prolonged strenuous exercise depends on internal and environmental factors. The capacity for heat acclimatization depends on an increase in rate of sweat generation for level of exertion and a lower sodium content. As judged by such changes, heat-acclimatized men and women show similar adaptive patterns. After acclimatization, women's heart rates and rectal temperatures in hot and humid conditions at rest and after activity are the same of those of men.[3] Lower sweat rates in women are required to maintain comparable body temperatures, suggesting an improved efficiency in heat-released mechanisms. An increased risk for heat exhaustion might be hypothesized in women during the second half of the menstrual cycle from elevations in basal body temperature owing to progesterone effects. However, increased susceptibility to heat injury during the luteal phase has not been demonstrated in the scientific literature. Wells[4] studied the heat responses of women at different stages in their menstrual cycles in hot-dry and neutral environments. Sweat rates and evaporative heat loss did not vary through the menstrual cycle.

Drinkwater and colleagues[5] studied heat adaptation in female marathon runners and showed a relationship between physical fitness as measured by $\dot{V}_{O2max}$ and resistance to heat injury.[5] Female runners with high

$\dot{V}_{O2max}$ (49 mL $\cdot$ kg$^{-1}$ $\cdot$ min$^{-1}$ versus 39 mL $\cdot$ kg$^{-1}$ $\cdot$ min$^{-1}$) had lower heart rates, lower skin and rectal temperatures, and quicker onset of sweating compared with less-conditioned individuals. These findings are similar to patterns in men, and they confirm a resistance to heat-stress injury from physical conditioning. A high level of physical fitness, however, does not protect an athlete from heat exhaustion or potentially fatal heat stroke, which may accompany overexertion in a given level of training. Considerations for women are almost identical to those in men for heat-intolerance susceptibility. Studies in women during cold exposure and physiologic adaptation at altitudes show patterns similar to those in men under the same environmental stresses.

In summary, women are as susceptible to environmental stress as men during prolonged exercise, but equally capable of physiologic adaptation. Acclimatization to hot weather is facilitated by underlying fitness capacity, but still requires 7 to 10 days for optimal adaptation. Competitive athletes and recreational runners alike, men or women, must respect the limitations of internal (adaptive) and external (climatic) stresses. Copious consumption of fluids, especially water, during prolonged exercise is the best preventive medicine. Guidelines for prevention of heat injury as outlined by the American College of Sports Medicine should be considered, whether racing or out for a recreational jog.[6]

## HAZARDS OF EXERCISE: HEAT INJURY

Aerobic exercise involves the generation of internal heat through performance of muscular work. As the core temperature rises, an increased amount of cardiac output is delivered to the skin so that heat can be dissipated in the form of sweating. Heat is lost principally through evaporation of sweat from the body surface, which cools off the individual at the price of losing vital circulating fluids. Prolonged strenuous exercise invariably leads to dehydration, which may then lead to fatigue, confusion, lethargy, and persistent excessive body temperature. Advanced states of heat exhaustion from exercise may lead to coma and even cardiac arrhythmias and sudden death. These rare and extreme hazards can be avoided by adequate knowledge of the steps that prevent dehydration and hyperthermia during exercise.

The first tenet of prevention is adequate hydration before exercise. This is best done by consuming 8 to 10 ounces of water 10 to 20 minutes before beginning a strenuous workout. The warm-up phase of exercise allows the muscles and tendons to adapt to the biomechanics of exercise while the blood flow increases to exercising muscle. As body temperature rises, the sweating mechanism kicks into place with the perception of "second wind." Prolonged exercise should involve taking breaks to consume additional water and, when appropriate, moistening the body surface with sponging or spraying to assist in the cooling process. Such measures provide a form of "external sweating," which helps to dissipate heat through evaporation without needing to use internal fluid resources as the sole source of water for evaporation.

Sweating involves the loss of more water than sodium and chloride in comparison to their concentrations in blood. As a result, serum levels of sodium rise continuously during exercise. For this reason, salt supplements are undesirable prior to or during strenuous exercise, and in events lasting less than 2 to 3 hours individuals should rely on the use of water alone as the optimal repletion fluid in the prevention of heat injury. Exclusive and "excessive" water intake during prolonged events such as ultramarathon may lead to hyponatremia or low sodium levels.

Appropriate dress during exercise is a final important component to prevention of heat stress. This involves dressing in light and loose-fitting clothing during hot weather exercise, especially on humid days when the sweating mechanism is less efficient. In addition, exercising in full sunlight increases the risk, and use of a hat for protection from radiant energy in sunlight will help to protect from dehydration. Finally, individuals should use extreme caution when they sit in saunas or hot tubs after exercising. They should immediately leave these modalities if they feel the least bit dizzy, weak, or faint. All people are dehydrated after exercising, and saunas and hot tubs can cause considerable additional fluid loss, even in the absence of visible sweating.

Educating runners about heat acclimatization, prehydration, and control of exercise intensity during training and racing should result in less frequent heat injury. Emergency care when such complications do arise should prevent the fatalities that still occur from the medical consequences of severe exertional heat stroke. Physicians should encourage heat-injury precautions, including races to be run at cooler times of the day and canceled when wet-bulb temperatures exceed 28.0°C. Drinking 10 to 12 ounces of cold fluids, either diluted commercial drinks or fruit juice diluted to 2 to 3 parts cold water, is recommended to replenish fluid and potassium losses. Athletes should not wait to become thirsty, since 2 to 4 pounds of fluid loss may occur before thirst becomes intense. Warm fluids should not be consumed, as they are absorbed more slowly than cold fluids. Commercial drinks are high in sugar and may cause abdominal cramps if not diluted. Salt tablets and potassium supplements are not needed and are not recommended for shorter events (under 3 hours). One should acclimatize gradually, starting at 50 percent maximal effort and increasing 5 to 10 percent daily. Cotton socks to absorb sweat and white, nonporous clothing to reflect the sun's rays are also recommended. These preventive strategies are summarized in Table 16–1.

The best treatment of heat injury is immediate rapid cooling performed on-site and without delay. In an Australian study, the mean time it took to cool patients who had rectal temperatures equal to or greater than 41.5°C was 37 minutes.[7] No runners experienced the severe sequelae of heat stroke with this rapid-cooling approach. If treatment is delayed, major medical complications including fulminant rhabdomyolysis, acute renal failure requiring dialysis, hepatic necrosis, and disseminated intravascular coagulation can occur, although infrequently.[8,9] Common heat injuries and their treatment are seen in Table 16–2.

Heat injury is an internal as well as an external job. Prevention includes adequate pre-exercise hydration, cooling strategies during prolonged exercise, proper dress, and—most of all—avoiding overexertion for one's level of training. Novices and experts alike may fall prey to overestimating their potential, especially as weather conditions for heat injury (high temperature, humidity) prevail.

**Table 16–1.** MEDICAL ADVICE TO RUNNERS

**Training**

If possible, try to acclimatize yourself to heat if the race is to be run in hot weather. Try to run at least 36 to 50 miles a week in training runs and take occasional longer runs. If you cannot comfortably run 15 miles one month before the marathon, you may have trouble running the race safely. Cut back mileage several days before the race to avoid exhaustion on race day.

**Diet**

Eat what you feel comfortable with. Extreme changes, such as carbohydrate loading, may affect you adversely. A slight increase in vitamin C and salt intake may be beneficial, especially in hot-weather races. Decreasing protein intake and substituting carbohydrates several days before the race may increase your stores of muscle glycogen.

**Clothing**

Wear light-colored clothing to protect against heat and, if possible, wear mesh clothing on a hot day. Natural fibers such as cotton will chafe less than synthetics. On a warm day, if you are comfortably warm at the starting line, you are probably overdressed.

**Fluids**

Drink early and often. Try to drink one pint of water 10 minutes before you run and at least half a cup of water every 15 minutes thereafter. Wetting the skin with hose sprays or sponges can bring temporary comfort but is no substitute for drinking. You are adequately hydrated before a race if your urine is a pale straw color. Since dehydration can actually blunt your thirst mechanism, don't let thirst be your guide for drinking. If you are not used to electrolyte-glucose drinks, you may want to avoid them during the race.

**Running the Race**

Begin slowly. On humid days, when the temperature is 75°F or greater, slow your pace by 45 to 60 seconds per mile. If you experience persistent localized pain, seek medical help. The signs of heat exhaustion are headache, tingling or pins and needles in the arms, back, and extremities, fatigue, a weak pulse, cool, moist skin, profuse sweating, and cold chills. The signs of heatstroke are headache, convulsions, altered behavior or mental state, red-hot skin, and absence of sweating. If you feel any of those symptoms, seek medical help or at least slow down or walk. Race officials will be instructed to remove you from the course if you appear to be at risk of injuring yourself. If you have a pre-existing injury or medical condition that could endanger your health, do not run.

**Finish Line**

Get out of the sun. Drink fluids. If you don't feel well or feel faint, seek medical help. Get into dry clothes as quickly as possible.

From Editorial Staff: Marathon Medicine. Emerg Med 17(16):89, 1985, with permission.

The best prevention is a knowledgeable runner who knows her limits.

## CARDIAC CHANGES WITH EXERCISE AND TRAINING: RISKS AND BENEFITS

It has long been appreciated that endurance training can lead to changes in virtually every measurable cardiovascular parameter. Electrocardiographic changes include a variety of rhythm and conduction disturbances, as well as depolarization changes characteristic, in other clinical settings, of various diseases.[10] The heart as studied by echocardiography shows changes in both chamber size and myocardial mass, which vary with type of training. Endurance-trained athletes tend to have dilated chambers with a minor degree of increase in left ventricular wall thickness, resembling the volume-overload pattern seen in valvular regurgitation. In contrast, isometric or strength training induces a greater increase in wall thickness and total myocardial mass without chamber dilation, as is seen in valvular aortic stenosis. Work hypertrophy, as documented by these studies, is associated with supernormal left

## Table 16-2. COMMON RACE INJURIES AND THEIR TREATMENT

### Heat Cramps

A mild response to heat stress.

*Treatment*
If unaccompanied by serious complications, treat with rest, oral fluids, cooling down, stretching, ice and massage, and muscle massage.

### Heat Exhaustion

A serious situation in which hypovolemia develops as a result of excessive fluid loss. The rectal temperature may range between 100 and 105°F or higher. The runner experiences lassitude or dizziness, nausea, headaches, and muscle weakness. Although the runner is probably volume-depleted, sweating should be evident.

*Treatment*
For mild cases, treat the same as for heat cramps. For serious cases, including those with hypotension, persistent headache and vomiting, or altered mental states, initiate IV fluid resuscitation, cool vigorously (with an ice-water bath, for example), and consider transport to an emergency facility.

### Heatstroke

Often characterized by motor disturbances, such as ataxia, and severe nervous system disturbances, such as confusion, delirium, or coma. Circulatory collapse and hypotension are possible. Rectal temperature usually exceeds 105°F but may be lower after a period of collapse and cooling. The skin is usually warm but the victim may not sweat, although sweating usually occurs in the initial stages.

*Treatment*
Cool the runner immediately with hosing or fanning and ice applied to major arteries such as the carotid, axillary, femoral, and popliteal. If rectal temperature monitoring is possible, place the patient in an ice-water bath. Massage her extremities, raise her legs, place her in the shade, and begin volume replacement with 1 to 2 liters of half-normal saline, although more may be required. Transport immediately to a medical facility.

### Hypothermia, Exposure

Rare and most likely to occur in underdressed runners during cold-weather runs who either don't run fast enough to generate adequate heat or exhaust themselves early.

*Treatment*
Runners with a rectal temperature of 96.8°F or lower should be stripped of wet clothing, given warm clothing, and wrapped in blankets. If the runner is not shivering, she may be hypoglycemic. Give slightly sweet drinks. Monitor rectal temperature in those whose temperature is 91.2°F or lower.

### Hypoglycemia

May present as sweating, tremor, mental confusion, and combativeness.

*Treatment*
Rest and sugar or electrolyte glucose drinks.

### Hypovolemic Collapse

Seen most often in hot-weather races at the finish line, especially in runners who drink little or no liquid during the race. Hypotension, caused by diminished vasoconstriction, can lead to syncope. Runner's pulse will be weak and runner may be faint, cyanosed, or vomiting. It can occur as late as half an hour after the runner finishes the race if fluid intake is insufficient and will be worse if she's vomiting or has diarrhea.

*Treatment*
Take rectal temperature; have patient rest with legs raised; hydrate intravenously initially, then orally. Hypovolemia is usually self-limiting.

Modified from Editorial Staff: Marathon Medicine. Emerg Med 17(16):82, 1985, with permission.

ventricular performance during exercise, and, like the arrhythmias that may coexist, it is usually benign in nature. It is generally felt that asymptomatic athletes with documented myocardial hypertrophy and abnormal electrocardiograms do not require provocative or invasive cardiovascular testing prior to training or competition. In the absence of chest pain or syncope, bradyarrhythmias or even low grades of heart block and ventricular irritability need not be pursued as they would in symptomatic patients with suspected heart conditions. The sole caveat concerns the rare occurrence of sudden cardiac death in young athletes during sport, which is discussed in Chapter 17.

While the incidence of coronary heart disease is low in women compared with men, diseases of the circulatory system account for roughly two thirds of all deaths among women in the United States. The incidence of mild myocardial infarction or death from coronary heart disease in premenopausal women is below 1 in 10,000 per year. A large number of cardiovascular deaths occur in women after age 75, but cardiovascular deaths also account for one third of all deaths from age 65 to 74. Death rates from cardiovascular disease in women are 40 percent lower than in men for persons between 35 and 64 years of age and relative mortality for women falls to 25 percent of male levels for ages 35 to 44.[11] Nevertheless, cardiovascular death rates may be increasing in women, especially during the postmenopausal period, perhaps related to increases in women who have smoked cigarettes throughout their lives. Although smoking-adjusted rates for coronary heart disease in women under 45 years of age have not increased in the United States, Framingham data from other studies indicate an increase in coronary disease in postmenopausal women, with a risk profile similar to that observed in men. Risk factors for coronary artery disease in women include the standard triad of hypertension, hypercholesterolemia, and cigarette smoking. Regular exercise produces a beneficial effect on such a risk profile, reducing resting blood pressure, increasing the "good" or HDL cholesterol, and creating a positive incentive to stop smoking. In light of the high smoking rates in young women, it is particularly important to advise women to exercise and give up smoking, as these actions may be mutually reinforcing and beneficial.

Cardiac risk in women can be reduced by regular exercise using guidelines of consistency and moderation. Exercise is an extra incentive to avoid smoking and pursue a prudent, low-fat diet.

## HEMATOLOGIC EFFECTS OF EXERCISE IN WOMEN: IRON STATUS AND ANEMIA

Obligatory iron loss through menstruation creates a potential risk for iron depletion and, if mild or subclinical, secondary anemia. Studies in apparently normal, healthy college-age women document the depletion of total body iron stores—by examination of stained bone marrow aspirates—in up to 25 percent of subjects.[12] Rates of iron deficiency among apparently healthy college athletes may be somewhat higher, as reported in one blood study.[13]

Confusion is likely to arise between true iron-deficiency anemia and the so-called pseudoanemia, or sports anemia, of endurance training. Systematic observations have documented a drop in hemoglobin, hematocrit, and red blood cell count with onset of a 9-week training program in previously sedentary college women.[14] Values may fall to low-normal or within abnormal ranges during progressive training, with a return to baseline upon resumption of sedentary status. "Pseudoanemia" also occurs in male athletes, owing to hemodilution from an increase in plasma volume. Studies of red cell mass in athletic "pseudoanemia" show normal or high values with low hemoglobin parameters from an expanded plasma volume. Specific measurement of body iron stores, or its reflection in normal values for serum iron and iron-binding capacity or ferritin levels, establishes this dilutional cause of a low hemoglobin concentration.

A differentiation of true anemia (an absolute decrease in red cell mass) from pseudoanemia (a relative or dilutional decrease in hemoglobin value) cannot be made from measurement of the hemoglobin and hematocrit determinations alone. Clarification of true iron-deficiency anemia versus "pseudoanemia" in female athletes requires direct measurement of body iron stores. This can be done by measurement of serum iron and iron-binding capacity or serum ferritin levels, which are normal in the case of the "pseudoanemia" but low in the case of true iron

**Table 16–3.** LABORATORY DIFFERENTIATION
OF TRUE VERSUS PSEUDOANEMIA

|  | Pseudoanemia | True Anemia |
|---|---|---|
| Hemoglobin/ hematocrit | Decreased | Decreased |
| Red cell mass | Normal | Decreased |
| Plasma volume | Increased | Normal |
| Total blood volume | Increased | Normal |
| Iron/iron-binding capacity (IBC) | Normal | Decreased |
| Ferritin | Normal | Decreased |

From Siegel AJ: Understanding abnormal lab values in the female athlete.
Contemp Ob Gyn 25:73, 1985, with permission.

deficiency.[2] This differential is shown in Table 16–3.

Physicians should realize that the athlete in training has multiple additional stresses on iron stores. In addition to menstruation, female athletes may lose iron in sweat with a significant loss of stores over time if not accompanied by a balanced intake of iron in the diet. In addition, syndromes of exercise-related hematuria and more recently of gastrointestinal blood loss during exercise have been reported.[15] These may add to the burden of iron depletion in the athlete and create a true iron-deficient state.

The diagnosis of iron-deficiency anemia in women or men requires specific measurement of the serum iron parameters as noted previously. Low values for serum iron with a reciprocally increased serum iron binding capacity or a low serum ferritin level, or both, indicate depletion of total body iron stores and the need for specific supplementation. Treatment should consist of 300 milligrams of ferrous sulfate given once or twice daily for at least a year. Patients should be rechecked after that time to establish return of serum iron stores to the normal range. Persistent abnormalities may deserve further clinical investigation for sources of iron loss (menses, renal losses, gastrointestinal losses) if compliance with the treatment has been established.

It is reasonable to suggest routine iron supplementation for female athletes undergoing intense training, just as is recommended for pregnant women, because both conditions increase iron requirements. Routine iron supplementation, however, does not yield demonstrable benefits for the athlete with adequate iron stores.

Even in the absence of anemia, a decrease in body iron stores may cause a diminished exercise performance or capacity related to the role of iron in the tissue cytochrome and myoglobin systems. Recent reports have highlighted the importance of identifying borderline iron-deficiency states in athletes, even in the absence of anemia, through measurement of serum ferritin levels. Low serum ferritin levels indicate a need for treatment, even in the presence of normal serum iron levels. However, normal ferritin levels may not always exclude iron deficiency. Acute inflammation, as can be caused by infection or injury from heavy training, can transiently raise serum ferritin levels to normal range. Therefore, when iron deficiency is strongly suspected, ferritin levels should be assessed after the athlete has recovered from any febrile illness or stopped training for 2 or 3 days. Symptoms of fatigue and declining performance may be identical in "overtraining" and in marginal iron-deficiency states. Clinical observations suggest that repletion of diminished iron stores may reverse these symptoms and improve exercise performance.[14]

The sports-active woman requires adequate levels of iron to avoid depletion of reserves and possible compromise of exercise performance. Endurance training, like pregnancy, may require the regular use of iron supplements. Development of true iron deficiency in a female athlete warrants medical investigation to rule out pathologic causes of iron loss.

## POSSIBLE CAUSES OF "RUNNERS' ANEMIA"

In addition to menstrual losses, women face the additional possibility of ongoing iron loss during endurance training through additional body fluids such as sweat, urine, and feces. Recent studies have shown that some long-distance runners develop guaiac-positive stools during long-distance training and competition, which revert to normal within 72 hours.[15] The possible causes of blood loss include intestinal ischemia, stress gastritis, drug-induced lesions, and loss of blood from pre-existing lesions. Runners with anemia and guaiac-positive stools deserve a systematic medical investigation to rule out an intrinsic bowel problem unrelated to the exercise training.

More common than rectal bleeding is the rather frequent occurrence of runners' diarrhea, which is an expression of increased bowel motility akin to the irritable bowel syndrome seen with emotional stress in a large number of individuals. Manifestations range from minor abdominal cramping to severe watery diarrhea during prolonged strenuous exercise, which can interfere with performance and is intensified by the stress of competition. This condition, sometimes termed "runners' trots," is often successfully treated with precompetition doses of antispasmodic agents.[16]

Another possible cause of iron loss producing "runners' anemia" is hematuria, as discussed in the following section.

## EFFECTS OF EXERCISE AND TRAINING ON THE URINARY TRACT

The occurrence of exercise-related urinary abnormalities has been extensively reviewed in the literature and in medical-specialty books, with the term "athletic pseudonephritis" applied to conditions associated with abnormal urinary sediments.[17,18] Severe volume depletion and dehydration can, indeed, lead to proteinuria and hematuria with the presence of formed elements such as proteinaceous casts. A prospective study of 50 male physician marathon runners showed that microscopic hematuria occurred in 18 percent in initial postrace urinalyses, but cleared within 24 to 48 hours.[19] Exercise-related hematuria appears to be a frequent and self-limited benign condition that does not warrant extensive invasive work-up. Gross hematuria occurred in only 1 out of 50 subjects, and must be considered a complication of nontraumatic sports such as running. Work-up of a series of patients with so-called 10,000-meter hematuria identified bladder trauma as the cause of this hematuria.[20] Other studies suggest that the bleeding may come from the kidneys. As concomitant bladder or renal pathology cannot be summarily excluded after gross hematuria related to exercise, it is reasonable to suggest intravenous pyelography and cystoscopy to exclude specific causes.

Positive Hemastix reaction without detectable blood on microscopic analysis of urine is suggestive of myoglobinuria. This reaction may be quite common, if not universal, in marathon runners after peak efforts, resulting from transient rhabdomyolysis during extended physical exertion.[21] Elevations of serum creatine kinase up to 30 times normal have been noted in marathon runners without perceived urinary symptoms or evidence of injury. Other studies have shown transitory decrements in creatinine clearance following marathon competition, which may be prerenal or related to volume depletion rather than due to tubular injury.[18] Whereas exertional rhabdomyolysis is common, acute renal failure is extremely rare.[9] It has been reported in patients with sickle cell trait who are at increased risk of renal tubular necrosis following rhabdomyolysis, which may then proceed to other complications such as disseminated intravascular clotting.

Heat stress, prolonged strenuous exercise, muscle injury, and urinary abnormalities are thus interrelated. It is crucial for physicians to identify runners with acute hypovolemia occurring in heat-stress injury so that they can institute the rapid rehydration that will prevent attendant renal injury. Cases of acute renal failure following severe dehydration in marathon runners have been reported, although such injury is clinically preventable.[9] There is no evidence that permanent or progressive renal injury results from prolonged strenuous training as in long-distance runners. Acute increases in serum creatinine levels have been reported but are readily reversible with rest and rehydration. Progressive renal damage from

**Table 16–4.** DIFFERENTIAL DIAGNOSIS FOR ABNORMAL TEST RESULTS

| Laboratory Findings | Clinical Condition | Exercise-Induced Findings |
| --- | --- | --- |
| Low hemoglobin, low hematocrit | Anemia (true iron deficiency) | Pseudoanemia (see Table 16–3) |
| Abnormal urinalysis (hematuria, proteinuria) | Renal disease | Transient changes |
| Positive test for GI bleeding | Intrinsic gastrointestinal pathology | Transient finding due to maximal exercise |
| Abnormal liver enzymes: lactic acid dehydrogenase (LDH), serum glutamic oxaloacetic transaminase (SGOT) | Hepatic inflammation (true hepatitis) | Transient muscle injury accompanied by release of enzymes from skeletal muscle that are also present in liver tissue (pseudohepatitis) |
| Elevation of total creatine kinase and the MB isoenzyme | Myocardial disease | Chronic skeletal muscle injury or exercise-induced rhabdomyolysis |

The pseudosyndromes listed above (last column) are more common in rigorously training endurance athletes than in beginners.
From Siegel AJ: Understanding abnormal lab values in the female athlete. Contemp Ob Gyn 25:73, 1985, with permission.

recurrent low-grade rhabdomyolysis and myoglobinuria is a theoretical possibility but has not been demonstrated to date. Again, prevention is the best treatment, and runners should be encouraged to take fluids liberally during and immediately after strenuous physical effort. Differential diagnostic features or urinary sediment changes and other diagnostic tests are shown in Table 16–4. Prevention and treatment are summarized in Tables 16–1 and 16–2.

Strenuous exercise reduces renal blood flow and may result in abnormal urinary findings after exercise. Adequate rehydration, as discussed in an earlier section on heat injury, prevents renal tubular damage. Recurrent or persistent hematuria deserves medical evaluation to exclude non–exercise-related causes.

## SERUM ENZYME ABNORMALITIES: MUSCLE INJURY AND PSEUDOHEPATITIS

Prolonged strenuous exercise may be associated with transient elevations of skeletal muscle enzymes, which are also present in hepatocytes or liver cells. Serum levels of glutamic-oxalo-acetic transaminase and lactic dehydrogenase are routinely used as screening tests for hepatic dysfunction, and elevated levels of these enyzmes may frequently be assumed to represent hepatitis in runners. Measurement of specific serum enzymes such as creatine kinase can resolve this dilemma, so that elevations of creatine kinase and these other enzymes indicates transient muscle injury rather than liver disease, in the endurance-trained athlete. Several recent studies indicate that athletes may have enzyme elevations two to three times the upper limits of normal compared with age- and sex-matched sedentary individuals (see Table 16–4). These values may increase to 10-fold after racing, because of transient exertional rhabdomyolysis.[21] These findings are often accompanied by muscle soreness in the athlete and indicate the need for rest and maintenance of hydration. Specific clinical symptoms such as persistent headache, nausea, vomiting, or flank pain should lead to investigation of impaired renal function or other complications, as noted in the prior sections.

One avenue for excluding liver disease in a runner with abnormal enzyme profiles is to measure liver-specific "enzymes" such as alanine amino-transferase and gamma glutamyl transpeptidase. A recent paper documents some transient increases in these liver specific proteins in marathon runners after racing, indicating possible release from hepatocytes due to indirect trauma or decreased hepatic blood flow.[22] Persistence of abnormal liver function tests might warrant measurement of serum hepatitis markers to exclude chronic hepatitis but need not lead to invasive testing such as liver biopsy. Many runners have been referred to specialists for consideration of this procedure on the basis of the muscle injury parameters, as described earlier. Such invasive testing is usually unnecessary and should be avoided.

With reference to the biliary tract, it should be noted that some individuals have a genetic condition (Gilbert's disease) in which bilirubin conjugation may be impaired under physiologic stress such as strenuous exercise, infections, or prolonged fasting. Such individuals may develop an increase primarily in unconjugated serum bilirubin and may appear mildly jaundiced. This condition is benign and asymptomatic, and can be detected by somewhat elevated levels of unconjugated bilirubin in the face of otherwise normal liver enzymes. This elevation of unconjugated bilirubin is usually transient, whereas liver disease usually leads to persistent elevations of unconjugated bilirubin in the face of elevated liver enzymes. These findings are in contrast to those in patients with chronic hemolytic anemias, in whom pigment gallstones may be formed because of an increased biliary excretion of breakdown products of hemolysis, leading to significant elevations of direct bilirubin. Pigment gallstones have been reported in long-distance runners and attributed to runner's hemolysis, although this must be a very rare and unusual occurrence.[23]

Elevated serum enzymes in endurance-trained athletes regularly occur from chronic injury to skeletal muscle and are not specific for liver injury. The diagnosis of hepatitis should not be made in the absence of clinical symptoms or findings of hepatic dysfunction.

## PSEUDOMYOCARDITIS

In addition to the abnormalities in total creatine kinase that indicate transient muscle injury as noted earlier, chronic endurance sports participation may lead to transient elevations of the MB isoenzyme or heart-specific fraction of creatine kinase in serum.[24] Such elevations may at times be quantitatively similar to findings in patients with a variety of heart diseases such as cardiomyopathy, myocarditis, or injury secondary to ischemic heart disease.

Large increases in the serum total creatine kinase and CK-MB activities may be found in both men and women after competition. Cardiac isoenzymes are present in trained skeletal muscle, perhaps on the basis of chronic muscle fiber injury and repair.[25] Studies using heart scan techniques fail to reveal any underlying heart injury in these individuals. Abnormal elevations of serum CK-MB in an otherwise asymptomatic female athlete without cardiorespiratory symptoms can be reasonably attributed to an exercise-induced injury to skeletal muscle and not to a myocardial source (see Table 16–4).

## EXERCISE-INDUCED ASTHMA

Exercise-induced asthma (EIA) is a relatively common, readily diagnosable and treatable form of reversible bronchospasm.[26] It occurs with high frequency in individuals with an allergic or asthmatic background in whom exercise provokes or increases symptoms. Bronchospasm also occurs in subjects who do not have a clinical history of overt asthma, in whom symptoms may be unappreciated or subclinical until the additional work of breathing during exercise is imposed. The frequency with which such reactions are detected depends upon the sensitivity of measurements used, as well as on the type of exercise.

The typical course of symptoms is a slow onset of bronchospasm as one starts exercising, reaching a peak 6 to 8 minutes after the exercise phase begins. Symptoms often stabilize or subside if exercise is continued, and some of these individuals can exercise through their attacks after some initial difficulty. The postexercise rebound is well described, as difficulty may return or intensify after cessation of activity. Figure 16–1 shows the typical pattern of observed pulmonary function parameters with relationship to time in healthy subjects and those with EIA. The four parameters of lung function shown reflect the impairment during and after exertion. Simple spirometry with measure of the timed or one-second vital capacity is adequate to confirm suspected clinical cases in most instances.

Exercise-induced asthma causes the same bronchial smooth-muscle contraction that results from allergen-triggered asthmatic response. Recent investigations, however, reveal that EIA is not triggered by an allergic response, but rather by reactions of large and small airways to changes in humidity during

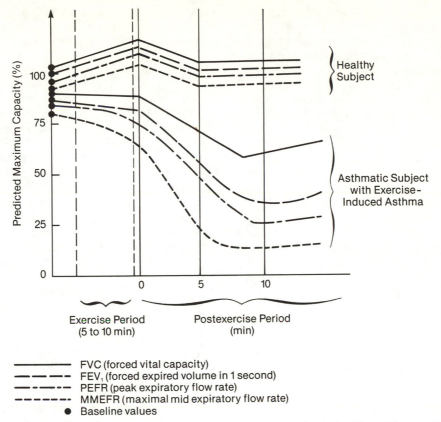

*Figure 16-1.* Comparison of spirometric measurements following exercise in healthy subjects and in patients with exercise-induced asthma. (Adapted from Gerhard H, and Schachter FN: Exercise-induced asthma. Postgrad Med 67(3):93, 1980, with permission.)

cold-air breathing. McFadden and Ingram[26] have shown that the magnitude of the bronchoconstrictive response to a fixed exercise task or to a fixed level of ventilation depends on the temperature and/or water content of the inspired air.[26] Lower air temperatures and humidity favor the obstructive response, which does not occur in susceptible subjects when inspired air is fully saturated with water at body temperature. Airway cooling from heat loss during high ventilatory work is the specific precipitant. These findings explain why corticosteroids are ineffective in treating exercise-induced asthma, whereas warming of inspired air through a face mask can be effective.

A wide range of treatments is available for patients with EIA, including warming of inspired air in cold weather as a preventive measure, and use of specific pharmacologic agents used in the treatment of traditional asthma. Those treatments approved by the International Olympic Committee for the

1984 Olympic Games are listed in Table 16–5. These agents can be taken as pre-exercise doses to block the onset or to minimize bronchoconstriction. A warm-up period is often

**Table 16–5.** ANTIASTHMATIC MEDICATIONS APPROVED BY THE INTERNATIONAL OLYMPIC COMMITTEE FOR THE 1984 OLYMPIC GAMES*

| Medication | Aerosol | Oral |
| --- | --- | --- |
| Theophylline | NA | Yes |
| Cromolyn sodium | Yes | NA |
| Albuterol | Yes | Yes |
| Terbutaline sulfate | Yes | Yes |
| Corticosteroid | Yes | Yes |

*Drug Commission of IOC requires name of athlete, country, drug, and dosage.
From Eisenstadt WS, Nicholas SS, Velick G, et al: The Physician and Sportsmedicine 12(12):100, 1984, with permission.

useful in reducing EIA, but inhalation of a bronchodilator just prior to peak exercise is highly beneficial. Sympathomimetics are disallowed in some competitive situations so that alternatives such as cromolyn sodium must be used. Cromolyn is not a bronchodilator and is most effective when administered 30 minutes prior to peak effort. Physicians must be aware of these special circumstances as well as the range of treatments available to the recreational athlete.

Persons susceptible to exercise-induced asthma should be encouraged to participate in sports and exercise that may have a beneficial effect on general physical conditioning and preservation of lung function. The adequately informed primary care physician can enhance the capability of patients to lead full and active lives despite the need for specific treatment.

Exercise-induced asthma is common, especially in individuals with a background of allergies in childhood. Patients may outgrow seasonal symptoms but develop wheezing or cough with exercise, especially in cold air. Preventive strategies include pre-exercise treatment with topical or inhalant bronchodilators.

## EXERCISE-INDUCED ANAPHYLAXIS

Individuals with a history of allergic reactions such as childhood eczema, seasonal rhinitis, or even asthma are prone to a second exercise-related reaction that begins with diffuse itching and may result in generalized hives or urticaria. Such symptoms may occur after years or decades of being allergy-free and may be limited to minor discomfort. The reaction can, however, progress to generalized angioedema, including facial swelling and laryngeal spasm, with compromise of the upper airways. This reaction was reported in a group of young athletes after a variety of sports and may be unpredictable in occurrence and severity for any individual.[27] Some authors have suggested that exposure to a specific allergen such as shellfish, to which the individual is subclinically sensitized, may then combine with exercise to trigger the allergic response. Exercise causes most cells to release vasoactive mediators similar to cold-induced urticaria, in which histamine is released in the skin after cold exposure. Susceptibility is not related to training or expertise, and exercise-induced anaphylaxis has been reported in national champions and in world record holders.[28] Management can entail preventive measures such as administration of mild antihistamines or perhaps cromolyn sodium prior to exercise. However, these treatments are only partially effective at best and do not completely prevent the reaction. Such pretreatment may be necessary for individuals only at times of peak risk, as the urticarial response may occur only seasonally when allergic predisposition is heightened. Just as a shellfish-allergic patient avoids eating shellfish, avoiding specific foods prior to exercise may control or eliminate the allergic response in these individuals.

The pathogenesis of exercise-induced anaphylaxis is identical to immunologic-mediated anaphylaxis, even though the trigger is physical rather than allergic.[27] Effector mast cells fire to release histamine, the slow-reacting substance of anaphylaxis, bradykinins, and other mediators, which then cause the angioedema. Facial swelling is an indication for specific emergency measures, such as intramuscular administration of 8 mg of dexamethasone or subcutaneous administration of aqueous epinephrine 1:1000, 0.1 ml to 0.3 ml, along with insertion of an IV tube for fluid administration. Hypotension may develop from generalized increased vascular permeability, which may require stabilization with fluids and vasopressive drugs. Dopamine (400 mg) and D5W (500 ml), given intravenously at an appropriate rate, may sustain blood pressure in the face of circulatory collapse. While potentially life-threatening, exercise-induced anaphylaxis has not yet resulted in a reported fatality. Patients who have had this reaction, as well as individuals with known bee-sting sensitivity (hymenoptera), should have epinephrine available for administration if severe allergic manifestations develop.

Exercise-induced anaphylaxis is a generalized, severe allergic response triggered by exercise in specifically susceptible individuals. Exercise acts like a trigger for the already "loaded" gun of the allergic response, which appears to be a de novo reaction.

The preventive measure most often suggested to susceptible individuals is to be equipped with a bee-sting kit for ready use if any angioedema develops.

## EXERCISE-INDUCED URTICARIA

In the spectrum of allergic reactions to exercise, some individuals may develop blotchy red rashes sometimes with itching during a workout. This is called exercise-induced hives or urticaria, and it results from histamine release in the skin owing to rapid superficial temperature changes. Like exercise-induced asthma, exercise-induced urticaria may occur more readily with temperature provocation, either cold or warm. Local symptoms of cold urticaria are redness, itching, wheals, or edema in the skin, not the subcutaneous swelling seen in anaphylaxis as described previously. Systemic symptoms and circulatory collapse do not occur.

This condition is benign and can be handled with reassurance to the athlete. Low doses of antihistamines may diminish symptoms and may be prescribed if the side effect of drowsiness is not more bothersome than the itching that may result from not taking the drug.

## CAUTION: WHEN NOT TO EXERCISE

Patients and athletes alike are aware of the need for a graduated return to exercise and training after muscular skeletal injury, orthopedic surgery, and even general surgery, when these are necessary in athletes. Guidelines include reduced intensity and duration of workouts with progressive incremental training at no more than 10 percent increases per week. A gradual return to exercise intensity promotes smooth recovery and reduces risk of reinjury or clinical setback.

Similarly, athletes must adjust to the realities of medical illness, including the impact on exercise capacity of minor illnesses such as viral syndromes, flu-like illnesses, and es-

pecially respiratory infections. Athletes must take time off from training during febrile illness, as acute illness places stress on all organ system reserves and poses the danger of prolonging illness and incurring additional injury. Many viral illnesses are systemic; i.e., all organ systems are subject to transient viral exposure. Exercise at such times can be hazardous and even lead to arrhythmias and unfortunate instances of collapse during workouts or competition. As a working guideline, I emphasize to athletes the importance of rest as well as stress in training and the necessity of allowing the body to recover from intercurrent illness in order to make future training safe and productive.

Appendix A discusses exercise following an infection in greater detail.

## SUMMARY

This chapter has addressed various medical conditions that may arise in sports-active women and that present clinical dilemmas to the office practitioner. On the one hand, athletes may develop abnormal clinical or laboratory findings that represent physiologic adjustments to training and are not indications of underlying illness. On the other hand, athletes do place themselves at risk for developing problems such as transient hematuria, gastrointestinal bleeding, anemia, and heat injury, which require specific monitoring to rule out non–exercise-related conditions.

Careful assessment of the individual athlete, together with a background fund of information, will enable the practicing physician to provide reassurance when appropriate and to respond to underlying clinical problems as they may arise.

The knowledgeable physician can assist the sports-active patient in enhancing her athletic goals while reducing concern over sports-related symptoms or conditions.

## Appendix 16–1. SPORT CANDIDATE'S QUESTIONNAIRE

Name _____ Age _____ Date of birth _____

School _____ Grade _____ Sex _____

Athlete's address _____ Tel. No. _____

Parent's name & address _____ Tel. No. _____

Regular physician _____ Tel. No. _____

| Medical History | Yes | No | Past or Present   Please Circle Item(s) in ( ) |
|---|---|---|---|
| 1. | —— | —— | Discuss with a doctor a (health problem, injury, diet)? |
| 2. | —— | —— | Discuss with a doctor (emotional problem, stress management)? |
| 3. | —— | —— | Any close family member with (diabetes, migraines, asthma, heart trouble, high blood pressure)? |
| 4. | —— | —— | Any family member who died suddenly under age 50, excluding accidents? |
| 5. | —— | —— | Any (illnesses lasting more than 1 wk, chronic or recurrent illness)? |
| 6. | —— | —— | Any (hospitalizations or surgery)? |
| 7. | —— | —— | Any (injuries or illnesses) requiring treatment by a doctor? |
| 8. | —— | —— | Any allergies (hay fever, hives, asthma, bee sting, or drug allergies)? |
| 9. | —— | —— | Any medications taken regularly or within last 6 mo? |
| 10. | —— | —— | Any neck injury? |
| 11. | —— | —— | Any (concussions, skull fracture, loss of memory or consciousness, convulsions or epilepsy, headaches)? |
| 12. | —— | —— | Any (eyeglasses, contact lenses, decreased vision, or temporary loss of vision)? |
| 13. | —— | —— | Any (hearing loss, perforated eardrum, recurrent ear infections)? |
| 14. | —— | —— | Any (broken nose, nosebleeds, dentures, braces, bridges, tooth caps)? |
| 15. | —— | —— | Have you ever fainted *during* exercise? |
| 16. | —— | —— | Any (heart trouble, murmur, arrhythmias, chest pain, high blood pressure)? |
| 17. | —— | —— | Do you (smoke, drink alcohol, take drugs)? |

| 18. | — | — | Any (pneumonia, tuberculosis, chronic cough)? |
| 19. | — | — | Any loss of, or serious injury to (eye, testicle, kidney, lung)? |
| 20. | — | — | Girls, any menstrual problems? Age at first menstrual period_____ |
| 21. | — | — | Any (hernias, kidney problems, ulcer, heartburn, bowel problems, hepatitis)? |
| 22. | — | — | Any (diabetes, thyroid disorders, anemia, abnormal bleeding)? |
| 23. | — | — | Any knee injury (sprain, fracture, dislocation, surgery, chronic pain)? |
| 24. | — | — | Any ankle injury (sprain, fracture, dislocation, surgery, chronic pain)? |
| 25. | — | — | Any bone (fracture, infection, deformity)? |
| 26. | — | — | Any (injuries, sprains, dislocations, surgery) in (shoulder, wrist, finger, or any other joint)? |
| 27. | — | — | Any skin disorders (recurrent rash, fungal infection, boils, athlete's foot)? |
| 28. | — | — | Any injury not mentioned? _____ |
| 29. | — | — | Any (heat exhaustion, heat stroke)? |
| 30. | — | — | Any reasons why you were unable to participate in the past or should not be able to in the future? _____ |

31.  Date of last tetanus booster _____

**Explain Any Questions Answered With "Yes" Below**
(please be as *specific* as possible: dates, treating physician, list medications, residual problems, etc.)

_____

_____

_____

Signature of student athlete _____ Date _____

Signature of parent or physician _____ Date _____

From Gregg JR, and Spindler KP: Screening school-age athletes. Drug Therapy, September 1985, p. 75, with permission.

## Appendix 16–2. PHYSICAL EXAMINATION FORM

Name _____ Age _____ Date of birth _____

School _____ Grade _____

Height (in) _____ Weight (lb) _____ Pulse _____ BP (sitting, right arm) _____

Vision (acuity) R__/__ L__/__ Check one: __ normal without glasses __ normal with glasses

__ abnormal without glasses __ abnormal with

glasses

| OK | Circle in ( ) if Abnormality Present or Normal Condition Absent | Comments | Initials |
|----|-------------------------------------------------------------------|----------|----------|
| 1. _____ | Dental (dental prosthesis, severe caries) | _____ | _____ |
| 2. _____ | Skin, scalp, lymphatics (active infection, acne, rashes, adenopathy) | _____ | _____ |
| 3. _____ | Eyes/fundi (vision-color, depth, peripheral; pupils, extraocular movements, fundi) | _____ | _____ |
| 4. _____ | Ears, nose, throat (hearing, tympanic membranes, nasal septum, tonsils, throat) | _____ | _____ |
| 5. _____ | Neck (soft tissue) (adenopathy, thyroid, carotid pulses) | _____ | _____ |
| 6. _____ | Cardiovascular (PMI, pulses [femoral-branchial], rhythm, murmurs) | _____ | _____ |
| 7. _____ | Chest and lung (breath sounds, shape, excursion) | _____ | _____ |
| 8. _____ | Abdomen (hepatosplenomegaly, masses, costovertebral angle tenderness) | _____ | _____ |
| 9. _____ | Genitalia-hernia (scrotal contents, inguinal region) | _____ | _____ |
| 10. _____ | Sexual maturity (Tanner staging) | _____ | _____ |
| 11. _____ | Neurologic (sensation, deep-tendon reflexes, mental status) | _____ | _____ |
| 12. | Orthopedic (all for active range of motion and strength besides information in parenthesis) | | |
| _____ | a. Cervical spine/back (scoliosis) | _____ | _____ |
| _____ | b. Shoulders (symmetry) | _____ | _____ |
| _____ | c. Arm/elbow/wrist/hand | _____ | _____ |
| _____ | d. Hip/foot (passive range of motion hip, foot stance with weight bearing) | _____ | _____ |
| _____ | e. Knee (ligamentous stability) | _____ | _____ |
| _____ | f. Ankle (ligamentous stability) | _____ | _____ |
| _____ | g. Flexibility | _____ | _____ |
| _____ | h. % Body fat (specify method) | _____ | _____ |
| 13. _____ | Laboratory tests | | |

Hg _____g/dl Hct _____% Transferrin
saturation _____%
Urinalysis _____
Other _____

14.      Review by team physician
_____ a. No athletic participation
_____ b. Limited participation, e.g., _____
_____ c. Clearance withheld until: _____
_____ d. Full unlimited participation

**Appendix 16–2.** *continued*

15.    Comment/Advice: _____

     _____

16.    Team physician's signature _____ Date _____

From Gregg JR, and Spindler KP: Screening school-age athletes. Drug Therapy, September 1985, p. 77, with permission.

**Appendix 16–3.** DISQUALIFYING CONDITIONS (INDICATED BY AN X) FOR SPORTS PARTICIPATION, BY TYPE OF SPORT

| Condition | Collision* | Contact† | Noncontact‡ | Others§ |
|---|---|---|---|---|
| **General** | | | | |
| Acute infection (respiratory, genitourinary, infectious mononucleosis, hepatitis, active rheumatic fever, active tuberculosis) | X | X | X | X |
| Obvious physical immaturity in comparison with other competitors in group | X | X | | |
| Hemorrhagic disease (hemophilia, purpura, other serious bleeding tendencies) | X | X | X | |
| Diabetes, inadequately controlled | X | X | X | X |
| Diabetes controlled | ‖ | ‖ | ‖ | ‖ |
| Jaundice | X | X | X | X |
| **Eyes** | | | | |
| Absence or loss of function of one eye | X | X | | |
| **Respiratory system** | | | | |
| Tuberculosis (active or symptomatic) | X | X | X | X |
| Severe pulmonary insufficiency | X | X | X | X |
| **Cardiovascular system** | | | | |
| Mitral stenosis, aortic stenosis, aortic insufficiency, coarctation of aorta, cyanotic heart disease, recent carditis of any cause | X | X | X | X |
| Hypertension, organic | X | X | X | X |
| Previous heart surgery for congenital or acquired heart disease | ¶ | ¶ | ¶ | ¶ |
| **Liver** | | | | |
| Enlargement | X | X | | |

* Football, rugby, hockey, lacrosse, etc.
† Baseball, soccer, basketball, wrestling, etc.
‡ Cross-country, track, tennis, crew, swimming, etc.
§ Bowling, golf, archery, field events, etc.
‖ No exclusions necessary.
¶ Each patient should be judged individually in conjunction with cardiologist and surgeon.
From Blum RW: Preparticipation evaluation of the adolescent athlete. Postgrad Med 78:2, 52–55, 1985, with permission.

# References

1. Bunch TW: Blood test abnormalities in runners. Mayo Clin Proc 55:113, 1980.
2. Siegel AJ: Understanding abnormal lab values in the female athlete. Contemp Ob Gyn 25:73, 1985.
3. Wyndham CH, Morrison JF, and Williams CG: Heat reactions of male and female caucasians. J Appl Physiol 20:357, 1965.
4. Wells CL: Sexual differences in heat stress response. The Physician and Sportsmedicine 5(9):78, 1977.
5. Drinkwater BL, Kupprat IC, Denton JE, et al: Heat tolerance of female distance runners. Ann NY Acad Sci 301:777, 1977.
6. Statement of the American College of Sports Medicine: Prevention of heat injuries during distance running. J Sports Med 9(7):105, 1976.
7. Sutton JR: Heatstroke from running. JAMA 243(19):1896, 1980.
8. Koppes GM, Daly JJ, Coltman CA, et al: Exertion-induced rhabdomyolysis with acute renal failure and disseminated intravascular coagulation in sickle cell trait. Am J Med 63:313, 1977.
9. Stewart PJ, and Posen GA: Case report: Acute renal failure following a marathon. The Physician and Sportsmedicine 8(4):61, 1980.
10. Huston TP, Puffer JC, and Rodney WM: The athletic heart syndrome. N Engl J Med 313:24, 1985.
11. Gordon T: Cardiovascular risk factors in women. Pract Cardiol 5(7):137, 1974.
12. Scott DE, and Pritchard JA: Iron deficiency in healthy young college women. JAMA 199(12):147, 1967.
13. Steenkamp I, Fuller C, Graves J, et al: Marathon running fails to influence RBC survival rates in iron-repleted women. The Physician and Sportsmedicine 14(5):89, 1986.
14. Martin DE, Vroon DH, May DF, et al: Physiological changes in elite male distance runners training for olympic competition. The Physician and Sportsmedicine 14(1):152, 1986.
15. McMahon LF, Ryan MJ, Larson D, et al: Occult gastrointestinal blood loss in marathon runners. Ann Intern Med 100:846, 1984.
16. Priebe WM, and Priebe J: Runners' diarrhea (RD)-Prevalence and clinical symptomatology. Am J Gastroenterol 79:827, 1984.
17. Gardner KD Jr: Athletic pseudonephritis alteration of urine sediment by athletic competition. JAMA 161:613, 1956.
18. Poortsmans JR: Exercise and renal function. Sports Med 1:125, 1984.
19. Siegel AJ, Hennekens CH, Solomon HS, et al: Exercise-related hematuria findings in a group of marathon runners. JAMA 241:391, 1979.
20. Blacklock NS: Bladder trauma in the long distance runner. 10,000 metres hematuria. Br J Urol 49:129, 1977.
21. Siegel AJ, Silverman LM, and Lopez RE: Creatine kinase elevations in marathon runners, relationship to training and competition. Yale J Biol Med 53:275, 1980.
22. Apple FS, and Rogers MA: Serum and muscle alanine aminotransferase activities in marathon runners. JAMA 252:626, 1984.
23. Leslie BR, and Sanders NW: Runner's hemolysis and pigment gallstones. N Engl J Med 313:1230, 1985.
24. Siegel AJ, Silverman LM, and Holman BL: Elevated creatine kinase MB isoenzyme levels in marathon runners. JAMA 246:1049, 1981.
25. Siegel AJ, Silverman LM, and Evans WJ: Elevated skeletal muscle creatine kinase MB isoenzyme levels in marathon runners. JAMA 250:2835, 1983.
26. McFadden ER, and Ingram RH: Exercise-induced asthma. Seminars in Medicine of the Beth Israel Hospital, Boston 301(14):763, 1979.
27. Sheffer AL, and Austen KF: New exercise-induced anaphylactic syndrome identified. Modern Medicine 1:96, 1981.
28. Siegel AJ: Exercise induced anaphylaxis. The Physician and Sportsmedicine 8(1):55, 1980.Figure 16–1. Comparison of spirometric measurements following exercise in healthy subjects and in patients with exercise-induced asthma. (Adapted from Gerhard H, and Schachter FN: Exercise-induced asthma. Postgrad Med 67(3):93, 1980, with permission.)

# CHAPTER 17

# Cardiovascular Issues

PAMELA S. DOUGLAS, M.D.

As participation in both competitive and noncompetitive sports increases, the numbers of female athletes, of athletes with known forms of heart disease, and of older athletes more likely to have occult heart disease also increases. In general, the cardiovascular responses to exercise are similar in both sexes in both healthy individuals and in those with heart disease. However, physiologic and pathologic differences do exist between the sexes and are important in the evaluation and treatment of the exercising woman.

Exercise of any type or intensity requires increased oxygen delivery to working tissue. This is accomplished through peripheral mechanisms, which include differential perfusion of vascular beds and increased oxygen extraction by muscle, and through central or cardiac mechanisms, chiefly an increase in cardiac output. Thus, maximal exercise, or maximal oxygen uptake, is determined by maximal increases in the peripheral arteriovenous $O_2$ difference, and by cardiac output and its components, stroke volume and heart rate.

## AEROBIC CAPACITY

In the average sedentary woman, maximum aerobic workload is 15 to 30 percent lower than in the average sedentary man,[1,2] even when corrected for body size. This may be due to a number of factors. Women normally possess a lower total oxygen-carrying capacity of blood, owing to lower blood volume, fewer red blood cells, and lower hemoglobin content. Women also have smaller

239

hearts, with smaller stroke volumes and therefore higher heart rates for a given cardiac output or oxygen uptake. Finally, women generally possess a higher percentage of adipose tissue and a lower percentage of working muscle than do men. These differences combine to produce, on average, a lower maximal level of work or aerobic capacity in women.

In part, these "physiologic" differences may also be explained by considering that, on the average, men are more active than women and therefore maintain a more trained state, particularly as women tend to become relatively more sedentary after puberty. Several factors support this hypothesis. Training programs produce similar increases in aerobic capacity in both sexes, even when older individuals are examined.[2-4] Maximal oxygen uptake in individual highly trained female athletes can approach and equal that of similarly trained males.[5] Finally, there is little difference in exercise capacity between boys and girls under the age of 12.[1]

Regardless of cause, recognition of the lower maximal aerobic capacity and higher heart rates during submaximal exercise in women as compared with men is essential to the accurate interpretation of exercise results in women. Sex-specific standards have been developed for maximal aerobic capacity as well as nomograms for the calculation, in women, of maximal capacity from submaximal heart rate and oxygen uptake values. Exercise performance in women cannot be adequately evaluated without references to such standards.

## CARDIAC FUNCTION IN RESPONSE TO EXERCISE

In addition to differences in aerobic capacity, the normal cardiac response to exercise in women may be different than in men.[6] The most widely used diagnostic test for the evaluation of left ventricular function during exercise is the gated blood pool scan. This test involves use of radiolabeled red blood cells (using technetium) to determine ejection fraction, or the percent of blood within the left ventricular chamber that is ejected with each heart beat, at rest and at maximal exercise. Normal individuals have been defined as those able to increase their ejection fraction by at least five percentage points during exercise.[7] Persons with a lesser increase, or even a decrease, are felt to have a component of myocardial dysfunction, or at the least, impaired cardiac reserve. Higginbotham and associates[8] studied healthy, sedentary adults and found that the generally accepted "normal" increase in left ventricular ejection fraction during exercise occurred only in men and not in women. Of the 16 women studied, only 7 increased their ejection fraction by five points or more (compared with 14 of 15 men) and the average ejection fraction was unchanged (63 percent at rest compared with 64 percent at peak exercise). In contrast, the average ejection fraction in men increased from 62 to 77 percent (Fig. 17–1).

In addition, the mechanisms used to increase cardiac output during exercise appeared different in men and women. In men, end-diastolic left ventricular size did not change whereas end-systolic size decreased, leading to increases in stroke volume and ejection fraction. In contrast, women achieved a similar increase in stroke volume by increasing end-diastolic size while end-systolic size remained unchanged. Thus, women appeared to dilate their left ventricles, or increase preload, whereas men increased ventricular shortening. The physiologic basis for these different mechanisms of achieving the same end—increasing cardiac output and therefore oxygen supply to muscle—is unknown, as is its significance for preserved health or training.

These findings have important clinical implications. If good health is defined by the healthy male pattern of response, the remainder of the population, or women who normally respond differently, may be falsely diagnosed as unwell. Since exercise gated blood pool scanning is commonly used to measure the cardiac functional response to exercise and is recommended as a diagnostic test for the evaluation of a variety of cardiac complaints, the problem is potentially a large one. At special risk for misdiagnosis as having impaired cardiac function is the healthy woman, whether sedentary or active, undergoing evaluation of cardiac function. In a similar manner, a woman with mild known cardiac disease may be classified as having more severe impairment than is actually the

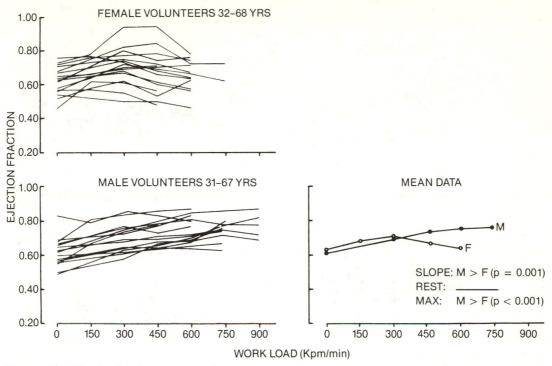

**Figure 17–1.** *Ejection fraction responses during exercise in which the workload was increased every 3 minutes. Progressive individual data are shown for women, top left, and men, bottom left. Mean submaximal and maximal group data are plotted on the right as mean data ± standard deviation for normal female (F) and male (M) volunteers. Significant intergroup differences are shown for the slope of the response, as well as for data from subjects at rest and during maximal exercise. (From Higgenbotham et al.,[8] with permission.)*

case, owing to use of the male response as a normal reference standard.

In contrast to aerobic capacity and the functional response to exercise, other aspects of cardiac-related exercise physiology appear to show few differences between men and women. Aging affects aerobic capacity of healthy individuals of both sexes similarly, causing a decline in maximal oxygen uptake.[1,2] This results from a decrease in the maximal achievable heart rate and decreased mechanical performance of the myocardium as well as limitations in the functioning of other organ systems (Fig. 17–2). Blood pressure is little changed in the normal person following either isotonic or isometric exercise training. There is some evidence that both systolic and diastolic pressures may be reduced by training in individuals with hypertension; however, these effects are small and not known to differ between the sexes.[9]

The hearts of both men and women appear to adapt similarly to exercise training.[1,2]

This has been documented in studies of women pursuing typically female-dominated sports such as field hockey and dance,[10,11] as well as those pursuing jogging, swimming, and triathlon trainings.[12,13] Weight training or isometric exercise appears to produce cardiovascular effects similar to those of aerobic, dynamic exercise.[15] A detailed discussion of the structural cardiac changes associated with dynamic and resistive exercise training is beyond the scope of this chapter and has been recently reviewed.[14,15] At present, no differences between the sexes have been found in the extent or incidence of cardiac adaptations to exercise.

Female athletes develop clinical findings of left ventricular hypertrophy, including an enlarged heart on chest radiograph, increased left and right ventricular cavity sizes and wall thicknesses on echocardiography, and increased voltage on ECG reflecting an increased myocardial mass. Following

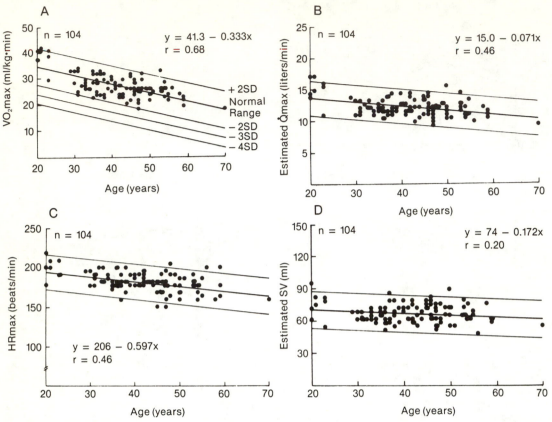

**Figure 17-2.** *Derived values for observed and maximal cardiovascular variables in 104 normal, healthy women. A, Observed age- and weight-adjusted value of maximal oxygen uptake ($\dot{V}_{O_2max}$). The regression line is shown and the normal range indicated by ±2 standard deviations (SD). The standard deviation for oxygen uptake is 3.59 mL · kg$^{-1}$ · min$^{-1}$). B, estimated age-adjusted values of maximal cardiac output is ($\dot{Q}_{max}$). The standard deviation for cardiac output is 1.35 L · min$^{-1}$. C, Observed age-adjusted values of maximal heart rate (HR$_{max}$). The standard deviation for heart rate is 14 beats/min. D, Estimated age-adjusted values of maximal stroke volume (SV). The standard deviation for stroke volume is 8 mL. (From Hossack et al.,[6] with permission.)*

weight training, the cardiac chambers tend to remain normal sized and the walls become hypertrophied. Athletes of both sexes develop cardiac arrhythmias with training, probably because of alterations of vagal tone and catecholamine metabolism. Although sinus bradycardia is most common, low-grade atrioventricular block, premature atrial or ventricular contractions, and repolarization abnormalities are also seen.[14]

Since many of these adaptive changes may also signify the presence of true heart disease, it is important to recognize that for women, as well as men, physical training may lead to physiologic structural and electrical changes in a healthy heart that must

not be confused with similar findings in cardiac disease states.

## EXERCISE ELECTROCARDIOGRAPHIC TESTING

The most common form of heart disease in the United States today is coronary atherosclerosis. Coronary stenoses limit the delivery of adequate amounts of oxygen to the heart, a problem often not noted until oxygen demands are increased by exercise. Thus, monitoring of electrocardiographic recordings capable of detecting cardiac ischemia during a controlled exercise protocol is

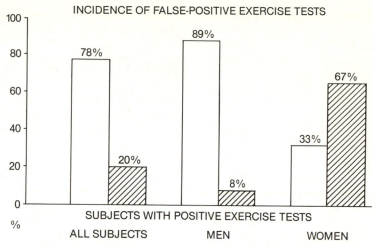

**Figure 17–3.** *The marked difference in the incidence of false-positive exercise test results between men and women is statistically significant ( p <0.001, regardless of coronary anatomy). Hatched bars indicate percent of positive exercise test results associated with normal coronary arteries or less than 50 percent stenosis (false-positive results). Open bars indicate percent of positive tests associated with 75 percent or greater coronary stenosis (true-positive results). Overall, 60 of 77 subjects (78 percent) had both positive exercise tests and significant coronary disease. In men, 55 of 62 (89 percent) had true-positive test results, whereas only 5 of 15 women (33 percent) did. This difference is statistically significant (p <0.001). (From Sketch et al.,[16] with permission.)*

the most widely used diagnostic procedure for the detection of coronary disease. In men, regardless of symptoms, such exercise testing is an excellent screening test, with few false-positive results. In contrast, in women, the incidence of false-positive test results (appearance of electrocardiographic changes characteristic of myocardial ischemia leading to a diagnosis of coronary disease in its absence) is quite high, perhaps as high as two thirds of all positive tests (Fig. 17–3).[16,17]

Several factors explain this difference. The most important of these is the difference in the prevalance of heart disease between men and women.[18] In general, the effect of disease prevalance in the population studied has great impact upon the accuracy and usefulness of any given diagnostic test. This is termed Bayes' theorem and is highly applicable to the comparability of exercise testing results in men and women. Because coronary disease is relatively less likely in women, any given positive test result is more likely to be a false rather than a true result. Thus, the diagnostic utility of exercise testing for coronary artery disease in women is lower than for men. To eliminate the Bayesian factor, Barolsky and co-workers[19] studied the utility

of exercise testing in groups of men and women with similar disease prevalences. This markedly improved the validity of test results, although women still had a higher incidence of false-positive test results.

Another reason for the high rate of false-positive test results is the higher incidence in women of other characteristics that are associated with nondiagnostic results.[20,21] These characteristics include atypical chest pain, resting electrocardiographic abnormalities including nonspecific ST- and T-wave changes, and ingestion of medications such as digoxin and diazepam. Since these characteristics appear more commonly in women than in men, test results are more frequently confounding in women.

Several alternative strategies have been proposed to render exercise testing more useful in women. These include more stringent use of probability analysis,[22] alternate or additional electrography lead placement,[23] consideration of R-wave amplitude as well as ST-segment changes,[24] and use of thallium-201 myocardial scintigraphy with exercise testing.[17,25] The addition of isotope imaging does markedly improve the specificity of exercise testing; however, the false-positive rate is still higher for women than for men. In part, this may be due to attenuation of tracer signal resulting from overlying breast tissue.[25,26] In addition, thallium scanning is costly, time consuming, and requires radiation exposure and the availability of special equipment and trained personnel.

The different sensitivity and specificity of exercise testing in women has important clinical implications. In diagnostic exercise testing performed to define and classify preexisting complaints, the women with chest pain due to noncardiac causes are far more likely to be diagnosed as having coronary disease. This is obviously an undesirable event and, in addition to causing a great deal of patient anxiety, may lead to taking unnecessary medications and/or undergoing additional testing, which is more expensive and may endanger health. In contrast, a negative test result is a good indication of the absence of heart disease. Exercise testing performed to ensure that a training program may be undertaken safely is at even greater risk of producing a false suspicion of cardiac disease. The low sensitivity of exercise testing in women makes it a very poor screening test for cardiovascular disease in women, regardless of symptoms.

## EXERCISE LIMITATIONS IN HEART DISEASE

The effects of exercise in those with heart disease appear to be similar in both men and women. However, since little attention has been focused on potential differences between men and women, it is possible that such differences do exist, but have been overlooked. It is known that women in general have a worse prognosis following myocardial infarction[27] and a higher mortality and lower success rate following coronary artery bypass grafting[28] than men have. Whether this dichotomy extends to other forms of therapy, such as exercise training, is unknown. In general, exercise regimens following myocardial infarction or revascularization surgery are of established value in hastening recovery and improving quality of life in the short term; longer-term benefits such as reduction of recurrence or improved long-term survival are more difficult to prove. Rehabilitative programs for those with nonischemic heart disease are more

controversial, and again, possible sex-related differences have not been explored.

## Mitral Valve Prolapse

In contrast to most forms of either congenital or acquired heart disease, mitral valve prolapse occurs with greater frequency in women than in men. For this reason, information regarding cardiac function and exercise in this disease process may be more likely to represent the female than the male circumstance. Mitral valve prolapse is a generally benign syndrome characterized by a broad variety of cardiac findings, which may include some or all of the following: mid-systolic, nonejection click; late systolic murmur; echocardiographic or cineangiographic evidence of systolic billowing of the mitral valve leaflets into the left atrium; thickened mitral valve; atypical chest pain; palpitations; dizziness; abnormal electrocardiogram; atrial or ventricular arrhythmia; systemic emboli; mitral regurgitation; Marfan's syndrome; syncope; and sudden death.[29]

The question of myocardial involvement in mitral valve prolapse has been raised by documentation of left ventricular segmental contraction abnormalities, and by its association with chest pain and ventricular arrhythmias. This has led to examination of global function using rest and exercise ejection fractions as measured by gated blood pool scanning.[30-32] As might be expected, owing to the preponderance of women with the disease, patients with mitral valve prolapse have an "abnormal" failure to increase ejection fraction in response to exercise. This has been taken to be suggestive of a "cardiomyopathic process"[30] and renders difficult the accurate diagnosis of the etiology of chest pain (ischemic versus nonischemic).[31,32] However, as noted previously, normal, healthy females also may fail to increase their ejection fraction with exercise; therefore, it is difficult to label the behavior of those with mitral valve prolapse as indicative of myocardial pathology.

In the overwhelming majority of cases, mitral valve prolapse is a benign, isolated auscultatory or echocardiographic finding that has no known influence on exercise performance or the advisability of pursuing competitive or recreational sports. This view is supported by the rarity of complications documented during exercise. It must be kept in mind, however, that the natural history of the disorder is not well known and its clinical significance remains somewhat controversial. The American College of Cardiology recently recommended that a small subset of patients with mitral valve prolapse limit competitive participation to low-intensity sports such as bowling and golf.[33] These patients included those with a history of syncope, a family history of sudden death due to mitral valve prolapse, chest pain worsened by exercise, repetitive ventricular ectopy or sustained supraventricular tachycardia (especially if worsened by exercise), moderate or severe mitral regurgitation, and dilation of the ascending aorta (associated with Marfan's syndrome). It was recommended that no restrictions be placed on those with any or all other manifestations of the mitral valve prolapse syndrome.

## Anorexia Nervosa

Another disorder primarily afflicting women and thought to affect cardiac performance is anorexia nervosa, which is discussed in Chapter 18. Previous studies of starvation have demonstrated decreased heart size, blood pressure, and heart rate, which may not be reversible with refeeding. A recent study[34] has shown that cardiac function is preserved and that the observed changes in cardiac architecture, load, and function are appropriate responses to decreased blood pressure. These parameters, as well as exercise performance, return to normal with weight gain. Thus, the observed cardiac abnormalities should not in themselves represent limitations to exercise.

## Sudden Death

The risk factors predisposing to unexpected sudden death in women are somewhat different from those in men.[35] Data from the Framingham Heart Study showed that age and, marginally, cholesterol were risk factors in both sexes. In addition, hematocrit, vital capacity, and glucose were significantly related to the incidence of sudden death in women only. In men, additional risk factors for sudden death were those associated with coronary disease including systolic blood pressure, obesity, smoking, and

electrocardiographic evidence of left ventricular hypertrophy.

Although the significance of these findings for the exercising woman is unknown, several other forms of heart disease are clearly associated with sudden death during exercise. As far as is known, relative risks for men and women relate to the prevalence of these cardiac illnesses; the consequences or severity of each disease process do not differ in men and women.

Chief among cardiac diseases causing sudden death in young people during exercise is hypertrophic cardiomyopathy. This disease is idiopathic, genetically transmitted and characterized by a thickened left ventricle with normal chamber size. Because cardiac adaptation to exercise may produce a similar picture, differentiating between physiologic and pathologic hypertrophy may be difficult and may depend on identification of other pathologic features such as asymmetric septal hypertrophy and systolic anterior motion of the mitral valve. Any athlete suspected of having this disorder should be fully evaluated by a cardiovascular specialist. The American College of Cardiology recommends that patients with this disease should never participate in high-intensity competitive sports, regardless of disease severity.[33] Those with marked hypertrophy, significant left ventricular outflow tract obstruction, arrhythmias, or a family history of sudden death or syncope should not participate in any form of athletic endeavors.

## Other Forms of Heart Disease

Consideration of the exercise limitations imposed by each form of heart disease is beyond the scope of this review. In addition, there is no evidence available to indicate differences in disease processes other than those discussed previously, which would suggest different exercise limitations in men and women. The reader is referred to the Task Force on Cardiovascular Abnormalities in the Athlete and its recommendations regarding eligibility for competition.[36] This conference, which was sponsored by the American College of Cardiology and by the National Heart, Lung and Blood Institute, compiled an up-to-date, comprehensive summary of both resistive and dynamic exercise limitations in all forms of congenital and acquired heart disease. It must be stressed that any person with known or suspected heart disease, regardless of sex, should undergo a full cardiovascular evaluation before undertaking exercise training or sports competition. These recommendations apply equally to male and female athletes.

## SUMMARY

In conclusion, although many aspects of the female cardiac response to exercise appear similar to the male response, many other aspects have not been fully examined with respect to differences between the sexes. In areas that have been studied, a number of important differences exist. Because many of these differences must be kept in mind for the correct interpretation of diagnostic cardiac exercise testing performed in women, an appreciation of the normal female response is vital. These differences are just as important to keep in mind in examining the female athlete as they are in examining the sedentary woman. Much research remains to be done before a complete examination can be made of all the unique aspects of cardiovascular problems in the exercising woman.

## References

1. Åstrand I: Aerobic work capacity in men and women with special reference to age. Acta Physiol Scand 49:169, 1960.
2. Åstrand PO: Human physical fitness with special reference to sex and age. Physiol Rev 36:307, 1956.
3. Adams GM, and de Vries HA: Physiologic effects of an exercise training regimen upon women aged 52 to 79. J Gerontol 28(1):50, 1973.
4. Wessel JA, Small DA, Van Huss WD, et al: Age and physiological responses to exercise in women 20–69 years of age. J Gerontol 23:269, 1968.
5. O'Toole ML, Hiller WDB, Douglas PS, et al: Cardiovascular responses to prolonged cycling and running. Med Sci Sports Exerc 17(2):219, 1985.
6. Hossack KF, Kusumi F, and Bruce RA: Approximate normal standards of maximal cardiac output during upright exercise in women. Am J Cardiol 47:1080, 1981.
7. Borer JS, Bacharach SL, Green MV, et al: Real-time radionuclide cineangiography in the non-invasive evaluation of global and regional left ventricular function at rest and during exercise in patients with coronary artery disease. N Engl J Med 296:839, 1977.
8. Higginbotham MB, Morris KG, Coleman E, et al: Sex-related differences in the normal cardiac response to upright exercise. Circulation 70(3):357, 1984.
9. Seals DR, and Hagberg JM: The effect of exercise training on human hypertension: a review. Med Sci Sports Exerc 16(3):207, 1984.
10. Cohen JL, Gupta PK, Lichstein E, et al: The heart of a dancer: Noninvasive cardiac evaluation of professional ballet dancers. Am J Cardiol 45:959, 1980.
11. Zeldis SM, Morganroth J, and Rubler S: Cardiac hypertrophy in response to dynamic conditioning in female athletes. J Appl Physiol 44:849, 1978.
12. Douglas PS, O'Toole ML, Hiller WDB, et al: Left ventricular structure and function by echocardiography in ultraendurance athletes. Am J Cardiol 58:805, 1986.
13. Douglas PS, Hiller WDB, O'Toole ML, et al: Left ventricular structure and function in ultraendurance athletes. Med Sci Sports Exerc 17(2):203, 1985.
14. Huston TP, Puffer JC, and Rodney WM: The athletic heart syndrome. N Engl J Med 313(1):24, 1985.
15. Stone MH, and Wilson GD: Resistive Training and Selected Effects. In Goldberg L, and Elliot DL (eds): The Medical Clinics of North America. WB Saunders, Philadelphia, 1985.
16. Sketch MH, Mohiuddin SM, Lynch JD, et al: Significant sex differences in the correlation of electrocardiographic exercise testing and coronary arteriograms. Am J Cardiol 36:169, 1975.
17. McCarthy D: Stress electrocardiography in women. Int J Cardiol 5:727, 1984.
18. Patterson, RE, Eng C, and Horowitz SF: Practical diagnosis of coronary artery disease: a Bayes' theorem nomogram to correlate clinical data with noninvasive exercise tests. Am J Cardiol 53:252, 1984.
19. Barolsky SM, Gilbert CA, Faruqui A, et al: Circulation 60(5):1021, 1979.
20. Linhart JW, Laws JG, and Satinsky JD: Maximum treadmill exercise electrocardiography in female patients. Circulation 50:1173, 1974.
21. Detry JMR, Kapita BM, Cosyns J, et al: Diagnostic value of history and maximal exercise electrocardiography in men and women suspected of coronary heart disease. Circulation 56(5):756, 1977.
22. Melin JA, Wijns W, Vanbutsele RJ, et al: Alternative diagnostic strategies for coronary artery disease in women: demonstration of the usefulness and efficiency of probability analysis. Circulation 71(3):535, 1985.
23. Guiteras P, Chaitman BR, Waters DD, et al: Diagnostic accuracy of exercise ECG lead systems in clinical subsets of women. Circulation 65(7):1465, 1982.
24. Ilsley C, Canepa-Anson R, Westgate C, et al: Influence of R wave analysis upon diagnostic accuracy of exercise testing in women. Br Heart J 48:161, 1982.
25. Friedman TD, Greene AC, Iskandrian AS, et al: Exercise thallium-201 myocardial scintigraphy in women: correlation with coronary arteriography. Am J Cardiol 49:1632, 1982.
26. Stolzenberg J, and Kaminsky J: Overlying breast as cause of false-positive thallium scans. Clin Nucl Med 3:229, 1978.
27. Puletti M, Sunseri L, Curione M, et al: Acute myocardial infarction: sex-related differences in prognosis. Am Heart J 108(1):63, 1984.
28. Fisher LD, Kennedy JW, Davis KB, et al: Association of sex, physical size, and operative mortality after coronary artery bypass in the coronary artery surgery study (CASS). J Thorac Cardiovasc Surg 84:334, 1982.

29. Jeresaty RM: Mitral valve prolapse-click syndrome. Prog Cardiovasc Dis 15:623, 1973.

30. Gottdiener JS, Borer JS, Bacharach SL, et al: Left ventricular function in mitral valve prolapse: Assessment with radionuclide cineangiography. Am J Cardiol 47:7, 1981.

31. Newman GE, Gibbons RJ, and Jones RH: Cardiac function during rest and exercise in patients with mitral valve prolapse. Am J Cardiol 47:14, 1981.

32. Ahmad M, and Haibach H: Left ventricular function in patients with mitral valve prolapse a radionuclide evaluation. Clin Nucl Med 7:562, 1982.

33. Maron BJ, Gaffney FA, Jeresaty RM, et al: Task force III: Hypertrophic cardiomyopathy, other myoperi-cardial diseases and mitral valve prolapse. J Am Coll Cardiol 6(6):1215, 1985.

34. St. John Sutton MG, Plappert T, Crosby L, et al: Effects of reduced left ventricular mass on chamber architecture, load, and function: a study of anorexia nervosa. Circulation 72(5):991, 1985.

35. Schatzkin A, Cupples LA, Heeren T, et al: The epidemiology of sudden unexpected death: Risk factors for men and women in the Framingham Heart Study. Am Heart J 107(6):1300, 1984.

36. Mitchell JH, Maron BJ, and Epstein SE: 16th Bethesda Conference: Cardiovascular abnormalities in the athlete: recommendations regarding eligibility for competition. J Am Coll Cardiol 6(6):1186, 1985.

# CHAPTER 18

# Eating Disorders

JACK L. KATZ, M.D.

Two coincidental developments over the past two decades have made the topic of eating disorders a legitimate one for inclusion in a scientific work on women and exercise. The first clearly is the enormous increase in serious athletic participation by women. What traditionally had been almost exclusively the domain of men has now become a flourishing and important aspect of living for a substantial number of women in industrialized societies. The second is the dramatic rise in the incidence of eating disorders, specifically anorexia nervosa (AN) and bulimia. As these syndromes are primarily disorders of women (90 to 95 percent of all cases), and as issues related to weight, food intake, and physical activity are central both to eating disorders and to sports, it is not surprising that this topic is now genuinely germane to this book's mission.

While this chapter will review in detail the nature, theories of etiology, and approaches to treatment of the eating disorders, it will also seek to address several particularly relevant questions. For example:

1. Is sustained, strenuous exercising, especially by women, a risk factor for the development of an eating disorder?
2. Are women with a vulnerability to eating disorders drawn to serious athletic activity as a way of dealing with that vulnerability?
3. Do anorexia nervosa and intense athletic involvement share common underlying psychologic themes and conflicts?

## EPIDEMIOLOGY

As indicated earlier, since the 1960s there has been a dramatic, perhaps 100 percent, increase in the incidence of the eating disorders that goes beyond heightened diagnostic acuity.[1] Estimates of the prevalence of anorexia nervosa generally rest between 1 and 5 percent of female adolescents,[2] with the lower end of this range being more likely accurate than the upper one. Reports of the prevalence of bulimia have been considerably less consistent, but a consensus figure would probably fall between 5 and 10 percent of college-age women,[3] with the higher end of the range more probable here.

Clearly, these are not trivial figures. They have prompted various speculations about such an accelerating rate. The most common proposals are that the media's emphasis on thinness as a culturally desirable physical characteristic has triggered more dieting than ever before, and that the increasingly complex role of women in our society has created particular stress and conflict for them around issues of identity and control which are being played out by excessive attention to appearance.[4] However, we should also note that, perhaps because of better nutrition or subtle evolutionary trends, female adolescents are experiencing menarche and puberty earlier than ever before. Thus, they are encountering biologic and psychosocial stresses at an earlier age than previously. If today's parents are also more self-absorbed than were prior generations, this earlier exposure to stress will be met by less, rather than more, nurturance, and food may then take on particular symbolic importance.[5]

Finally, although AN and bulimia can occur in males and can also occur in persons living in nonindustrialized societies, they have a particular affinity for women growing up in industrialized cultures. Earlier writings suggested that white upper-middle-class girls were at particular risk, but more recent reports suggest that minority groups are now also vulnerable.[6] Rather than socioeconomic background being the critical variable, achievement-orientation of families may be the most relevant common denominator.

## SETTING AND ONSET

### Anorexia Nervosa

Although there are perhaps "typical" circumstances associated with the onset of AN, it must be emphasized that a substantial minority of patients present histories that deviate from such scenarios.

Classically, the future anorectic patient is in her teens, most likely approaching either 14 or 18 years of age (i.e., about to make a significant transition in her schooling). She has seemingly been a well-functioning girl, indeed is often described by her parents as having been "perfect . . . never a problem." She is highly conscientious about her schoolwork, appears to have friends, and is usually well organized. But beneath this veneer of health, there is often found a girl with low self-esteem, one who is compulsive in her style, works excessively conscientiously to maintain her grades (i.e., is an "overachiever"), and is overly dependent in her relationships. She is also, more often than not, slightly overweight and has a "sweet tooth."

Usually, but not always, a psychosocial stressor can be identified that correlates with the onset of consciously initiated dieting (although the connection between the dieting and the stressor may not be conscious). Common events are a loss (e.g., parental death or divorce), a blow to self-esteem (e.g., a failed first heterosexual relationship), or a separation (e.g., a vacation abroad, beginning college). Of course, some of these circumstances are intrinsic to adolescence and, while indeed stressful, are hardly unique to the life histories of anorectic girls.

The girl at risk for AN, like many other American female adolescents and adults, consciously decides to embark on a diet. She does so in typical fashion, initially eliminating carbohydrate-rich foods. What makes her different from her peers, though, is the intensity of her drive to lose weight, her stoic pleasure in enduring hunger pains, and her increasing preoccupation with achieving thinness at the expense of all other goals.

Initially, there is a sense of exhilaration, a "high," which may be consequent to a newly found sense of mastery or to the accolades she begins to receive from peers and adults for her willpower and her improving figure. But it is also conceivable that this phenomenon is mediated by a rise in the body's endorphin level. Such a rise has been shown to occur, at least initially, in conjunction with two aspects of the unfolding AN: decreased food intake[7] and increased physical activity.[8] It has even been speculated that it is the unconscious attempt to recapture this initial, possibly endorphin-mediated, high that drives the anorectic into her ever-downward spiral.

However, as indicated at the outset of this section, exceptions to this stereotypic picture abound. Not all future anorectics are bright overachievers with compulsive styles, and not all begin their dieting in association with a psychosocial stressor. Some may actually follow the lead of a girlfriend in embarking on a diet; others may have initially lost weight as a consequence of a bona fide medical illness (most commonly, perhaps, infectious mononucleosis); still others begin to lose weight because of a real loss of appetite from a state of depression; and not all anorectics are initially overweight or come from weight- or food-preoccupied families.

The possible role of intense athletic activity (e.g., long-distance running) in the pathogenesis of anorexia nervosa will be discussed in a later section.

### Bulimia

Although the setting and precipitating events for anorexia nervosa have been described with reasonably reliable agreement, including agreement about exceptions to such formulations, the triggers for bulimia remain controversial and unclear.

We have now come to recognize at least two manifest forms of bulimia, which literally means "ox-hunger" but which more practically refers to pathologic binge-eating and gorging. In one form, what starts out as fairly typical anorexia nervosa evolves into bulimia over a course of time, typically 1 to 2 years. Thus, after weight has been driven down, and in the presence of ongoing rigid and severe dieting, the anorectic individual may one day, to her shock and dismay, suddenly embark on an uncontrollable binge. Not infrequently, two circumstances coincide to facilitate the appearance of the binge: an upsetting experience producing a dysphoric state (depression, anger, anxiety) and the availability in abundance of forbidden foods (typically carbohydrates). The vulnerability to binge may be further enhanced if the food is available in private (e.g., in one's own apartment or after everyone else has retired for the evening). After the binge, there is considerable disgust, shame, and guilt, followed by firm resolve not only to never permit this to happen again but also to diet even more rigorously to compensate for the weight presumably gained from the binge. However, with increasing frequency, the binges begin to recur, until ultimately the binging may become a more conspicuous part of the clinical picture than the dieting.

In the other form, the individual becomes a binger without having ever passed through an emaciated, officially diagnosed anorectic phase. However, the initial circumstances and the emotional states are probably the same in both forms. Although nonanorectic bulimics may have never been substantially underweight, most, if not all, have been chronic dieters whose weights have fluctuated frequently. Thus, altered dietary intake and unstable weight also seem historically related to bulimia in technically nonanorectic persons.

## CLINICAL PICTURE

While the etiology of the eating disorders had defied a unified, air-tight formulation, the phenomenology of anorexia nervosa and bulimia has been impressively delineated over the past two decades, and a rich, coherent, and reliable clinical picture of these syndromes is now available. Both eating disorders can be regarded as syndromes characterized by an admixture of psychologic, behavioral, and biologic disturbances.

### Anorexia Nervosa

#### Core Features

**Self-imposed, rigidly enforced dietary restriction.** Classically, this is viewed as being at the heart of AN. Thus, in the face of mounting hunger, the anorectic consciously and deliberately elects to pursue a sustained course of restricted food intake. As previously noted, carbohydrates are eliminated initially, but many anorectics go on to become exclusive vegetarians. Rituals in the preparing and eating of food are also characteristic. Obviously, such dieting must be differentiated from true anorexia, that is, real loss of appetite, such as in medical illness or depression . However, as noted earlier, some girls actually give histories of having lost weight in conjunction with medical illness or depression, only to have the consequent weight loss apparently catapult them into consciously pursued dieting. One dilemma for current parents, of course, is to know when the ubiquitous dieting among Western female adolescents has gone beyond the bounds of "normal" dieting. The presence of the features that follow will help answer that question, but early prediction of whose dieting will evolve into an eating disorder can provide an insurmountable challenge even for "experts" in the field.

**Substantial weight loss.** Although this is the symptom that usually calls attention to the illness, there is no clear-cut amount of weight loss that must have occurred to confirm the diagnosis, the official psychiatric criteria notwithstanding. The Diagnostic and Statistical Manual of Mental Disorders, Third Edition,[9] specifies a weight loss of at least 25 percent from original body weight (including projected weight for still-growing adolescents), but this figure would be viewed as only a rough guide. AN does occur in women who have not lost one quarter of their original weight, and a diagnosis should be made with the full clinical picture in view.[10]

**Morbid concern with losing control over eating and becoming fat.** The fear of loss of control is central to the psychology of every anorectic. It is concretized around the dual concerns that food intake and weight will become uncontrollable. Thus, the anorectic woman believes that she cannot be "thin enough," much less "too thin," because the threat is always there that someday the floodgates will open and her insatiable appetite will spring forth and produce not only a gain in weight but a body of "humongous" dimensions.

**Obsessional preoccupation with food.** Given the fear of loss of control over food intake and weight, it is not surprising that the anorectic's central preoccupation is with food. One might, however, view this repetitive, morbid dwelling on past, present, and future diet in either biologic terms (i.e., as a reflection of starvation's effect on central nervous system function and presumably cognition) or psychodynamic terms (i.e., as a reflection of the unconscious wish or impulse that underlies the symbolic conscious repudiation). In either case, the important fact is that, increasingly, the anorectic individual devotes her time to fantasies and plans about

buying, cooking, and eating various food items; this obsession progressively impinges on all other aspects of her existence.

**Distorted body image.** Facilitating the descent into anorexia nervosa is the impaired capacity of its victims to gauge accurately their physical dimensions. While normal female adolescents generally see themselves as somewhat larger than they really are (and perhaps this is one reason for the vulnerability of females for developing eating disorders), anorectics markedly overestimate their bodily dimensions—as established by objective studies with distorting lenses, calipers, and so on.[11] Clinically, the 70-lb adult anorectic will continue to talk about the need to lose some body fat here or there, while actually being emaciated. Paradoxically, this tendency appears to intensify with the progression of the emaciation, thereby further confounding attempts at treatment.

### Common Features

**Amenorrhea.** In view of the 95 to 100 percent prevalence of this symptom in women who manifest all of the core features of AN, one could well argue that loss of menses should also be considered a "core" feature. However, as there is no analogous feature in men (although sperm count does drop significantly), it is perhaps wisest to list amenorrhea among the "common features." Interestingly, amenorrhea not only usually occurs relatively early in the course of AN, but also, in approximately 25 to 35 percent of anorectic women, it occurs prior to any significant weight loss (although often after dieting has begun). Furthermore, menses may take many months to resume after weight restoration. Some women who develop AN at an early adolescent age and then remain anorectic may never attain menarche, and we have also observed women who developed AN after stopping oral contraceptives. It is these aberrations in hypothalamic-pituitary-ovarian axis function that fueled the long-standing interest of endocrinologists in anorexia nervosa.[12]

**High level of physical activity.** A dramatic and highly prevalent symptom in persons with anorexia is the striking level of physical activity that accompanies the excessive dieting. While many anorectics were physically active people prior to the onset of their eating disorder, exercising takes on an increasingly frenetic quality as the syndrome unfolds.[13] Like the dieting, the physical activity (most commonly running, calisthenics, swimming) becomes ritualized and rigid. When starvation begins to be serious, the hyperactivity will usually give way to weakness and lethargy, indicating the need for urgent medical care; however, the extreme denial characteristic of these patients may permit exercising to continue, sometimes even in the face of advanced emaciation.

**Insomnia.** Although overlooked in the early literature on AN, difficulty in both falling asleep and sleeping soundly is a common complaint. It is not clear whether this symptom is a consequence of malnourishment, anxiety, mood disturbance, excessive exercise, or some other aspect of the syndrome, but it is sufficiently distressing so that many anorectics will find themselves becoming increasingly dependent on sedatives, particularly benzodiazepines, to attain satisfactory sleep.

**Cold intolerance.** Conceivably as a result of diminished adipose tissue peripherally and more likely as a consequence of starvation's effect on hypothalamically mediated thermoregulation centrally, AN commonly elicits significant cold intolerance. This symptom, compounded by the psychologic defense of denial, accounts for the typical dress of anorectics with layers of sweaters or sweatshirts, which keep the patient warm and hide her emaciation.

**Use of emetics, cathartics, and diuretics.** In addition to their excessive restriction of food intake, some anorectics will employ various external agents to keep their weight as low as possible. Thus, some will induce vomiting (particularly the bulimics—see later) by mechanical means (inserting a finger, toothbrush handle, or appliance cord into the throat to trigger the gag reflex) or chemical means (usually with syrup of ipecac). Others will use enemas or laxatives to "clean out" their gastrointestinal system (leading to chronic constipation eventually). Some will employ diuretics to minimize the contribution of body fluids to their weight.

**Involvement with food-related activities.** Paradoxically, the very object that is dreaded, namely food, is often central not only to the anorectic's thoughts but also to her behavior. Thus, those with AN appear to derive vicarious (and probably sadistic) pleasure from watching others eat what they have cooked or baked for them. They are often involved in preparing exotic dishes and can attach elaborate rituals to their own eating. Bulimic anorectics not uncommonly also hoard and steal food, and a substantial number of patients with eating disorders actually work as waitresses.

**Difficulty in recognizing satiation.** Despite its formal name, and contrary to some of the earlier writings, AN is not a "nervous loss of appetite" and its victims do experience hunger pains (at least before the disease has entered the chronic phase). However, they are subject to real difficulty in experiencing (or, more likely, interpreting) sensations of satiation. They will often complain of being unable to know whether they are full or still hungry after eating a meal.

**Drug abuse.** About one quarter of anorectic patients (almost all of whom are also bulimic) give past or recent histories of drug abuse, typically with stimulants (which, of course, may also serve as anorexogenics) and sedatives. (Heroin use is rare, however.) These patients, who frequently also are diagnosed as having "borderline personalities," appear vulnerable to the drug abuse by virtue of their emotional lability, impulsive tendencies, and general anxiety, as well as their specific panic over possibly losing control of their weight.

**Depressive symptomatology.** Although it is the symptomatology surrounding food, eating, and weight that usually brings the individual with an eating disorder to professional attention, perhaps fully half of the patients with eating disorders manifest significant feelings of depression. Thus, they may feel dejected, pessimistic, and hopeless. Currently it is unclear whether these feelings are a consequence of starvation, which has been shown capable of eliciting such effects on mood;[14] a reflection of an underlying affective disorder;[15] or simply a reaction to the disruptions in normal living and interpersonal relations created by the eating disorder. Although the depressed mood, low self-esteem, shame, and not-infrequent suicidal ideation do suggest an affective disorder, the typical "vegetative" signs (e.g., appetite loss and weight decline, insomnia, decreased libido, constipation) are difficult to assess in the presence of an eating disorder, and anhedonia, loss of reactivity to the environment, motor retardation, and diurnal mood variation (i.e., the features of melancholia) are characteristically not evident.

**Obsessional features.** More than half of all anorectic patients manifest behavioral and cognitive patterns typical of obsessive-compulsive disturbance. Thus, eating and exercise rituals, emotional constriction, obstinacy, perfectionism, and ruminations are common. Most of these individuals give histories of similar tendencies prior to the onset of the eating disorder, but it should also be noted that starvation studies in normal volunteers have established that obsessive-compulsive, as well as affective, disturbances can be a common consequence of starvation.[14]

## Bulimia

As described earlier, bulimia will evolve either in the context of established anorexia nervosa or independently of it (but typically in one who has frequently dieted and experienced weight fluctuations). Characteristically, the binge takes place in private, usually during the evening hours, and involves the consumption of huge quantities of food (often tens of thousands of calories in the same sitting). The usual binge foods are precisely those that are most assiduously avoided during the rest of the bulimic's day, namely carbohydrate-rich items (but virtually any and every morsel of food in the house is a potential target for the bulimic's binge). Typically, the binge terminates in self-induced vomiting, but, although most bulimics vomit, not all do, and vomiting should *not* be considered a prerequisite for the diagnosis of bulimia. Indeed, some bulimics simply exhaust themselves eventually and settle into a troubled sleep. Others will try to compensate by using laxatives or enemas.

The binge, which may occur anywhere from several times per 24-hour period to several times per month, elicits enormous personal shame. Not only are patients disgusted with themselves, but they are also initially unwilling to discuss their symptoms with anyone else. (This may account for the paucity of references to bulimia in the literature until the past decade when it began to "come out of the closet.") More importantly, each binge triggers off an ever-greater resolve to diet, and this only intensifies the fast-feast cycle. As with the anorectic's eating, the binge can become ritualized. Thus, the time, setting, and type of food become increasingly important and fixed. Moreover, in those bulimics who vomit, the vomiting can take on its own significance, achieving reinforcement from the physical relief it provides for the abdominal discomfort, psychologic relief from the concern about having consumed so many calories, affective relief from the shame and guilt over the loss of control, and perhaps symbolic relief from deeper conflicts about such matters as sex, pregnancy, and relationship with parents.

## BIOLOGY OF EATING DISORDERS

While the psychologic and behavioral features of the eating disorders obviously produce a dramatic clinical picture, it is commonly the impaired physiology that eventually occurs which brings the afflicted individual to medical attention. The biology of anorexia nervosa is essentially the biology of starvation, while the biology of bulimia is principally a reflection of the physiologic derangements produced by chronic vomiting or laxative abuse, or both, as well as by the erratic swings in food consumption. The physical, laboratory, and hormonal findings in anorexia nervosa are reviewed further on and are summarized in Tables 18–1, 18–2, and 18–3. Abnormalities characteristic of bulimia are also noted. Obviously, those individuals who manifest both AN and bulimia, as discussed earlier, will likely show the biologic alterations typical of both syndromes.

### Physical Signs

These are summarized in Table 18–1. The tooth decay and salivary gland enlargement are particularly associated with the binging and vomiting of bulimia. The degree of emaciation in anorectics will obviously depend on the net caloric balance between intake and expenditure; in bulimics, this will reflect the relationship among starvation, binging, and vomiting, so that such an afflicted individual could be underweight, overweight, or of perfectly normal weight. Weight loss among pure restricting anorectics may range from 20 to 50 percent below ideal body weight. The possibility of deception by the anorectic patient about her weight (whether

**Table 18–1.** PHYSICAL SIGNS OF EATING DISORDERS

**Anorexia Nervosa**
1. Emaciation
2. Dry skin
3. Lanugo
4. Loss of scalp hair and brittle nails
5. Cold extremities and impaired temperature regulation
6. Decreased heart size
7. Bradycardia
8. Hypotension
9. Edema
10. Osteoporosis

**Bulimia With Vomiting**
1. Tooth decay
2. Salivary gland enlargement

by lying or by adding weights to her body or dress before visiting a physician) should always be kept in mind; even though the anorectic may regard herself as too heavy, her fears of loss of control of her eating can result in all kinds of deception to keep others from coercing her to gain weight.

The salivary gland enlargement, it should be noted, particularly when coupled with the not infrequent periodic edema (which is of uncertain origin, as hypoalbuminemia is not characteristic), can serve to reinforce the eating-disordered patient's conviction that she is "getting fat," thereby intensifying further her dieting in a vicious circle.

## Laboratory Findings

The list of potential laboratory abnormalities is given in Table 18–2. (Endocrine abnormalities are treated separately.)

A moderate anemia is not unusual in AN. Hematocrit values under 35 percent and hemoglobin levels under 11.0 g/dL are common, and a panleukopenia also is not rare. Excretion of large amounts of dilute urine, reflecting partial diabetes insipidus, can appear if starvation becomes severe and chronic enough to affect hypothalamic function or renal function or both. Diabetes mellitus–like changes in glucose tolerance test results will also begin to appear with long-term avoidance of carbohydrates: fasting blood sugar falls to relatively low levels (less

than or equal to 70 mg/100 mL), an excessive and sustained rise is noted after glucose load (greater than or equal to 180 mg/100 mL), and a "rebound" hypoglycemia (less than or equal to 50 mg/100 mL) may appear as a delayed but excessive insulin outpouring then occurs. Patients will often claim that they have "hypoglycemia" as their problem, and physicians may actually diagnose the presence of diabetes, but these glucose abnormalities are the consequence, not the cause, of the chronic starvation and erratic carbohydrate consumption.

Vomiting is particularly pernicious because of its possible effects on electrolyte balance. The low potassium level and metabolic alkalosis it produces can lead to cardiac arrhythmias and even to cardiac arrest and death. Vomiting may also lead to dehydration, which can then confuse interpretation of electrolyte values by producing spuriously high figures.

Other laboratory abnormalities can include an elevated level of plasma carotene, in part due to the high carrot consumption characteristic of anorectics (because of the low calorie value of carrots) but possibly also related to low thyroid (particularly $T_3$) values; hypoproteinemia and liver enzyme abnormalities in severe and chronic cases (al-

**Table 18–2.** POTENTIAL LABORATORY ABNORMALITIES OF EATING DISORDERS

**Anorexia Nervosa**
1. Anemia and leukopenia
2. Partial diabetes insipidus
3. Glucose tolerance abormalities
4. Elevated plasma cholesterol and carotene levels
5. Abnormal liver function tests
6. Depressed plasma and urinary zinc and urinary copper levels
7. Ventricular enlargement on CAT scan; electroencephalogram abnormalities
8. Diminished gastric emptying on fluoroscopy

**Bulimia With Vomiting**
1. Evidence of dehydration (e.g., elevated BUN)
2. Hypokalemia, hypochloremia, and metabolic alkalosis
3. Elevated plasma amylase
4. Electrocardiogram abnormalities (secondary to electrolyte abnormalities)
5. Electroencephalogram abnormalities

**Table 18–3.** CHARACTERISTIC ENDOCRINE ABNORMALITIES OF EATING DISORDERS

1. Hypothalamic-pituitary-gonadal axis abnormalities
   a. Depressed plasma and urinary concentrations of gonadotropins (LH and FSH) in the face of depressed concentrations of estrogens and androgens
   b. Immature circadian LH secretory pattern
   c. Absence of monthly cycling in LH secretion
   d. Deficient LH "feedback" response to administered clomiphene citrate or ethinyl estradiol
   e. Usually deficient LH response to administered releasing hormone (LHRH), although correctable by daily "priming" with LHRH
2. Hypothalamic-pituitary-adrenal axis abnormalities
   a. Elevated concentrations of plasma and urinary cortisol (but usually with maintenance of normal circadian rhythm)
   b. Diminished cortisol suppression by dexamethasone administration
   c. Elevated cortisol production rate (despite the elevated plasma level of cortisol)
3. Growth hormone (GH) abnormalities
   a. High-normal or slightly elevated concentrations of plasma GH
   b. Impaired GH response to induced hyperglycemia and hypoglycemia, L-dopa, and TRH
4. Hypothalamic-pituitary-thyroid axis abnormalities
   a. Low-normal concentration of plasma $T_4$ and distinctly low $T_3$
   b. Low or low-normal concentration of plasma TSH (despite low $T_3$ and possibly low $T_4$ levels)
   c. Normal (or delayed but correctable with priming) TSH response to administered TRH

though characteristically uncommon in earlier cases); and hypercholesterolemia, perhaps also secondary to low $T_3$ values. Urinary excretion of zinc and copper has also been reported to be depressed in patients with AN.

Finally, perhaps one quarter of all anorectics and bulimics show nonspecific electroencephalogram abnormalities, most commonly unilateral or bilateral spikes in the temporal-occipital area. The basis for these abnormalities is not clear, but their presence prompted trials of anticonvulsant medication for the treatment of the eating disorders.[16] CAT scans suggestive of ventricular dilation and cerebral atrophy in patients with chronic AN have also been reported.

## Endocrine Abnormalities: Hypothalamic Implications

Because of the early occurrence of amenorrhea in patients with anorexia nervosa, the endocrinology of AN has undergone substantial investigation. As indicated in Table 18–3, the characteristic endocrine abnormalities have now been well delineated. These findings, when taken as a group, strongly suggest that hypothalamic function is impaired in those with AN.[17,18] This possibility is further reinforced by the previously noted abnormalities in temperature regulation and urine concentrating ability commonly seen with AN.

We assume that this hypothalamic dysfunction is a consequence of the starvation and extreme weight loss in patients having AN. However, other variables conceivably play a role; for example, the bizarre dietary intake (i.e., malnutrition as distinct from weight loss), psychologic factors (such as anxiety or depression), impaired sleep-wake patterns, and even excessive exercise. Although there is no firm evidence that the hypothalamic dysfunction precedes AN, it is conceivable that AN can adversely affect hypothalamic function and thereby secondarily impair hypothalamic control of appetitive behavior, thus creating a vicious circle.[19]

## DIAGNOSIS, COURSE, AND PROGNOSIS OF EATING DISORDERS

In its typical presentation, and given the considerably enhanced sophistication in recent years of both professionals and lay persons in this area, AN will pose little problem for diagnosis. While several medical and psychiatric conditions are also associated with weight loss (Table 18–4), the anorectic's characteristic adolescent age, otherwise good

**Table 18–4.** DIFFERENTIAL DIAGNOSES OF PATIENTS WITH WEIGHT LOSS

1. Psychiatric conditions
   a. Depression
   b. Mania
   c. Schizophrenia (paranoid)
2. Medical conditions
   a. Malignancy
   b. Hypothalamic tumor
   c. Diabetes, hyperthyroidism, other endocrinopathies
   d. Infectious diseases (infectious mononucleosis, tuberculosis, etc.)
   e. Gastrointestinal disorders (malabsorption syndromes, regional enteritis, ulcerative colitis, etc. )
   f. Chronic alcoholism

physical health, and obvious pleasure in her skeleton-like appearance should cause little diagnostic confusion. Problems can arise from the following confounding sources: deception about true weight by the patient, later age of onset (an increasing number of cases now appear to be starting in the third, fourth, and even fifth decades of life), and the hidden presence of bulimia (which can produce a picture of normal weight). Clearly, alertness to these possibilities is indicated when a person is suspected of having an eating disorder but does not quite fit the typical mold.

One of the extraordinary aspects of the eating disorders is that outcome is so variable and unpredictable. At one end of the spectrum, there is probably a significant number of teenage girls who "flirt" with AN, some perhaps even crossing over the border, only to respond to their parents' or physician's guidance or to their own good sense, and return to more normal eating and weight. At the other end, there are the 5 to 10 percent of patients who will die of direct complications of their eating disorder.[20] The causes of death are cardiovascular collapse or cardiac arrest (particularly due to electrolyte imbalance from vomiting or cardiac toxicity from abuse of syrup of ipecac), overwhelming sepsis (due to compromised immune function secondary to starvation), extreme hypoglycemia, and suicide.

Between these extremes, various courses and outcomes are possible: a single full-blown episode, recurring discrete episides, or chronic disorder. The appearance of bulimia is usually regarded as a serious prognostic sign because of its known likelihood to become associated with chronicity, although,

paradoxically, it may alleviate somewhat the emaciation problem. Moreover, whether as antecedent, concomitant, or consequence of the eating disorder, full-blown depression may further complicate the course.

While Minuchin and co-workers have claimed a better than 85 percent cure rate with their form of family therapy,[21] most workers in the field report less successful results.[11] A consensus might be that about 40 percent of all treated eating-disordered patients recover, about 30 percent show moderate but not definitive improvement, and about 30 percent run a chronically debilitating course (in which group will be found the 5 to 10 percent who die of the illness). Clearly, the eating disorders should not be considered benign conditions.

## THEORIES OF ETIOLOGY

The wide range of symptoms and signs found in the eating disorders has elicited an equally broad array of proposals to "explain" these syndromes. Yet, as our experience and sophistication with these syndromes have increased, we are becoming more cautious about accepting simple etiologic formulations and moving more toward a "risk-factor" model.

Perhaps the most significant contribution historically to our understanding of eating-disordered individuals, particularly the pure restricting (i.e., nonbulimic) anorectics, was made by Hilde Bruch, who moved away from a symbolic-libidinal-conflictual framework—e.g., seeing AN as a defense against an underlying wish for oral impregnation—toward more of an ego psychology framework. For Bruch,[22] AN came to represent a desperate attempt by the vulnerable adolescent to achieve a sense of identity and mastery independent from that of her overbearing and intrusive parents (particularly mother). The mother's insensitivity to physiologic and emotional cues provided by the infant caused the developing child to show deficiencies and confusion in identifying inner experiences and thus gaining a reliable sense of self. This would lead to a basic sense of ineffectiveness, perplexity over bodily sensations, and disturbances in body image. In the context of the developmental transition of puberty and adolescence—producing such stresses as bodily change, separation, heterosexual encounters, increased independence and responsibility, and scholastic demands—the anorexia-vulnerable person, who feels the need for high achievement but who has little confidence in her capacity to be successful, would turn increasingly toward her own body as the one area in her life that she could truly control. Her thinness not only re-established a sense of mastery and effectiveness but helped her define herself as someone special, i.e., her unique appearance shored up her precarious self-esteem and meager sense of identity.

Because this scenario is played out in the context of the adolescent's family, other investigators, such as Minuchin and co-workers,[21] have emphasized the importance of understanding and treating the family as a system. Thus, AN has significance not only for the diagnosed anorectic but for the entire family unit. Minuchin's group has identified four characteristics of such families: they are excessively enmeshed in each other's affairs, severely mutually overprotective, rigid in their interacting mechanisms as they relate to each other and to the outer world, and unable to achieve appropriate resolution and closure on family conflicts. AN, in this framework, represents an attempt on one level to achieve at least some "space" and autonomy within the family unit, while ensuring on another that threats to the homeostasis of the family constellation—e.g., by the designated patient truly maturing and moving out on her own—are thwarted.

Still other themes have been emphasized by various writers: the need to keep the body in a state of biologic immaturity to avoid confronting sexual impulses and heterosexual relationships,[23] the response to a cultural milieu that promises women happiness and success if thinness can be attained,[4] and the symbolic attempt to rid the self of the bad mother—with whom the anorectic identifies her body—by literally starving it.[24]

Unfortunately, all of these formulations, whether intrapsychic, family, or sociocultural, are based on observations after the fact. Thus, inferences are made about premorbid characteristics after AN has been diagnosed. The impact of such a pernicious condition on self-esteem, family dynamics, and perception of the environment cannot be readily determined: predisposing, precipitating, and sustaining characteristics tend to become confused. Moreover, many of the common conflicts described (e.g., over separation, independence, and sexuality) are characteristic of normal adolescents as well, and the more pathologic features of self and family (e.g., feelings of emptiness and enmeshment) are common to other pathologic, but non–eating-disordered, syndromes such as "borderline" states and "psychosomatic" disorders.

It is for these reasons that workers in the field are moving toward a "risk-factor" approach to the eating disorders.[25,26] Rather than specify a single etiology, we now recognize that there is a variety of factors—cultural, familial, and individual—that increase one's vulnerability to developing an eating disorder (Table 18–5). As the number and intensity of these risk factors increase, so does the vulnerability. However, clearly not all persons with eating disorders need have exactly the same risk factors, and some persons with some risk factors might never develop a manifest eating disorder; protective individual and family characteristics, individual biologic differences, and serendipity in life events could serve to modify outcome.

Moreover, the sustaining effects of starvation and malnutrition in patients with AN should not be overlooked.[19] As dieting becomes sustained, its impact on digestive capacity and function, endorphin levels, hypothalamic function, cognitive capacity, affective state, body image, cultural response, menstrual regularity, and so on, actually serve to reinforce further food avoidance, thereby creating an increasingly treatment-resistant situation.

Finally, whereas most of the focus in the eating-disorder literature has been on the

**Table 18–5.** RISK FACTORS THAT INCREASE VULNERABILITY TO
DEVELOPING EATING DISORDERS

**Cultural Risk Factors**
1. Westernized and contemporary
   a. Equates thinness with both beauty and happiness
   b. Emphasizes attention to self and body
   c. Demands varied, and at times conflicting, roles of women
2. Capable of readily disseminating cultural values and styles through visual media (e.g., movies, television, magazines)

**Familial Risk Factors**
1. Achievement-oriented
2. Intrusive, enmeshing, overprotective, rigid, unable to resolve conflicts
3. Frugal with support, nurturance, encouragement
4. Overinvested in food, diet, weight, appearance, or physical fitness
5. Known to have members with a formal history of eating disorder or affective disorder

**Individual Risk Factors**
1. Female
2. Adolescent
3. Slightly overweight
4. Subject to feelings of ineffectiveness and low self-esteem
5. Subject to conflicts and doubts about sense of personal identity and autonomy
6. Subject to bodily perceptual disturbances (e.g., distorted body image, uncertain feelings of satiation after meals)
7. Subject to overgeneralization and other cognitive distortions
8. Subject to an obsessional style and conficts about control

etiology and pathogenesis of anorexia nervosa, we are now beginning to understand more adequately the nature of the vulnerability of the individual for developing bulimia. On the biologic side, the loss of substantial weight (even if not to emaciated levels—e.g., an obese individual who diets to reach merely normal weight[27]), in the face of ongoing, severely restricted dietary intake, intensifies the drive to eat; on the psychologic side, this drive will most likely be responded to in excessive fashion, i.e., by binging, when the individual is characterized by so-called borderline features (impulsivity, emotional instability, an all-or-nothing orientation to life, feelings of inner emptiness, and so on). Thus, it is the mesh between biologic and psychologic vulnerabilities that loads the dice for the emergence of bulimia.

## TREATMENT

While the number of controlled studies on the efficacy of various treatment approaches to the eating disorders remains meager, there has been a substantial increase over the past two decades in empirical clinical experience in the management of AN and bulimia. There remains no sure-fire treatment for either condition, but certain guidelines have begun to emerge.[28,29]

Perhaps the two most important principles in dealing with the eating disorders are (1) the earlier the intervention, the greater the likelihood of response; and (2) the treatment approach should be tailored to the phase, severity, and setting of the disorder.

Whereas young adolescents who have just begun to diet excessively may respond to a good "educational" talk from a trusted pediatrician, patients with more clearly established cases of AN will require, at the very least, individual psychotherapy with a professional who is experienced with eating disorders. The therapy will typically focus on dealing with concerns about control and identity, on identifying and accepting bodily feelings and emotional responses, and on facing the anxieties inherent in becoming an independent adult. The therapist must be prepared to deal with educational and cognitive issues, as well as dynamic ones, and to be supportive, reliable, and respectful.

The critical place of the family as the battleground upon which an eating disorder evolves has suggested to experts such as Minuchin[21] and Palazzolli[24] that family therapy is as important as individual therapy, if not more so. Certainly for the adolescent living at home, family therapy that emphasizes the family unit as a system and its need to be more flexible and less intrusive in response to perturbations produced by any of its members is a most important complement to more traditional individual therapy.

Group therapy has elicited considerable interest in recent years for the treatment of bulimia. Whereas nonbulimic anorectics tend to say little in groups and actually become competitive with each other regarding success in losing weight, bulimic persons tend to be more open about their feelings in a group and also benefit from being confronted about their secretive gorging and purging behaviors. Moreover, most therapy groups also incorporate cognitive-psychoeducational elements, often in the context of a time-limited course of treatment, which can be helpful practically in dealing with and aborting eating and thinking patterns that tend to perpetuate the starve-binge cycle.

While the aforementioned approaches are germane to the patient with early anorexia nervosa or bulimia, as well as to the chronic but relatively stable patient, the importance of the hospital for the acutely starving anorectic or the severe bulimic in electrolyte imbalance—or both when they have lost control of their life to the eating disorder—should not be minimized. Because anorectics can lose weight precipitously, medical involvement should be a principal part of both the initial evaluation and any subsequent outpatient treatment. Not only is extent of weight loss important, but the rate must be considered. Some chronic patients may be stable at 35 percent below their ideal weight after many years with AN, whereas a patient who had dropped to 25 percent below ideal weight in just a few months may represent an acute medical emergency. Clearly weight change, electrolytes, blood chemistries, cardiac function, pulse, and blood pressure must be examined to make a judgment about the need for admission, but compulsive exercises or food-related rituals or numerous daily binges that interfere with the patient's functioning or interpersonal relations are also indications for hospitalization.

The inpatient setting itself, ideally a unit specifically geared for eating disorders but conceivably even a general medical or psychiatric floor, can provide several important aspects of treatment. In addition to close physiologic monitoring and supportive nursing, a hospital permits electrolyte correction with intravenous fluids, external restraints on binging and vomiting, application of a behavioral modification regimen to encourage weight gain, use of medications as indicated, and hyperalimentation (total parenteral nutrition) through an indwelling catheter in a subclavian vein or feedings through nasogastric tube for the patient who is severely emaciated and categorically refusing to eat.

A behavior modification approach assumes that the aberrant eating pattern, whatever its original determinants, has become a "habit" by the time that hospitalization becomes necessary. Thus, it might best be undone, like most habits, by the institution of an appropriate schedule of positive and negative reinforcers. Although common contingencies might include, for example, loss of visiting privileges or of access to off-unit activities, the most potent reinforcer—and one with obvious relevance to this book—may well involve access to exercise. The importance of exercise in the mental economy of most anorectic individuals has been demonstrated by Blinder, Freeman, and Stunkard.[30] Using a behavioral paradigm in which access to exercise was contingent on sufficient daily weight gain, they documented that significant and rapid improvement in weight could be attained during hospitalization.

The use of medication, whether on an inpatient or outpatient basis, has begun to receive particular attention. While the earlier literature mainly emphasized the use of chlorpromazine (Thorazine) in the acutely agitated, excessively exercising anorectic inpatient, the more recent emphasis has been on the use of antidepressants, particularly the monoamine oxidase inhibitor (MAOI) phenelzine (Nardil)[31] and the tricyclic antidepressant imipramine (Tofranil),[32] for the treatment of bulimia. The rationale for their use has been the seeming overlap in clinical, familial, and laboratory features in bulimia and affective disorders; however, this explanation remains controversial. Moreover, whereas controlled studies do suggest a statistically significant reduction in frequency of binges when these drugs are taken at therapeutic doses (the same doses as for treatment of depression), in my experience their effect is often far from ideal. In addition, side effects are poorly tolerated, and bulimics who may binge on tyramine-containing foods are obviously not candidates for treatment with an MAOI. Finally, as noted earlier, the not infrequent combination of EEG abnormalities and eating disorders has spurred interest in the application of anticonvulsants, particularly for bulimia. Both phenytoin (Dilantin)[16] and carbamazepine (Tegretol)[33] have been reported as helpful, but controlled studies on efficacy are lacking or inconclusive.

It must, of course, be noted that the eating disorders become chronic conditions for many, if not most, of those afflicted with them. The therapist must often be prepared to engage in long-term treatment, to use multiple modalities (including hospitalization when indicated), and to be willing to settle for goals that emphasize minimizing morbidity rather than achieving full cure. Indeed, those patients and therapists who seek quick remedies are likely to meet only with frustration.

## EXERCISE AND EATING DISORDERS

As indicated in the introduction to this chapter, the inclusion of considerable material on the eating disorders in a text on exercise and women was prompted by important questions. Does vigorous exercise or athletic competition "cause," or increase the likelihood of developing, AN? Do people with a predisposition for an eating disorder gravitate toward sports? Might physical activity in some fashion actually protect against the emergence of an eating disorder? Why is exercise so important to most persons who are anorectic? These, and other questions, are being asked with increasing frequency because of the growing number of women who are active athletically and the growing number of women who develop AN or bulimia.

Although complete, satisfactory answers to these questions are not available, relevant data have begun to appear. That serious long-distance running can apparently trigger the appearance of classic anorexia nervosa has now been reported,[34] but apparently this represents the precipitation of an eating disorder in persons who already have a strong predisposition for its development. Indeed, with so many people running and exercising currently, we would be faced with an AN epidemic if such activities could actually "cause" an eating disorder. Nevertheless, progressive weight loss, amenorrhea, and increasing preoccupation with calorie intake versus output should prompt close attention by physicians, trainers, and athletes to the possibility that the high level of physical activity may be evolving into a manifest eating disorder. Possible biologic and psychologic mechanisms underlying this precipitation have been proposed.[34]

The intriguing thought that perhaps athletics can be protective against the emergence of an eating disorder may actually have some support in the literature. A study of college women engaged in intramural sports between 1977 and 1982, when the incidence of AN was clearly increasing, found no evidence of a concomitant decrease in average weight among the study subjects.[35] Although it is conceivable that non–anorexia-prone women are attracted to college intramural sports (i.e., as opposed to varsity sports or individual running), or that eating disorders do exist in substantial numbers among such women but are obscured by bulimia which maintains weight at a generally normal level, it is also possible that intramural athletics provide an outlet that contains physiologic or psychologic elements that are, in some manner, protective against the development of AN.

Further support for such a thesis might be seen in a very recent study of both abnormal eating attitudes and manifest AN in a large number of long-distance female runners.[36] While 14 percent revealed aberrant attitudes on the Eating Attitudes Test (EAT) and the Eating Disorders Inventory, only 2.4 percent actually gave clinical evidence of having or possibly having had AN. On the other hand, another study found a strong correlation between scores on the EAT and the number of hours spent jogging per week, but not between EAT scores and other forms of physical activity.[37]

But are persons who are prone to eating disorders perhaps strongly "pulled" toward athletic participation? In addition to the previously mentioned reports of a relatively high percentage of female long-distance runners with abnormally elevated scores on screening tests for impaired attitudes toward eating-related issues, it is well known that anorectic individuals are typically excessively active physically during the disorder's acute phase. Numerous hours are devoted daily to calisthenics, running, swimming, or other athletic activities; often the exercising takes on a frenetic quality. This high level of physical activity might be seen as merely the expected manifestation of the conscious desire to work off as many calories as possible each day as part of the obsessional drive to attain supreme thinness. However, at least one report suggests that anorectic women are more active than their peers prior to the overt onset of the disorder and that they continue to remain physically active even after apparent recovery from AN.[13]

One of the most interesting, provocative, and controversial reports in this area was that by Yates and co-workers in the prestigious *New England Journal of Medicine*.[38] The authors reported that their psychologic interviews of male obligatory runners (men who run a minimum of 50 miles per week) revealed socioeconomic and personality characteristics strikingly similar to those reported in female anorectics. They speculated that obligatory running in men and AN in women both represent unconscious attempts to establish a more definitive sense of identity and effectiveness. Cultural values simply make it easier, they suggested, for men to use running and women dieting. Moreover, they proposed that members of either sex who use running to solve problems of identity and effectiveness will be subject to depression and more manifest eating disturbances when they cannot run if, for example, they have been injured; this possibility is actually consistent with the case reports of Katz.[34]

Nevertheless, the view that running is an analogue of AN has been questioned by Blumenthal and co-workers.[39] Using more precisely defined and quantitative psychologic assessment scales, they could not replicate the qualitative impressions of Yates and associates.[38] Moreover, it has been argued that the weight loss and food aversions common to many serious athletes reflect the pressures and demands of the sport but should not be confused with the deep premorbid psychopathology of those with bonafide anorexia nervosa.[40]

Presumably the truth rests somewhere in the middle of this debate. Those with conflicts over control and self-identity may seek solutions in exercise and sports competition or in weight control or possibly in both. Statistically, though, this group must certainly represent a very small percentage of the vast numbers, male and female, who engage in athletic activities. And, among those who have manifest eating disorders, only a small percentage is likely to be involved in serious, competitive sports, given the vulnerability to pathologic fractures, cardiac arrythmias, dehydration and electrolyte imbalance, loss of physical strength, and so forth, that characterize these syndromes.

Once involved with athletics, the person who is vulnerable to, but not yet manifesting, an eating disorder may actually find a relatively healthy solution to some of his or her psychologic conflicts. On the other hand, such a predisposed person may find that the coincidental weight loss, the competitive defeats, the pressure to perform more successfully, the problem of injuries interrupting rigid athletic schedules, the disruption of regular eating schedules and patterns by the demands of the sport, the frequent contemplation of the relation of body weight to performance, and the known effect of exercise on appetite[41] and perhaps on the body's endorphin system[42] will only serve to aggravate dramatically that predisposition.

## EATING DISORDERS AND OTHER SPECIAL SUBCULTURES

The importance of the mesh between environmental demands and individual vulnerabilities is perhaps best demonstrated by the high prevalence of eating disorders among women in certain subcultures.[43,44] These subcultures—such as ballet, acting, and modeling—are characterized by an *explicit* emphasis on the desirability of thinness. Thus, it is not surprising that most models, actresses, and ballerinas are underweight; yet, not all or even most have eating disorders. There is evidence, for example, that sociocultural background can exert a protective or risk-enhancing influence even within such narrow subcultures.

Thus, Hamilton and co-workers,[45] in a

study of ballerinas in nine regional and national dance companies, found mean weight for the entire group to be 12 percent below ideal value; however, no black American dancers reported having AN or bulimia, while 15 percent of the white American dancers admitted to having AN and 19 percent acknowledged the presence of bulimia. The anorectic ballerinas were not only thinner than their nonanorectic ballerina peers but also manifested generally greater psychopathology and were more likely to be dancers with the most competitive companies.

Finally, there is now evidence from the literature on ballet dancers that the presence of amenorrhea in such dancers is mediated not by their extensive physical activity but by their inadequate nutritional intake.[46] This may well have implications for the amenorrhea common to other strenuous exercisers—e.g., long-distance runners. Hence, we again note a complex interaction of multiple variables, which is perhaps precisely what we should expect to encounter in human psychobiology.

## SUMMARY

In that both the eating disorders and serious exercise have become strikingly more common among women over the past two decades, and with both sharing concerns about weight, diet, and activity level, it is not surprising that questions about a possible relationship between them have also begun to emerge. Because anorexia nervosa and bulimia are commonly not benign disorders, having behavioral, cognitive, emotional, and biologic consequences that can readily become debilitating and chronic, such concerns are hardly academic.

The available evidence relevant to these concerns is currently limited. Nevertheless, it does suggest that a high level of physical exercise becomes a risk factor for the development of an eating disorder only when it occurs in an individual who has other predisposing risk factors—e.g., conflicts or doubts about sense of identity and self-control. Extreme physical activity can also be a symptom of an already emerging state of anorexia nervosa; but here the activity tends to be frenetic and the mental component involves the conscious desire to "burn off" cal-

ories, rather than a desire to experience the sheer fun of exercise or the gratification inherent in successful physical competition. It is conceivable that, for some athletes, female or male, extreme exercise can provide an outlet for solving conscious or unconscious conflicts, in the same way that excessive dieting—or excessive stamp collecting, excessive gambling, or excessive drinking—might. However, for most of the large number of women who now exercise regularly, particularly those whose exercise is not part of a subculture that explicitly attaches great status to thinness such as ballet or modeling, the risk of developing an eating disorder appears to be minimal, while the likely benefit to mental and physical well-being is probably substantial.

## References

1. Jones DJ, Fox MM, Babigian HM, et al: Epidemiology of anorexia nervosa in Monroe County, New York: 1960–1967. Psychosom Med 42:551, 1980.
2. Crisp AH, Palmer RL, and Kalucy RA: How common is anorexia nervosa?: a prevalence study. Br J Psychiatry 140:564, 1983.
3. Johnson CL, Lewis S, Love S, et al: Incidence and correlates of bulimic behavior in a female high school population. J Youth Adolescence 13:6, 1984.
4. Schwartz DM, Thompson MG, and Johnson CL: Anorexia nervosa and bulimia: the sociocultural context. Int J Eating Disorders 1(3):20, 1982.
5. Levenkron S: Treating and Overcoming Anorexia Nervosa. Charles Scribner's Sons, New York, 1982.
6. Pumariega AJ, Edwards P, and Mitchell CB: Anorexia nervosa in black adolescents. J Am Acad Child Psychiatry 123:111, 1984.
7. Kaye WH, Pickar D, Naber D, et al: Cerebrospinal fluid opiod activity in anorexia nervosa. Am J Psychiatry 139:643, 1982.
8. Appenzeller O: What makes us run. N Engl J Med 305:578, 1981.
9. Diagnostic and Statistical Manual of Mental Disorders, ed 3. American Psychiatric Association, Washington, DC, 1980, p 67.
10. Askevold F: The diagnosis of anorexia nervosa. Int J Eating Disorders 2(4):39, 1983.
11. Garfinkel PE, and Garner DM: Anorexia Nervosa—A Multidimensional Perspective. Brenner/Mazel, New York, 1982.
12. Katz JL, and Weiner H: The aberrant reproductive endocrinology of anorexia nervosa. In Weiner H, Hofer MA, Stunkard AJ (eds): Brain, Behavior, and Bodily Disease. Raven Press, New York, 1981, p 165.
13. Kron L, Katz JL, Gorzynski G, et al: Hyperactivity in anorexia nervosa: A fundamental clinical feature. Compr Psychiatry 19:433, 1978.
14. Keys A, Brozek J, Henschel A, et al: The Biology of Human Starvation. University of Minnesota Press, Minneapolis, 1950.
15. Katz JL, Kuperberg A, Pollack CP, et al: Is there a

relationship between eating disorder and affective disorder? New evidence from sleep recordings. Am J Psychiatry 141:753, 1984.

16. Green RS, and Rau JH: Treatment of compulsive eating disturbances with anticonvulsant medication. Am J Psychiatry 131:428, 1974.

17. Mecklenburg, RS, Loriaux DL, and Thompson RH: Hypothalamic dysfunction in patients with anorexia nervosa. Medicine 52:147, 1974.

18. Katz JL, and Weiner H: A functional, anterior hypothalamic defect in primary anorexia nervosa? Psychosom Med 37:103, 1975.

19. Wortis J: Irreversible starvation. Biol Psychiatry 20:465, 1985.

20. Seidensticker JF, and Tzagournis M: Anorexia nervosa—clinical features and long term follow-up. J Chron Dis 21:361, 1968.

21. Minuchin S, Rosman BL, and Baker L: Psychosomatic Families: Anorexia Nervosa in Context. Harvard University Press, Cambridge, 1978.

22. Bruch H: Eating Disorders: Obesity, Anorexia Nervosa, and the Person Within. Basic Books, New York, 1973.

23. Abraham S, and Beaumont PJV: Varieties of psychosexual experience in patients with anorexia nervosa. Int J Eating Disorders 1(3):10, 1982.

24. Palazzoli MS: Anorexia nervosa. In Arieta S (ed): The World Biennial of Psychiatry and Psychotherapy, Vol I. Basic Books, New York/London, 1970, p 197.

25. Johnson C, Lewis C, and Hagman J: The syndrome of bulimia—review and synthesis. Psychiatr Clin North Am 7(2):247, 1984.

26. Katz JL: Some reflections on the nature of the eating disorders: On the need for humility. Int J Eating Disorders 4(4a):617, 1985

27. Marcus MD, Wing RR, and Lamparski DM: Binge eating and dietary restraint in obese patients. Addict Behav 10:163, 1985.

28. Garner DM, and Garfinkel PE (eds): Handbook of Psychotherapy for Anorexia Nervosa and Bulimia. Guilford Press, New York/London, 1985.

29. Andersen AE: Practical Comprehensive Treatment of Anorexia Nervosa and Bulimia. Johns Hopkins University Press, Baltimore, 1985.

30. Blinder BJ, Freeman DMA, and Stunkard AJ: Behavior therapy of anorexia nervosa: Effectiveness of activity as a reinforcer of weight gain. Am J Psychiatry 126:1093, 1970.

31. Walsh BT, Stewart JW, Roose SP, et al: Treatment of bulimia with phenelzine—a double-blind, placebo-controlled study. Arch Gen Psychiatry 41:1105, 1984.

32. Pope HG Jr, Hudson JI, Jonas JM, et al: Bulimia treated with imipramine: a placebo-controlled double-blind study. Am J Psychiatry 140:554, 1983.

33. Kaplan AS, Garfinkel PE, Darby PL, et al: Carbamazepine in the treatment of bulimia. Am J Psychiatry 140:1225, 1983.

34. Katz JL: Long distance running, anorexia nervosa, and bulimia: A report of two cases. Compr Psychiatry 27:74, 1986.

35. Crago M, Yates A, Beutler LE, et al: Height-weight ratios among female athletes: are collegiate athletics the precursors to an anorexic syndrome? Int J Eating Disorders 4(1):79, 1985.

36. Weight LM, and Noakes TD: Is running an analogue of anorexia? A survey of the incidence of eating disorders in female distance runners. Med Sci Sports Exerc 19:213, 1987.

37. Richert AJ, and Hummers JA: Patterns of physical activity in college students at possible risk for eating disorder. Int J Eating Disorders 5:757, 1986.

38. Yates A, Leehey K, and Shisslak CM: Running—an analogue of anorexia? N Engl J Med 308:251, 1983.

39. Blumenthal JA, O'Toole L, and Chang JL: Is running an analogue of anorexia nervosa? An empirical study of obligatory running and anorexia nervosa. JAMA 252:520, 1984.

40. Smith NJ: Excessive weight loss and food aversion in athletes simulating anorexia nervosa. Pediatrics 66:139, 1980.

41. Epling WJ, Pierce WD, and Stefan L: A theory of activity-based, anorexia. Int J Eating Disorders 3(1):27, 1983.

42. Colt EWD, Wardlaw SL, and Frantz AG: The effect of running on plasma $\beta$-endorphin. Life Sci 28:1637, 1981.

43. Druss RG, and Silverman JA: Body image and perfectionism of ballerinas: Comparison and contrast with anorexia nervosa. Gen Hosp Psychiatry 1:115, 1979.

44. Garner DM, and Garfinkel PE: Sociocultural factors in the development of anorexia nervosa. Psychol Med 10:647, 1980.

45. Hamilton LH, Brooks-Gunn J, and Warren MP: Sociocultural influences on eating disorders in professional female ballet dancers. Int J Eating Disorders 4:465, 1985.

46. Hamilton LH, Brook-Gunn J, and Warren MP: Nutritional intake of female dancers: A reflection of eating problems. Int J Eating Disorders 5:925, 1986.

# APPENDIX A

# Exercise Following Injury, Surgery, or Infection

## I. EXERCISE FOLLOWING BREAST TRAUMA OR SURGERY

CHRISTINE HAYCOCK, M.D.

### Minor Trauma

Patients who have minor abrasions or contusions do not require any time away from their athletic endeavors. Wearing a good supportive bra to minimize breast motion will suffice to keep them comfortable, along with a simple analgesic such as ibuprofen or aspirin.

### Minor Surgery

Following minor surgery, such as a breast biopsy or excision of a small cyst, some limitation of upper arm use, especially throwing or lifting, is indicated for at least 3 to 5 days to allow good cosmetic wound healing. This is in addition to good breast support and analgesics.

If the excision has been deep or extensive, requiring a drain for more than 24 hours, then 5 to 7 days of limited upper arm use may be indicated. This is an individual decision that must be made by the operating surgeon.

If infection is present due to an infected hematoma, or develops postoperatively, then upper arm motion must be restricted until all evidence of infection is gone.

### Mastectomy

Programs such as ''Reach to Recovery,'' sponsored by the American Cancer Society,

have shown the usefulness of exercise in the rehabilitation of the postmastectomy patient. Fortunately, since radical mastectomies are now performed rarely, most patients do regain their full preoperative range of motion and strength in the ipsilateral arm.

The athlete would be encouraged to begin arm raising at about 4 to 5 days after mastectomy and gradually to increase the motion daily. This routine is true as a matter of fact for all such patients to prevent formation of scar tissue that would limit future motion. However, in an athlete, at about the 2-week point, I would encourage the use of weights, beginning with a pound and gradually increasing, to build back upper arm strength. Squeezing a ball or other device for this purpose is also indicated. A good supervised physical therapy regimen is strongly advocated.

There may be other limitations required for the mastectomy patient if she requires radiation therapy or chemotherapy. These would have to be individually determined, as no set rule is feasible. It would depend on such factors as the amount of radiation given, the duration of the treatment, and the effect on her skin. Certainly, mild exercise would probably be permissible.

### Reduction or Augmentation Mammoplasty

Patients who have reduction mammoplasty would be limited in the same manner as mastectomy patients. Exercise would be limited until healing is sufficient such that no drainage or raw areas exist; then the same

## EARLIEST TIME TO RESUME EXERCISE POSTOPERATIVELY

| | Aerobic Exercise | | | | Weight Training | |
| | Nonwater Sports | | Water Sports | | | |
| Procedure | Light | Intense | Light | Intense | Light | Sub-maximal |
|---|---|---|---|---|---|---|
| D and C First-trimester abortion | Same or next day | Same or next day | When bleeding has ceased | When bleeding has ceased | Same day | Same day |
| Vaginal delivery Second-trimester abortion | 2 days | 2 days | When bleeding has ceased | When bleeding has ceased | Same day | Same day |
| Laparoscopy | 1–2 days | 1–2 days | 1–2 days | 1–2 days | 1–2 days | 1–2 days |
| Cesarean delivery Other laparotomy | 7 days | 21 days | 21 days | 21 days | 7 days | 21 days |

regimen outlined for mastectomy patients could be followed.

Rehabilitation of the athlete following augmentation mammoplasty should include careful supervision by the plastic surgeon and a physical therapist, for physical and legal reasons. The type and size of the prosthesis used would play a role.

## II. EXERCISE FOLLOWING OBSTETRIC/GYNECOLOGIC SURGERY

MONA SHANGOLD, M.D.

When to resume one's exercise program after obstetric or gynecologic surgery is best depicted in the table shown above.

## III. EXERCISE FOLLOWING COMMON ORTHOPEDIC INJURIES AND OPERATIVE PROCEDURES

LETHA Y. GRIFFIN-HUNTER, M.D., Ph.D.

### Ankle Sprain

The proper time to return to activity following an ankle sprain depends on the severity of the injury. The level of severity is defined by a grading system: grade I refers to pain at the ligamentous site but no laxity; grade II is pain at the ligamentous site with mild laxity; and grade III describes pain at the ligamentous site with significant laxity.

With grade I ankle sprains it may take from several days to several weeks for the patient to return to activity, whereas with grade III ankle sprains it will take a minimum of several weeks and may take up to several months. In grade I ligamentous injuries about the ankle, initial protection, ice, compression, and elevation are followed by rapid rehabilitation, stressing increasing range of motion and strength, with a special attempt at achieving return of proprioceptive feedback from the ankle. Range of motion is achieved by having the athlete do figure-of-eights and circles with her foot. Rubber tubing can be used as a resistive device for gaining strength in dorsiflexion and plantar-flexion and inversion-eversion.

Gains in proprioceptive feedback can often be maximized by having the athlete stand on the affected extremity with her eyes closed and relearn how to balance. Also helpful in this regard is a tilt board, a flat board attached to a half circle of wood, on which the athlete tries to balance her weight with the good foot planted on the ground and only partial weight on the foot on the tilt board. She then gradually increases her weight on the injured ankle until she has good balance and can stand independently on it. When the athlete has full range of motion and 90 percent strength and can hop independently on her extremity without pain, she can return to pivotal sports.

The rehabilitation programs for grade II

and grade III sprains about the ankle are similar. However, the period of immobilization and protection is longer, to allow for initial healing.

## Arthromeniscectomy

Following an arthromeniscectomy, the athlete is encouraged to ice and elevate her extremity for the first 48 hours. This initial period of rest, compression, elevation, and icing helps prevent swelling and, hence, minimizes the time off from sport following this procedure. If after 48 hours the athlete has minimal to no swelling and good range of motion, she can begin isometric, isotonic, or isokinetic strengthening exercises, as well as functional strengthening activities such as biking and swimming, and within a week she can begin running. Pivotal activities are usually not allowed for 3 to 4 weeks, until the new meniscal rim has remodeled.

## Patella-Stabilization Procedures

### Soft Tissue Releases

Following a soft tissue release for patella stabilization (typically a medial reefing or tightening of the medial muscles, as well as a release of the lateral muscles), the athlete's affected limb is initially protected, iced, and elevated for from 5 to 7 days. This allows the initial inflammation to diminish. Isometric exercises for the quadriceps, especially the vastus medialis, are encouraged during this period of time. A Myostim unit to maintain the oxidative enzyme contents of the involved muscle cells may be beneficial.

Quadriceps-setting exercisers and short arc extension exercises may be started anytime from 5 days to 2 weeks postoperatively. Biking, swimming, and walking can be begun as soon as the athlete has achieved control of her extremity and has a functional range of motion. Biking is often very useful in increasing range of motion, and therefore is to be encouraged. Return to pivotal sports may not be possible for up to 3 to 6 months, depending on the stability of the repair.

### Bony Realignment Procedure for Patella Dislocation

Following a bony realignment of the patella, the timing for initiating range of motion and strengthening exercises is dependent upon the bony fixation device used (e.g., screws, staples, and so on). The period of immobilization varies and should be dictated by the orthopedist.

## Lumbar Diskectomy

Immediately following diskectomy, the athlete is encouraged to begin walking in her hospital room, progressing within 7 to 10 days to walking about the home and outside the home, going gradually from 10-minute walks to 30- to 45-minute walks, at an increasing pace. Sutures are removed in 10 to 14 days. If there is not marked swelling or spasm in the paravertebral muscles, the athlete is also encouraged to begin swimming at 2 to 3 weeks following surgery. Swimming, like running, develops abdominal and paravertebral muscle strength and is therefore to be encouraged.

Pivotal sports are generally permitted within 3 to 4 months, as soon as the athlete has good muscle strength and no pain with activities of daily living. General consensus is lacking on whether an athlete should be permitted to return to contact sports following diskectomy, although many athletes have returned to long-distance running following diskectomy. One should encourage the athlete to choose a sport that does not require such impact-loading on the lumbar spine.

## Bunionectomy

Bunionectomy is not a "simple" procedure. It frequently necessitates bony realignment of the first metatarsal. Walking in a special shoe with a nonflexible wooden sole may be needed to protect the osteotomy. Ambulation can begin soon after the procedure, as long as protection is provided by such an appliance.

When early bony union is seen and pain and swelling have subsided, the hard-soled shoe may be replaced by a comfortable shoe with a nonelevated heel. Within 3 to 4 weeks, the athlete will probably be allowed to return to swimming and biking, as well as weight-training routines, as long as they do not involve rising up on the toes or impact-loading on the feet. Impact-loading activities such as running, soccer, tennis, and so forth, should not be permitted until swelling is completely resolved, range of motion of the metatarsophalangeal joint of the great toe is restored, and good bony union is present at the osteotomy site, which may be anytime from 3 to 6 months.

## Removal of Morton's Neuroma

Morton's neuroma is painful scarring about the intermetatarsal nerve in the foot. If the neuroma is unresponsive to nonoperative methods such as metatarsal pads, shoe modification, injection of steroids, and local anesthesia, then surgical excision can be accomplished.

Following this procedure, the athlete is instructed to keep the foot elevated for several days to diminish swelling. Within 3 to 4 days, she can be performing normal routine activities. However, if foot swelling occurs when she attempts to do so, further elevation is necessary. Generally about the second or third week, swelling has resolved. If the athlete is pain-free, swimming and biking are then permitted. It may be from 3 to 6 weeks before the athlete can resume running and pivotal activities without discomfort.

## IV. EXERCISE FOLLOWING AN INFECTION

GABE MIRKIN, M.D.

It is probably all right to exercise during a systemic infection, provided that the athlete is afebrile and does not have myalgia before exercising. These same criteria should be used to determine when to return to exercising after recovering from an infection. However, each case should be decided on its own merits, rather than by general rules.

Exercising with a fever increases cardiac output far beyond exercising with a normal body temperature. The heart must pump extra blood to skin to prevent heat build-up, in addition to its usual tasks of supplying oxygen and nutrients to exercising muscle. Some viruses that infect the respiratory tract can also infect the myocardium.[1] The combination of increased workload and viral myocarditis can result in a fatal arrhythmia.[2]

When skeletal muscles are infected by respiratory viruses, they usually hurt during exercise. Exercising when muscles hurt markedly increases susceptibility to injury. Infected muscles have reduced strength[3] and endurance[4] and decreased levels of necessary enzymes such as glyceraldehyde 3-phosphate dehydrogenase.[5]

## References

1. Burch JA: Viral diseases of the heart. Acta Cardiol 1:5, 1979.
2. Roberts JA: Viral illnesses and sports performance. Sports Medicine 3:296, 1986.
3. Friman G: Effect of acute infectious disease on isometric muscle strength. Scand J Clin Lab Invest 37:303, 1977.
4. Arnold DL: Excessive intracellular acidosis of skeletal muscle on exercise in a patient with post-viral exhaustion syndrome. Lancet 1:1367, 1984.
5. Astrom E: Effect of viral and mycoplasma infections on ultrastructure and enzyme activities in human skeletal muscle. Acta Pathol Microbiol Immunol Scand 84:113, 1976.

# Index

Page numbers followed by F indicate figures; page numbers followed by T indicate tables.